Lawrence of Arabia, Strange Man of Letters

Lawrence of Arabia, Strange Man of Letters

The Literary Criticism and Correspondence of T. E. Lawrence

Edited by
Harold Orlans

Rutherford • Madison • Teaneck
Fairleigh Dickinson University Press
London and Toronto: Associated University Presses

Associated University Presses
440 Forsgate Drive
Cranbury, NJ 08512

Associated University Presses
25 Sicilian Avenue
London WC1A 2QH, England

Associated University Presses
P.O. Box 338, Port Credit
Mississauga, Ontario
L5G 4L8 Canada

.0165-2151   8/10/93

The paper used in this publication meets the requirements of the American National Standard for Permanence of Paper for Printed Library Materials Z39.48-1984.

Library of Congress Cataloging-in-Publication Data

Lawrence, T. E. (Thomas Edward), 1888–1935.
    Lawrence of Arabia, strange man of letters: the literary criticism and correspondence of T. E. Lawrence / edited by Harold Orlans.
        p.   cm.
    Includes bibliographical references and index.
    ISBN 0-8386-3508-3 (alk. paper)
    1. English literature—History and criticism.   2. Lawrence, T. E. (Thomas Edward), 1888–1935—Correspondence.   3. Books and reading —Quotations, maxims, etc.   4. Critics—Great Britain—Correspondence. 5. Books—Reviews.   6. Criticism.   I. Orland, Harold, 1921– II. Title.
PR99.L333   1993
820.9—dc20
                                                                    92-53456
                                                                    CIP

PRINTED IN THE UNITED STATES OF AMERICA

To Kay,
My good wife

Contents

Preface

More may have been written about T. E.—Thomas Edward—
Lawrence, Colonel Lawrence, Lawrence of Arabia, later Aircraftman
T. E. Shaw—a name he legally adopted in 1927—than any other
Englishman of the century except Winston Churchill. A comprehensive
bibliography by Philip O'Brien lists four hundred biographies, dis-
sertations, literary studies, and juvenilia, 1,700 articles, and many
books in which he makes a long or short appearance.

In so large a body of material, there is much trash, invention,
romanticism, denigration, error, superficiality, misunderstanding, and
significant gaps in knowledge and understanding. The present book
seeks to fill one gap, or one and a half: that of Lawrence's literary
views and activities and the light, or half-light, they throw on his
character.

D. G. Hogarth, Lawrence's mentor—"the parent I could trust,
without qualification, to understand what bothered me," "the only
person to whom I had never to explain the 'why' of what I was
doing"—felt that "In some measure the life of letters is best suited
to him" (Garnett, 551, 557, 352). Upon occasion (with Lawrence,
almost everything must be thus qualified), Lawrence agreed; "in the
distant future," he told Edward Garnett, "...I shall be appraised
rather as a man of letters than as a man of action" (Brown, 361).

All his life, Lawrence was intensely absorbed in literature and poetry.
Wherever he was, in the desert or in barracks, in France, Whitehall,
Dorset, India, he read and re-read classical, medieval, and modern
works in Greek and French as well as English. He had a special interest
in and wide acquaintance with established writers (Hardy, Shaw,
Wells, Forster) and rising figures (Pound, Graves, Sassoon, Hanley,
Williamson, Day Lewis). Reading their work, often in draft or proofs,
he might take notes to be discussed in letters or conversation, as he
sought to analyze and master their craft and his own. "It would be
possible to compile a substantial book of criticism from these...
letters," the Weintraubs (78) wrote, and that idea also occurred to me.

E. M. Forster (1985, 78) thought Lawrence "a good judge of literary
matters." Edward Garnett said "of the authors I have known, T. E.

11

possessed, I think, the most responsive and the widest critical taste. He combined the true scholar's sense of literary values with the unconventional judgement of a man of culture who tests books by life" (*Friends*, 462). Others disagreed. Edward's son David (1951, 25) thought literary criticism "the subject in which...he was least sure of himself." F. L. Lucas found him "wayward." He "could make wild remarks....[or] very penetrating judgments" (Weintraubs, 98). To C. Day Lewis, Lawrence's comments on poetry were "sometimes contradictory, sometimes perverse..., alway independent-minded" (*Minorities*, 15).

This compilation permits the reader to judge for himself. Whatever you may think of Lawrence's literary judgments (and only someone with no opinions of his own can agree with all), you should enjoy them, for Lawrence's writing, especially his correspondence, is never dull, often funny, witty, irreverent, provocative, caustic, penetrating, direct.

Seven Pillars of Wisdom and, to a lesser extent, *The Mint* have been subjected to much literary, psychological, and textual exegesis, the occupational disease of English departments. Two recent examples are *T. E. Lawrence: Hero, Writer, Legend*, a book, edited by Jeffrey Meyers, devoted largely to rexamining these works, and Malcolm Allen's *The Medievalism of Lawrence of Arabia*, which enumerates the many references to medieval and chivalric subjects in *Seven Pillars*. Without ignoring *Seven Pillars* or *The Mint*, this book will focus on Lawrence's broader literary interests and opinions and the light they throw on his character.

Part I contains all of Lawrence's known published criticism: introductions, book reviews, and minor bric-à-brac. Most is out of print and difficult to find. As the thinness of this collection suggests and Lawrence often insisted, he was not and did not want to be a literary critic. He wanted to be a writer, and a central purpose of his criticism was to learn how to write better.

The most substantial piece, his introduction to *Arabia Deserta*, was the price he had to pay to get that massive work reprinted. The six reviews, his most formal criticism, were undertaken (under pseudo-initials) during a relatively idle period in India; thereafter he wrote no others.

All but two items were requested of him; had he accepted all requests, Part I would be many times larger. The two were *A Note on James Elroy Flecker*, found among his papers after his death, and the very detailed comments on the prose of *Tarka the Otter*, which originated as a letter, a type of letter he wrote periodically (see pp. 212 and 219).

Part II presents a large selection of comments on writers and writing drawn from Lawrence's extensive correspondence with prominent and ordinary people. Much of it has not before been published, was published in limited editions, or has long been out of print.

Few letters tell an author the truth, the whole truth, and nothing but the truth about his book. Lawrence not only flatters Shaw, Forster, or Manning: he flatters them so excessively one wonders what is going on. Conversely, he criticizes Williamson or Hanley with such humor and sensitivity that they enjoy it. His letters tell us something about Lawrence and the kind of relation he sought with each author.

Lawrence's remarks to others about the same author are seldom so respectful. Shaw and Forster are taken down a notch—"Now [Shaw] is pedestalled, and not as good as you are" (p. 223); "I like [Forster], but a little shamefacedly" (p. 157)—and Doughty, "invertebrate, shapeless, horrific" (p. 149), still more.

Juxtaposing the views Lawrence expressed to different correspondents about the same writer, living or dead, well or little known, provides evidence of his consistency or inconsistency and his manner of dealing with friends and strangers, with men of standing and comrades in the ranks. The chronological arrangement of passages on each writer or theme provides evidence of the stability or change in Lawrence's views over the years. His love of William Morris and other romantic fantasy persisted; his glorification of creative artists faded as his esteem for common men rose.

A reader interested in particular writers, Hardy or Shaw, D. H. Lawrence or Robert Graves, may want to read what Lawrence wrote to or about them. A reader looking for entertainment need only browse to see ikons broken and great men speared or illuminated:
- Homer...was an antiquarian, a tame-cat, a book-worm: not a great poet, but a most charming novelist. A Thornton Wilder of his time.
- ...T. S. Eliot with his cranky passion for the knuckle-end of the Church of England....A parvenu longing for roots.
- [Wyndham Lewis and Ezra Pound] are flabby-faced and soft-handed, and pant when going up flights of stairs. Of course this is not really criticism of their heads.....or is it?
- [Graves's *I, Claudius*] gripped me against my will....The writing is superb....And yet—and yet—quo vadis, Domine?....it will be...talked about for its vices, rather than its force.

The distinctive value of this correspondence is the insight it affords into Lawrence's trenchant mind and puzzling character. His mind pierced convention, reticence, and posturing; it was the mind of a formidable intelligence officer skilled at questioning, at interpreting speech and expression and piecing together scattered information. His mind was ruthless. "I like him [Doughty] too much...to start an analysis:" he tells a mutual friend, "you see the analysis proceeds always on its own rails, beyond your control" (p. 148).

As for Lawrence's character: that is discussed periodically in the introductions to each section. He could be open, friendly, positively forward, or withdrawn and unresponsive; breathtakingly honest or devious and convincingly misleading. Indeed, so many aspects of his character were checked by opposing aspects that he is better understood as two men constantly battling each other than one living harmoniously with himself.

Neither from his letters nor from independent testimony can he be fully understood. What Thomas Mann wrote of Dostoevsky applies with singular force to Lawrence:

> In every man's memory there are things which he does not reveal to everyone, but only to his friends. There are also things which he does not reveal to his friends, but at best to himself and only under a pledge of secrecy. And finally there are things which man hesitates to reveal even to himself.[1]

This work was undertaken with the consent of Arnold W. Lawrence, T. E.'s youngest brother and literary executor, who died in March 1991, aged 90; he is, however, in no way responsible for any of it. I must thank Michael V. Carey of the Lawrence Trust for permission to examine the Lawrence holdings at the Bodleian Library, Oxford, the most important collection of Lawrence letters (originals and copies) and papers, and Simon Master of Random House, UK, for permission to examine the Cape archive at the University of Reading.

Others who have helped to provide access to letters, papers, and publications by or about Lawrence are:

In Oxford, A. J. Flavell, the Bodleian, and D. A. Rees and the Principal and Fellows of Jesus College. In Cambridge, A. E. B. Owen, the University Library; M. A. Halls, Kings College Library; and Odette Rogers, the Fitzwilliam Museum. At the University of Reading Library, Michael Bott. In London, Roderick Suddaby, Imperial War Museum, and staff of the British Library. Also John Pateman, Librarian, the T. E. Lawrence Society.

In California, Edwards H. Metcalf, for access to publications (not letters) in his collection; Alan Jutzi, Thomas Lange, and Leona Schonfeld, The Huntington Library; and Marilyn B. Kann, the Hoover Institution. At the Harry Ransom Humanities Research Center, The

University of Texas at Austin, Cathy Henderson and Katherine Mosley. At the University of Missouri Library, Margaret A. Howell, and Randy Roberts, Joint Collection, Western Historical Manuscript Collection and State Historical Society of Missouri Manuscripts. At the Houghton Library, Harvard, James J. Lewis, Jennie Rathbun, and Elizabeth A. Falsey. At the Beinecke Rare Book and Manuscript Library, Yale, Vincent Giroud. At the Olin Library, Cornell, James Tyler, Ilse H. Nehring, and Lynne Farrington. Staff of the Arents Collection, Wayne Furman, Office of Special Collections, and the Henry W. and Albert A. Berg Collection, the New York Public Library, Astor, Lenox and Tilden Foundations. At Princeton University Libraries, Jean F. Preston. Staff at the libraries of the Universities of Virginia and Oregon, and Muriel Sanford of the University of Maine Library were also helpful.

I would like to thank the following for permission to quote designated passages: the British Broadcasting Corporation for a remark by A. E. Chambers in a December 3, 1958 BBC broadcast, "Lawrence of Clouds Hill"; David Bolt Associates for a passage by Sydney Cockerell; Jonathan Cape Ltd. for extracts from letters of Jonathan Cape and Wren Howard; the Peters Fraser & Dunlop Group Ltd. for a passage from *The Buried Day* by C. Day Lewis; Dr. Caroline Barron for passages from letters of D. G. Hogarth, his wife Laura, and their son William; The Society of Authors as the literary representative of the Estate of John Middleton Murry for a passage by Murry; Hutchinson Books and the Estate of H. M. Tomlinson for passages from two Tomlinson letters; The Henry Williamson Literary Estate and A. M. Heath & Co. for extracts from Williamson letters. The quotation from Mrs. Bernard Shaw's April 9, 1928 letter is by kind permission of the Trustees of the Will of Mrs. Bernard Shaw. Copyright published and unpublished letters of T. E. Lawrence are reproduced by permission of the Seven Pillars of Wisdom Trust.

I beg the indulgence of any other heirs or agents of writers whom I have been unable to reach or have overlooked.

For their help in replying to questions and providing information and advice by letter or in conversation, I want to thank Malcolm Brown, Charles M. Grosvenor, Lawrence James, Phillip Knightley, John Mack, Denis McDonnell, Jeffrey Meyers, Philip O'Brien, Colin Simpson, Stephen Tabachnick, Stanley Weintraub, and Jeremy Wilson. Judith Hallett and Donald Lyons kindly supplied the Greek and Latin I lack. Clifford Irwin, who has been working on an index of all Lawrence letters, has been repeatedly helpful in many ways. He and Philip O'Brien read and commented on a draft of the manuscript.

My good wife Kay has done so for several drafts and discussed Lawrence with me more often than she may have liked: but, then, I also edit her drafts and she is far more productive.

Finally, a few editorial points.

The spelling and punctuation in Lawrence's published criticism and published or unpublished letters follow—as scrupulously as my eye, sometimes weary hand, and the availability and clarity of originals and photocopies permitted—that in the source from which they are taken. Hence, the same title may be italicized or capitalized in one source but not another, and ampersands may or may not appear as they struck the fancy of Lawrence, David Garnett, or another editor. Likewise, the spelling of quoted passages follows that in the source, which leads to English spelling inside and American spelling outside quotes. The growing tendency of editors, even of *The Chicago Manual of Style*, to tamper with quoted matter for the sake of consistency or grammar is an unscholarly crime I will not commit.

Lawrence often put a series of dots in the midst of a passage, as if to mark a pause in his thinking and writing. These are transcribed here as five dots; four dots mark an elision including one or more periods; three dots, an elision within a sentence.

Sources are cited in the text and notes as briefly as possible: e.g., (Brown, 22); as Aldington (231) says; **Bodleian**; (*Letters*, 93). Full citations for abbreviated forms are given in the bibliography. A number with "p."—e.g., (p. 232)—refers to a page in this book.

In his writing, letters, and life, Lawrence used and was addressed by countless names and initials: T. E. Lawrence, E. Lawrence, T. E. L., T. E., Ned, Colonel Lawrence, Lawrence of Arabia, John Hume Ross, T. E. Shaw, T. E. S., Miss Davis, C. D., E. Smith, and no doubt others. Throughout this book, he is called Lawrence, the name his parents assumed and gave to their sons; his brothers used it all their lives and he, for most of his. He tried to shed it, but it is cut into his tombstone and has lasted.

Chronology of Lawrence's Life

1888 Aug. 16	born Tremadoc, Wales
1896 summer	Oxford
Sept. (–July 1907)	Oxford High School for Boys
1907 Oct. (–June 1910)	Jesus College, Oxford
1909 summer	Syria
1910–11 winter	Jebail, Syria
1911–14 springs	Carchemish
1912–13 falls	Carchemish
1914 Jan.–Feb.	Sinai
Oct.	War Office, London
Dec.	Military Intelligence, Cairo
1916 Oct.	Arabia
1918 Oct. 1	Damascus
Oct. 28	London
1919 Jan.–Oct.	Paris Peace Conference
Oct. (–Jan. 1921)	All Souls College, Oxford
1921 Feb. (–July 1922)	Colonial Office, London and Mid-East
1922 Aug.	RAF training depot, Uxbridge
Nov.	RAF School of Photography, Farnborough
1923 Jan.	discharged from RAF
Mar. (–Aug. 1925)	Royal Tank Corps, Bovington, Dorset
summer	Clouds Hill
1925 Aug.	RAF Cadet College, Cranwell, Lincolnshire
1926 Dec.	sails for India
1927 Jan.	RAF depot, Karachi
1928 May	RAF, Fort Miranshah
1929 Jan.	sails for England
Mar.	RAF, Mount Batten, Plymouth
1931–34	intervals in Hythe, Southampton, Cowes
1934 Nov.	RAF, Bridlington, Yorkshire
1935 Feb. 26	leaves RAF
May 13	motorcycle accident
May 19	death

Chronology of Lawrence's Writing

1909–10	wrote Oxford thesis, published as *Crusader Castles*, 1936
1914	completed *The Wilderness of Zin* (with Leonard Woolley), published 1915
1914	said he burned manuscript of Seven Pillars of Wisdom, a book on seven Near East cities
1916–19	articles in secret *Arab Bulletin*, published as *Secret Despatches from Arabia*, 1939 and 1991
1919–22	wrote, lost, and rewrote *Seven Pillars of Wisdom*; eight copies printed, 1922
1919–27	hand-copied collection of favorite poems, published as *Minorities*, 1971
1921	introduction to Charles Doughty, *Travels in Arabia Deserta*
1922–23	notes on life as Royal Air Force recruit
1922–26	revised *Seven Pillars* and supervised production of limited edition issued November–December 1926
1923	translated le Corbeau's *The Forest Giant*, published 1924
1924	introduction to Richard Garnett, *Twilight of the Gods*
1927	*Revolt in the Desert* (abridged *Seven Pillars*) published; sale stopped in Britain after royalties liquidate debt of limited edition
1927–28	six book reviews for *The Spectator*
1927–28	wrote out clean manuscript of *The Mint*, first general publication 1955, unexpurgated 1973
1928–31	translated *The Odyssey*, limited edition 1932; U.S. publication 1932, U.K. 1935
1931	foreword to Bertram Thomas, *Arabia Felix*
1935	general publication of *Seven Pillars*
1938	*The Letters of T. E. Lawrence*, David Garnett, editor
1954	*The Home Letters of T. E. Lawrence and His Brothers*, M. R. Lawrence, editor
1988	*The Letters of T. E. Lawrence*, Malcolm Brown, editor

Introduction:
Booklover, Writer, Literary Cognoscente

"I had meant to be a general and knighted, when thirty," T. E. Lawrence wrote (*Seven*, 562). He became an archeologist; an authority on medieval castles; a marksman, mapmaker, and intelligence officer; a dynamiter of trains; the adviser and leader of Beduin tribes who helped free Arabia and Syria from Turkish rule in a nine-hundred-mile desert campaign that culminated in Damascus; an adviser to Prince Feisal, the Arab spokesman at the 1919 Paris Peace Conference; Fellow of All Souls College, Oxford; Colonial Secretary Winston Churchill's adviser on Arab affairs, who put Feisal and his brother Abdullah on the thrones of Iraq and Transjordan; author and publisher of a luxurious limited edition of *Seven Pillars of Wisdom* (1926) and author of its abbreviated popular version, *Revolt in the Desert* (1927); a private in the Royal Tank Corps and Royal Air Force: a floor-sweeper, table-cleaner, swill-emptier, clerk, mechanic, motorcyclist, *Odyssey* translator, tester and developer of high-speed motor launches.

In 1919, Lawrence became, and thereafter remained, a national celebrity, when Lowell Thomas's romanticized lecture and film show on "the uncrowned King of Arabia" attracted sell-out crowds for six months in London. He was a hero who met and corresponded with leading cultural and political figures of the time—and a shy, lonely man who sought poverty and anonymity in a soldier's uniform and many aliases. He died at forty-six in 1935, when he crashed his motorcycle to avoid two boy bicyclists.

He went his own way, disregarding common conventions, ambitions, comforts, and deceits. He benefitted and suffered from his intelligence, excessive consciousness and self-consciousness, from his potent understanding, action, and influence. A strange, brilliant, complex, remarkable man.

In the strands of Lawrence's life the varicolored cord of books and literature, words read and written, runs strikingly.

The Book Lover

He knew the alphabet by three, read at four, learned French early (from

21

three to five, 1891–93, he lived in Dinard), began Latin at five. As a boy, he was often immersed in a book: walking, at table, before the fire. "...any book he took up he seemed to read at a glance," his mother said (*Friends*, 25). He read Macaulay's *Introduction to the History of England* at seven, Layard's accounts of the Ninevah excavations,[1] and *Helps to the Study of the Bible*. His letters from the Holy Land in the summer of 1909 (when, going on twenty-one, he walked most of nine hundred miles to inspect castles in Palestine and Syria), show how well he knew the Bible.[2]

Of 4,645 students taking the Oxford Senior Local Examination in 1906, Lawrence tied for third in Religious Knowledge and came first (with two others) in English Literature (Wilson, 40). His brother Frank, bicycling with him in France in 1910, writes, "Ned is rejoicing over some books he has discovered at the price of a franc. Each time I have a bath he goes and buys a book instead" (*Home*, 598). At Oxford University (1907–10), Lawrence read prodigiously, often six books a day in eighteen-hour sieges on a rug in his bungalow room silenced with green sheeting used for industrial soundproofing. An August 1910 letter evokes the flavor of that reading (p. 246). At the Karachi air base, with a five-and-a-half hour workday, he might finish three books daily.

Lawrence read fast, "a line if not a paragraph, at once"[3]—so fast, he read books he liked at least twice[4]—and had a remarkable memory for what he grasped. His testimony (he could invent or exaggerate)[5] is independently confirmed. When Francis Yeats-Brown brought him proofs of *Lives of a Bengal Lancer*, he read them "with lightning speed" within two hours and "corrected the book with the care of a proofreader."[6]

An example of Lawrence's photographic memory is his identification of Frederic Manning as the anonymous author of the 1930 war novel *Her Privates We* from its stylistic resemblance to Manning's *Scenes and Portraits*, which he had first read in 1909, often thereafter, and "knew...almost by heart."[7] According to Leonard Woolley, director (1912–14) of the Carchemish excavations, Lawrence "would quote from memory a particular potsherd that had been found in a former season and could describe its stratum and associations, although I and not he had excavated the piece and written the notes about it" (*Friends*, 87).

The rapid rewriting of *Seven Pillars* after most of the manuscript was lost,[8] and its armamentarium of local, geological, geographical, botanical, architectural, military, and other technical terms attests to Lawrence's great reading and recall. His knowledge was so wide, varied, and detailed that, in the years before his fame, friends called him "the Encyclopaedia" and "supercerebral."[9] Around 1933, Robert Graves, isolated on Majorca, used him as a convenient source of facts he needed:

> How near is Gadara to the Sea of Galilee?....Who were the Gadarene philosophers?....Whose verses did James quote in his epistle?....And what is the connection with Meleager?....Do send me the dope, in a brief referential memo and I'll...work it in.[10]

In their quarters at Carchemish, Lawrence and Woolley had 150 books in eight languages, which a visiting German librarian called "the best...of any small library he had ever seen" (p. 247). On wartime marches, Lawrence carried Aristophanes, Malory, and the *Oxford Book of English Verse*. Ten years later, at a base near Karachi, he soon collected 250 books: his own and others sent from England by friends, publishers, and especially Charlotte Shaw, George Bernard Shaw's wife.

At various bases in England and India, he was sometimes short of reading matter. His books were stored with friends and in boxes at the Cattewater RAF base near Plymouth; the few kept by his cot were thinned by borrowing; it was difficult to learn of and get enough good books to read. "If you come across any tolerable book that you don't want.....thank you!" he writes Charlotte Shaw; and Frederic Manning: "You mix with booky people, or read papers, and so cannot know the fantastic difficulty there is in hearing of things to read. Go to a book shop and look at the window? Only the W. H. Smith [popular, not serious] shops, in Southampton and Plymouth, only show the last Galsworthy..."[11]

In his forties (as old as he got) frequent travel, long work-hours, fatigue, and periodic eye trouble hampered his reading; nonetheless, he managed a bit at the start or end of the day. "I make the half-hour, by getting up before reveille."[12] Anticipating retirement in 1935, he fixed up a bookroom downstairs in his Dorset cottage (and a music room upstairs) and began to retrieve books lent and stored and to replace lost copies. "I have always meant, in my leisured age, to re-read all these men who excited me in my youth..."[13]

Upon his death, over 1,250 books were found in the cottage: classics in Greek and Latin, including 32 titles of the Loeb Classical Library; much French literature; a sprinkling in Italian, Spanish, and German. The English titles ranged from Beowulf and Malory to nineteenth- and twentieth-century writers, with much poetry; over twenty items from William Morris's Kelmscott Press, including the famous Chaucer, and many from the Ashendene, Doves, Golden Cockerel, Gregynog,

Nonesuch, and other private presses; books in leather or vellum; books inscribed by Doughty, Hardy, G. B. Shaw, E. M. Forster, Graves, Churchill, and others.[14]

A lonely man, self-contained and severely self-controlled, Lawrence may never have loved anyone or only Dahoum, a young Arab. But he certainly loved books: their contents; the appearance and feel of well-bound, well-designed, well-printed pages. He loved the crafts and arts of bookmaking, especially in fine editions, and learned them in great technical detail. As a young man, he bought land at Pole Hill, Chingford, on the eastern outskirt of London by Epping Forest, where he proposed to print fine books with his friend Vyvyan Richards. Near the end of his life, he planned a building above the water pool at his cottage for a small press (the humidity would keep the paper moist). "I am a printer by trade," the novelist John Buchan (a director of Nelson's publishers) remarked (374), ". . . . [but Lawrence] acquired far more information about printing than I ever possessed."

With "an extraordinary passion for detail" (Buchan, 374), Lawrence could quickly understand how a weapon, motor, poem, or novel was made. It was one of his strengths as a man of action and one of his weaknesses as a writer, for too much attention to the craft of words can slow their flow. In *Seven Pillars*, the prose can grow knotted like burled wood. Even in letters his prose is deliberately worked and may be abbreviated or twisted to strike the reader: e.g., "if I had choice," "it was accident," "she would give away herself."

Lawrence's intense interest in literature may resemble that of a scholar or man of letters, but hardly that of a man who spent eighteen years in the military. It did not come from his father, a leisured gentleman who never worked and seldom read a book, or from his mother, a little-educated, ultra-religious woman of working-class origin whose reading concentrated on the Bible. Shy, Lawrence withdrew from collective sports and meals at Oxford; even in the military, he ate alone and, when he could, retreated to his cottage or motorcycle. Books could be opened, closed, and shelved more easily than people. Despite his wide experience and deserved reputation as a man of action, "in certain respects he persistently appeared to be book-learned rather than life-learned."[15]

He read to learn—about the Greeks and history, architecture and warfare, the Middle Ages, the Near East, his contemporaries, and himself; to escape bourgeois England and enter a world of knights on quests, of honor, valor, chivalry, fortitude, resolve, purpose; later, to reenter a world that had gone—youth, the war, the discovery of a strange people, the battle against nature and fate, the effort to shape events. Above all, he read to enjoy and, if possible, learn various styles of writing, of rendering experience, observation, feeling, and imagination in prose.

The Writer

His wish to write, to condense and express his knowledge, perceptions, feelings, and mind exactly and impressively, was deeply rooted and long lasting. From his early twenties onward, he seldom went long without writing or rewriting something, taking notes for possible future use, and/or translating, editing, criticizing, or promoting someone else's work.

Lawrence's first substantial work, his undergraduate thesis on Crusader castles (1910), was a concise analysis of innumerable castles he had visited in Europe and Asia, with many photographs and drawings and a forceful argument that the Syrian castles were modelled on the European—flatly contradicting the reigning view.[16] "Instead of calling a spade a spade, you invariably call it a bloody shovel," his tutor said (Leeds, 10). The habit of flouting fashion, even what he himself had said, recurs. In 1929, he dismissed the thesis as "an elementary performance. . . . worthless," "Not worth printing,"[17] and suggested that he had burned it (another recurrent thought and, less often, deed).[18] In fact, it helped him earn first class honors in history; would have been accepted by Oxford University Press had he agreed to pare the expensive illustrations;[19] and has since been published in several editions.[20]

In 1912 letters from Carchemish, Lawrence says, "My books would be better, if I had been for a time in open country" and "I am gathering a store of Arab News and notions which some day will help me in giving vividness to what I write" (*Home*, 207, 239). He had in mind several books. One was a "travel book" he soon wrote on seven eastern cities—"Cairo, Smyrna, Constantinople, Beyrout, Aleppo, Damascus, Medina."[21] He said he burned this "youthful indiscretion-book" in 1914, preserving only the title, "The Seven Pillars of Wisdom."[22] He spoke also of books on the crusades and the background of Christ.[23]

Early in 1914, the Palestine Exploration Fund sent Woolley and Lawrence on a rushed, six-week archeological survey of the Sinai, then under Turkish rule, as camouflage for a topographical military survey conducted at the same time by British Army Captain Stewart Newcombe. The report, *The Wilderness of Zin*,[24] was the first book bearing Lawrence's name. He tried to have it removed:[25] plainly, his penchant for anonymity, pseudonymns, and pseudonymous initials arose before his flight from fame.[26] Years later he said the book "was

got out in a hurry for reasons of politics and is bad."[27] He published
little that he did not condemn.

Lawrence's wartime reports and memoranda as an intelligence
analyst in Cairo (1914–16) and liaison officer in Arabia (1916–18)
were forceful, penetrating, and marked by his genius for seeing
technical and political courses of action through the fog of circumstances. As with his press articles and letters propagandizing for the
Arab cause (1918–20), the pressure of events loosened his pen. He
wrote rapidly, incisively, and effectively without the endless rewriting
and word-twisting that marked his literary work. Returning from his
first visit to Arabia (1916), in five days waiting for a ship he wrote
a report of seventeen-thousand words "remarkable for their detailed
observation and clarity of style" (Wilson 1988, 67). Reports on
intelligence activities in Mesopotamia (1916), how to handle Arabs
(1917), and the complex geography of Syrian peoples and politics (1917)
illustrate this potent art.[28] If the test of analytical and political writing
is the reader's conviction that a strong mind has grasped the root of
the matter and clearly said what should be done, this kind of writing
was Lawrence's natural métier.

Lawrence's greatest literary effort—writing, rewriting, embellishing,
and publishing *Seven Pillars*—went on (with delays and interruptions)
for eight years. He sought to create a "Titanic" work that would rank
with *Moby Dick* or *War and Peace*.[29] When he had finished, he felt
he had failed and no amount or degree of praise (from Thomas Hardy,
G. B. Shaw, H. G. Wells, Siegfried Sassoon, Winston Churchill, and
many others) changed his feeling. The praise he dismissed as polite,
imperceptive, misguided flattery, meant for the action or the person,
not the book; always, from everyone, unwarranted; "he could accept
only unfavourable judgments upon his work."[30] No critic has
condemned *Seven Pillars* more severely than its author. He called it
"muck," "long-winded, and pretentious, and dull," "perverse,"
"priggish,...hysterical," "lewd lecherous unholy," "undigestible,"
"a stodgy mess of mock-heroic egotism....sludge," "irredeemable,
irremediable," "rotten," "putrid rubbish."[31]

Whatever one may think of *Seven Pillars*, it is not *that* bad. The
great Arabist H. St. J. B. Philby declared, "Not Homer nor Dante
nor Doughty surpasses...this stately flow of prose pressed from the
soul and refined by the mind of a...painter-poet."[32] I find it grip-
ping, often magnificent, with trenchant analysis of men, movements,
ideas, terrain, war; breathtakingly direct, mercilessly self-critical: yet
flawed by excessive detail,[33] shielded candor, and embossed prose:
the paint is too thick on the canvas. Like Robert Graves, I prefer the
more relaxed Oxford text of 1922.[34] Lawrence disliked *Seven Pillars*

because he disliked himself and his writing was too integral a part of himself to judge it differently. When Vyvyan Richards criticized his denigration of the book he replied, "Self-depreciation is a necessity with me."[35]

Most men embody contradictions and inconsistencies, but Lawrence's were extraordinary. His diverse selves did not merely bifurcate into recognizable opposites (commanding/meek, vain/ modest, loquacious/silent, sociable/solitary, masculine/feminine)[36] but fragmented into apparently disconnected characters. "Cockerell declares that he is fifteen different men, and that you never know which one will be on duty in any given emergency."[37] Stephen Tabachnick (1984, 1) calls him "a fragmentation artist."

Such fragmentation or, put more charitably, diversity was also evident in Lawrence's prose. He had distinct styles for different purposes: his official memoranda and press articles were incisive and provocative; his technical writing was clear and precise;[38] his letters reflected his mood and the recipient's character and situation. His literary style never settled into one mold. In the fall of 1922, while circulating the ornate *Seven Pillars* for comment, he was taking notes for what became the spare, staccato *Mint*. Sending the latter to Edward Garnett, he justly remarked, "I doubt whether any un-versed reader would be able to connect the two books by any tricks of authorship" (Garnett, 596–97).

His opinion of *The Mint* was mixed; as it was slighter than *Seven Pillars*, he slighted it less. He tells Charlotte Shaw it is "good prose" and "There never was...such stuff put on paper before—or is this the vanity of every author?" He tells Edward Garnett, "it's no good, but I don't like people to say so" and "it's pretty second-rate."[39] He writes one friend, "it is right, *so far as it goes*....Its [sic] the work of my maturity...and surely parts of it are powerful?.... There is a fastidiousness about its prose, a power & drive, (almost a heat) about it which pleases me." To another friend, he says it is "scrappy and arty and incompetent."[40] The harsher judgments went to writers. Irving Howe's (364) balanced verdict is: "a severely chiselled picture of barrack life...but too markedly an exercise, a self-conscious effort to *write*."

The itch to write never died, though Lawrence often pronounced it dead and never devoted to subsequent work (or undertook any that required) the effort that went into *Seven Pillars*.

"I find myself composing pages and phrases [of his Crusader castles thesis] as I ride" (on his bicycle), he writes home in 1908 (*Home*, 62). That "composing in the head," the mark of someone captured by language, recurs throughout his life. Writing *Seven Pillars* "has put an ink fever into me. I find myself always going about trying to fit words to sights and sounds in the world outside me.''[41]

He knows "that frenzied aching delight in a pattern of words which happen to run true" (p. 192). Words "have always fascinated me: playing with them like a child with bricks."[42] "My greatest pleasure," he tells the novelist James Hanley, "lies in mooning about through a [London] crowd, trying to fit words or rhythms to what my eyes see. Not for any purpose: for the exercise of it."[43] When he sees a seaplane crash that kills several men and leaps into the water to help with the rescue, he cannot later resist jotting down words to capture the memory.[44]

Lawrence's time in the ranks (1922–35) was increasingly devoted to an effort to make himself ordinary, and content to be so. "Lawrence was very busy now [1929] trying to persuade himself that he was ordinary: towards the end he was almost convinced," Graves (159) observed sardonically. Biographers dispute whether he achieved a lasting or fitful contentment. Can one be really content with periods of black despair?

However, Lawrence seems never to have been content with his writing. He tried many forms and condemned his performance in all. A piece he once praised was the prose equivalent of neatly arrayed hardware: "A 'Handbook to 37½ foot motor boats of the 200 class'. . . I pride myself that every sentence in it is understandable, to a fitter." He also termed it "the packiest stodge" and "Ever so dull. . . and entirely impersonal. Nobody could guess that anybody had written [it]."[45]

In Lawrence, a vein of vanity alternates with one of humility and self-castigation so that he wants first to be a great writer and then, convinced he has failed, to write no more. In 1924, he says *Seven Pillars* is "the only book I'll write"; "I can't write, and wouldn't if I could."[46] In 1928, he tells Edward Garnett *The Mint* is "the end of my attempts to write" and E. M. Forster, "I do not think it is at all likely that I will ever be moved to write anything again."[47] No wonder he reminded Blanche Patch (81), G. B. Shaw's secretary, of "a prima donna for ever trilling her last farewell."

Two 1930 letters catch Lawrence's shifting moods. "Probably if I went on trying I could achieve more second-rate work: and do not think it worth while," he says in one and, in the other, "I propose to go on fancying that I could, in some circumstances, & under certain impulses, *write*: and so long as I don't disabuse myself by trying to write, that makes a nice warm fiction to cherish under one's breath."[48]

The syndrome was repeated periodically. Thus, he tells the director of the New York office of Oxford University Press, which had just published his *Odyssey* translation, "I have promised myself, again and again, that I will never publish another book as long as I live.... If anybody needs money, it is surely myself... but I would rather starve than earn another penny by any publication." Was that to dispose of an importunate publisher? He tells another publisher that, when he retires, "desperation may well make me write something."[49] And he confides in Charlotte Shaw that he is contemplating "a book called 'Confession of Faith'..... embodying *The Mint* and much that has happened to me before and since as regards the air.... and the meaning of speed, on land and water and air. I see the plan of it. It will take long to do.... The purpose of my generation, that's really it."[50]

Lawrence's dissatisfaction with his writing had two evident sources (if any are needed beyond his dissatisfaction with himself). He was not satisfied to be a very good writer: he had to be a great one. "When I am writing I go mad, and *try* to make it better than yours or anybody's.... I did want to be a great writer," he admits to E. M. Forster."[51] "My aim [in *Seven Pillars*] may have been too high for anybody; it was too high for me."[52] "I thought that the mind I had... would sweep over the ordinary rocks of technique.... I had hopes... it was going to be a big thing.... I sent it to the printer, and when it came back... I saw it was no good."[53]

The word "technique" points to the nature of Lawrence's talent. He regarded writing as he regarded war, printing, or the management of men: as a set of crafts to be mastered: and he was remarkably good at that. Paragraphs, composed of artfully crafted sentences, were assembled into chapters and these, into a Book, as blocks and pillars make a Temple. Lawrence was sharp at detecting faults in the mortar and architecture of a literary work. What this approach lacked was only the heart of the matter: the feeling that overrides technique, the sense of living persons and events inhabiting a successful work of art.

Lawrence's self-control was in conflict with his creative efforts, as his brother Arnold saw: "the conscious subjection of his senses to his intellect may have deprived him of the ability to create artistically" (*Friends*, 589). If Tolstoy has a "technique" it is not perceptible, identifiable, or duplicable; it is not definable techniques but an inimitable vision Melville himself could not duplicate that makes *Moby Dick* great. When *Seven Pillars* holds the reader, he is held not by technical tricks but by Lawrence the man glimpsed and hidden in that great sea of words.

Francis Yeats-Brown, literary editor of the *Spectator*, called Lawrence's prose "the standard of modern descriptive English."[54] Recognizing his "itch for description, which... developed into a mania and broke through every convention," G. B. Shaw considered Lawrence "one of the greatest descriptive writers in English literature" (*Friends*, 246). Late in life, Lawrence understood that "my writing practice has all been to put down more and more exactly what I have seen or felt: invention would come very hard."[55]

But in *Seven Pillars* he sought to rival epics of imagination, not description. His friend Bernard Shaw and his favorite writer, William Morris, thought a writer should do what came easily.[56] Lawrence rejected that course; "real life," he once remarked, "consists in striving to do those things which you find not easy" (Ellis, 8). He strove to be an imaginative writer. An over-controlled writer and man, he could not loose his pen to wander in imagined fields. "I am totally unfitted by nature...to produce a work of creative imagination" (Ede, 9). Obstinately trying to write against the grain of his talent could only produce feelings of frustration and failure.

Literary Cognoscente

Before World War I, Lawrence's personal acquaintance with writers was limited. He was too young, shy, and socially ill-placed[57] to encounter many prominent figures or seek them out without special cause. At Oxford, he preferred reading to attending lectures and, living at home except for a term in college rooms, had less opportunity than other students to meet faculty. However, his archeological interests led him to frequent the Ashmolean Museum, where he met D. G. Hogarth, the Near East scholar appointed as its director in 1909. Hogarth became his mentor and confidant; a 1923 will designated him Lawrence's literary executor.[58]

Preparing for his first trip to Syria, Lawrence wrote to Charles Doughty, the patriarch of Arabian travellers. After his three-month trek, which he undertook alone against Hogarth's and Doughty's advice, he visited Doughty in December 1909, initiating an acquaintance in which he began as a novice, later became Doughty's promoter and benefactor, and ended privately critical of much of Doughty's work and some of his conduct (pp. 145–52).

In Syria, Lawrence and the poet James Elroy Flecker, British Vice-Consul at Beirut, 1911–13, became friends and had long talks on poetry and literature (pp. 92, 101). However, many of Lawrence's associates in those years were fellow archeologists such as the two Carchemish directors, Campbell Thompson and Leonard Woolley, and officials of the Ashmolean and British Museums.

The war changed everything. Up to the capture of Akaba in July

1917, Lawrence was a promising young man; some found him brilliant, impressive, daring, delightful; others, obnoxious, slovenly and ill-mannered, a bumptious poseur. By the war's end, Lawrence was known to leaders of the government and the king, and joined discussions of the Eastern Committee of the War Cabinet. He attracted great attention at the 1919 Paris Peace Conference and more, thereafter, in Britain where, over six months in 1919–20, Lowell Thomas's film and lecture show on "The Uncrowned King of Arabia" was seen by a million people and converted an unknown archeologist into Lawrence of Arabia, a national hero.

Writing and rewriting *Seven Pillars*, commissioning portraits and drawings for it, and superintending its composition, printing, and binding occupied Lawrence intermittently from January 1919, when he began the first draft in Paris, until December 1926, when he despatched printed, leather-bound copies to some two hundred subscribers and friends. Several aspects of this gruelling enterprise tell us a good deal about Lawrence as a man and writer.

The book dwells on two years of desert war, October 1916–October 1918, and Lawrence's sense of betraying the Arabs with promises Britain and France did not intend to keep. Only a footnote mentions his satisfaction with Churchill's (and his) 1921 settlement. "So we were quit of the war-time Eastern adventure, with clean hands, but three years too late" (*Seven*, 283).

A footnote is scant counterweight to an epic of political betrayal; a chapter or appendix would be more warranted. For whatever reasons, Lawrence preferred to display and preserve his feelings of duplicity and political failure rather than other feelings (of courage, earning the Arabs' trust and respect, victory, the eventual political achievement) he might have presented with equal force.[59] When a friend once suggested he write an account of what Lawrence called the "dogfight in...Downing Street" (1920–21) culminating in the Mid-East settlement, he replied that he might have done so had he lost the fight.[60] It was as if the only subject he could seriously entertain was one of defeat.

Lawrence was a perfectionist in an imperfect world, a craftsman and tinkerer in the world of inspiration and art. Striving always to improve, he could not leave well enough alone; in him, the artistic best was the enemy of the good. G. W. M. Dunn, an RAF friend, remarks, "He seemed to be pleased by nothing which he did, unless it was an act of kindness...or the surmounting of a difficulty by some simple ingenuity. His larger acts were never sufficiently perfect to please him. There was constantly the need for improvement in details" (*Friends*, 447). "It does not seem to me...as though anything I've

ever done was quite well enough done,'' Lawrence once wrote
Doubleday. ''That is an aching, unsatisfied feeling, & ends up by
making me wish I hadn't done anything: and very reluctant to try
anything more.''[61]

MEETING WRITERS

His craftsman instinct drove him to study and learn, and from whom
can writing be learned better than from writers? Books are not just
written; they are contracted for, edited, designed, perhaps illustrated,
typeset, proofed, printed, bound, published, advertised, reviewed, sold,
read, criticized. Lawrence sought to learn every phase.

Fame opened every door. The change was abrupt. October 4,
Lawrence was in Damascus, his weight eighty pounds, thirty or more
below normal; October 29, he was talking with cabinet ministers and
drowned in social invitations. Often he did not know how to behave.
The king was reputedly offended by his manner of refusing honors.
Lord Curzon, the Foreign Minister, burst into tears at Lawrence's curt
response to his praise. He accepted one dinner invitation, did not
appear, and showed up later in Arab dress. He once accepted fifteen
luncheon appointments for the same day.[62]

While pressing the Arab case, Lawrence sought publicity and social
contacts that might yield political benefits. After he went to work for
Churchill, he avoided publicity and reduced his social activity.
However, he continued to welcome and initiate contacts with poets,
writers, publishers, editors, painters, sculptors, curators: almost any
serious person connected with a creative art. In literature and the arts,
he was prepared to trade on his fame and approach people he did not
know well.

For example, visiting Churchill in November 1918, Lawrence met
his private secretary Edward Marsh, translator, editor of *Georgian
Poetry*, and patron of the arts. Lawrence asked if he knew Siegfried
Sassoon; he did and the three dined together the next day.[63] At
Oxford early in 1920,[64] Lawrence met Robert Graves, back from the
war to get his degree; they became close friends. Through Graves,
he met John Masefield, Robert Bridges, Edmund Blunden, Vachel
Lindsay, and, in 1923, Thomas Hardy; in turn, Lawrence introduced
Graves to Ezra Pound.

In March 1922, Lawrence had lunch with Sydney Cockerell, director
of the Fitzwilliam Museum, Cambridge; encountered G. B. Shaw and
his wife, whom Cockerell introduced; and taxied to the painter
Augustus John, whom both knew. Thereupon, Lawrence said, ''We
have seen the biggest English dramatist and the biggest English painter

of our day. Let us finish up with the biggest English printer!'' So they dropped in on St. John Hornby of the Ashendene Press, whom they also knew, and stayed for tea and dinner (*Friends*, 336).

On August 30, 1922, Lawrence forsook civilian society and, but for four months, remained under military discipline in the two lowest ranks the rest of his life. His duties, the crowd and noise in barracks, and the isolation of the bases hardly encouraged literary activities. That he nonetheless persisted in them shows their importance to him.

Entering the ranks represented his rejection of worldly rewards: money, honors, social position, political influence, public responsibility, personal comfort, leisure, the freedom to see whom and go where he pleased. To him, literature and art occupied a better world somehow removed from social pretense, the games people play jostling for position, attention, power. "I've wished all my life to have the power of creating something imaginative: sculpture, painting, literature." "Artists excite and attract me."[65] G. B. Shaw thought he "had a perfectly ridiculous adoration of literature and authors" (*Friends*, 247). His brother said he went so far as to believe "the production of works of art forms the only valid title to fame, or even justification of existence" (*Friends*, 589).

Lawrence certainly overvalued art and artists. "In one world I would put the creatures that create...while in another world, working for them, would be the cooks and shoemakers and boatmen and soldiers, who might swell a chest only for the hour after they had been of use to them."[66]

Lawrence timed his enlistment to coincide with the completion of the third draft of *Seven Pillars*, known as "the Oxford text" because eight copies were set in painfully small two-column format by the *Oxford Times*. Just before enlisting, he wrote G. B. Shaw (whom he had met for only twenty minutes that day in March) to ask would he read a copy and say what he thought. He also sent a copy to Edward Garnett, the editor and critic then serving as reader for the new publishing firm Jonathan Cape had established.

Thus, *Seven Pillars* was a calling card, a way to introduce himself to, correspond with, and meet literary figures; likewise, it induced some readers, like E. M. Forster and H. S. Ede, to write to Lawrence. However, the card was not always hospitably received. Rudyard Kipling was a case in point. The older champion of Britain's empire might have been expected to welcome the younger champion of brown dominions. In 1919, the two had discussed Asian issues; but Kipling was decidedly cool when Lawrence asked him to read *Seven Pillars*. "It looks to me...as if you had been on the job of that book too long," he wrote. "...I do not hold with showing one's friends what one is doing, till it is all done....if you are a pro-Yid [i.e., pro-Zionist, as Lawrence was]...I shall most likely...refuse to touch it."[67]

THE GARNETTS

Edward Garnett and Jonathan Cape were central figures in Lawrence's literary world. Garnett, whom he met at Cape's office in 1921, was one of the first readers of the Oxford text. In the fall of 1922, when Lawrence contemplated publishing a shortened version, Garnett (who had abridged *Arabia Deserta*) marked up a copy for this purpose.[68] When the work was done and only his signature on the Cape contract remained, Lawrence changed his mind. Despite this and other contretemps, Garnett, whose forte was nursing writers, remained a reliable friend and correspondent. Like others, he felt Lawrence was wasting himself in the ranks and tried to entice him out and, failing that, to encourage his writing. His letter inviting Lawrence to edit a proposed literary journal is noted in *The Mint*, chapter 19, "Shit-Cart":

> One of our hut fellows had flung me a letter....I now fished it from the pouch of my swill-stinking stiffened overalls....The letter...was soaked, and its envelope shredded open in my raw hand. I read with smarting eyes the offer of a friendly publisher to give me the editorship of his projected highbrow monthly *Belles-lettres*. I stared from the lovely clouds to my foul clothes, and wondered how it would feel to go back.

Two other Garnetts grew involved with Lawrence. Largely as a favor to Edward, who had done so much for him, he contributed an introduction to Richard Garnett's *The Twilight of the Gods*, first published in 1888 and reissued in 1924 (p. 64). Richard, who had been keeper of the British Museum reading room, was Edward's father. Lawrence also contributed the use of his marketable name, which he had abandoned for most purposes.

Edward's son David, four years younger than Lawrence, initiated a correspondence with him in 1927 after reading a copy of *Seven Pillars* Lawrence had suggested Edward give him. The correspondence continued vigorously (pp. 161–64) and friendship developed, though David, like his father, was not uncritical of Lawrence's foibles. He eventually edited the fullest collection of Lawrence's letters yet published.

When, in 1928, Lawrence asked Edward Garnett to show RAF commander Sir Hugh Trenchard the *Mint* manuscript he had sent from India, Garnett had three typescripts made. He would not risk losing a unique draft, as Lawrence had lost the *Seven Pillars* draft in 1919, or its destruction or retention by Trenchard. (The Garnetts and several other literary friends did not share Lawrence's adulation of Trenchard and the RAF.) Before long, these transcripts were seen by more people than had read the Oxford text.

Of course, *The Mint* could be read much more quickly. Nevertheless, its extensive circulation by Lawrence or with his consent is surprising; he had promised Trenchard it would not be published, for disclosure of the neanderthal state of RAF training would have embarrassed or injured the service and led to his discharge. Either he had grown inured to the danger or his passion for examining himself and his writing overcame his prudence.[69] Certainly, he was the ranking expert on substituting limited circulation for full and open publication. *Revolt in the Desert* was the main blot on a record that, just before his death, he sought to extend with a limited edition of *The Mint*.

JONATHAN CAPE

Jonathan Cape had been a book salesman; in 1920, he and Wren Howard were working for Lee Warner of the Medici Press when they decided to set up their own firm. *Arabia Deserta* brought the firm and Lawrence together.

Lawrence loved *Arabia Deserta* and knew it "very nearly by heart."[70] The five-hundred copies of the original Cambridge University Press 1888 edition had long been exhausted and used copies, when found, cost £20 to £30. During the war, Lawrence had hoped to get the work reprinted by the Government Press in Cairo, ostensibly for intelligence purposes as its account of Arabian geography and peoples was unexcelled; it "became a military text-book, and helped to guide us to victory in the East" (p. 63). He had crossed Doughty's path and met "Ferhan...Doughty's old host" (*Secret*, 126). In 1919, he had failed to persuade Duckworth, which had issued an abridged version in 1908, to publish the full text. He then tried Doubleday (p. 157).

Finally, in July 1920, Warner agreed to print five-hundred copies at nine guineas if he would write an introduction. Cape convinced Warner it would help sales to give the book a joint Medici-Cape imprint. Thus, *Arabia Deserta* became the first book published by the firm of Jonathan Cape, which opened for business January 1, 1921.[71]

Lawrence's name and introduction greatly helped to stimulate sales. Cape's listing expatiated on the Lawrence connection. "This reprint has been issued under the supervision of T. E. Lawrence, Fellow of All Souls, Oxford, who acted during the War as Chief Liaison Officer

with the Emir Feisal on the Staff of Lord Allenby'' (Howard, 44).
The first printing of five-hundred copies sold out in three months
and Cape kept the work in print thereafter until 1971 (Tabachnick
1981, 166).

If, as Edward Garnett said, Cape ''knew nothing about books''
(Jefferson, 196), he did know how to sell them. Having made this
connection with Lawrence, he never let go. ''Always from the very
beginning Lawrence was the key to our success,'' G. Wren Howard,
the founding director with Cape, stated (Howard, 82). Not two weeks
after the new firm was established, Cape wrote Lawrence:

> Can I suggest a business arrangement between us? You can, I am sure,
> cause quite an amount of interesting projects to come my way. . . . I should
> like you to act for me if you feel that you can at any time send anything
> my way. If I publish anything that comes through your introduction, I
> will pay you a royalty of 5% on what the book earns. . . . I mean the receipts
> by me from the sale of copies.[72]

Lawrence disliked formal responsibilities and money seldom
interested him. However, he must have felt obligated to Cape,
apologizing for withdrawing the *Seven Pillars* abridgement at the
twelfth hour. ''I'm very sorry to behave in this way, and to do harm
to your firm and its prospects. The initial fault was mine, in agreeing
to publish the abridgement: and it's another fault to cancel it so
late.''[73] Over the years he acted much as Cape had requested, but
without any formal arrangement and usually with no payment but
books. He criticized books and manuscripts, recommended new and
old titles for publication or reprinting, served as translator, editor,
and even blurb writer. The one rule governing his activities is that no
rule governed them: what he did one day he might not do the next,
because a longer commitment would reduce his freedom and his
situation or mood might change.

Visiting Augustus John, he saw a manuscript that he borrowed, was
struck by, and recommended to Cape. ''I think this is a coming thing,
though you won't think it, the man being a poet and his work verse.
Man is 21, and a believer in Keats and Shelley and *Moby Dick*. . . but
the thing is very good. He wants a publisher. . . and I think it might
pay you. . . to write to him.''[74] Cape brought out *The Flaming
Terrapin* in 1924, launching Roy Campbell's career. The episode
indicates Lawrence's ability to separate his literary judgment from his
personal taste. Decades later, Campbell vilified him privately in terms
too sick to be repeated.

Lawrence's introduction to *Arabia Deserta* was so successful Cape

invited him to write introductions to Melville's *Typee, Omoo*, and
Moby Dick. Despite his admiration for Melville, Lawrence declined,[75]
suggesting a translation instead. "If you...ever have anything in
French which needs translating (for a fee!) please give me a chance
at it....my French is good, and turning it into English is a pleasure
to me: also the cash would be welcome."[76] Lawrence liked Cape's
proposal that he translate Mardrus's French version of the *Arabian
Nights*, but it turned out another publisher would soon issue a
translation.

He then agreed to translate Adrien le Corbeau's *Gigantesque*, a
thirty-five-thousand-word imaginary biography of a seven-thousand-
year-old giant California sequoia. However, his translating, like his
writing, began with enthusiasm and ended in frustration and self-
denigration. At the outset, it was "quite a good book....I'll translate
it with pleasure." He put twenty pages

> into swinging English then turned back and read it, and it was horrible....
> The book is written very common placely by a man of good imagination
> and a bad mind and unobservant. Consequently it's banal in style and
> ordinary in thought, and very interesting in topic....I'd like to wring Le
> Corbeau's neck.

Three months later he had finished. "At last this foul work: complete
....Damn Adrien le Corbeau & his rhetoric. The book is a magnificent
idea, ruined by jejune bombast. My version is better than his."[77]

Lawrence's next French translation did not go so well. Pierre
Custot's *Sturly* was strangely like *Le Gigantesque*: a short fictional
biography of a giant sturgeon who, born near Chinon, swims half the
world's seas before being tossed up on a French beach and sold at
market. Lawrence finished the translation, reread it, "and I have
burned it page by page....Gigantesque [proofs] went off yesterday.
It's rotten bad. Should have burned that too."[78] Not quite crediting
this, Cape asked if Lawrence had kept an earlier draft;[79] when none
was produced, he got Richard Aldington to do the translation.
Lawrence wrote the jacket blurb (p. 101).

Cape next suggested Flaubert's *Salammbo*, which Lawrence greatly
esteemed. He said "yes" and then, a week later, "no," feeling that
"he had over-committed himself" and should concentrate on revising
Seven Pillars (Wilson, 734).

At the top of one Lawrence letter, Wren Howard scribbled in pencil,
"This wretched man had better write a novel—it wd help to clear his
addled head." Replying, Cape was more diplomatic. "Why don't you
write a novel and in it work out all your feeling and your attitude to

the world in general?''[80] Over the years, E. M. Forster and John Buchan also suggested Lawrence try his hand at fiction, but Lawrence's fictional talent was deployed in conversation and letters, play-acting, spying, leg-pulling, occasional boasting, and what Robert Graves called "foxing" to put someone off the scent. He told Cape, "My own writing is only a dissatisfaction to me: so much disappointment & pain without any faculty of pleasing myself or anyone else. For that reason I tried translating, hoping to dodge thereby the creative effort: only to find myself as particular over the reproductive."[81]

Cape reaped his reward when, deep in debt over the extravagant subscriber's edition, Lawrence finally agreed to publishing a truncated *Seven Pillars* with the camels in and the agony out. *Revolt in the Desert* appeared in March 1927 with 'T. E. Lawrence' on the title page as a thin salve for the author's conscience and T. E. Lawrence, minus apostrophes, on the jacket. In publicity, advertisements, reviews, and newspaper stories, it was Lawrence of Arabia, T. E. Lawrence, T. E. Shaw, and anything but anonymity. The book, which Lawrence called a "very harmless colourless lifeless spineless abortion,"[82] became a bestseller; ninety-thousand copies were printed before Lawrence stopped further British sales under a special contract provision; U.S. sales continued. Cape sustained the public appetite for Lawrence with a biography he commissioned from Robert Graves and published in November 1927, giving Graves only three months to write it.

Lawrence's two years in India, 1927–28, a posting he arranged to escape the publicity he rightly anticipated from the publication of *Seven Pillars* and *Revolt*, were comparatively productive. His duties left much free time; his correspondence grew so much he complained he could not afford the postage and sought to supplement his RAF pittance by writing. "I find that I must make twenty pounds or so. The obvious way (forgetting 'Sturly') is to attempt another French translation. Probably you won't want me again...," he wrote Cape. "Have you any objection to my trying to touch someone for a French novel on commission?"[83] In subsequent letters Cape asked if he had a book in mind; again offered him a regular retainer; repeated Edward Garnett's invitation to edit a literary review; and suggested he translate Rousseau's *Confessions*.

Perhaps Lawrence's was less a request than a notice that he did not want to be bound solely to Cape, for he accepted none of these proposals.[84] Instead, he sounded out Doubleday about a French translation[85] and began to review books for *The Spectator* (as will be discussed later), to copy and revise the 1922 notes that became *The Mint*, and to translate the *Odyssey*.

Revolt and Graves's biography, *Lawrence and the Arabs*, brought

Cape's Lawrence stock to a high point not reached again until after his death. Faced with the *Revolt* contract clause obliging him to offer Cape his next book, and having no intention to publish *The Mint*, Lawrence offered it for "a million [pounds] down in advance of a royalty of 90%.... writing books might be an inevitable act of nature: but...publishing them was an indulgence" he told Edward Garnett.[86]

He sent Cape or Garnett repeated suggestions of books they should publish; commented, sometimes in unbelievable detail, on books, galleys, or manuscripts they sent (as in his 4500-word letter on Henry Williamson's *Tarka the Otter*—see p. 105); and dropped by their office for literary talk when he could get to London. But he undertook no major project for the firm.

The *Odyssey* translation, which did not involve Cape, occupied much of Lawrence's free time from spring 1928 until August 1931, for he "did about five lines an hour, revising each line later an average of fourteen times..." (Weintraub 1963, 187). A robust start and discouraged end was again evidenced. In 1928, before he started, the Odyssey "goes with me, always, to every camp, for I love it....so great a work of art"; in 1930, "the Odyssey disappoints me. It is not really good stuff. How does it go on being praised?" By 1932, it is "A pot boiler.... Thin, arty, self-conscious stuff.... pastiche & face powder."[87]

After the *Odyssey*, Lawrence took on no literary work of comparable magnitude. Shuttling between boatyards, RAF installations, ship and engine builders, and sea trials was unsettling; his correspondence accumulated until he could pick up a batch and deal with it. He did edit Middle East war memoirs Cape issued in 1933 as *Garoot, The Adventures of a Clydeside Apprentice* by Ian Tyre. "All my effort has been to break up his flow into significant chunks: to chapter, paragraph and sentence the rolling flood: and in so doing to increase its speed and readability."[88] He accepted only books in payment.[89] He turned down a stream of suggestions: to edit Burton's *Anatomy of Melancholy* or "anything else... you think you would like to edit or translate"; to edit *Danakil*, the manuscript of an Abyssinian journey; or to write anything of his own.[90]

By request, he sent Cape a jacket plug to boost sales of *The Charlesmen* by the Swedish writer Verner von Heidenstam:

'GOSTA BERLING'S SAGA by Selma Lagerloff and THE CHARLESMEN by Verner Von Heidenstam are two unusual books in your list. THE CHARLESMEN is exquisite and rare work. It has a good deal of the quality of a frieze in sculpture and the conversations are so odd. I've read nothing else like it.'—T. E. Shaw[91]

An edition published after his death changed the signature to T. E. Lawrence. *The Charlesmen* is a brilliant series of sketches and vignettes of the Swedish troops Charles XII led to death and captivity in Russia and Turkey, 1707–14; the author won the Nobel Prize in 1916.

Cape kept Lawrence before the public with a new biography, published March 1934, by the prominent military writer Captain B. H. Liddell Hart, far more carefully researched than Graves's.[92] On July 30, 1935, ten weeks after Lawrence's death, the firm was at last able to publish *Seven Pillars*. The first printing of sixty-thousand was followed by five more that year and many others in succeeding years; by *T. E. Lawrence by His Friends* in 1937, David Garnett's edition of Lawrence's letters in 1938, a sanitized *Mint* in 1955, an unexpurgated *Mint* in 1973, and many other works by and about Lawrence that made Cape the foremost publisher of Lawrenciana.

Cape was not Lawrence's only publisher friend. He met Frank Doubleday, the American publisher, at a London dinner in December 1918; they corresponded thereafter and tried to meet when both were in England. Lawrence was singularly kind to elderly friends; some may have served as parental figures, especially after his father's death in 1919 and his mother's departure for China in 1922. (His relations with her were tense and any older woman who did not seek to impose her standards of morality, conduct, cooking, and housekeeping would be more relaxing.) Among these were Doubleday and his wife Florence, Bernard and Charlotte Shaw, and Thomas and Florence Hardy.

Lawrence struck up acquaintanceships with Peter Davies, Frederic Manning's publisher; F. V. M. Morley and Geoffrey Faber of Faber; A. S. Frere-Reeves of Heinemann; and C. J. Greenwood of Boriswood. As his departure from the RAF approached, he wanted to stay in touch with several publishers to have a range of translating and editing opportunities to earn "about £70 more" a year, which he felt he would need beyond his small investment income and RAF pension.

"My last visit to London," he told a friend, "I went the round of the publishers I know, sounding them for a job in 12 months time, when the R.A.F. leaves me. . . . a job that will let me stay most of the time in Dorset."[93] To Morley he explained how, in "my walk across Bloomsbury. . . . I usually ask for Cape first. . . and then you, returning to Tottenham Court Road (and civilisation) by way of Frere-Reeve in Heinemann's. . . . it should be possible for me, if I maintain friendly relations with four or five good publishers to work them in rotation for a modest job of editing or translating."[94]

Back from India in January 1929, Lawrence renewed contact with his old literary friends—the Shaws, E. M. Forster, Edward Garnett, Robert Graves, Edward Marsh, Siegfried Sasson, Mrs. Hardy, John

Buchan—and made new ones: David Garnett, H. S. Ede, Henry
Williamson, Frederic Manning, Noel Coward, James Hanley, Geoffrey
Keynes. He did not hesitate to send compliments and criticism on their
latest book to writers he did not know. In this manner, he opened
a correspondence, for example, with C. Day Lewis and Thornton
Wilder.

HELPING FRIENDS

His interest in writers went beyond their writing to their welfare: their
publication, income, and contentment. He did what he could to help
those who needed help: in his postwar days at Oxford he was called
the "little ray of sunshine."[95] His persistence and ingenuity in helping
Graves and Doughty are illustrative.

When they met, Lawrence was thirty-one and famous and Robert
Graves twenty-four, an impoverished poet with a wife and two small
children. Lawrence liked Graves's poetry and commended it to others,
while offering him detailed comments and advice. "He had a keen
eye for surface faults, and...it was rarely that I did not agree that
something was wrong at the point indicated," Graves said. "...he
stood as a sort of guardian angel over me: if anything went wrong
he was always at hand to help."[96]

When Graves's shop failed in 1921 and he owed £300, Lawrence
gave him £50 and three manuscript chapters of *Seven Pillars*, which
he sold for £200.[97] He tried to get Graves books to review[98] and a
job writing a history of the RAF; helped him get a 1925 appointment
as Professor of English at the new Royal Egyptian University in Cairo;
gave him *Seven Pillars* with the note "Please sell when read," which
he did for some £330; and arranged for him to write his biography,
for which Graves received a £500 advance. "You know you have my
help and fellowship whenever you need it, in any direction I can reach,"
Lawrence told Graves.[99] Despite a certain estrangement that later set
in over Laura Riding, whom Lawrence disliked and Graves loved, he
honored that pledge.

Lawrence's part in the 1921 reissue of *Arabia Deserta* has been noted.
He also helped to get it reviewed by the right person in the right
place.[100] Not long after, Lawrence learned that Doughty was in
financial distress as his investments had collapsed. He contrived with
Sydney Cockerell to raise £400 (much of it his own money) to buy
the manuscript of Doughty's *The Dawn in Britain* for presentation
to the British Museum, while Cockerell raised a similar sum to buy
the *Arabia Deserta* notebooks for the Fitzwilliam Museum.

Lawrence arranged for Doughty to receive, in October 1922, a civil list pension of £150 a year.[101] Though the two differed radically in temperament and outlook, and Doughty could not approve of *Seven Pillars*,[102] Lawrence remained steadfast to the end; he was one of the small group present at Doughty's funeral in January 1926. When, some months earlier, an American scholar sought to discuss the Mid-East with him, Lawrence asked:

> Did you send old Mr. Doughty a copy of your article? It would probably interest him. He is very old, & is resting & waiting quietly for the end of his life in Kent: and all news of the parts of Arabia covered by him on his journey give him great pleasure. Most people interested in Arabia feel sufficiently indebted to the old man to wish to do him a kindness.[103]

Lawrence put one tank corps comrade in touch with Raymond Savage, his literary agent, to help him place his work; he helped G. W. M. Dunn, a fellow aircraftman, get his poems published by Cape.[104] He gave H. S. Ede shrewd advice on how to publicize his book.[105] When Manning Pike, who had done the press work for *Seven Pillars*, was in a poor state and unemployed, he gave him a few pounds and a push.[106] When K. W. Marshall, a young bookseller he befriended, lost his job he lent him his cottage and tried to find him work. When V. M. Yeates, author of *Winged Victory*, died, he inquired about his wife and children. "They are more than half the tragedy. Is there any prospect of help for them?"[107]

To boost sales of *Her Privates We*, he let Peter Davies put out a little pamphlet on his detection of the anonymous author; he let other publishers use extracts from letters to promote books by James Hanley (p. 116) and Simon Jesty (p. 117). An episode recounted by C. Day Lewis indicates the potential market value of Lawrence's name:

> In 1934 Lawrence was reported by a gossip columnist to have said to Winston Churchill that I was a good prospect. Hardly had the newspaper come out when the telephone bell started ringing in the office of the Hogarth Press. Leonard and Virginia Woolf, having sold the usual small number of each of my three books of verse they had so far published, had covered the stack of unsold copies with chintz...and were using it as a settee. The orders now pouring in for these books caused Leonard and Virginia to subside until, within a few hours, they were sitting on the floor. As a result, when *A Time to Dance* came out in 1935, it sold very well from the start.[108]

In the last weeks of his life, though in a distressed state trying to adjust to retirement and hounded from his cottage by newsmen, he looked into the police action barring the local sale of Hanley's *Boy* as obscene, to see how it might best be dealt with (pp. 181–82).

The recumbent stone effigy of Lawrence carved as a memorial by his friend Eric Kennington shows him in Arab gown and headdress, his hand on a curved dagger and beside his head the three books he carried during the desert campaign. His devotion to poetry and literature was serious and lifelong, perhaps too serious, for to him literature was somehow better than life: better composed and controlled, more examinable, more self-contained, and far more durable.

Lawrence of Arabia, Strange Man of Letters

Part I

Published Criticism

The pieces in Part I are all of Lawrence's known published criticism. As only two of the pieces are currently in print (the introduction to *Arabia Deserta* and the translator's note to the *Odyssey*) and most are difficult or impossible to obtain, it seemed useful to collect them in one place. The pieces in each chapter—Introductions, Reviews, and Bric-à-Brac—are arranged in the chronological order in which they were written, so far as that can be determined.

1

Introductions

Despite his avowed dislike of introductions as a genre and a mode of advertisement, Lawrence wrote three, to books by Charles Doughty, Richard Garnett, and Bertram Thomas.

Arabia Deserta

How he came to write the introduction to the 1921 reissue of *Travels in Arabia Deserta*, Charles Doughty's classic account of his 1876–78 travels in Arabia, has already been explained (p. 35). He did not want to write it, but could not escape. "I hate introductions to masterpieces (puff-introductions by pygmies: It's like tourists cutting their names on the walls of Kenilworth) but there seemed little chance of getting the book out without an effort in that direction."[1]

Lawrence loved Arabia, prolixity, detail, and elaborately worked prose; as there are more of these in *Arabia Deserta* than in any other work on Arabia, no wonder he loved it. In the introduction, its "completeness" is what he most praises: "Doughty's completeness is devastating." "...he seems to have recorded everything." "The realism of the book is complete....Doughty tries to tell the full and exact truth of all that he saw." He also admires Doughty's simple conviction, his unchanged Englishness—"'His seeing is altogether English"—his directly recorded vision untainted by self-questioning— "the book is never morbid, never introspective", and his "immunity" to Arab values, beliefs, and ways of thinking.

In all this, the contrast with Lawrence himself is implicit. Distinguishing the small class of Englishmen abroad who "feel deeply the influence of the native people" and "imitate the native" from the larger, "cleaner" class whose Englishness is strengthened in foreign surroundings, he puts Doughty in the latter. Clearly, he himself is in the former, those who imitate the native "so well that they are imitated back again."[2]

The laudatory introduction should be compared with Lawrence's remarks on Doughty in his correspondence over a seventeen-year period (pp. 145–52). In 1911 and 1912, as a young man of twenty-two and twenty-three, *Arabia Deserta* is his model; he wants "to do something of the sort," yet is "not trying to rival Doughty." Has he been captured by Doughty, the Arabs, or the desert? In later years, at least, I think the answer would be the desert, which maintained its hold on his memory when that of the Arabs and Doughty had slipped.[3]

The failings of Doughty's other work—the "bathos" of *The Cliffs*, the disorganization of *Dawn in Britain*, the preaching of *The Clouds*—do not diminish Lawrence's regard for *Arabia Deserta*. However, in his 1923 letters to Sydney Cockerell, reservations begin to emerge. The greatness of the book now seems a product of Doughty's smallness and simplicity. In subsequent letters he notes the book's formlessness and redundancy, Doughty's "inhuman arrogance." The "unshakeable conviction of his own rightness" stems from his simplicity, narrowness, and personal isolation. *Adam Cast Forth* is "splendid"—in the fall 1919, Lawrence had "spent many hours. . .reading and re-reading" it (Wilson, 621); the rest of his poetry is a "great failure." Though *Arabia Deserta* "remains wonderful" Lawrence no longer likes its style; "why should we borrow our syntax from. . .Sweden or Denmark"?[4] If Doughty had written in "two-syllabled words" more people would read it; the archaisms and Arabic terms are regrettable.

Robert Graves expressed the contrast between *Arabia Deserta* and *Seven Pillars* bluntly: "Doughty was too stupid and simple to conceal anything, whereas Lawrence was too clever to tell the whole truth."[5]

In 1924, Cape invited Lawrence to write a memoir of Doughty; he declined, and did so again in February 1926.[6] Lawrence's August 27, 1927 letter to Hogarth (p. 150) was prompted by Hogarth's work on Doughty's biography, cut short by his death November 6. Thereupon, Lawrence was asked to finish the manuscript. Though reluctant, he drafted a statement of the conditions under which he would,[7] but gladly withdrew when Hogarth's son William took on the task.

Nonetheless, William put him on notice: ". . .you are the only person competent to handle the Doughty manuscript. . . .if I find, as seems likely, that the needed revision is beyond my power, I shall press for you."[8] Mrs. Hogarth, for her part, wrote, "I am utterly depending on you to write an introduction. . . .[Mrs. Doughty] is disappointed with the last 4 or 5 chapters dealing with the poetry. . . .[Hogarth] says in the preface that he is no judge of poetry and. . .does not propose to treat it 'seriously'."[9] That was probably Hogarth's way of skirting the issue, since he agreed with Lawrence's strictures about Doughty's poetry.[10]

Lawrence did not write the introduction, nor did he ever undertake a life of Hogarth, as Mrs. Hogarth also requested.[11] If he did not respond to these requests from the widow of his mentor, a man for whom he had the deepest regard, it can only be because he could not for emotional reasons that are not easily understood. Somehow, in his self-despising inner world, Hogarth and Doughty were *good* while he was *vile*, unfit to soil their memory. That feeling is expressed in an astonishing remark to Charlotte Shaw: "...as for D. G. H. and Doughty; do you really think I would foul them with trying to draw my slime across their track? Oh, they are much too good!"[12]

In 1930, Harper's would have published Doughty's *Mansoul* if Lawrence wrote an introduction; he declined.[13] By now, refusal said nothing about Doughty; it was Lawrence's immediate response to almost any invitation. "I will not write a foreword, or a backword, or a middle piece, or any old piece, for anyone for anything, I hope. I always say 'I hope', because I daren't say 'never': that word would ring down the curtain on too many hopes."[14]

The Twilight of the Gods

In 1915, Lawrence writes home from Cairo, "Salute Arnie [his youngest brother] for me. Ask him to search at Blackwell's for a copy of *The Twilight of the Gods* by Richard Garnett, & if it's not dear, to send it me. The book must be out of print long ago, but is probably common" (*Home*, 307). In 1922, he tells Edward Garnett he has changed his mind about his son David's *Lady into Fox*: "It's remarkable." Earlier, he had called it decadent and (unflatteringly) "fantastic." "By the way isn't it unusual that literary power should carry on from generation to generation like that. He's the third, isn't he? Yet, to my scholar's taste, *The Twilight of the Gods* is more attractive" (Garnett, 383–84).

Around November 1923, Garnett asked would Lawrence do an introduction for the new illustrated edition of *Twilight* John Lane was planning. Lawrence replied,

> when I first read your letter I said "That's a thing I'll have to do".....
> Since, I am become reluctant (you see, I meant not to use my brain any more) but still I feel that it can hardly be avoided....Introductions are vicious things, & I've sinned once already.[15]

He told Charlotte Shaw, "Introductions are not honourable things, either for the introducer or the introduced....For the humour of the situation lies in my having consented to write an introduction to. . . .'The twilight of the Gods': to be done soon. . . . I'm to get twenty guineas. Oh, the sweet pill!''[16]

Now in the tank corps at Bovington, Lawrence was "not a happy man."[17] The writing did not go well; on May 3, he was "still baffled" by it.[18] Three weeks later he sent it off:

> . . .here the results of several efforts are, boiled together. I know their inadequacy, so much that if I read them again they will go W. P. B. [waste paper basket]. It's the best place you can put them. . . . Please tear it up and get [H. G.] Wells or David [Garnett] to write a successor.[19]

The debate of the conservative and modernist Gods, down from their pedestals at the British Museum, about reforming Olympus is, I believe, the only example of sheer fiction in Lawrence's writing.

Arabia Felix

Despite his ceaseless protestations, Lawrence wrote one more introduction.

In 1929, he had urged Hugh Trenchard to send one of the new airships, R100 or R101, soon to make trial flights, over the Ruba el Khali, the "Empty Quarter" of Arabia. "No European has ever crossed it, nor any Arab any of us has actually questioned. . . . To go over the empty quarter will also be an enormous advertisement for them [the airships]: it will mark an era in exploration" (Garnett, 663). The trip was not made; in October 1930, R101 crashed, killing forty-eight people; only six survived.

Shortly after, Bertram Thomas, the British agent at Muscat, crossed the desert by camel. Lawrence was enthusiastic about "the finest geographic feat since Shackleton." Thomas was due a knighthood "or some other honour of which I know nothing," he told Edward Marsh, then secretary to the Minister for the Colonies (Garnett, 715). Thomas received an OBE (Order of the British Empire) and awards from several geographical societies, but his CMG (Companion of St. Michael and St. George) was delayed seventeen years.[20]

When Thomas asked Lawrence to introduce his account of the trip, he replied, "I implore you not to have a preface. . . . Resist Cape. . . and he will flee before you.''[21] When Thomas persisted, he wrote:

> I'll read your script or proofs (better script) with eagerness: and if it is impossibly bad I'll try and write a preface. If it is, as it must be, hugely good, then you'll be so proud of it. . .that you will utterly spurn and

despise the idea of a preface. Prefaces are the fruits not of vanity but of over-modesty.[22]

Lawrence made marginal notes and suggestions on the manuscript: "It is a simple, direct, interesting book, full of information, and *nice*," he informed Charlotte Shaw. "Not very adeptly written, though he tries hard." As for the preface, "as usual I have nothing to say, and hesitate to display an empty mind."[23] He wrote Thomas "to report my failure to make any foreword. . . . all I feel is a great release and relief, at knowing that your book is good enough. . . . It is exceedingly well told and will live for generations" (Garnett, 737).

Thomas was not put off and finally Lawrence relented. He wired that he "would get something done" and did. "A poor, lame thing . . . . It will need your censorship: and the proper spelling of all the people's names" (Brown, 459). To Cape, he said, "I hope very much that he [Thomas] and you will decide not to use it . . . . the book will do better on its own."[24]

The faint prospect that Cape would take that advice was eliminated by suggestions G. B. Shaw added in proof. "Will you sign this Foreword 'T.E.L' or T. E. Shaw ('T.E.L') or (sometimes T.E.L)?" Lawrence asked.[25] It was signed T.E.S. but the title page read, "With a Foreword by T. E. Lawrence (T.E.S.)"; Scribner's American edition added "Colonel."

Lawrence apologized to Charlotte Shaw. "I was forced into it by Thomas, and found my writing joints stiff."[26] Forced! A mule could sooner be forced to fly.

The mood of the foreword is a recognition of aging. One by one, Lawrence recalls the great travellers of his youth: Doughty, Blunt, Hogarth, Bell. "They are all gone, those great ones. . . . and that is why Thomas must come down to me." A year earlier, in *Cakes and Ale*, Somerset Maugham had depicted a writer who became great by outliving his contemporaries. The parody pained Mrs. Hardy (though Hugh Walpole was apparently Maugham's target); Lawrence said it "made my flesh creep" (p. 185). There was no denying it; the ever-boyish Lawrence, now forty-three, was feeling the years. "He was plumper, could not see as well as in earlier days, was occasionally hard of hearing, and felt the cold. In short, he was slipping into middle age."[27]

He was not yet dead or buried in the past. Often accused of having backed the wrong prince in the desert, in the foreword he recognizes "the crowning solidarity which the desert owes to Ibn Saud." And he sees the future importance of airpower in war and peace, when "a winged generation lands on the next planet."

Travels in Arabia Deserta
by Charles M. Doughty

It is not comfortable to have to write about *Arabia Deserta*. I have studied it for ten years, and have grown to consider it a book not like other books, but something particular, a bible of its kind. To turn round now and reckon its merits and demerits seems absurd. I do not think that any traveller in Arabia before or since Mr. Doughty has qualified himself to praise the book—much less to blame it. The more you learn of Arabia the more you find in *Arabia Deserta*. The more you travel there the greater your respect for the insight, judgment and artistry of the author. We call the book "Doughty" pure and simple, for it is a classic, and the personality of Mr. Doughty hardly comes into question. Indeed, it is rather shocking to learn that he is a real and living person. The book has no date and can never grow old. It is the first and indispensable work upon the Arabs of the desert; and if it has not always been referred to, or enough read, that has been because it was excessively rare. Every student of Arabia wants a copy.

However, there is no need at this time of day to commend Doughty to students. They all know of him. It is to the outside public, willing to read a great prose work, the record of the wanderings of an English poet for two years among the Beduins, that this edition must make its appeal, and perhaps with them that the verdict of present-day travellers in Arabia will have weight. I have talked the book over with many travellers, and we are agreed that here you have all the desert, its hills and plains, the lava fields, the villages, the tents, the men and animals. They are told of to the life, with words and phrases fitted to them so perfectly that one cannot dissociate them in memory. It is the true Arabia, the land with its smells and dirt, as well as its nobility and freedom. There is no sentiment, nothing merely picturesque, that most common failing of oriental travel-books. Doughty's completeness is devastating. There is nothing we would take away, little we could add. He took all Arabia for his province, and has left to his successors only the poor part of specialists. We may write books on parts of the desert or some of the history of it; but there can never be another picture of the whole, in our time, because here it is all said, and by a great master.

There have been many well-endowed Englishmen travelling in Arabia, and most of them have written books. None have brought away a prize as rich as Doughty brought, and the merit of this is his own unaided merit. He had many things against him. Forty years ago the desert was less hospitable to strangers than it is to-day. Turkey was still strong there, and the Wahabi movement had kept fanaticism vivid in the tribes. Doughty was a pioneer, both as European and Christian, in nearly all the districts he entered. Also he was poor. He came down a lone man from Damascus with the pilgrim caravan, and was left behind at Medain Salih with scant recommendation. He struck out into the desert dressed like the very poor, travelling like the very poor, trying to maintain himself by the practice of rational medicine, in a society more willing to invest in charms.

Then he was a sick man. His health was weak when he started, and the climate of the plateau of Arabia is a trying one, with its extremes of heat and cold, and the poverty of its nourishment. He had been brought up in England, a fruitful country of rich and plentiful food. He came as a guest to the Arab tents, to share their lean hospitality, and to support himself on the little that sufficed them. They treated him to what they had themselves. Their skinny bodies subsisted well enough on a spring season of camel-milk, and rare meals of dates or meat for the barren months of the year, but such a diet was starvation for an Englishman. It would be short commons to a sedentary man; but Doughty was for ever wandering about, often riding from sunrise to sunset, if not for half the night, in forced marches across rocky and toilsome country, under a burning sun, or in keen exhausting winds. Travel in Arabia in the best circumstances, with a train of servants, good riding-beasts, tents and your own kitchen, is a trying experience. Doughty faced it native-fashion, in spite of his physical disadvantages, and brought home more booty than we all. The sheer endurance of his effort is wonderful.

Somewhere he half apologizes for his defects, calling his book the seeing of a hungry man, the telling of a most weary man; nevertheless he seems to have recorded everything. We have all sometimes been weary in the desert, and some of us have been hungry there, but none of us triumphed over our bodies as Doughty did. He makes his hardships a positive profit to him, by distilling from them into his pages that sense of strain and desolation which will remind every Arabian traveller vividly of his own less fortunate moments. Yet even at such times, coming so often in these two dangerous years, Doughty's keenness of observation was not reduced. He goes on showing us the circumstances and the characters and the places of his tale, without any loss of interest: and that this could be so is a high testimony, not only to his strength of mind, but also to the imaginative appeal of Arabia and the Arabs to him and to us.

For his own strength of character his book stands unconscious witness. He has revealed himself to us in his pages indirectly (the book is never morbid, never introspective), almost unwillingly, for the way of telling is detached, making no parade of good or evil. He refused to be the hero of his story. Yet he was very really the hero of his journey, and the Arabs knew how great he was. I spent nine months in Western Arabia, much of it in the districts through which he had passed, and I found that he had become history in the desert. It was more than forty years ago, and that space of time would even in our country cause much to be forgotten. In the desert it is relatively longer, for the hardships of common life leave little chance for the body to recruit itself, and so men are short-lived and their memories of strangers, and events outside the family tree, soon fail. Doughty's visit was to their fathers or grandfathers, and yet they have all learned of him. They tell tales of him, making something of a legend of the tall and impressive figure, very wise and gentle, who came to them like a herald of the outside world. His aloofness from the common vexations of their humanity coloured their imagination. He was very patient, generous and pitiful, to be accepted into their confidence without doubt.

They say that he seemed proud only of being Christian, and yet never crossed their faith. He was book-learned, but simple in the arts of living, ignorant of camels, trustful of every man, very silent. He was the first Englishman they had met. He predisposed them to give a chance to other men of his race, because they had found him honourable and good. So he broke a road for his religion. He was followed by Mr. Wilfrid Blunt and Miss Gertrude Bell, other strong personalities. They confirmed the desert in its view of Englishmen, and gave us a privileged position which is a grave responsibility upon all who follow them. Thanks to them an Englishman finds a welcome in Arabia, and can travel, not indeed comfortably for it is a terrible land, but safely over the tracks which Doughty opened with such pains. No country has been more fortunate in its ambassadors. We are accepted as worthy persons unless we prove ourselves the contrary by our own misdoings. This is no light monument to the memory of the man who stamped so clear an impression of his virtue on a nomad people in the casual journeyings of two years.

We export two chief kinds of Englishmen, who in foreign parts divide themselves into two opposed classes. Some feel deeply the influence of the native people, and try to adjust themselves to its atmosphere and spirit. To fit themselves modestly into the picture they suppress all in them that would be discordant with local habits and colours. They imitate the native as far as possible, and so avoid friction in their daily life. However, they cannot avoid the consequences of imitation, a hollow, worthless thing. They are like the people but not of the

people, and their half-perceptible differences give them a sham
influence often greater than their merit. They urge the people among
whom they live into strange, unnatural courses by imitating them so
well that they are imitated back again. The other class of Englishmen
is the larger class. In the same circumstance of exile they reinforce
their character by memories of the life they have left. In reaction against
their foreign surroundings they take refuge in the England that was
theirs. They assert their aloofness, their immunity, the more vividly
for their loneliness and weakness. They impress the peoples among
whom they live by reaction, by giving them an ensample of the complete
Englishman, the foreigner intact.

Doughty is a great member of the second, the cleaner class. He says
that he was never oriental, though the sun made him an Arab; and
much of his value lies in the distinction. His seeing is altogether English:
yet at the same time his externals, his manners, his dress, and his speech
were Arabic, and nomad Arab, of the desert. The desert inhibits
considered judgments; its bareness and openness make its habitants
frank. Men in it speak out their minds suddenly and unreservedly.
Words in the desert are clear-cut. Doughty felt this contagion of
truthfulness sharply (few travel-journals show a greater sensibility to
climate and geography than this), and among the tribes he delivered
himself like them. Even in the villages he maintained an untimely and
uncompromising bluntness, in a firm protest against the glozing politic
speech of the town-Arabs. His own origin was from the settled country
of England, and this preference for the nomad might seem strange;
but in practice the Englishman, and especially the Englishman of
family, finds the tribes more to his taste than the villages, and Doughty
everywhere is the outspoken Beduin. His "stiffness to maintain a just
opinion against the half-reason of the world" was often unwise—
but always respectable, and the Arabs respected him for it even where
they resented it most.

Very climatic, too, are his sudden changes of tone and judgment.
The desert is a place of passing sensation, of cash-payment of opinion.
Men do not hold their minds in suspense for days, to arrive at a just
and balanced average of thought. They say good at once when it is
good, and bad at once when it is bad. Doughty has mirrored this also
for us in himself. One paragraph will have a harsh judgment; the next
is warm kindness. His record ebbs and flows with his experience, and
by reading not a part of the book but all of it you obtain a many-
sided sympathetic vision, in the round, of his companions of these
stormy and eventful years.

The realism of the book is complete. Doughty tries to tell the full
and exact truth of all that he saw. If there is a bias it will be against

the Arabs, for he liked them so much; he was so impressed by the strange attraction, isolation and independence of this people that he took pleasure in bringing out their virtues by a careful expression of their faults. "If one live any time with the Arab he will have all his life after a feeling of the desert." He had experienced it himself, the test of nomadism, that most deeply biting of all social disciplines, and for our sakes he strained all the more to paint it in its true colours, as a life too hard, too empty, too denying for all but the strongest and most determined men. Nothing is more powerful and real than this record of all his daily accidents and obstacles, and the feelings that came to him on the way. His picture of the Semites, sitting to the eyes in a cloaca, but with their brows touching Heaven, sums up in full measure their strength and weakness, and the strange contradictions of their thought which quicken our curiosity at our first meeting with them.

To try and solve their riddle many of us have gone far into their society, and seen the clear hardness of their belief, a limitation almost mathematical, which repels us by its unsympathetic form. Semites have no half-tones in their register of vision. They are a people of primary colours, especially of black and white, who see the world always in line. They are a certain people, despising doubt, our modern crown of thorns. They do not understand our metaphysical difficulties, our self-questionings. They know only truth and untruth, belief and unbelief, without our hesitating retinue of finer shades.

Semites are black and white not only in vision, but in their inner furnishing; black and white not merely in clarity, but in apposition. Their thoughts live easiest among extremes. They inhabit superlatives by choice. Sometimes the great inconsistents seem to possess them jointly. They exclude compromise, and pursue the logic of their ideas to its absurd ends, without seeing incongruity in their opposed conclusions. They oscillate with cool head and tranquil judgment from asymptote to asymptote, so imperturbably that they would seem hardly conscious of their giddy flight.

They are a limited narrow-minded people whose inert intellects lie incuriously fallow. Their imaginations are keen but not creative. There is so little Arab art to-day in Asia that they can nearly be said to have no art, though their rulers have been liberal patrons and have encouraged their neighbours' talents in architecture, ceramic and handicraft. They show no longing for great industry, no organisations of mind or body anywhere. They invent no systems of philosophy or mythologies. They are the least morbid of peoples, who take the gift of life unquestioning, as an axiom. To them it is a thing inevitable, entailed on man, a usufruct, beyond our control. Suicide is a thing nearly impossible and death no grief.

They are a people of spasms, of upheavals, of ideas, the race of the individual genius. Their movements are the more shocking by contrast with the quietude of every day, their great men greater by contrast with the humanity of their mass. Their convictions are by instinct, their activities intuitional. Their largest manufacture is of creeds. They are monopolists of revealed religions, finding always an antagonism of body and spirit, and laying their stress on the spirit. Their profound reaction against matter leads them to preach barrenness, renunciation, poverty: and this atmosphere stifles the minds of the desert pitilessly. They are always looking out towards those things in which mankind has had no lot or part.

The Beduin has been born and brought up in the desert, and has embraced this barrenness too harsh for volunteers with all his soul, for the reason, felt but inarticulate, that there he finds himself indubitably free. He loses all natural ties, all comforting superfluities or complications, to achieve that personal liberty which haunts starvation and death. He sees no virtue in poverty herself; he enjoys the little vices and luxuries—coffee, fresh water, women—which he can still afford. In his life he has air and winds, sun and light, open spaces and great emptiness. There is no human effort, no fecundity in Nature; just heaven above and unspotted earth beneath; and the only refuge and rhythm of their being is in God. This single God is to the Arab not anthropomorphic, not tangible or moral or ethical, not concerned particularly with the world or with him. He alone is great, and yet there is a homeliness, an every-day-ness of this Arab God who rules their eating, their fighting and their lusting; and is their commonest thought, and companion, in a way impossible to those whose God is tediously veiled from them by the decorum of formal worship. They feel no incongruity in bringing God into their weaknesses and appetites. he is the commonest of their words.

This creed of the desert is an inheritance. The Arab does not value it extremely. He has never been either evangelist or proselyte. He arrives at this intense condensation of himself in God by shutting his eyes to the world, and to all the complex possibilities latent in him which only wealth and temptation could bring out. He attains a sure trust and a powerful trust, but of how narrow a field! His sterile experience perverts his human kindness to the image of the waste in which he hides. Accordingly he hurts himself, not merely to be free, but to please himself. There follows a self-delight in pain, a cruelty which is more to him than goods. The desert Arab finds no joy like the joy of voluntarily holding back. He finds luxury in abnegation, renunciation, self-restraint. He lives his own life in a hard selfishness. His desert is made a spiritual ice-house, in which is preserved intact but un-improved for all ages an idea of the unity of God.

Doughty went among these people dispassionately, looked at their life, and wrote it down word for word. By being always Arab in manner and European in mind he maintained a perfect judgment, while bearing towards them a full sympathy which persuaded them to show him their inmost ideas. When his trial of two years was over he carried away in his note-book (so far as the art of writing can express the art of living) the soul of the desert, the complete existence of a remarkable and self-contained community, shut away from the currents of the world in the unchanging desert, working out their days in an environ-ment utterly foreign to us. The economic reason for their existence is the demand for camels, which can be best bred on the thorns and plants of these healthy uplands. The desert is incapable of other development, but admirably suited to this. Their camel-breeding makes the Beduins nomads. The camels live only on the pasture of the desert, and as it is scanty a great herd will soon exhaust any one district. Then they with their masters must move to another, and so they circulate month by month in a course determined by the vegetation sprung up wherever the intermittent winter rains have this season fallen heaviest.

The social organisation of the desert is in tribes, partly because of original family-feeling, partly because the instinct of self-preservation compels large masses of men to hold together for mutual support. By belonging to a recognised tribe each man feels that he has a strong body of nominal kinsmen, to support him if he is injured; and equally to bear the burden and to discharge his wrong-doing, when he is the guilty party. This collective responsibility makes men careful not to offend; and makes punishment very easy. The offender is shut out from the system and becomes an exile till he has made his peace again with the pubic opinion of his tribesmen.

Each tribe has its district in the desert. The extent and nature of these tribal districts are determined by the economic laws of camel-breeding. Each holds a fair chance of pasture all the year round in every normal year, and each holds enough drinking-water to suffice all its households every year; but the poverty of the country forces an internal subdivision of itself upon the tribe. The water-sources are usually single wells (often very scanty wells), and the pasturages small scattered patches in sheltered valleys or oases among the rocks. They could not accommodate at one time or place all the tribe, which therefore breaks into clans, and lives always as clans, wandering each apart on its own cycle within the orbit of the tribal whole.

The society is illiterate, so each clan keeps small enough to enable all its adults to meet frequently, and discuss all common business verbally. Such general intercourse, and their open life beside one another in tents makes the desert a place altogether without privacy. Man lives candidly with man. It is a society in perpetual movement, an equality of voice and opportunity for every male. The daily hearth or sheikh's coffee-gathering is their education, a university for every man grown enough to walk and speak.

It is also their news-office, their tribunal, their political expression, and their government. They bring and expose there in public every day all their ideas, their experiences, their opinions, and they sharpen one another, so that the desert society is always alive, instructed to a high moral level, and tolerant of new ideas. Common rumour makes them as unchanging as the desert in which they live; but more often they show themselves singularly receptive, very open to useful innovations. Their few vested interests make it simple for them to change their ways; but even so it is astonishing to find how whole-heartedly they adopt an invention fitted to their life. Coffee, gunpowder, Manchester cotton are all new things, and yet appear so native that without them one can hardly imagine their desert life.

Consequently, one would expect a book such as *Arabia Deserta*, written forty years ago, to be inaccurate to-day in such little respects, and had Doughty's work been solely scientific, dependent on the expression rather than the spirit of things, its day might have passed. Happily the beauty of the telling, its truth to life, the rich gallery of characters and landscapes in it, will remain for all time, and will keep it peerless, as the indispensable foundation of all true understanding of the desert. And in these forty years the material changes have not been enough to make them really worth detailed record.

The inscriptions at Medain Salih have been studied since his day by the Dominican fathers from Jerusalem, and some little points added to his store. The great stone at Teima which lay in the *haddaj*, was looked for by later travellers, and at last purchased and carried off to Europe. Doughty's collections of these primitive Arab scripts have been surpassed; but he holds the enduring credit of their discovery. His map, and some of his geographical information have been added to, and brought into relation with later information. People with cameras have wandered up and down the Aueyrid *harrat* in which he spent weeks, and of which he wrote so vivid a description. We know their outside face exactly, from photographs; but to read Doughty is to know what they make one feel. Crossley and Rolls-Royce cars have made a road of some of that Wadi Humth, whose importance he first made clear to Europe. Aeroplanes have quartered the hills in which he found such painful going. Unfortunately those in cars and aeroplanes are not able to write intimate books about the country over which they pass.

Another change in Arabia has come from the Hejaz Railway, which in 1909 was opened from Damascus to Medina, and at once put an end to the great army which used to perform the pilgrimage by road. The Emir el Haj and his people now go by train, and the annual pageant of the camel-caravan is dead. The pilgrim road, of whose hundreds of worn tracks Doughty gave us such a picture, is now gone dull for lack of all those feet to polish it, and the kellas and cisterns from which he drank on the march to Medain Salih are falling into ruin, except so far as they serve the need of some guard-house on the railway.

The Rashid dynasty in Hail has pursued as bloody a course since his day as before it. Saud, the last Emir, was murdered in 1920, and the sole survivor of the family is an infant, whose precarious minority is being made the play of the ambition of one and another of the great chiefs of the Shammar tribe. On the other hand, the Wahabi dynasty of Riath, which seemed in its decline, has suddenly revived in this generation, thanks to the courage and energy of Abd el-Aziz, the present Emir. He has subdued all Nejd with his arms, has revived the Wahabi sect in new stringency, and bids fair to subject all the inner deserts of the peninsula to his belief. The Emir's younger son was lately in the Deputation he sent to this country, under the conduct of Mr. H. St. J. Philby, C.I.E., sometime British Resident at er-Riâth, during the Great War. Whilst in England they visited Mr. Doughty.

The Sherifate of Mecca, in whose humanity Doughty reposed at Taif at the end of his adventures, made a bid for the intellectual leadership of the Arabs in 1916 by rebelling against Turkey on the principle of nationality. The Western Arabs, among whom Doughty's ways had so long fallen, took a chivalrous part in the war as the allies of Great Britain and with our help. The Sherif's four sons put themselves at the head of the townsmen and tribesmen of the Hejaz, and gave the British officers assisting them the freedom of the desert. All the old names were in our ranks. There were Harb, Juheyma, and Billi, whom Doughty mentioned. His old hosts, the Abu Shamah Moahîb, joined us, and did gallantly. Ferhan, Motlog's son, brought with him the Allayda, and with the other Fejr they took Teyma and Kheybar from their Turkish garrisons, and handed them over to King Hussein.

Later the Shammar joined us, and volunteers came from Kasim, from Aneyza, Boreyda and Russ to help the common war upon the Turks. We took Medain Salih and El Ally, and further north Tebuk and Maan, the Beni Sakhr country, and all the pilgrim road up to Damascus, making in arms the return journey of that by which Doughty had begun his wanderings. *Arabia Deserta*, which had been a joy to read, as a great record of adventure and travel (perhaps the greatest in our language), and the great picture-book of nomad life, became a military text-book, and helped to guide us to victory in the East. The Arabs who had allowed Doughty to wander in their forbidden provinces were making a good investment for their sons and grandsons.

In this great experience of war the focus of motive in the desert changed, and a political revolution came to the Arabs. In Doughty's day, as his book shows, there were Moslems and Christians, as main divisions of the people. Yesterday the distinction faded; there were only those on the side of the Allies, and those with the Central Powers. The Western Arabs, in these forty years, had learned enough of the ideas of Europe to accept nationality as a basis for action. They accepted it so thoroughly that they went into battle against their Caliph, the Sultan of Turkey, to win their right to national freedom. Religion, which had been the motive and character of the desert, yielded to politics, and Mecca, which had been a City of worship, became the temporal capital of a new state. The hostility which had been directed against Christians became directed against the foreigner who presumed to interfere in the domestic affairs of Arabic-speaking provinces.

However, this note grows too long. Those just men who begin at the beginning of books are being delayed by me from reading Doughty, and so I am making worse my presumption in putting my name near what I believe to be one of the great prose works of our literature. It is a book which begins powerfully, written in a style which has apparently neither father nor son, so closely wrought, so tense, so just in its words and phrases, that it demands a hard reader. It seems not to have been written easily; but in a few of its pages you learn more of the Arabs than in all that others have written, and the further you go the closer the style seems to cling to the subject, and the more natural it becomes to your taste.

The history of the march of the caravan down the pilgrim road, the picture of Zeyd's tent, the description of Ibn Rashid's court at Hail, the negroid village in Kheybar, the urbane life at Aneyza, the long march across the desert of Western Nejd to Mecca, each seems better than the one before till there comes the very climax of the book near Taif, and after this excitement a gentle closing chapter of the road down to Jidda, to the hospitality of Mohammed Nasif's house, and the British Consulate.

To have accomplished such a journey would have been achievement enough for the ordinary man. Mr. Doughty was not content till he had made the book justify the journey as much as the journey justified the book, and in the double power, to go and to write, he will not soon find his rival.

The Twilight of the Gods and Other Tales by Richard Garnett

How kind a nurse has the British Museum been, sometimes, to poets! In the Department of Fishes O'Shaughnessy sang of fountains, whole rivers of tears. Barbellion among the beasts found himself his richest subject for dissection; and this Dr. Garnett in the horrific dome (bald within and without like an empty ostrich-egg), which is the Reading Room, was used to chuckle over the Twilight of the Gods.

They seem to have been moved by contraries, these central-heated artists. Much poring over Japanese prints makes a Binyon re-create Arthurian legends. In the Assyrian Basement I have heard a keeper whose charge (if hardly his care) was Babylonian burst into modern song. Assur-nasir-Pal reminded him of an only girl. He was an ordinary man, incapable of literature even at his highest; but in him was working the spirit of contrariety, which has made the real artists blossom so strangely in their police-guarded halls. The Director, no doubt, could be moved only to Limericks, while Epic would be the choice of the man with red dress-cuffs and lapels, who takes your umbrella at the door. Incidentally this is the best place in London to lose an acquired or embarrassing umbrella. It costs no more than the pain of carrying off a brass disc; and that's not all loss, for there is one special pattern of slot machine in which these discs perform miracles.

Many other personal details of the Museum are curious; but Mr. Lane *did* promise to pay me twenty guineas for an introduction to the "Twilight"; and so unprecedented an event in my writing career demands and deserves more attention than it appears to be getting. So here is back again for Dr. Garnett. . . .

The Reading Room, his province, is wise, rich, sober, warm, decent (even dingy), industrious; but it lacks humour, it lacks polish, and all that crackling display of surface virtue which comprehends smartness, and is much more. Consequently, because the Museum was hushed, Dr. Garnett would be—on paper—lively. Because the great ceiling coved so solemnly overhead, he would be flippant. Because his readers were so deadly serious, he would be sprightly.

Which is not to say that he too was not serious and bookish and sincere. The great national Museum may be a great necropolis for the public, a charnel-house wherein the mouldering bones of dead civilisations are somewhat indecently displayed. For the staff it is a Temple, and themselves the devotees. For them the world outside the windows is that which is indecent in display. They live with the best materials of the past, studying them, endeavouring by every context of literature and history to understand them more fully, to see them more remarkably in the round. For this select few on earth, Greece and Rome, Babylon and Egypt are not dead. These empires are in their department (or in old So-and-So's next door), things of vital importance, growing daily larger and clearer, their bread-and-butter, their ideal, their study, the business of their working hours and the chosen pastime of their leisure. Inestimable is this privilege of a twenty-four-hour-day preoccupation with the censored fittest of sixty centuries . . . and I am happy to remember how for some years the B.M. made me estimable in its employment.

Dr. Garnett's department, the Reading Room, is one which forces a sympathetic president to be somewhat universal. Rome and Greece, Chaldea and Egypt: those were real enough to him; but their reality was not exclusive, to him alone of the staff. His dealings throughout the open hours were with living people, inquirers all, whether they were great scholars with minds so deep in the well of learning that never could they be raised to the life of day, or simple souls who had perhaps not heard of Sanchoniathon or Vopiscus. People would sidle up to him at his desk to ask for the best book upon caterpillars, for a Keats manuscript, to know how many protons might be in a cubic foot of Bessemer steel. The Library is the ultimate reference book of the world, and its presiding genius the Index.

Courteously and unerringly Dr. Garnett would advise upon bee-keeping or bimetallism, while inwardly his mind was picturing Caucasus or Pandemonium and little themes of Albert of Aix or Hesychius were running through his head. Never did he abdicate from his chair of scholarship. In this book are his *obiter scripta*, reactions of his spirit against drudgery, and what a bouquet and flavour they have! Book-learned in the best sense, he was a worthy priest of the Museum, that last temple of the classical theogony.

I like to imagine the puzzled debate in the Greek sculpture halls, at night in the quiet moon-lit emptiness after the public had withdrawn, as the carved Gods on their marble pedestals heard his carpet slippers flip-flapping softly where the nailed soles of P.C. 7872889 had made harsh day music. Dr. Garnett came through so shyly, carefully, among the ranked Gods, since perhaps he did not quite know if his faith founded on print, or on Pentelic marble . . . and the Gods too remained aloof, shy and speechless, for they are as little used to worshippers as men are to Gods. The Die-hard section, Ares, Zeus himself, Hera, were for dismissing him: better, they said, no worshipper at all than one who had exposed their rents and patches to a mocking world. The beautiful Athene, the confused Apollo leaned by reason to this party: though their instincts lay with Æsculapius, with Hermes, with Prometheus, the modernists, who stoutly pleaded that seas and centuries were considerations to be admitted in argument even by Gods, and that for a reformed Olympus there lay yet a hope in the constituencies. "Here," they said, "is one who has made our question again a living issue. He in Britain, Anatole over there in France, are rousing public interest. Pull yourselves together, provide copy, show yourselves, wear your plaster noses" (Demeter burst into tears), "become NEWS: and from these Apostles will be born an army at whose head we will regain our provinces."

Conservatism, of course, carried it. Gods are ever slow to overtake a reform movement. They slipped back again into the Elgin Room, and stood there mutilated but immobile on the dingily-labelled pedestals when the attendants came round with the feather brushes in the morning. Dr. Garnett was born an age too soon or too late.

Yet in these Gods he did virtually believe: his drawing of them is to the life, visualised, with that routine apology of the sensitive *dévot* who hides his beliefs and his beloved from the arrows of vulgar contempt by dressing them in motley, to evoke not anger but laughter from the crowd. Last and most slippery refuge of faith! but how tender must be the God who is small enough for the worshipper to fondle and protect, and play the shield to! Dr. Garnett's intimacy with his Gods betrays sincerity. Not the last, no doubt, but the latest of the Pagans confesses himself.

The scholarship in these tales is beautiful: so deep, so unobtrusive, so easy and exact. The high-roads of the classic have been much trodden, so that they are become white, straight, dusty tracks. Scholarship which is sure of itself, and not ambitious to go far or fast, often takes more delight in by-ways where there are winding paths, quaint resting-places, a luxuriance of overgrown foliage. Dr. Garnett was a very sure scholar, who had done the plain things and the big things and was tired of them. In this book lies his leisure, as much for our delight as his. It wants no learning to enjoy the *Twilight of the Gods;* but the more learning you have, the more odd corners and hidden delights you will find in it.

The Gods are the main elements. Poisons, the science of toxins, are perhaps third element. Second place, I think, falls to black magic. Here again, so far as my competence extends, Dr. Garnett is serious. His spells are real, his sorcery accurate, according to the best dark-age models. His curious mind must have found another escape from the reading-desk in the attempts of our ancestors to see through the veil of flesh, downwards.

"It will be a tough business," observed the sorcerer. "It will require fumigations."

"Yes," said the bishop, "and suffumigations."

"Aloes and mastic," advised the sorcerer.

"Aye," assented the bishop, "and red sanders."

"We must call in Primeumaton," said the warlock.

"Clearly," said the bishop, "and Amioram."

"Triangles," said the sorcerer.

"Pentacles," said the bishop.

"In the hour of Methon," said the sorcerer.

"I should have thought Tafrac," suggested the bishop, "but I defer to your better judgment."

"I can have the blood of a goat?" queried the wizard.

"Yes," said the bishop, "and of a monkey also."

"Does your Lordship think that one might venture to go so far as a little unweaned child?"

"If absolutely necessary," said the bishop.

"I am delighted to find such liberality of sentiment on your Lordship's part," said the sorcerer. "Your Lordship is evidently of the profession."

It seems to me that the learned Doctor would have been in some danger, too, if the nineteenth century had been the ninth or the seventeenth.

On the point of scholarship let us give the book a first-class. Ditto in magic, in alchemy, in toxicology; ditto in wit and humour. Yet they say it never sold. As literature my experience (despite Mr. Lane's solitary swallow) is not professional enough to make my opinion of the book worth while. Swinburne loved it: my introduction to it came at second hand from him. Flecker, the inquiring poet, stole his first copy. Mr. Wells, a writer of very different texture, has praised it in print. Wilde's satisfaction is some testimony to the wit. *The Yellow Book* published some of it. Perhaps all these people borrowed or stole copies: apparently their satisfaction and their praise of it were not

enough to exhaust the editions which the publisher offered. Now he
is trying an illustrated edition. Such good wine can well endure to be
bushed largely; and therefore, apart from that possible twenty guineas,
I cannot refuse the opportunity to say clearly, and I hope infectiously,
how very much I have enjoyed the book for nearly twenty years; and
what a passport to the sympathy of many chance-met literary men
my knowledge of it has been.

So please, purchasers-of-this-edition, don't lend your copies too
freely. For one thing, you probably won't get them back. It's packed
with a delicious callous cruelty, of the playful sort which thrills bookish
men. There is an ever-springing irony which provokes smiling. Smiling
is decorous in the Reading Room (always think of that), where an open
laugh would shatter the air like a stone in a quiet pool. The readers
sit all round the edge, like the frogs round the pool; and you know
how a large stone floods the water into all their mouths and stops the
croaking. This book will make you chuckle: nothing vulgar. There
is a polish and perfection of incongruity, like goggles on an aged bust:
a wit so fine that its point has reflections down a chain of three or
four passages to which the original alludes: allusions recondite, and
yet so broad and human that I've heard the chuckles spread from the
reader across a barrack full of troops. There is finished care side by
side with recklessness, mad gaiety over all the marvellous bundle of
contradictions. What a brood for the old Reading Room to have
hatched!

Arabia Felix
Across the "Empty Quarter" of Arabia
by Bertram Thomas

Thomas shocked me when he asked for a foreword to his great journey-
book, not because introductions put me off (he may as reasonably
enjoy them, perhaps) but because he had recourse to me. It took some
while to think out so strange a lapse.

You see, in my day there were real Arabian veterans. Upon each
return from the East I would repair to Doughty, a looming giant, white
with eighty years, headed and bearded like some renaissance Isaiah.
Doughty seemed a past world, in himself; and after him I would visit
Wilfrid Blunt. An Arab mare drew Blunt's visitors deep within a Sussex
wood to his quarried house, stone-flagged and hung with Morris
tapestries. There in a great chair he sat, prepared for me like a careless

work of art in well-worn Arab robes, his chiselled face framed in silvered, curling hair. Doughty's voice was a caress, his nature sweetness. Blunt was a fire yet flickering over the ashes of old fury.

Such were my Master Arabians, men of forty, fifty years ago. Hogarth and Gertrude Bell, by twenty years of patient study, had won some reputation, too; and there were promising young officers, Shakespear and Leachman, with a political, Wyman Bury, beginning well. To aspire Arabian-wise, then, was no light, quick ambition.

They are all gone, those great ones. The two poets were full of years and in high honour. Naturally they died. The war burdened Hogarth and Gertrude Bell with political responsibilities. They gave themselves wholly, saw their work complete and then passed. The three younger men died of their duty, directly; and that is why Thomas must come down to me.

I suppose no new Sixth Former can help feeling how much his year falls short of the great fellows there when he joined the school. But can the sorry little crowd of us to-day be in the tradition, even? I fear not. Of course the mere wishing to be an Arabian betrays the roots of a quirk; but our predecessors' was a larger day, in which the seeing Arabia was an end in itself. They just wrote a wander-book and the great peninsula made their prose significant. (Incidentally, the readable Arabian books are all in English, bar one; Jews, Swiss, Irishmen and What-nots having conspired to help the Englishmen write them. There are some German books of too-sober learning and one Dutch.) Its deserts cleaned or enriched Doughty's pen and Palgrave's, Burckhardt's and Blunt's, helped Raunkiær with his Kuweit, Burton and Wavell in their pilgrimages, and Bury amongst his sun-struck Yemeni hamlets.

Our feebler selves dare not be Arabians for Arabia's sake—none of us save Rutter, I think, and how good, how classical, his book! The rest must frame excuses for travelling. One will fix latitudes, the silly things, another collect plants or insects (not to eat, but to bring home), a third make war, which is coals to Newcastle. We fritter our allegiances and loyalties.

Inevitable, of course, that these impurities should come. As pools shrink they stench. Raleigh could hearten my ancestor—'Cozen, we know but the hand's-breadth of our world'—but since him Arctic and Antarctic, the wastes of Asia and Africa, the forests of America have yielded their secrets. Last year I could have retorted—'There is but a hand's-breadth we do not know'—thinking of that virgin Rub' al Khali, the last unwritten plot of earth big enough for a sizable man's turning in twice or thrice about, before he couches. However, only these few paragraphs of mine now stand between appetite and the tale of its conquest. To-day we know the whole earth. Would-be wandering youth will go unsatisfied till a winged generation lands on the next planet.

Few men are able to close an epoch. We cannot know the first man who walked the inviolate earth for newness' sake: but Thomas is the last; and he did his journey in the antique way, by pain of his camel's legs, single-handed, at his own time and cost. He might have flown an aeroplane, sat in a car or rolled over in a tank. Instead he has snatched, at the twenty-third hour, feet's last victory and set us free. Everything having been once done in the slowest fashion we can concentrate upon speed, amplifying the eye of the tortoise by the hare's and the bird's. All honour to Thomas. The Royal Geographical Society itself forgives, bemedals its supersessor . . . also he has an O.B.E.

I will not say how much I like this book, lest the publisher dig out the odd sentence for his blurb. Thomas let me read the draft, and I then did my best to comment usefully; once remarking that the tale was good enough for his journey—no faint judgment, set against what I think the finest thing in Arabian exploration. As he tells it, the achievement may read easy, because he is a master of every desert art. Here once more is the compleat Arabian traveller enshrined. Not twice but twenty times his tiniest touches set me remembering that wide land which I liked so much, twenty years ago, and hoped never to feel again. Thence, I suppose, the reason of my writing him this useless foreword; that and my understanding of his risks. Only by favour of a propitious season could this very rare individual, after infinite care and tact in preparation, have gambled his life upon the crowning solidarity which the desert owes to Ibn Saud, and won through. Thomas is as fortunate as deserving.

2
Reviews

The six reviews reprinted here, all Lawrence is known to have written,[1] were undertaken during his stay at the RAF base at Drigh Road, in the desert seven miles from Karachi. The first four appeared in various August and September 1927 issues of *The Spectator*; one, on H. G. Wells's short stories, in February 1928. The last, on Walter Savage Landor, written, Arnold Lawrence judged, around March 1928, was published posthumously in *Men in Print* (1940), a limited edition with five of Lawrence's literary pieces.[2]

In April 1926, at the suggestion of Evelyn Wrench, editor of *The Spectator*, Francis Yeats-Brown, the journal's literary editor and Wrench's cousin, invited "Colonel Lawrence" to review books on the Near East "anonymously or otherwise." Lawrence, or rather T. E. Shaw, declined with a series of false excuses. "I have not written anything since I enlisted. . . . In barracks it would be quite impossible. Indeed, it's very seldom I can bring myself to answer a letter" (Wrench, 130).

A year later, Wrench (who knew Lawrence and had introduced him to F. N. Doubleday) tried again. With time to spare in India and short of reading matter, Lawrence was now interested. He ruled out use of his name and writing on the Mid-East, political subjects, or archaeology.

> If you want poems reviewed, anonymously, or literature, (biography, criticism, novels of the XXth. Cent. sort of Forsters, Joyces, D. H. Lawrences etc.) at an interval of three months from the fountain head:— but of course you don't. . . .
>
> If . . . you still feel charitable: why I'll be delighted! I'm not ambitious, financially . . . , and not proud, critically: for I've never imagined that my writing was any good. So I'll do the very smallest stuff, gladly.[3]

Wrench (131) suggested Lawrence "think out some anonymous name over which your articles will always appear. It might be rather amusing creating a fresh personality." That was a game Lawrence enjoyed.

71

He proposed "C. D." for Colin Dale, derived from Colindale, the last station he had entered on the London underground.

> The fewer people aware of C. D. in your team the better. For if talk began about that person I should cut his throat. . . . I'd suggest the first five or six things worth signing be restrained to their initials. If the miracle continues . . . we might climb so far as Colin D., keeping the full truth about the D till it was certain that the fellow could write and had a character. In my heart of hearts I know he hasn't.[4]

Spectator readers never learned C. D.'s first name.

Lawrence's first substantive letter to Yeats-Brown mentioned three of the authors he reviewed.

> D. H. Lawrence I'll be delighted to have a try at. I've read all his stuff since the White Peacock.
> Hakluyt is only a name to me. So on that you'll get the reflection of a fresh mind; if it does reflect anything. . . . Guedalla I had the misfortune to meet at Oxford.[5]

Lawrence received the three D. H. Lawrence novels—*Women in Love, The Lost Girl, The Plumed Serpent*—on a Wednesday, read them Thursday, and mailed the review Friday. "Too quickly, no doubt, but I did not want to keep you longer without a sample, besides I've been reading him since before the war, so that my mind was made up before this week" (Brown, 340). Six days later, he mailed the Guedalla review. Later, he said, "You should have torn up my Guedalla review. It was punk." Yeats-Brown rejoined: it "was simply splendid."[6]

Hakluyt proved "hard work. Old H. had not the judgement of a white ant, or the keen vision of a dormouse. The times gave him the best material in the world, & he made an awful mess of it. However the later stuff not even his editing could spoil. The recenter volumes are V.G."[7] Lawrence also labored over Wells's stories. They "are works of art: but 1200 pages of them!" he protested in September; and in December, "three [days] . . . have been wasted, in an effort to write a review of H. G. Wells' short stories: I can't write reviews, yet I want to, badly!"[8]

In the D. H. Lawrence review, "*The Rainbow* and *Women in Love* and *Aaron's Rod* stutter and stammer. . . . Finally there came to us *The Plumed Serpent*. . . . a perfect achievement, the balance of mind and strength and spirit. . . . the accepted creed of a man who is at last sure of himself." No mention of the lunacy he is at last sure of:

the blood of reptiles, the spermy water, the meaningless, repetitious prose, the vacuous chants of Quetzalcoatl, the striving "to open the oyster of the cosmos, and get our manhood out of it."

At the level of ideas (if that is the right word for muddled feelings) and even plot, *The Plumed Serpent* resembles Algernon Blackwood's *The Centaur* (1909), which impressed Lawrence as a boy and man (p. 255). In Blackwood, an Irish man, in D. H. Lawrence, an Irish woman abandons the deadening bourgeois world of work and family for a primitive country in search of something fundamental: a nameless feeling, an unconscious, unthinking sense of being at one not just with nature but the cosmos.

The review compares D. H. Lawrence's novels with E. M. Forster's. Forster, "clever and subtle," "rolled thunderstorms in teacups," exhibited his characters carefully, "like a collector"; Lawrence, "not subtle," exhibited "hussies and bounders" like "a showman, trumpeting his stock."

Lawrence tried to review Forster's *Aspects of the Novel* (1927). "It is a wonderful little study. I read it about six times, & made a sheaf of notes: and wrote them out. No good. Did it again. Again no good. My third try was a bit more of a thing, and yet not good enough for The Spectator."[9] He began a review of *The Brothers Karamazov* but stopped when he heard of Hogarth's death.[10]

By January 1928, Lawrence was reorganizing his notes and preparing a clean copy of *The Mint*; he had received a letter asking him to translate the *Odyssey* for a substantial sum and was being pressed to complete Hogarth's unfinished biography of Doughty. These tasks doubtless reduced his interest in reviewing. However, it is unlikely that his interest would have been sustained. The pattern seemed preordained: initial enthusiasm followed by increasing self-depreciation and eventual refusal to continue a line of literary work at which (no matter what others might say) he judged himself a failure.

"*The Spectator* was the most widely read political weekly of the Edwardian era, with a circulation of 20,000. . . . Its politics were conservative and ultra-patriotic. . . . [It was] a very respectable journal for which to write. . . . the level of reviewing was high by any standard" (Marwil, 126–27). After reading the D. H. Lawrence review, Martin Secker, who published the novels, asked who "C. D." was and would he write "a short critical book" on Lawrence.[11] H. G. Wells called the review of his stories "the most interesting estimate of his work that he had ever seen" (*Friends*, 424).

Such praise, or Yeats-Brown's opinion that the reviews were "extraordinarily acute, and aroused great interest," meant nothing to Lawrence. As soon as he started, he began to apply the brakes.

His letter accompanying the D. H. Lawrence review declared "of course it's no good. By nature I wasn't meant to write. . . . I don't expect you to like what I write." The Guedalla piece "wouldn't work out. . . . I'm quite aware (always have been) that I can't write. . . . better not send me any more books."[12] Subsequent letters said, "I write such miserable stuff that it isn't worth printing" and "When I have finished Hakluyt . . . and Wells, then I'm really finished: for I take it you'll have agreed to send me no more. . . . I'm sorry. It shows that one doesn't write good reviews merely by being interested in books."[13]

Thus Lawrence's reviewing ended though, returned to England in 1929, he continued to correspond and sometimes to meet with Wrench and especially with Yeats-Brown. He firmly instructed *The Spectator* to stop his free subscription.[14]

"Writers are people who go on spinning their experiences into books, for sheer love of it, or inability to refrain. It's for this feeling that I wasn't really of the craft that I've stopped reviewing," he explained to Edward Marsh. His final judgment on his reviewing was brief and harsh: "I've tried reviewing. It pays, it distracts the mind, it irritates. Finally it disgusts."[15]

Novels of D. H. Lawrence

Martin Secker has been too careful in producing his cheap edition of D. H. Lawrence's novels. In its clumsy type-panel the type looks too big, and the reverse looms shadowly through the thin paper: also the margins have been pared to the quick. This is a pity, for D. H. Lawrence is a prodigious novelist, whose works need to be studied in series (to learn their significance of growth) as well as to be re-read frequently, each for itself, because of the rich depth and strangeness and fine artistry of the author. These little volumes are likely to crack up under the work booklovers will give them.

D. H. Lawrence has had a wonderful career, since the distant day when *The White Peacock* took the breath of literary England with its sudden independence and wealth of form. A young man's work this, obviously, with its cadenced prose, beautiful in sound and mannered in pattern. He was writing, then as now, for ear and eye together: but he seemed to overvalue the classical tradition, to check his powers, in too strict obedience to architectonic law. So with his next book, and his next, *Sons and Lovers* being perhaps the prose culmination of this first phase, which found itself, more transparently, in the poems:

The sea in the stones is singing,
A Woman binds her hair
With yellow, frail sea-poppies
That shine as her fingers stir.

While a naked man comes swiftly
Like a spurt of white foam, rent
From the crest of a fallen breaker,
Over the poppies sent.

Do you see the doubled 's' in each first and last line? There is the young Lawrence, his imagination playing lead to his mind. Appetite and self-education rushed him into growth. Ideas leaped in flocks, full-grown, into his work, too quickly to be always clear, too grown to be always good company, one to the other. *The Rainbow* and *Women in Love* and *Aaron's Rod* stutter and stammer with the heat of the teacher who has felt something so exciting that he cannot delay to think it into its fitting words. Words upon words, he pours them out in a river.

Slowly the passion checked. It crystallized into conviction. In *Kangaroo* and the short stories we can see the molten stuff cooling, to grow hard and solid, yet plastic in the master's burning hands. Finally there came to us *The Plumed Serpent*, the 'magic' as *The Spectator* called it, a perfect achievement, the balance of mind and strength and spirit, a vivified independent creation of art.

What pains before *The Plumed Serpent* can be created! Book after book, each of them the hardest and honestest and best work of which his wits are capable, for nearly twenty years; and all the time growth, growth, growth. He never tries to please another judgment than his own, never walks in a made road, never re-treads the easy track of an earlier success. Every time he gives us, in both hands, all he can hold of himself. It is a pageant: novels, poems, scientific work—not good, this last. His pseudonymous Oxford history-book and his psychological treatise are unhappy: as though a maker, who could make live men and women, were bothering to model clay images of men and women. *Twilight in Italy*, too, was hard to read. It clung to the roof of the mouth, like an overkneaded suet pudding. But at his best he is an impeccable prose writer (which is not to say that he has all the virtues). Compare him with Brahms in music; and when the landscape painter in him feels the setting of a story, miracles follow. The Italian hill-villages in *The Lost Girl* are dizzy with their sense of height, and the supreme success of *The Plumed Serpent* is the lake, which becomes a major character in the book. However, there's no need to discuss *The Plumed Serpent*. It has arrived. It is more curious to see by what road it came.

In those early days, before the War, readers' hopes lay in Lawrence and Forster. These two heirs, through the Victorians, of the great tradition of the English novel were fortunate to have made good their footing before war came. Its bursting jarred them off their stride, indeed. Lawrence glances at the War twice or thrice, and wrote a haunting poem of a train-journey in uniform, but no more. Each man had tired of politics and action, and plunged into the dim forest of character in time to save himself from chaos. In imagination we used to make Forster and Lawrence joust with one another, on behalf of their different practices of novel-writing, as our fathers set Thackeray and Dickens at odds. Forster's world seemed a comedy, neatly layered and staged in a garden whose trim privet hedges were delicate with gossamer conventions. About its lawns he rolled thunderstorms in teacups, most lightly, beautifully. Lawrence painted hussies and bounders, unconscious of class, with the unabashed surety of genius, whether they were in their slippered kitchens or others' drawing-rooms. Forster's characters were typical. Lawrence's were individual. 'There have been enough stories about ordinary people', said he, in self-defence: but it was easy for him to say that. Everybody in the world would be remarkable, if we used all our eyes to see them. Lawrence will call one eloquent, because his body curves interestingly when he stands still. Another is rich, because his dark silence means something. A third may thrill, once in the book, in voice. Some have interesting minds. Not many.

Forster may love a character, in a gentle, aloof irony of love, like a collector uncovering his pieces of price for a moment to a doubtful audience, as if he feared that an untaught eye might soil, by not comprehending, their fineness. Lawrence is a showman, trumpeting his stock, eager for us to make them ours—at his price. There is no comedy in him. He prods their ribs, prises open their jaws to show the false teeth. It is not very comfortable, on first reading. To be impassive spectators of the slave-market takes a training.

Forster is clever and subtle. Lawrence is not subtle, though he tries, sometimes, to convey emotional subtlety. In the big things his simplicity is shattering. His women browbeat us, as Juno browbeat the Gods at Jupiter's at-homes: but in the privacy of their dressing-rooms they jabber helplessly. Pages and pages are wasted in the effort to make the solar plexus talk English prose.

Both Lawrence and Forster give their main parts to women whenever possible. This is their deliberate choice, for each can draw an admirable man. Look at the youths in the *Longest Journey*: or read what Lawrence has written about Maurice Magnus, or Cipriano, or that splendid Canadian soldier in *The Fox* (was it the 'Fox', or had the story one name in England and another in America?). But Lawrence never draws an average man or an average woman. He gets excited always over our strangenesses, and is the first thrall of his own puppets.

'If one could get over the feeling that one was looking at him through the glass of an aquarium', he says in *The Lost Girl.* So he himself feels the queerness of his creations. We see the poor fishy things writhing across his whirl of words, in the grip of emotion belonging to some other element than the every-day. They are not hard and strong. He is poet, and thinker, a man exquisitely a-tingle to every throb of blood, flexure of sinew, plane-modulation of the envelope of flesh. He feels, sees, and sings us instant and endless improvizations: and there is weakness somewhere in it all. The excitements are sometimes febrile: nor does he always play fair. Look at him dodging round his crowded characters, sniping at their back-parts (gutter-sniping almost) when they are most off-guard or most distracted. What about that portrait of M. M., or of Hermione? Compare the shameless spite of *Look! We Have Come Through* with the lambent raillery of the Queen Bee which dignifies *Sea and Sardinia* into happiness. Then, after the long journey through all his works, return, in *The Plumed Serpent*, to Mexico and the accepted creed of a man who is at last sure of himself.

Mixed Biscuits
H. M. Tomlinson, W. H. Hudson,
William Gerhardi, Arthur Machen, and Others

One by one the publishers—after the ordeal of publication at seven shillings and sixpence or half a guinea—re-launch their best books in cheap format. These tiny volumes are easier to make friends with than the ceremonious and expensive editions, for it is in such little reprints, literature coming down to us in its working dress, that a man may reason with its authors unashamed. We open them casually, without fear or hesitation. And there is none of that preliminary heaving or dusting called for by a folio.

We would buy Messrs. Duckworth's New Readers Library if it was ill-looking; that it happens to be skilful in its design, with a light binding, well-proportioned page and adequate paper, is an unlooked-for pleasure. This is a much better series than the old cheap one, from which some of the favourites are reissues. But even so, the New Readers Library is not yet consistently good enough. It is neither sized nor dressed by the right.

Of its first six files, H. M. Tomlinson is probably the biggest name—here indeed, as we are told often enough, is the full art of English prose—though, of course, *The Sea and the Jungle* is early Tomlinson: and so is, perhaps, a little *too* full, too generous. Upon one sunset, for instance, Mr. Tomlinson lavishes three picture-similes, in as many sentences. Properly economized and spaced out across weeks of his voyage, these would have given us three lovely sunsets, instead of one slight indigestion. Not that there should be any rule against three-storied pictures. They can be done, if the design of each shows awareness of those above or those below, so that they supplement or smile at each other's distinctions. Mr. Tomlinson's neighbour-similes, here and occasionally elsewhere in this early, spendid book, are strangers. However, here is a Tomlinson, which is to say a classic. Messrs. Duckworth begin nobly.

Then there is Hudson's *Green Mansions*. Hudson, still glorious (and either this or *The Purple Land* is his best book), begins to date a little. He wrote just before the prose revival which we owe to the self-conscious craftsmen of the 'nineties. The Elizabethans, at the bidding of their Euphuists, loaded Malory's beautiful English with relative and subsidiary and dependent clauses, which allowed Sir Thomas Browne later to chase his every sentence, and Johnson to reduce its synthetical forest to a ruled and stiffened grammatical sequence. Out of this Macaulay and the professors made their cakes.

From such stodge we have been set free by the literary equivalent of the pre-Raphaelite movement, which rediscovered for everybody the secrets of limpidity and simpleness that had been known only to the exceptional genius, the Swift or Defoe or Bunyan of the generations. If you take a jungle page of Hudson and pit it against a jungle page of Tomlinson, you will find the difference to lie more in the manner than in the matter. Hudson has conviction and better knowledge: Tomlinson more eye and a subtler feeling. Only, Tomlinson is a little hard of hearing. It takes a slammed door or the straining of a ship in the gale before he gets sound perfectly on paper, whereas Hudson had the most open ear of any prose writer.

Mr. Gerhardi has written at least two remarkable books, but he would not, I think, be at ease in a jungle. He likes his apes caged: and he squats by one corner of the cage and catches their gibberings on his phonograph and their antics in his kodak till our heads swim, and presently we think we are going as mad as are his victims. *The Polyglots* is a book to read—very modern and outspoken. Mr. Machen's *Terror* varies yet further the variety of the series. It is a formula-made mystery, by a veteran craftsman; cultured, complicated work by an author who is superior to his own terrors. It is not quite the best of Mr. Machen, for it gives him little scope for the exquisite sense of cruelty which distinguishes his ripest work. Mr. Baring's *Lost Diaries* is another forlorn quest of that inimitable unattainable idea which no doubt began before the *Dialogues of the Dead*. It disappoints. As for *The Roadmender*, here is variety with a vengeance. Leave it for those who like that sort of thing: it should not be included in this library.

A Critic of Critics Criticized
Men of Letters by Philip Guedalla

"No, thanks," said I to the Assistant Editor. "Not Guedalla. I've met him": and by next post, of course, the book came. I sighed and read the first essay. Nothing to it. Just as I'd thought. Pleased at my right perception I turned over the pages to read the last essay, on "Critics," and now I have to apologize. It was first-rate. Four times I read it, and it still kept on being first-rate. So I opened again at page 1 to go steadily through the lot.

Between page 1 and page 42 I could find no return for my labour; but the third line of page 42 was made up of the single word "No." Succinct, as a judgment, everybody will agree: but also it was sufficient and final and witty and yet tender. After so much crackling artifice the bit of simplicity was devastating and delightful, like a bull in an exhibition of modern Sèvres. Page 42 made me like Guedalla, and my stimulated eye prepared to be pleased with the rest of the book.

The whole body of his writing seemed better on second acquaintance. Therefore I tried it a third time. That's hard on a new book, to be read three times straight off. It is fairer, and fortunately more usual, to interpose several other books between the re-readings of a favourite. But reviewers can't always choose. During this third reading I found myself glancing at each essay to see how long it was, and if it was more than four pages, then I skipped the first three. Either Guedalla is a slow starter, or he takes a long time to find his stride; or he is like a fresh horse who, on leaving the stable, must walk mainly on his back legs along the drive, and as far as the first turn in the road. After that he gets down to his work properly.

I dallied with reasons for this preliminary prance. The cause, in horses, would be too much oats, and the treatment more chaff. Men are complicated. At Oxford, for example, they teach the art of constructing essays. Undergraduates read aloud a weekly essay (the poor thing it sounds, in their shy delivery) to the weary tutors, who explain at the end that all essays are alike. They start with some general considerations, the same for every dissertation upon a past theme whether it be the Sacred Band, the Cinque Ports, or the Foreign Policy of Charles XII. A paragraph just beyond half-way may glance, allusively, at a pertinent fact, and then the effort will round itself to a close with more formulae of general application. So the padding here may be a relic of Oxford: or were these articles commissioned to fill a set space in some journal? Or is the trouble racial? Remember Disraeli's spangled sense of colour, Zangwill's foppery, Rosenberg's electric storms: and the commoner manifestation of Mrs. Goldstone, wife of the celebrated banker, upon whose ample front last night at dinner long ranks of pearls were paraded.

Apart from her decoration Mrs. Goldstone is sober and solid. Guedalla, too, is fundamentally responsible. With his queer clever manner surely should go a queer judgment? But no. His views are much the same as mine and Everyman's. They aren't clever at all. It seems a waste of the teased and tinselled high-spirited style, if the conclusion is to be ordinary. During my fourth reading I dotted his margins with my notes on him. Once he flashes into humour, linking "the great humped back, the curling tusks, the trunk the lumbering heavy tread of the Last, the very last of the Great Victorians" with his memory of Thomas Hardy, that still, tiny, bird-like thing. His delicacy (which I have failed to copy) kept him from stressing the joke. Three times his wit has delighted me: the superb classification (why did he labour it?) of Henry James in James I., James II., and the Old Pretender: the portrait of Max Beerbohm as the writer in tight patent-leather boots: the idea of Chesterton's having gone to Jerusalem with Belloc's luggage. My other twenty-nine marginal disfigurements are approvals of opinions which strike me as acute and sensible.

No better evidence of taste could be desired than his article on Kipling. He stands down here in favour of Henry James, from whom he has dug up an admirably balanced judgment, out of some obscure preface. It says all that need be said. In considering Arnold Bennett he half-glances at Trollope. He touches lightly on Hardy's novels, properly to commend us *The Dynasts*, a "chronicle play." He does not call it a God's-eye view of Europe, nor the scenario of the greatest film which will never be made. He is just to Barrie, piercing through his charm to the ominous beyond, without exploring it. If I were a kitten I should not play with Sir James, lest I found steel in those claws, and behind the veil an iciness more cruel than night in the Arctic. He seems to miss his aim, most, with Shaw: not seeing the hidden poet, and the moralist, always on the side of the angels. He is wise enough to see in Wells the prose artist, which H. G. himself, dissatisfiedly conscious of the pains he takes in writing, is ardent to deny. Conrad he examines with friendly curiosity. Perhaps he never met him, or he would have looked for tone-deafness in his style, after hearing but one of those amazing mispronounced sentences of mixed English and French, which were his excited speech. He sums up against Galsworthy, as novelist, and makes plain how the ultra-refinement of Max Beerbohm has ended in vulgarity. Chesterton he considers mainly in relation to his poor book on Jerusalem, and Belloc, that other example of fine talent employed to blind its owner, is passed over. Saintsbury is firmly sat on, Proust's English admirers laughed at, Wilfrid Blunt praised (what is he doing in this gallery of the popularly great?), Gosse and other critics criticized. Yet Gosse did give us *Father and Son*, which will be remembered on the credit side when his bread-and-butter contributions to journalism are forgotten. And so it goes on. All good: none perfect: hardly any of it really good enough: except that essay on the critics.

Hakluyt—First Naval Propagandist
The Principal Navigations, Voyages, Traffiques and Discoveries of the English Nation, &c. by Richard Hakluyt

Parts of Hakluyt are no end good. We have all heard of his writings as the sea-epic of England, which does for our ocean story what Malory did for the dim beginning of the homeland: and like Malory, Hakluyt was a clergyman, with an unclerical bee in his bonnet. Only there the parallel ends. Hakluyt preaches. He thought that England's heritage was the high sea and feared (in the days of Elizabeth I) that we were neglecting it. So he compiled a blue-bookish thesis, to prove that we had been, were, and would ever be great in so far as we were active on the seas and beyond them. His book was propaganda, himself more sustained and more industrious than most writers-with-a-moral; and he has been justified in the ten generations which have succeeded him.

More than most writers. Yet I'm not sure that Hakluyt is a writer, really. Take this first volume. It starts with Geoffrey of Monmouth, and goes through Bede, to the Cinque Ports, via the Steelyard to the Hansa towns, and back to the Libel of English Policy. The first 250 pages are dry and dusty quotations (except the history of King Edgar, where Dr. Dee makes us chuckle) in the manner of some schools of Modern History. His own age, by the voice of Michael Drayton, called him "industrious." Mr. Masefield quotes this in his interesting introduction, but goes further, to call him an "almost perfect" editor. I doubt whether many people will agree. Hakluyt's English is not fine, but plain and sensible. His adjectives are judicious, his sentences cumbrous and involved, like so much sixteenth-century prose, in its elaborate adolescence. His language is sober: whereas Adlington (for example) had a trick of words which clash on his reader's minds, and jet out sparks of delight. Hakluyt does not surprise us. It would be difficult to write well with your eye on a Secretary of State. He tries to keep his eyes on two or three Secretaries of State at once, to judge by his epistles dedicatory.

Perhaps he was too conscientious. He was marshalling facts in his brief, and scorned to rush his hearers away on a current of emotion. Also he thought completeness the duty of an editor. Did not Raleigh begin his history with the Creation? We would have preferred from him "Memoirs of the Court of Elizabeth." Hakluyt was collecting the materials of the maritime history of England, and aimed to be exhaustive, every-sided and authoritative. The *Times* Law Reports do much the same in their province. If his questions were still being ventilated, in suspense, we might approve such seriousness. But the very completeness of his victory has made him superfluous with the superfluousness which would have been Nelson's had he survived Trafalgar. Especially to-day when our national mind is wandering in the shades of a spiritual Jutland, trying to turn over a new leaf. Are we to thank God for the R.A.F., in the new phase?

Pending our assault upon the next element, we can give Hakluyt thanks for having started our ancestors so well with the history of the last one. He made researches into all the past that was available to him, and collected the yet abundant but fading stories of his contemporaries. The contemporaries were the better activity, for him. Since the age of Elizabeth the archives and muniment rooms of England have been ransacked, and we no longer want his help to study Florence of Worcester and the rest. But without Hakluyt any quantity of Elizabethan sailors' tales would have been lost. We owe him Purchas, too. He inlaid everything he came across, good or bad, in his collections. Where his sources wrote well, we have it well. Where they wrote badly, we have it unadorned. That is one conception of the duty of an editor; and Hakluyt, being scientific, accordingly robbed us of what might have been a masterpiece. Malory passed all his stuff through the mill of his personality, and gave us a miracle of goodness. He reaps the reward of being yet read, though a fairy-tale; and of having brought forth masterpieces. This Arthurian cycle has a way of transfiguring its servants, even when they are old men, and called

Tennyson. From Spenser to the "Waste Land" our thought-maggoty poets have forgotten their riddled minds in the splendid legend.

Poor Hakluyt's truth has had a more homespun fate: and I do not think that even this brave effort of Messrs. Dent (the volumes are handy and well-printed) will bring him into fashion. He is more a quarry than a book, though a most excellent quarry. For me the peak of this first volume of the new edition is Richard Johnson's four pages (352–356) of life among the Samoyedes. He was a servant of Richard Chancelour, who writes many dull pages about his voyages to Russia. Among them this story of Johnson glows like a jewel. If only the servant had written more and the master less! There is colour, too, in the title grant of the Merchant Adventurers, and Master Steven Burrough, in a single priceless paragraph, brings Sebastian Cabot to life among his lusty ship's company. Henry Lane pleads his case in the Russian manner before the Czar, and gives us the thrill of strange proceedings, as strange as Anthony Jenkinson's Malestrand, the great whirlpool, into which whales were sucked, with a strange pitiful cry.

Anthony Jenkinson was a friend of Mr. Hakluyt, and his journeys in Russia bulk largely in this first volume. Unfortunately Hakluyt let him off the writing of a proper account of his adventures, and printed, instead, the severely business-like reports rendered by him to his firm in London. These are the notes for a book rather than a book, and they are tantalizing, because they lift the veil of life for a moment, only to drop it. Jenkison saw a review of the Russian army (428), made notes of mujik life (434–436), visited semi-nomad Tartars in their hordes (441, 450), was nearly ship-wrecked in the Caspian, rode across Persia, compounded with brigands on the banks of the Oxus, and spent Christmas in Bokhara, after manifold adventures. He could write, too, and had a bright eye and the spirit of his time. He tells us how he set up the red cross of St. George over the waves of Caspian "for honour of the Christians," supposing it had not been seen there before. Hakluyt should have provoked his friend to write him a special tale, which would have been worth all the careful scholarship which goes before and after. It would have been alive, with the liveliness of some of the tales which follow in the succeeding volumes. But they must wait for another time, lest I grow as long as Hakluyt, in reviewing him.

The Short Stories of H. G. Wells

One thousand one hundred and fifty pages of H. G. Wells's short stories for 7s. 6d. It is amazing value for money. Probably they are renumbered stereos of another edition, otherwise Messrs Benn could hardly have done it. It is nearly as difficult to see how Wells did it. In this collection are sixty-three stories, none negligible, some very long. My memory vaguely suggests to me others not here included. Besides this decent life-output for a short-story writer Wells has the achievement of his massive *History*, and a shelf of novels, and miscellaneous prose-work, literary or political. His drafts would tell us if this huge production is due to industry or to a happy fluency. His writings let us into so many workshops and laboratories that we would like to see his own.

This sudden bulk of tales seems a chance to distinguish the profile of H. G. Wells, the prose artist. In his mature novels we cannot see the writer for the dust of his manly activities. He preaches and argues and attacks, has theories and practical programmes, tries to get something done. This role of politician and sociologist he imposes upon the primal artist. Indeed, he spares little admiration for pure writing, which he thinks a fad of emasculate amateurs. Yet he cannot keep out of his work that secret rhythm which its sentences (bare of relative clauses, and dependants, and adjectives, and participles) hold somewhere in their structure. So that any person with an ear and knowledge of letters, after about six lines, says 'Wells', and is right every time. At his highest he writes magnificently; and deliberately always; never falling below adequacy: only the stuff of the novels is too contentious to show us a clean edge. In these shorter pieces he is determined to entertain and to relieve his imagination of a burdening idea: there is no ephemeral moral underlying them.

It would be scientific to date each tale, and consider Wells as a growth, like an oak-tree. The publishers have grouped them, irrelevantly, to give their bulk palatable variety. If we undo their work, and classify each sort apart, we are in a position to examine the complete phenomenon of H. G. where he stands full-high, as an entertainer. Then we see at once that the futurities—those jugglings with the time-sense for which he is very famous—are only a scrap of his collection. There are five such stories, depending primarily on the time-sense, and three others into which it enters. Not much, in sixty-three. There are only four stories radically concerned with mechanisms, another notorious side of his invention. To me this quantitative insignificance of his most reputed side came as a shock. Nor did these seem his very good stories. They date. Man-made things grow queer to our eyes, sooner than the queer shapes of ourselves. Wells lasts better where he deals with human nature, which varies as slowly as the structure of men's bodies. The best of us would be as good (after a year's apprenticeship) as the best Cro-Magnon men, if our time were suddenly put back.

The next thing to come out, overwhelmingly, was the standpoint of the student of biology. The trend or evidence of science everywhere obsesses the mind which wrote: but it is a humble mind, prepared to hold everything as possible—the genuine, unmixed humility of the student-investigator on the threshold of science. There is not a trace of the professorial mood and no presumption of deep knowledge. There are five stories which declare themselves aloud as the trial or apprenticeship pieces of the laboratory student beginning to write, with the materials provided by his class-rooms and text-books. Only, as it happens, they are not his first work!

A true-blue biologist would see man only in his place in nature. Wells must have been ingrossed in the problems of personality before he came to study science. Five of these stories deal with aberrations of personality. Aberrations—yes: but not one queer man amongst them. His queerest things are done by ordinary people. Six stories deal intensely with Nature, the Huxleian Nature; only H. G. is an alienist among biologists. For him the aberrations of Nature, its sports and freaks, its violent rejections of the norm—these are the fascinations.

The student of life shifts his gaze from the eye-piece of his microscope to universal nature. Six stories deal with world-exchanging, with transmutations of spheres or entities. In them the author is heavy with material, and takes a very long time to get off the ground. He has not the nature to be happy in blind space. He cannot be tremendous. He likes to anchor his strangenesses to some familiarity, to make concrete his vision by focusing it on the light outlining the back of a woolly rhinoceros, on the control levers of an indescribable machine. Yet he does not really describe even the levers, he makes us think he has described them. The method slips into the grotesque in his sub-oceanic story *In the Abyss*. Perhaps his own imagining is not often very strange and he feels uneasy when he loses sight, for long, of earth and pavements.

Thirty-one stories, so far: and he has finished with the stars. Half of this collection is of the earth and of mankind, familiar. In them he is on common ground with his peers; and we look eagerly for adherences and affiliations. In two instances there is a trace of Wilde; and here and there a little of the *Yellow Book* carefulness of step. Good schools of prose, these, for a man having no preoccupation with the graceful; who does not even, like Butler, try to say his say at its very plainest. Later there is a hint of Kipling, and two essays in the fatuous which remind me of *Three Men in a Boat*; but these reflections are not the manner—Wells remains an integer as stylist—but a situation or setting. He has never belonged for more than a moment to fashion or movement or clique. What a panorama, what diversity of literary modes fill the backward gaze of a man who began writing in the end of the eighties, and is still a producing artist, with mind yet unfixed, to-day! Homer was more near to Peisistratus than 1886 to us.

Of these thirty-two entertainments twelve seem to be just entertainments. Perhaps no one else could have written them; but perhaps it would not have mattered if Wells had been lazy on their day. Six others partake of the age of overseas adventure, which followed the decline of Kipling. They are excellent. Three or four throw a passing glance at magic, that toy for tired intellects. One story, *The Door in the Wall*, is a very lovely thing, and seems rather by itself— like a gloss on an E. M. Forster fragment.

'An intimation of beauty', say the publishers: half the tales deserve that heading. See, for example, how horror flowers under Wells's hands. There are six stories of the succession of Poe; they are too good to be called Grand Guignol, so compact are they with painful beauty and strength and passion: *The Cone, The Reconciliation, The Lord of the Dynamos*. Besides these are a few parables, for a quiet close to the set. One is a satire, not very acute; another, *The Pearl of Love*, seems to me a fancy to be proud of. Its full cup of sentiment does not brim over, nor its rich prose become precious.

In such analysis of the forms of these sixty-three stories the grave, rare comeliness which is their common denominator has been neglected; and Wells himself, the writer, has slipped through the meshes of my thinking. Always he does. We take for granted so above-board a man. He seems to show himself fully, and we forget he is only showing us what he pleases. Generalizations about H. G. must needs be tentative; for they cannot be maintained against challenge.

As regards his characters, the greatest in this volume is 'I', who colours the whole with himself. There seems not one queer *soul* in the sixty-three. Wells deals more with events and externals than with motives, and uses lay figures as pegs for his costumes. It is easier to arrange the necessary incidents on a stock character—a character which the author has used so often that he need not explain it to himself or to his readers. Wells sees his men as a part of things, and is tempted to make matter as mobile as man. He knows that there is no wonder in the machinery of the senses, but only incompleteness in them. His descriptive work lacks colour. The sense he most calls upon is the visual one. Yet his exactest picture will not make into a drawing. The generalness of his landscape is surprising. You don't catch breath with 'That's Surrey, that's its picture.' The bay of page 355 might be Devon or California, or Malaya. You can feel it, and yourself in it, but it does not take hold of you with any sharpness of its own. Probably Wells would remove, as a blemish, any detail which did take the reader's attention from the business of the story. He is wonderfully adequate, as craftsman, over all his unexampled range. For exact subordination of means few English wrtiers better earn the attribute classical—in respect to his short stories. In the novels, his men and women sometimes mutiny and exceed his plan: it was nearly inevitable with the fierceness of characterization demanded by the novel of twenty years ago.

He angles throughout for a wide public. To most writers, after their beginning book, there comes this fork in the road—whether to care first for what is to be bound between their covers, or for the suffrages of all the people outside. Wells would not have us think him interested in form (though incidentally an invisible H. G. takes good care of what Mr Wells would disregard), and his characters are meant to mean something to most people. Not for him the lofty solitary soul, but the gregarious fellow, clubbable either in pub or in Athenæum. The tales have almost no recognizable women. They are not touched in, except for Elizabeth in *The Days to Come*. Yet even Elizabeth you would not know in the street, as you know Altiora Bailey.

Doubtless it is deliberate, this drawing upon the untapped resources of the readers' minds. It saves space in development. The sudden subtlety of a plain-faced man is like to be overwhelming. Wells will operate for pages in a quietude as fine as Jane Austen's, and suddenly fling in a rarity, like a whale's *bulla*, and make it justify tragedy. Yet even the tragedy is controlled.

Perhaps in the end we should come back to his student ambitions for the secret of Wells's individuality as a short-story writer. The interest in biology has mated happily with his concern for the mass of human nature to make him a general practitioner in the diseases of creation: his consciousness of life as an organism has made him the cosmic doctor. One-third of this volume is extracted from the case-book of his practice and details the patients' ills and treatment: aberrations of nature, of matter, of personality. There is a complete absence of quackery and of specialist absorption. Alienist was, perhaps, too strong a word for him, since for alienists often no normal man exists: whereas Wells is sure of the sane core within his creation.

The Works of Walter Savage Landor

I think this is rather a wonderful effort, on the part of publishers and editor. It is probably the definitive edition of Landor, which includes everything he wrote, prose as well as verse, that any man could ever wish to read. When they talk about the complete works of authors

they seldom mean more than this. Everybody has things like cheques
and bills, and washing lists, that are indubitably his work, but which
are not readable, in the particular sense.

Here is all Landor or all enough. It is magnificently printed, in a
type of excellence, on good paper, in a size which is imposing, as
Landor should be, without being unwieldy. I have carried its various
volumes about with me, lately, trying to think out a review of them,
and have not suffered either from their weight or size. The binding
is apparently strong. A car wheel passed over Volume three, without
its disintegrating.

The first, and I think most certain thing to say about this edition
is that it can probably never be bettered. Those who purchase it (sixteen
volumes, the publisher thinks, at 30s. each: a lot of money) are getting
something final for their money. Not only does it include all the Landor
hitherto collected, but there are extras of all sorts. Not the laundry
bills and cheques and other ascripta which take up an appreciable time
of everybody's pens, whether they are great authors or not, but the
real writings of this strange and uncompromising man.

The second thing to be sure about with this edition, I think, though
I say it only by guess, and have not collated Mr. Welby's texts with
MSS or first collected editions . . . is that the editing is as final as the
quantity of the texts. No quality but love for his author could have
so subdued an editor to suppress himself. This is a definitive edition
as easy and beautiful to read as an unscientific one. There are no
disfiguring footnotes—or very few. No brackets, no apparatus of
criticism, no impertinent explanations of what an author meant or
did not mean. Mr Welby has trusted Landor to say what he meant:—
and magnificently did the old man mean it.

The old man; why do we think of Landor always as old? Other
authors have grown old; why was Landor never young? why do we
prefer to cherish the old man in our imaginations? I think I can, at
times, love Landor but only as an old crotchet whose whims must be
allowed to have their sway with me, for the sake of peace, while I
am in his company. The risk, the loss, the expense, the disaster of
quarrelling with Landor are too great to dare to face. They would for
ever destroy one's pleasure in the work.

So we get an author to whom one must surrender if one is to enjoy
him—a tyrannical writer.

Hence perhaps the smallness of his audience, at times, and the way
in which ever so many people pick him up, cry 'glorious; I'll come
back and have some more of this' and don't. We are so seldom in
the yielding mood. Yield:—it's not yielding; it is complete abject laying
aside one's own senses of values and standards, if one is to absorb
Landor. He humiliates.

A great artist: he said his say beautifully. The cadences of his prose, the lambent smiling of the old thing, the ripeness of age, the prejudices and cock-sureness of too long a life, are all here, perfectly set down. His art was such another vehicle as the prose of George Moore: a vehicle which was so lovely itself that (for a long time) no one asks where it is going, or whether it is going anywhere. For a long time:—but for sixteen volumes? Not for me.

It's as lovely, and as remote, and as useless, as the sound that wind makes in the top of too close a grove of firs. A music of whispering, which steals down the cathedral-dark, pillared, yet starved trunks within the grove. It is good to listen there, once in a way. We may be sure that whenever we walk there, the music of the wind will be waiting there for us, as in a store: but it's a pleasure which, if made an end, wouldn't help us very much. It is too smooth, too sure, too unfaltering to hold much mind.

3

Bric-à-Brac

These motley pieces, written for varied purposes with much or little care, reflect the wide range of Lawrence's critical interests and sensitivities.

Kennington's Arab Portraits

Eric Kennington, sculptor, painter, and official war artist in both World Wars, visited the Near East early in 1921 commissioned by Lawrence to paint portraits of figures in the Arab revolt for the subscriber's edition of *Seven Pillars* for which he was art editor. Lawrence was to accompany him but could not, having become Churchill's adviser and engaged in the March 1921 Cairo Conference and subsequent negotiations in the region. However, he met Kennington several times and helped to arrange sitters.

His discussion of the portraits was written as a preface for the catalog of their October 1921 exhibition at the Leicester Galleries, London. Actually, it was written in August 1921 in Aden, where Lawrence had gone by ship from Jidda after futile talks with the "absurd" King Hussein of the Hejaz.[1] It illustrates Lawrence's ability to write fluently and evocatively, disregarding all distractions, when the spirit moved him.

Nonetheless, his depreciation of his writing was ripening. Writing from Cairo in October 1921, he told Kennington that the preface, which

I have now forgotten all the sense and shape of, except that it was too long [a transparent ploy for someone with such an unusual memory; he used it on other occasions]. As it is forgotten it must have been light, and little-thought-on. Aden is not good for work: and I'd written a good one in London after seeing the collection, and left it buried somewhere. (Garnett, 334)

"There seems a hopeless line drawn between those who have creative

90

imagination and those whose imagination is sterile,'' Lawrence declares
(p. 98). There is no doubt on which side of the line he placed himself.
The true artist is absorbed in his work, his brush or pen flows naturally,
not consciously (certainly not self-consciously): art is inspired, not
manufactured or deliberately designed. Kennington ''did not know
why he was working, nor how he was working. When he felt that he
knew things went very badly'' (p. 98).

Lawrence had done many architectural drawings, maps, sketches,
and tried to sculpt.[2] But he was not a serious competitor in these arts
as he was in literature and could cultivate them disinterestedly.
'' . . . by going to look at pictures, when we are quite incapable of
painting one, we . . . recognise our interim duty of service'' (p. 98).
In the early postwar years particularly, he had a keen interest in
contemporary painting and became friends with many prominent
artists, notably Kennington, Augustus John, William Rothenstein,
Wyndham Lewis, William Roberts, and Lady Kathleen Scott. For a
while, spending more money than he had commissioning work for
Seven Pillars, he was, Jeremy Wilson (675) surprisingly declares, ''one
of the most significant private patrons of contemporary artists in
Britain.'' There must have been few significant private patrons at the
time.

Some readers may think criticism of portraits has little to do with
criticism of literature. In this instance, the parallels are pronounced.
Lawrence exalted both kinds of art and artists and scorned his own
critical judgment—which did not keep prominent men from requesting,
or him from expressing, it.[3]

Sturly

As has been recounted, in late 1923 Lawrence translated Pierre Custot's
Sturly, an unepical story of a sturgeon who, born in France, sees the
world's seas before returning to die in France. He described it as

> a true tale of how fish live, very well told: but English people like hearing
> of fish that were caught, hardly of fish *qua* fish, minus humanity . . . . the
> author was not solid upon his own simplicity, and has chased off after
> rare words and images out of his nervousness.[4]

Discontent with the translation, he burned it (though Jeremy Wilson
suggests he dropped work on it in order to devote his time to *Seven
Pillars*).[5] A translation by Richard Aldington was published by Cape
in 1924. All that remained of Lawrence's work was the jacket blurb
Lawrence sent to Cape with the following note:

After giving birth to the enclosed I'm likely to be confined to my barracks for a while. It's rot, & horrible, but I'll never make a publicity agent. Apologies.

Chuck it to one of your staff, & tell him to make a polished blurb of it.

I'm so ashamed yet to tarry with the book unfinished that I can't write to you.[6]

Despite that characteristic dismissal of his work, the blurb was used unchanged except for minor repunctuation. It was a good blurb, making more of the book than was warranted. David Garnett (438) calls it "a parody of the advertisements on book wrappers."

Flecker

Lawrence met the poet James Elroy Flecker and his wife Hellé in 1911 in Beirut, where Flecker was British Vice-Consul from 1911 to 1913, when tuberculosis forced him to leave for a sanitorium in Switzerland, where he died two years later. The note, evidently written at Clouds Hill in late 1924 or early 1925, was "a much-corrected draft" found among Lawrence's papers after his death.[7] The words in brackets are Arnold Lawrence's editorial additions. An earlier version published by Doubleday, Doran in 1937 contains different readings of several words, including obvious errors, and two variant passages reproduced here from Arnold Lawrence's text.

Upon reading the draft, Mrs. Flecker wrote Arnold Lawrence:

Italy and the Elizabethans were the two great influences in the shaping of J. E. F's mind and also the violent reaction against the modern middle-class Protestant frame, so deadly to the artist.

Your brother's suggestion about Roy's poetry having suddenly matured, though very flattering for me[8] I cannot adopt. I fear it is more probably illness that matured him. His exile from literary groups and witty small talk may have helped as also the influence of the clear light of Eastern lands that drove away romantic chiaroscuro.[9]

Arnold Lawrence added the following comments:

[In Mrs. Flecker's] opinion, . . . Flecker showed no 'Jewish' traits. . . . it cannot have been an Aldini Aristophanes, and they did not live at the Deutscherhof. I suspect that the 'last postcard' quotation is inaccurate too. It is always possible that the original has disappeared, but I have found one postcard from Flecker, written at Davos five months before he died, which contains a sentence, 'I am miserable', though otherwise it is quite

differently worded. In this Note it may have been summarized from
memory, or deliberately paraphrased, so as to make it decently impersonal
and to conceal the identity of Flecker's correspondent. For the Note was
certainly meant for publication under a pseudonym—'Miss Davis' to judge
by the opening words. The fiction is carefully sustained. That photograph
'by some earlier visitor' was actually the writer's own work; 'my
photographing' or 'my photography' is scribbled on the print stuck as a
frontispiece into his copy of *Forty-two Poems*. (*Men*, 11–12)

Lawrence condemned his lack of creative imagination so severely, so
often, and so persuasively that the fictional element in his writing may
be undervalued.

Tarka the Otter

The detailed commentary on *Tarka the Otter* was written as a letter
to Edward Garnett, who had mailed loose proofs of the book to India.
The criticism, Arnold Lawrence observed, "was primarily addressed
to Garnett; it was left to his judgment whether the letter went also
to Williamson, who was not known to the writer" (*Men*, 13). The
footnote and bracketed words in the text are Arnold Lawrence's.
Garnett sent the letter—"two foolscap sheets lined with a minute and
meticulous hand, smaller than ordinary typewriting, extremely neat"
(Williamson, 13)—to Williamson, who was delighted. He replied,
"Your criticism was like my own voice talking to me,"[10] and sent
Lawrence a copy of *The Old Stag*. A correspondence and, later,
friendship ensued.

Tarka won the 1928 Hawthornden Prize, which launched Williamson
into a more successful phase of his career as a nature writer. In response
to Lawrence's critique, he made changes in the fourth edition of *Tarka*
(June 1928), with the acknowledgment "slightly revised, following
suggestions of 'T. E. L.' " (Wilson, 1194). In a 1935 novel where
Lawrence makes a cameo appearance, Williamson calls his criticism
"penetrating and direct and instantly interesting criticism: a child's
clarity and directness, with its essential innocence, and to this add the
wisdom of deep and completely realized experience."[11]

Lawrence wrote similar microscopic critiques to, among others,
Forster, Graves, and Hanley. They show how closely he read, his
sensitiveness to the choice, sound and rhythm of words, and his deep
regard for the writing craft. Yet writing was not just a craft to be judged
by craftsmen; its quality had to be tested by the acuteness with which
it rendered reality. He noted errors of observation or description with

a correction or joke (" 'The moon hung like a gold-fish bone' . . . . improbable. Fishbones . . . are only gold if in a finan haddock, smoked."). Some of his criticism, as he was quite aware, might be criticism of *Seven Pillars* ("It is written too hard. There are no flat places where a man can stand still.").

Lawrence managed to combine sharp technical criticism with enough real or, at any rate, convincing praise and encouragement to retain the victim's friendship. In part, that reflected his ability to identify and sympathize with the writer and, in part, his stance as a critic who looked at a work as almost a shared task of the writer and reader. In his later years in the ranks, he grew progressively disenchanted with writing for other writers and (like Tolstoy) felt that good writing should make good reading for ordinary people.

Odyssey

Over the three years from mid-1928 to mid-1931 Lawrence spent much of his free time, often forty or forty-five hours a week, translating the *Odyssey* for £800, a substantial sum at the time. His translator's note may be read together with the remarks on Homer in his letters (pp. 186–91), especially those to Bruce Rogers and Emery Walker, for whose splendid 1932 limited edition of the *Odyssey* the translation was undertaken. Splendid in all respects but page numbers, which were omitted because Rogers could not think where to put them without marring the pages!

As Lawrence explained to Charlotte Shaw, the note originated in "aggravated letters to Bruce Rogers. . . . He extracted some of it and sent it me as matter for a projected circular-prospectus. . . . I drew it together and cleaned it. . . . and then he asked if it might introduce the translation. I weakly agreed to its going at the end, as a lesser evil."[12] The note, unsigned in the Rogers edition, was signed "T. E. Shaw" and placed in the front of the widely sold 1932 American edition of Oxford University Press.

Lawrence called the *Odyssey* "archaistic" (p. 186) and "Wardour-Street Greek" (the London street where replica antique furniture was sold), thus blaming Homer for the rich English he felt he had to use. Homer's "notebooks were stocked with purple passages." His friend John Buchan (1984, 216), a fine Greek scholar, said Lawrence "was not simple-souled enough to translate Homer, so he invented a pre-Raphaelite Homer whom he could translate." Another friend, Ronald Storrs, "the most brilliant Englishman in the Near East" (*Seven*, 56), voiced a similar opinion. "Lawrence . . . lacked the surrender of soul to submit himself lowly and reverently even to the first poet. Of Matthew Arnold's three requisites for translating Homer—simplicity, speed and nobility, . . . he failed somehow in presenting the third, substituting as often as not some defiant and most un-Homeric puckishness of his own" (Storrs, 472).

Others have rated the translation more highly. The classicist C. M. Bowra termed it "by far the best translation of Homer into English. . . . It is exciting, humorous, and technical as the *Odyssey* is. . . . its complete lack of trite phrases and exhausted words gives it the youth and gaiety of Greek" (R. Weintraub, 20). Robert Fagles (162–64) writes:

> Lawrence's burly, combative prose finally gives Homer a compelling stature. . . . For Lawrence art is craft. . . . the tone [of expertise] that Lawrence first asserted in his *Odyssey* . . . was at best attractively adept, but at worst full of the arrogance of the insecure. Lawrence could never call a spade a spade; it had to come out an adze or a mattock or an ash-hafted carbon-steel shovel.

Fagles noted that the last two books showed "a marked falling off in intensity" and, indeed, Lawrence was then weary of and determined to end his long labor.

Irving Howe (364) again offers a good summary judgment. "He turned the *Odyssey* into firm, often pungent English prose—some classicists have balked, but it is a living book."

Lawrence asked his brother Arnold, a Greek scholar, to check the first book "from the point of scholarship."[13] Arnold later wrote:

> With his *Odyssey* . . . he took immense care, sacrificing correct wording to correct feeling. . . . some who profess complete knowledge of the dead language assure us that he was blatantly inaccurate, but slips would rarely have passed his checking of his verison by previous translations. . . . there remain too few specimens of early Greek to prove or disprove his contention that the original is decadent. (*Friends*, 587–88).

Rogers had the translation read by an authority who proposed many corrections. Though Lawrence himself had suggested that the manuscript be checked for accuracy,[14] he resisted but eventually accepted most of the changes, "while defending himself strenuously" (R. Weintraub, 17). Some of this insistence on his own authority, on the ability, gained by knowledge and experience, to judge and correct Homer, is evident in the note ("He is all adrift when it comes to fighting, and had not seen deaths in battle"), which one reviewer deemed "smart alecky."[15] It is pronounced in Lawrence's January 1931 letter to Rogers responding to his critic:

I have handled the weapons, armour, utensils of those times, explored their homes, planned their cities. I have hunted wild boars and watched wild lions, sailed the Aegean (and sailed ships) bent bows, lived with pastoral peoples, woven textiles, built boats and killed many men.

In his introduction to a recent edition of the translation, Bernard Knox rejects three significant points in Lawrence's depiction of Homer. That Homer is "a bookworm. . . . [whose] work smells of the literary coterie, of a writing tradition," he says, "does not seem possible . . . at such an early stage of Greek literacy." That Homer's characters are "thin and accidental," he finds quite off the mark: "a whole company of minor characters . . . have . . . held the attention of many generations of readers" and the leading characters, Lawrence himself admits, "are fully formed." Lawrence's complaint about Homer's "infuriating male condescension to inglorious woman" particularly annoys Knox. Detailing the contrary evidence at some length, he declares:

> In fact, the *Odyssey* is sharply distinguished from most of the other great works of Greek literature by the repeated emergence of women, not as subordinate presences or passive victims but as effective, even decisive, agents. . . . There is no condescension here, and no inglorious woman either. Coming from Lawrence, the complaint rings false; . . . he seems to have spent most of his life avoiding contact with [women].

Knox agrees with Lawrence that the *Odyssey* is not a conglomeration of stories dating from different times but "a single, authentic, unedited work" or, as Lawrence puts it, "the first novel of Europe." And he thinks the translation "preserves, as well as prose can hope to do it, much of the force, charm, and dignity of the original poem."[16]

La Maison Sans Issues

This and the next item are oddities, letters used as prefaces to bolster sales of novels unlikely to do well without—or with—them. Both were published after Lawrence's death, yet there is some evidence he approved, or did not object to, their use.

La Maison Sans Issues is a French translation of James Hanley's *No Directions*, a virtually surrealist novel of the delirious activities of a drunken sailor and residents of a dilapidated apartment house during a night-time air raid on London. First published in 1943 by Nicholson & Watson (and reissued by André Deutsch in 1990), the translation was issued by the same firm in Brussels, probably in 1946. Lawrence's July 2, 1931 letter to Hanley, extracts from which followed an introduction by Henry Miller, dealt mainly with another Hanley story, *Sheila Moynihan*. Most of this letter is reproduced again on pp. 174–75, so the reader can judge how fairly the selected passages represent the original. One extract had already provided a blurb for Hanley's *Boy*. Hanley must have contacted C. J. Greenwood, his publisher at Boriswood, and then asked Lawrence if they might use it in a revised edition, for, after disparaging introductions, Lawrence acquiesced.

> I don't care, personally: so long as I'm not accused with reason of setting up as a critic, which I am not qualified to be. Only if he [Greenwood] does print something, make it clear that it is from a private letter, & let it be a fair sentence. . . . Hang it all, a fellow does not write injudicial letters! (p. 176)

Lawrence could not have approved use of the painfully accurate remark that his friend G. B. Shaw, still very much alive, "is pedestalled, and not so good as you are." However, the letter had already been included in David Garnett's 1938 selection of Lawrence's letters.

The letter was translated into French; to retranslate it would be too entertaining. As a compromise, I have used Lawrence's original words but retained the French paragraphing and punctuation.

River Niger

Lawrence's May 20, 1934 letter to Greenwood served as a preface to the October 1935 Boriswood publication of *River Niger*, a novel by Simon Jesty (a pseudonym behind which W. W. Vickery wisely hid). Two days before, Lawrence had acknowledged receipt of "the new Jesty book [presumably in manuscript]. What you say of it is exciting. He *might*, you know, pull it off one day. I oughtn't to agree to read another word for five months, but I'll try to make a quick do of it, if you can entrust it to me for a week."[17]

He responded quickly, complaining—how seriously and how much in jest?—that Jesty hampered speed-reading. "To-day, we have no time for the conceits of Nashe or Thomas Browne." Or, he might have added, of Malory, Doughty, William Morris, and *Seven Pillars*. He was not entirely joking: his taste had changed.

Several words and sentences deleted in the preface are here restored, in brackets, from the original letter in the Bodleian.

Eric Kennington's Arab Portraits

Some admirable man, perhaps an Elizabethan, said that critics were lackeys who brushed gentlemen's clothes: and here is Kennington asking me to write a note on his collection of Arabian portraits.

There seems a hopeless line drawn between those who have creative imagination and those whose imagination is sterile. The main purpose of a work of art seems to reveal itself only to the creative: the rest of us see the side issues. The artists cannot or will not explain what they are really at: their humanity interferes with them. So with these drawings the world will not be given its cue to say if they are good or bad, works of art or only attempts at them, until Kennington is dead, and his things considered by artists who neither like nor dislike him and his influences and friends.

All of this, if one believed in the importance of final judgement, should be kept hidden, not said. It makes a poor start for a note on the list of drawings shown: and yet by going to look at pictures, when we are quite incapable of painting one, we do, in a way, recognise our interim duty of service. We can be honest lackeys, and take pleasure in handling and dusting clothes which are not for our wearing. We will then see that catalogue and show are of the subsidiary issues, by-products of the imaginative works whose design is beyond our grasp. They are meant to rouse the money instinct, to produce food and bed: and a north light in which Kennington may sit at leisure and try to create more pictures.

I saw him doing one of these and can testify that he did not know why he was working, nor how he was working. When he felt that he knew, things went very badly. When he began to whistle softly, things were moving well; and as some Arabs think that whistling is a speech with devils, many of his subjects must have felt themselves in bad company before their sittings ended. He was drawing odd people, who are very impatient of those they think fools, men without ties, or duties, or claims, rank individualists who cling to their barren country that they may owe nothing to any man, and be owed nothing in return. Very difficult sitters they are.

It was a strange chance which put him in contact with this Society, but he rose to his occasion and brought a full selection of his opportunities back with him in his portfolio.

He has drawn camel-men, and princes of the desert, donkey-boys, officers, descendants of the Prophet, a vice-president of the Turkish Chamber, slaves, sheikhs and swordsmen. They represent a fair choice of the real Arab, not the Algerian or Egyptian or Syrian so commonly palmed off on us, not the noisy, luxury-loving, sensual, passionate, greedy person, but a man whose ruling characteristic is hardness, of body, mind, heart, and head.

This is no doubt where my being asked to write a note comes in, for I know these odd people who sat to him, and some of them have been my friends. The causes of his going out to Arabia were, a poet, something a man said, and an unpublished book of mine. His Arabs were amongst those who fought gallantly for their freedom in the War. Freedom is a profane, not a saintly body, for which they cared too exclusively to have a spare mind to see themselves in action. It never occurred to them that their children might want to know what they did, and so they wrote down nothing of their story. I felt that this was a mistake, and set about making loose notes in the leisure and detachment which I had, for our race has been free so long that by now we have forgotten that wonderful first taste; indeed age has made it cloying, and sometimes we wish for chains as a variety.

This book was something for the future, but it was an outside view, from an odd angle, and words, especially an amateur's words, are unsatisfactory to describe persons. It seemed to us that it would be balanced somewhat by an expert view, from another angle: and so Kennington went out to correct my men. He was to have had me as his guide, but circumstances prevented this, and plunged him alone into a great Arab camp, which was in a state of semi-warfare. There he had nothing better than a bell-tent for working in, and an atmosphere of unrest and uncertainty which made work difficult.

I had meant to help him in his selection of subjects to draw: as events turned out he was thrown on his own judgment. It is interesting to see that instinctively he drew the men of the desert. Where he was there were ten settled men to every nomad: yet his drawings show nearly ten desert men to every peasant. This has strengthened in me the unflattering suspicion that the nomad is the richer creature.

The Arab townsman or villager is like us and our villagers, with our notion of property, our sense of gain and our appetite for material success. He has our premises, as well as our processes. The Beduin on the other hand, while his sense is as human and his mind as logical as ours, begins with principles quite other than our own, and gets further from us as his character strengthens. He has a creed and practice of not-possessing, which is a tough armour against our modern wiles. It defends him against all sentiment.

Somehow or other Kennington persuaded them to sit; and when he came home, and turned over his sheets of paper in front of me, the experience was very wonderful. I saw first one and then another of the men whom I had known, and at once learned to know them better. This may point indirectly to the power of the drawings as works of art: it pointed without contest to their literary completeness as illustrations of my memory of the men in action: and I think it is praise of psychology. There is quite admirable character here.

Some are curiously typical. Of course they are individual enough, speaking portraits of the men in many of their moods and attitudes: but often Kennington has reached beyond the particular, and made them also types. Perhaps it was because of the language bar, which forced him to rely entirely on his visual powers. However it is, in this study and in that you see not only So and So, son of So and So, but a representation of all the Ageyl who ever rode out from Bagdad, or of all the freedmen of the palm-oases of Nejd. In his Sherifs and in his Sheikhs you see the spirit of the race of sherifs, or of the class of sheikhs sitting within these men's clothes, inhabiting their features, giving a broader significance to their shapes. These drawings are deep and sharp renderings of all that Western Arabians are.

They are quite literal, not prettied or idealised in any way. Yet it would not be fair to call them average. Kennington chose some of the finest men within his reach for his sitters. Auda abu Tayi (p. 222) is the best man in Arabia to have beside you in a fight: you are good enough yourself if you can keep near him for long. He is a mosaic of quixotic splendours: and when he dies the "Middle Ages" of the desert will have ended. Said el Sikeini (p. 378) is a dour puritan, who saw his men dragging chests of gold and rich merchandise from the train which he had blown up by a mine. He left them plundering while he carefully rolled up and carried away the wire and electrical gear with which he had fired this mine, and with which he meant to fire the next. There is Sherif Shakir (p. 198), the finest horseman in Arabia, and one of its bravest and richest and most beloved men. There is the boy Mahmas (p. 292) whom our standards would make a murderer. He is short-tempered and proud, and cannot endure to be worsted in argument. When it happens he leans forward with his little knife and kills the other party. Three times he did it before people learnt to respect his convictions, however ill expressed. His elder brother, a responsible parent, each time saved him from odium by discharging on the nail the blood-money which heals the dispute and compensates the bereaved. There is the Emir Abdulla (p. 68) who will read this note, and would not thank me for either praise or blame of him. His complexity comes out in this portrait.

At the other end of the scale is the spy (p. 260) who was our most excellent informant in the War, but is looked down upon by his fellows because he took money for his work. He lost the money in a bad trading venture after the armistice, and now without either friends or substance must serve as a donkey boy where he once walked free. His face shows his sense of the broken world about him: but when he was sent for to be drawn he ran home and put on his best clothing. It was not very good, but evidently he still has hope and self-respect.

Ali ibn Hussein, Fahad, Matar, Mohammad Sheri, Sindah: the desert is full of songs and legends of their fighting, books could be written round them by the Arabs, and, personally, I am very content to have had a share in causing to be made these records of their faces, while the knowledge of what they did is fresh in men's minds. Whoever writes those books will have to write well if he is to do honour to his illustrations.

Sturly
by Pierre Custot

A picture of the ocean written from beneath the waves. The author is learned in deep-sea fish, a little of a poet, a skilled hand at prose. He has used his beloved fish as a vehicle to convey to us his comments on the world, and nature and humankind; but with so much skill that the fish always keep the forefront of the view, and tinge the whole story with a vivid strangeness. These hardly known inhabitants of deep water have hitherto been the preserve of scientists, and their marvels have been guessed at rather than described. M. Custot is widely read, and has digested what is to be studied of their lore, while his interest in human life is strong enough everywhere to subordinate the scientist to the philosopher and man of letters. Consequently the instincts and accidents and reflexions of his fishes are lively for us; and they are embedded in such word-pictures of the sea and coasts that the complete work is memorable. There is no moralizing, no rhetoric, no verbiage; just a sinewy tale, so simply told that the labour of its writing is unperceived.

A Note on James Elroy Flecker

'Let Miss Davis wait meanwhile in your room,' said the consul . . . as I passed out under escort of the long-legged, short-bodied young Vice-Consul to a side room of the British Consulate at Beyrout. A wooden chair, obviously for the desk: a cane chair—that should do for me. The Vice-Consul slid uneasily into his place. 'Sorry, not much to read'

said he, pushing dossiers over the file of *La Vie* to the right of his
blotter, and *La Rire* to the left, the only papers on the table. I stared
at three fine framed photographs of Greek temples.

My second yawn stirred him to confidence. 'Beyrout's a
hole . . . but this Consulate! My God, how I hate respectable people.'
I said something about the importance of being a Consul, here in
Turkey with extra-territorial privileges like a diplomat. 'They rate us
pretty cheap, all the same', replied he. 'A riot here in Beyrout that
time when the ice-cream fellows bombarded the port. I was driving
down to the Hotel with K. the Finnish Vice. The mob took us for
Italians, and would have lynched us, but for the driver who stuck to
his box, and a splendid police fellow, who came across to our rescue.
The Russians rewarded him with fifty pounds. Our embassy sent him
a silver cigarette case.' Flecker sniffed sharply . . . for he valued
himself well: by inner conviction, not panache.

'What's this "Georgian Poetry" book?' asked I once, disparaging
in my innocence. 'Oh,' said he, 'a collection of all our stuffs—jolly
useful. Shows how much better a poet I am than my contemporaries.'

This was not panache on Flecker's part: he was wrapped up in
poetics, making a wide, exact, skilful study of how other men had
written. He left untouched no one of the sources of European verse.
His education had given him scholarship to master ancient Greece and
Rome. His profession had taught him some classical Arabic, some
Turkish. His practice made him acquainted with modern Greek. French
was a daily language to him: and his inherited Jewish aptitude for
languages made it not arduous to keep abreast of Spanish, Italian,
Portuguese. Only Russian, I think, remained deliberately strange. It
was too northly for this Mediterranean Semite.

We were both living in the Deutscherhof, that plain but clean
German hotel on the east side of Beyrout harbour. Flecker stalked
in, Mrs F. before him, protecting the vice-consul. Russian, German,
American, since for them cleanliness was good and plainness essential,
lived there and dined in its dining-hall at mutually-repulsive tables.
The Austrian one (just a functionary, who had married a ramrod),
the Dane (who at least doesn't attempt not to look a spy) were easily
dismissed. Flecker had been at fisticuffs with the German a little while
before: had floored him in the hotel hall. Almost it had been a
scandal . . . but the summer was coming in sultry and damp, and the
blue-bottle scandal-flies too limp to buzz through the heat. For
England perhaps, for F was furiously British: [a] patriotic, 'God save
[the] King' exile, nostalgic, and knowing himself landless, cling [ing]
desperately to fiction. No. Some difference upon a point of taste, I

believe. Was it Aristophanes? Flecker had just got the large Aldini
Aristophanes and was chasing his old memories of pleasure about the
intricate convolutions of the Greek type. Puns it was that he most
wanted then. His passion for words extended even to their abuse which
had a monstrous beauty, like the hindquarters of an elephant.

Slowly he and I made friends. This strange gawky figure felt the
banishment of hot Beyrout, the steamy harbour, the formal consulate,
the slow sourness of boiled cabbage which smelled through the hotel.
He had shifted his quarters across the road to a kitchen-free annexe,
where he had rooms, and a bit of roof, some Greek island embroideries,
draperies to disguise irrepressibly German furniture . . . books,
cascades of books. 'That's a lovely thing', said he. It was an Austrian
printed cotton, too simple, one would have thought, for his grasp.

Flecker's gestures were personal things, sudden always, graceful as
far as they went, but always unfinished . . . as though his mind were
passing to another subject before the physical accompaniment was
complete. They were too undisguised to be English—but what was
English in this man with the abrupt graceful unfinished movements,
the full spirit, the fiery temper, the lust after all luscious surfaces and
experiences of life? A strong physical frame, as yet little sapped by
insidious disease.

Mrs Flecker, the poised dignity and sweetness of her. The pure
corrective to what was garish and excessive in Flecker, super-abundant.
May one call him a little Jewish in his love of colour and scent, his
rioting taste? Downright English in his physical brutality and efficiency,
his fighting fists, his long springy stride which carried him through
the knee-deep asphodel, up and down the rock-slopes of Lebanon
behind Beyrout, his classical bent thrilled to discover traces of Imperial
Rome here in a rock-cut road, there in an inscription, or in the lovely
aqueduct which spanned Beyrout river just above the town. Flecker
was a Gadarene Greek, and kinsman of Meleager whose poems he
came too near worshipping to hope to translate—spendthrift of
emotion, loving men and sometimes women, showy, joyous (sinking
when ill soon to despair), feeling every joy and sorrow sharply, always
embroidering, curling, powdering, painting, his loves and his ideals,
demonstrative, showy, self-advertising, happy.

It wasn't the fakir, the pilgrim, the hermit, the ascetic of the East,
nor the poor man who called to Flecker's spirit. By instinct, by taste,
by upbringing, by inheritance, his was the town-life of rich Syria, the
satins and silks, perfumes, sweet-meats, grocers and Syrian boys. Dim-
silked, dark-haired musicians. Ah, if he could have thought of those
in the next street but one. In the next street he grew sated with the

nearness of them. In his street—and he longed for Marlborough Downs. It is restless, is life, for the man whose blood mates North and South (N.W. and S.E.).

Areya, the marble pillars and stones arches of verandah: clean bright rooms suffused with Mrs F's love of form. F. very ill now (she [had] Malta fever), half-sobbing with joy at the wind sighing in the pines—('real trees, trees such as you might see in England'), walking on the carpet of their needles. Carelessly flung beneath a tree talking of women's slippers, and of whippings, of revising *Hassan*. Viola Tree walks like a leopard (no great miracle if you know the Egyptians). . . . It must have been a phrase of that week: he said it twice, gustingly. . . .

Dressing up. Bedouin camel-hair cloak, camel-driver's heavy black merino head-knot, Hama brocade head-cloth. Photographed by some earlier visitor, one bare forearm thrust forward, to show woman's beaten-silver old Damascus bangle on wrist.

There, these are such poor fragments of delight. Flecker is dead. 'Do write me a word. I'm sick, and very miserable' was the last post-card, from his cruel mountain-side in Switzerland. With him there went out the sweetest singer of the war generation.

TWO VARIANT PASSAGES

Flecker had just got the big Aldini Aristophanes from Oriolis, of Florence, and was spending hours and eye-sight crawling about its convoluted type in hot chase of classical jests. They were too un-disguised to be English—but what was English in this curious high-coloured, sun-coloured man, with his gawky build and inquiring carriage of the head, his restless fingers smoothing the dark moustache which reduced, without wholly concealing, the sensuality of the mouth. The dark eye-brows, indeterminate nose. Not English, no: yet not Jewish either. Like a sensitised edition of his young brother, who is the only living thing I have seen to remind me of him.

Mrs. F. Choiseul-Gouffier period—fifth century, and archaic, with a form still bigger perhaps to the artist than meaning. F. was later: third century, Hellenistic.

Some of the corrupt early stuff was, I feel sure, Herman Flecker's work. I feel assured that Flecker, the mature poet whom we know as F, was James Helle Flecker . . . as some of the early rococo stuff was rather Herman than James. It was the union of F and his wife which wrought the miracle, which alloyed his too soft gold with a metal fit for our use.

Tarka the Otter
by Henry Williamson

This letter is about *Tarka*, which I have been reading lately. I take it that Williamson is in something of the position I was in. He's written one book, and wants to write more. He's tried his uttermost to write this one better than his power allowed him. He's probably rather in the dumps about it now. I got to that point after Uxbridge: and then I turned back to the printed version of the *Seven Pillars* and read it all, and judged it entirely worthless. But I learnt a very great deal in those years I tried to write. And if he will take my remarks as coming from a self-confessed failure—a man who never will be able to write, despite all his equipment and knowledge, just because he lacks the seed of creation—he may find something of interest in his own performance's impact on me.

I should say first that *Tarka* was in itself an achievement, though not (thank goodness) a final one. There are good reasons in *Tarka* for expecting his next book to be better. Whereas anyone can see in the *Seven Pillars* 320,000 good reasons why my next book would be worse!

It is written too hard. There are no flat places where a man can stand still a moment. All ups and downs, engine full on or brakes hard on. He has been afraid of what he did easily, and too modest in his judgment of his own power. For normal readers, a very little of his hardest work will go a long way. He should write one easy paragraph in five, three normal ones: and only key us up to his full strain for the little remainder. *Tarka* is tiring to read. It is too close knit: you can't skip a sentence without loss. It is monotonous for the eye to jog at one pace. Skipping is a merit, because it rests the brain. Let him sometimes have mercy on the short-breathed.

It is too staccato. Agreed that is his mode: but no long piece of music was ever written in one mode, like a song. His style should flow, sometimes, in legato passages: passages in which the sound of the vowels means more, in the way of sense, than the clicking of the consonants. *Tarka* is essentially consonantal . . . and I've stumbled over trying to read it aloud to myself, as I'd stumble over Peter Pipers pheasant picked a peck of pickled peppers. His tautness of line induces monotony: so does his dryness and exactitude of phrase. More carelessness, for God's sake. He is big enough to unbutton his waistcoat in public. If he does not, readers will never get at ease with him. Some of his pages are more like gravel than like water or rock. Also his paragraphs are cut out of the piece; they should begin and end irrevocably; be little creations.

Nor do I call it a merit to restore so many dying words to life. We are too rich, in the English language. Half the trade and technical words might die, and good riddance. His local terms are half a jargon. Admitted they are pedigree words, some of them. But why 'tissed', for instance, repeated 1,000 times? I liked it the first time, and progressively disliked it as it went on. There's more power making the well-known word do. You'll quote me Doughty against that; but I call Doughty's greatness in spite of his style, of his vocabulary of Arabic (in *Arabia Deserta*), of his Syntax of Icelandic-German. Camel is a better word (because more worn) than thelul. This inlay of strange words into a ground-work of daily English is a mistake. The effect is fussy, not primitive, more peasant-art than peasant. It is for hierophants like Williamson to make a virtue, not a regret, of their education. Words like Dimmity, skillet, cranching, peggle, vuz-peg, quap, fitch, vair, eve-light, uvver, hover, pill, day-hide, up-trends, channer, glidder, mazzard, yanning:—all these are words of local value only: and while one or two of them might add colour, twenty only bring darkness. It's a good writer who can add three words to English. Of course Williamson would say he was reviving, or bringing out, some of these: but, as I say, we have too many now: a weasel hardly earns a better name than that!

Page 3. I was sorry, as I got to the end of the second sentence, not yet to have met a verb standing upright. It was a pity to *begin* with a feminine paragraph, and bad taste to follow a weak beginning with the superbly-drawn picture of the falling oak, one of the book's highlights. Paragraph I should be postponed, or strengthened.

Paragraph 3 (on page 4) illustrates well my complaint about the staccato style. 21 lines, eleven full stops: only one semi-colon, ten commas. He should use fewer commas (i.e. more sentences which grow without stops to adult size) and not be afraid of subjunctives and relatives. Agreed they are overdone in social prose, but Theodore Powys and Williamson underdo them. The old technique of writing is not yet decayed: we don't yet need a new style. English prose approaches its golden age, when somebody will display all its richness. *Ulysses* is a text-book and catalogue of all the modes. Paragraphs should be books in microcosm: have a start, a climax, couplings fore and aft, a finish.

Page 4. I don't like likening mist to anything so *particularly* small as the down on an owl's feathers. To feather-down—yes: but the particularity felt small to my taste, and made my mouth smile—bad taste, therefore, of mine or his.

Page 6. 'The mist moved down with the rime: her heart slowed: she forgot quickly.' That seems to me admirable prose.

Page 8. 'Whither he had straightly flown.' I wonder in what sense straightly is used? Old or new?

Page 11. 'The moon paled of its gleam.' This is literary: precious.

Page 14. The growth of Tarka: more supple and fluent prose: and the Kingfisher, next page, just the reverse: strained ideas, and rhythm.

Page 27. I like 'star-shining', though it is rather conscious. There are very many hyphenated words in this book. I tried to use not more than one per paragraph, as a matter of manners. Prose is bad when people stop to look at it.

Page 24. 'Nothing feared the old lady': this sentence wants recasting. It is broken-backed. There is both a who and a which in it. I made myself a rule not to use two relatives in a sentence: though one may use a relative 'who', and a relative 'that' and get away with it, undetected. It's the being detected that's criminal, always.

Pages 26, 27. The night-jar and owl: a well-told, drawn out effort. So many of his incidents are all over in a sentence: or are gradually introduced, and lead nowhere. It's a little cinematographic: whereas I think painting is harder and better: to concentrate significance on a few semi-static entities, and make them equal the crowd. Joyce walks down Sackville Street and catalogues 356 articles as he walks. Forster could give the same completeness with five things, carefully placed and built together with the necessary association-ideas. Modes, these two, of course.

Page 35. The clamour of the kill, and the mother's feeling are excellent.

Pages 37, 38, 39. An elaborate landscape, but it isn't made use of: painted for sheer pleasure in paint: which is virtuosity, not book-making. I have a yearning for simplicity, except where elaboration is reluctantly—and finally—necessary.

Page 42, 43. The fox I find clear, and interesting: a character who enriches the book: not an excrescence.

Pages 44. The hedge-hog's death I'd call virtuosity, again. The otters had gone: why deepen the jungle behind their backs? We all know that nature is bloody and ravenous.

Pages 45, 46. 'Golden' pollen, 'green' heads, 'brown' in autumn. I do not like catalogues of colours. Hint at them by parallel, not by direct classification. 'Fountains of pollen spilled like sunlight on the juicy heads, which would soon pass, with autumn, into the colours of decay.' That's awful: but Williamson could have done it well, knowing the plants. Just the bald statement is too easy: it's like a pencil sketch, with colour-notes written along the margins. Marland Jimmy is a character. He and Nog are my two joys in the book: for I don't like Tarka or Deadlock: and the she-otters are confusing and undistinguished.

Page 48. Before the shadow of a grass-stalk . . . bravo! There's the seeing eye!

Page 51. 'Like *a* mussel-shell on *a* sea-shore.' Only one *a* I think is prudent.

Pages 53–55. The trap scene is well done. But why (page 55) 'the otter she left it' . . . a misprint, or more literary-particularity? If the latter, it's a crime to get self-conscious in the heat of action. When there is leisure, you may preen yourself: but never when you're moving.

Page 60. 'Mewing with their pads on the dead bird.' 'The moon hung like a gold fish-bone in the dusk.' This seems to me improbable. Fish-bones don't often hang, and are only gold if in a finnan haddock, smoked.

Page 62. I like this picture of the moon like a luminous grub in a cocoon.

Page 64. 'A wheel of sticks, riveted by bubbles'—too elaborate. Pictures should be common enough for the reader to think of their parallel, not of them.

Pages 67, 68, 69. Very good. A charm of pleasure after too much animal.

Page 70. The first paragraph is music: and the second good. But bump goes the warm blood next page, when the otter takes the stage again. Perhaps Williamson tired of his first-line animals, sometimes.

Page 76. The sea, and Bideford are beautifully introduced, and painted in: there is real skill in the changing scene.

Pages 78, 79. The swallows again bring back the deeper note. Do you notice how Williamson puts his highest lights on the birds?

Page 79. Shouldn't more weight have been laid on the growth of Tarka, as an animal? We get hundreds of the greedy little beast's meals, and not one decent phrase or thought out of his head. He's about as intelligent as a mincing machine.

Page 84. The mill is a pleasant variety. I'd have emphasized it.

Page 85. God, I suppose, is love: but no one would have thought it.

Page 89. The light-house is two pictures telescoped: the bright eye—in the dark: and the bleached bone—in sunlight. Either is good: both together are bad. The last sentence of this paragraph again introduces colour-words, from a catalogue. Colour—like the 'bleached bone' very fine example—should be left for the reader's quickened imagination to fill in. I'm not sure that the best writer isn't he who gets most work out of his reader.

Pages 91–93. The sea-fight is good, but a little too Jack-London-Hugo, with its violence. An animal too many, I fancy, for easy digestion. But fighting makes me sick. I'm quaker-natured.

Page 96 seq. The raven is magnificent. One can see him. I suppose birds in the air are nearer us than animals in the water: or is it that an airman finds something cleansing and holy in the power of flight?

Pages 100–102. The main episode is amazing. I fancy it's too strange to be untrue: but it makes a gargoyle of strangeness in a book which contains, otherwise, hardly a high-light. *Tarka* is like two or three motives, twined together.

Page 103. Poured like liquid glass—lovely phrase: though I'd have avoided 'icy' as next-door neighbour. The spines of the grass scratching at the air very good, but what a come-down to the air's clutch, in the last line!

Page 104. The prose in this mounts full and significant, into positive splendour. Page 105 is all a crescendo: and the central paragraph of page 106 seems to me the climax of the book—almost fit, for its wonder, to be put next Traherne's 'orient wheat', as one of the finest passages of English prose. Sense, sound, colour, all quite beyond criticism: beyond ordinary admiration too. It makes me very shy of writing critically of any of the book. Only I feel that Williamson should have wrought himself up to this point more than once: could have.

Page 110. Marland Jimmy again warms up the otter world. Good old beast.

Pages 121–123. These do not seem to me as good as some of the rest. A surfeit probably. The book repeats itself, sometimes, not in word or deed, but in spirit and result.

Page 125. The 'I' seems causeless. Is it the remains of an earlier draft, or the irruption of a later mood?

Page 129. 'Bog and hummocks': 'dimmed and occluded': 'drifts and hollows': why all this marrying? Occluded should not be in progression with dimmed, either. Dimmed into occlusion? Occluded into dimness? Better left out. Peat that was heather: a bit too tightly pressed, that cheese. Often he packs too much into his sentences. *Tarka* takes days to read: whereas books shouldn't be so long and slow: readers can only give books their spare hours: and how are we to keep a mood for the spare hours of every day for a week, to do Williamson justice? He should ask less of his public, in time: but more in degree.

Page 131. 'A fine sibilance in the wry wind music': Oh very good.

'Wry' is genius, just there. The gladness of the other, too, is very welcome, at last.

Page 133. Good page, till the preciousness of the grey and *silent* 'song-light' trips you up on your face in the bog. Nor do I like the unwise dandelion. I laugh, of course, but twistedly. It's like the sea, which in Aeschylus had an ανηριθμον γελασμα and in Matthew Arnold, unplumbed, salt, estranging: and in Milton* performed pure ablution: and in the Sitwells yaps like a Pekinese: and to James Joyce is scrotum-tightening. Each artist funds the self-portrait in it.

Page 134. 'The moor-folk call this morning glory the Anmil.' And the French, with like crudity, call a dandelion a pissant-lit. Damn the moor-folk.

Pages 136–137. I like your stoats. They did to Tarka what he'd earned—or some of it. I didn't think I'd ever like stoats, either.

Page 139. The cocoa-tin is a beautiful thing, just enough told and no more. Excellent.

Page 142. The picture of the viper-shaped river is good, but a little too rare for my fancy. My eyes like to see quickly, not to half-shut themselves and erect a likeness from some very deep stomach of imagination.

Pages 144–145. Tarka the man of blood again. I'm all on the dogs' side now: and shall vote for the extermination of otters.

Page 146. The cat is good: though I'd have liked her better less maimed.

Page 147. 'A hot broken glitter' (good) 'like a flight of silver' (bad; all metallic life) 'birds played lightly on the (green) flags . . . one brilliant *beak of light pecked at his eye* till he awoke (yawning, to turn on his back).' The underdotted [Italic] part too much prolongs the metaphor. I have tried to smooth the march of the sentence after awoke. His grain is too harsh, and his tempo monotonous with its metronomic regularity. More variety of syntax, please, and more agility of verbs. Up the subjunctive mood.

Page 148. A good short shower, well done, but drowned in too much that is less significant. This book is rich enough for ten, like wedding cake, in which plums crowd out the honest flour to the degree of uneatability and dim the acerbity of the peel.

Page 149. Apparently he does not like a closed car, even on a

---

*This seems to be a slip for Keats—the reference must be to 'the moving waters at their priest-like task of pure ablution round earth's human shores' in his last sonnet [note by A. W. Lawrence].

showery day. What plenty of dry clothes he must have, at home! Or does he not keep a car? Engine smoke is rather a lovely pale blue, if the driver knows his job.

Page 151. 'The murky water twired by the knee joints of his thin green legs.' Oh, very good, again: twired was probably half a day's work, and worth it.

Pages 152, 153. I suppose the dog-catalogue is good: there is a rare variety of description: I am not fond of hounds, though, and do not warm to their noise or sight: and I felt the particularity too deliberate, as of someone who had read the Iliad.

Page 155. Tarka's escape reads to me a bit tall: but I suppose Williamson has otter-hunted, and I haven't—and won't.

Page 161. 'Points of shining rested on the black bubbles riding on the crests of hollows.' Not a good sentence. The two 'ings' are one too many: not more than one 'ing' per 5 or 6 lines, as a rule, unless they are tied 'ings', like 'leaping and twisting': here one is substantial, and one verbal. 'On the . . . on the'—this is also crude: and crests of hollows is too stiff. Three 'silvers' in the next three lines.

Page 163. 'Assayed the air.' V.G. but rather wasted. It should have been tied to the scent of white-tip, so that the reader felt it coming, and caught it.

Page 165. 'With pricked ears, and a tail-tip gone.' Tut tut! 'Linked into chains and chased': two 'cha' together. Tut Tut. Only repeat a word-sound if it is reminiscent of the act-sound you are trying to describe.

Page 166. 'The ringing rasp of . . . was loud. Circular saws rang raspingly' . . . I don't know. I'd have put it other.

Page 169. 'Just deep enough to cover an old boot.' That seems to me very skilful. The owls supply very necessary humour. I wish there had been more to smile at, all through the book.

Page 173. This isn't the first or second time that the curlews have provided admirable passages and pictures in the welter of blood.

Pages 174–176. The ravens again are good. All the birds seem to me higher creations than the otters.

Page 180. 'The noise hurt the fine drums of his ears.' At last I feel with Tarka.

Page 181 seq. The movement of the hunt, with the tangled weaving of Tarka's trail, is very good.

Page 187. The whirlpool is very good.

Page 188. I don't like the needless entry of the fisherman. Williamson distracts us, often, by too much. A few pages back he drew a lovely picture, in a line, of the golden-stream-shadow of Tarka's swimming-wave. Lovely: but there was a hunt on.

Pages 189, 190. Good: but surely a bit tall?

Page 192. The stag-hunt is an excrescence. We don't want so much matter.

Page 195 seq. The wandering of Tarka after white-tip is well drawn, shapely, and (though richer and closer-woven than most writing) not discursive for Williamson.

Page 203. 'Gemmeous dragonet' . . . and he liked the horror so much that he repeats it, 2 pages later, when I was decently over the shock!

Page 204. 'It saw Tarka and out of its beak, hooped as its wings in downward gliding fell a croak, which slurred upwards to a whistle, and broke in a sweet trill as it flew away.' Not a digestible sentence. He should have chewed it again, for our sakes. Good old Nog returns to save the situation. Continuity is a blessing in so gravelly a book. Pictures hail down at us from every page.

Page 205. Good, where the otters meet, with the differing voices.

Page 207. The cottage-lights, 'like wind-blown embers' is so good that I'd have struck out Antares like an ember on page 22.

Page 208. The cubs eating fascinated me, as a study in syllable-music. Very acutely 's'd and 'e'd.

Page 212. The flowers and birds again relieve me of more fish-suppers. I don't like fish, and never did, either fried or boiled: while as for raw!

Page 214. Nog's children make another smile; whereas the cubs are just bloody. Is it my fancy, or are otters hateful?

Page 219. I do not like the sentiment of the three last lines: it too broadly prefigures a tragic next chapter.

Pages 220–223. The gathering of the hunt—good. I smell some irony behind it—perhaps wrongly. Good stuff, though. The hunt I won't attempt to pronounce upon. It must have been very hard to do, for we had had previous hunts (too much, perhaps?) which had stolen much of what should have been its thunder. It is drawn out very long, but the prose has more excitement in it, so that the eye can run down a paragraph without microscopically examining each word. That's a kindness Williamson does us, at last. Good metaphor, careful picturing, are blemishes in active parts, where no adjectives are needed at all. I call the last three or four paragraphs very fine stuff, and the end of the book almost too skilful. A piece so cunning, so composed, so artful, requires to be read in court dress, rather as Machiavelli used to write! Symbolic, parabolic, realistic:—but not real. Yet so spiced and tormented a generation as ours can hardly find a simplicity which does not ring false: so perhaps it is better to admit our complexity, and develop it to the nth.

I'm rather appalled to have written so much, and to have arrogantly suggested change. Yet to put it bluntly saves space. I have felt something lacking in the spots upon which my reading has checked to a standstill. If I were a writer, I could, presumably, have said what was the matter—and that would have hurt Williamson's feelings. Whereas by just putting up a notice 'Danger, road up', I've attracted his attention, without trying to particularize trenches, or holes, or new metal, or deflections, or side-roads.

He will realize, if you send him this letter, that I'm not a verbal artist: but a fellow who thought for a long time about writing, and then found (not too late) that he couldn't do it. Yet sometimes I fancy that it isn't the success who teaches best, but the half-failure. So perhaps he will not be peevish. I shouldn't have written so much about the book if it was not, in my judgment, particularly worth writing about. If I might hazard a general opinion it is that the otter-subject did him much harm. All his good stuff clusters in the side-lines of the book. He could write, I think, nobly about open air, and wind, and sunlight, and night and men and birds.

If Williamson is tetchy and satisfied, don't send him this. He'll be insulted at the criticisms of a nobody he's never heard of. But my ambition to write would sooner have come to its head (and incidentally cut its throat in despair) if someone had taken my stuff line by line and ragged it. You did, practically, in your long notes on that draft of my encumbrance: but I met you five years after the crisis was over, when I was already embarking on a new line [the R.A.F.], which has, thanks be to God, decently contented me. Lucky to have spare strings for my bow!

[Postscript] Very many thanks for sending it [*Tarka*] to me. It has kept me sizzling with joy for three weeks. The best thing I've met for ever so long. Fresh, hopeful, fecund, and so, so, careful. It is heartening to see a writer caring much for his words, and chasing and chiselling them with such firmness. I hope he likes it well enough to persevere, for I shall look forward to reading him again:—apart from *Tarka*, which I'll read many times yet.

The Odyssey: Translator's Note

The twenty-eighth English rendering of the *Odyssey* can hardly be a literary event, especially when it aims to be essentially a straightforward translation. Wherever choice offered between a poor and a rich word richness had it, to raise the colour. I have transposed: the order of metrical Greek being unlike plain English. Not that my English is plain enough. Wardour-Street Greek like the *Odyssey's* defies honest rendering. Also I have been free with moods and tenses; allowed myself to interchange adjective and adverb; and dodged our poverty of preposition, limitations of verb and pronominal vagueness by rearrangement. Still, syntax apart, this is a translation.

It has been made from the Oxford text, uncritically. I have not pored over contested readings, variants, or spurious lines. However scholars may question the text in detail, writers (and even would-be writers) cannot but see in the *Odyssey* a single, authentic, unedited work of art, integrally preserved. Thrice I noted loose ends, openings the author had forgotten: one sentence I would have shifted in time: five or six lines rang false to me: one speech seems to come before its context. These are motes in a book which is neat, close-knit, artful, and various; as nearly word-perfect as midnight oil and pumice can effect.

Crafty, exquisite, homogeneous—whatever great art may be, these are not its attributes. In this tale every big situation is burked and the writing is soft. The shattered *Iliad* yet makes a masterpiece; while the *Odyssey* by its ease and interest remains the oldest book worth reading for its story and the first novel of Europe. Gay, fine and vivid it is: never huge or terrible. Book XI, the Underworld, verges toward 'terribilita'—yet runs instead to the seed of pathos, that feeblest mode of writing. The author misses his every chance of greatness, as must all his faithful translators.

This limitation of the work's scope is apparently conscious. Epic belongs to early man, and this Homer lived too long after the heroic age to feel assured and large. He shows exact knowledge of what he could and could not do. Only through such superb self-criticism can talent rank beside inspiration.

In four years of living with this novel I have tried to deduce the author from his self-betrayal in the work. I found a book-worm, no longer young, living from home, a mainlander, city-bred and domestic. Married but not exclusively, a dog-lover, often hungry and thirsty, dark-haired. Fond of poetry, a great if uncritical reader of the *Iliad*, with limited sensuous range but an exact eyesight which gave him all his pictures. A lover of old bric-a-brac, though as muddled an antiquary as Walter Scott—in sympathy with which side of him I have conceded 'tenterbooks' but not railway-trains.

It is fun to compare his infuriating male condescension towards inglorious woman with his tender charity of head and heart for serving-men. Though a stickler for the prides of poets and a man who never misses a chance to cocker up their standing, yet be must be (like writers two thousand years after him) the associate of menials, making himself their friend and defender by understanding. Was it a fellow-feeling, or did he forestall time in his view of slavery?

He loved the rural scene as only a citizen can. No farmer, he had learned the points of a good olive tree. He is all adrift when it comes to fighting, and had not seen deaths in battle. He had sailed upon and watched the sea with a palpitant concern, seafaring being not his trade. As a minor sportsman he had seen wild boars at bay and heard tall yarns of lions.

Few men can be sailors, soldiers and naturalists. Yet this Homer was neither land-lubber nor stay-at-home nor ninny. He wrote for audiences to whom adventures were daily life and the sea their universal neighbour. So he dared not err. That famous doubled line where the Cyclops narrowly misses the ship with his stones only shows how much better a seaman he was than his copyist. Scholiasts have tried to riddle his technical knowledge—and of course he does make a hotch-potch of periods. It is the penalty of being pre-archaeological. His pages are steeped in a queer naivety; and at our remove of thought and language we cannot guess if he is smiling or not. Yet there is a dignity which compels respect and baffles us, he being neither simple in education nor primitive socially. His generation so rudely admired the *Iliad* that even to misquote it was a virture. He sprinkles tags of epic across his pages. In this some find humour. Rather I judge that here too the tight lips of archaic art have grown the fixed grin of archaism.

Very bookish, this house-bred man. His work smells of the literary coterie, of a writing tradition. His notebooks were stocked with purple passages and he embedded these in his tale wherever they would more or less fit. He, like William Morris, was driven by his age to legend, where he found men living untrammelled under the God-possessed skies. Only, with more verbal felicity than Morris', he had less poetry. Fashion gave him recurring epithets, like labels: but repetitions tell, in public speaking. For recitation, too, are the swarming speeches. A trained voice can put drama and incident into speeches. Perhaps the tedious delay of the climax through ten books may be a poor bard's means of prolonging his host's hospitality.

Obviously the tale was the thing; and that explains (without excusing it to our ingrown minds) his thin and accidental characterisation. He thumb-nailed well; and afterwards lost heart. Nausicaa, for instance, enters dramatically and shapes, for a few lines, like a woman—then she fades, unused. Eumaeus fared better: but only the central family stands out, consistently and pitilessly drawn—the sly cattish wife, that cold-blooded egotist Odysseus, and the priggish son who yet met his master-prig in Menelaus. It is sorrowful to believe that these were really Homer's heroes and exemplars.

La Maison Sans Issues
by James Hanley

Plymouth, 2–7–31

Dear Hanley,

. . . You must work very fast yet your writing is all good, clear and fitting, and when necessary beautiful. Yet all your own.

. . . Also your "cataracts" puzzled me. There were three of them, quite close together: once as a verb, once an adjective and once a noun. I fancy you overdid 'em. Otherwise your writing is just a transparent medium, through which what you want to say slips invisibly and silently into my mind. I like that. It seems to me the essence of style. . . . Your character drawing is superb, here and in "Boy" and in "The Last Voyage" and "Drift". You can draw characters as and when you please, with an almost blistering vividness. . . .

You need not bother about the Latin Quarter or about schools and "cliques". They will bother more about you: and if you don't pay attention, they will fall to praising everything you do, whereas praise is always waste of time to hear and harmful in overdose. After years of it, you look for it and credit it and then are soiled. Take poor Bernard Shaw, who must have been wonderful when he was your age, fifty years ago. Now he is pedestalled, and not so good as you are. Whereas 50 years hence you may be rotten. . . .

I will try and find something not pimpish of me in Arab kit, for you. It was long ago and a scabby episode in my life. Politically the thing was so dirty that I grew to hate it all before it came out more or less honestly in the end. So when I see pictures of myself in Arab kit, I get a little impatient. Silly of me, for it was long ago and did really happen.

Your sanity, and general wholesomeness stick up out of your books a mile high: people with dirty patches in them skirt round and round them, alluding but never speaking right out. They are afraid of giving their spots away and you can map them just by outlining the blanks. Whereas, God almighty, you leave nothing unsaid or undone do you? I can't understand how you find brave men to publish you!

River Niger
by Simon Jesty

13, Birmingham Street,
Southampton.
[Thursday 20.5.34]

Dear Greenwood,

and there followed a long pause, after writing that address. I have just finished the *River Niger*, with astonishment, admiration—and some bewilderment. Let me try and fault-find, in a reader's criticism of a book whose technical performance I have unreservedly admired.

Its verbal Ping-pong was too clever for me. I saw I was only a retired colonel. They were all equally clever: not a dull mind in the crowd of them. You mentioned Faulkner, and bits from him introduce the sections of the book. I remembered Firbank, and George Meredith before him. There seemed to be a Jewish odour and some Priestleyness.

Upon the theme, I fancy he has too credulously read [Seabrook], a cheap and sensation-mongering [American]. I doubt whether Voodoo is any more African than—say—Negro Spirituals. Fetichism (if you must have a portmanteau word for the black creeds of Africa) never at its worst falls so low as the heights of Voodoo.

I suspect an anachronism in his curative use of light so early in Judy's life. How old is Jesty? His film-star longs for a voice like Forbes-Robertson and a figure like Henry Ainley. Ainley went up to about [fifteen] stone during the war, and only lately filmed at all—but has kept what I think is the most beautiful voice upon the stage: better, surely, than Forbes-Robertson's at his prime.

[I thought I recognised parts of Yeovil and hope there is no local foundation for Mr. Godsip.]

Jesty's world is incredibly small. It holds only about eight named characters who bump together whether they stay put or wander abroad. Wilkie Collins and his generation flourished on coincidences: but Jesty out-Victoria's them. He has not one but twenty incredible coincidences.

His probate and inheritance law-knowledge seems a bit wild.

Mainly, though, I tended to grumble at his cleverness. He budgets only for exact and minute readers, whereas most book-readers are like me, of a wolfish appetite. We gulp down our books in basket-fulls—and in the gulping we lose his finer phrases and subtler allusions. Mercy on the speed-reader, please! To-day we have no time for the conceits of Nashe or Thomas Browne. I know that Faulkner began with many of these epigrammatic and seeming-obscure allusive sentences, written in a staccato rhythm, with nouns, adjectives (many) and verbs (few) dancing in measure. But Faulkner shed this mannerism as he wrote more and more hurriedly. Jesty has been too careful, writing this book.

However, we are now back again at admiration. It is a very astonishing and very successful work: too ambitious, I think in that it tries to use too many motives, mixing the black strain with parable and finance and voodoo and provincial politics and blindness and passion. It is too generous, too dispersed, too omnivorous. Too-too, in fact. But good, very very good. The *Drunken Damozel* was the sort of first book (not too certain of itself) that many people could (and do, unfortunately) write. Jesty survives it, with increased power in his display. The third book might be triumph. The man can write, damnably well. Alas that he should prink and curl his sentences like a gardener preparing a show chrysanthemum for Chelsea. Not necessary. There are dozens of blooms in the book. It is almost wanton in its merit.

And what are you to do with it? Heaven only knows. If your name was Macmillan, I would say 'Put aside five hundred pounds and nurse Mr Jesty. He may well come off and be a great comfort to your firm a thousand pounds hence'. [But that sort of counsel is no good to you, for you have not a hundred pounds: nor to Macmillan, for they would not approve of Mr. Jesty.] He falls between the peaks of merit and caviarety.

I agree that you would be almost bound to lose money on *River Niger*. I doubt if it would sell two hundred copies in England: and I suppose the States would be quite hostile to its theme and tendencies. [As for introduction by some noted star . . . . . I don't suppose E. M. F[orster]. would do it—and when he did it for Constance Sitwell nothing favourable for the publisher happened.] It ought to be printed and published, just to show people how our generation (or yours, I must say, I suppose: I keep on forgetting anno domini and my decrepitude) can or could write. Some rich man or Guild should endow this sort of thing.

Perhaps we can talk this over if you and the Marshalls get to my cottage in July. If I am still here I would make a great effort to come across and spend part of a day with you.

Part II
Literary Correspondence

Letters to a writer about his work can not, out of friendship and charity, nakedly and fully express the reader's real opinions. "A man who is asked by a writer what he thinks of his work," Samuel Johnson remarked, "is put to the torture and is not obliged to speak truth."[1] Each passage on writers, writing, and books in Lawrence's correspondence, his brother Arnold noted, must be

> read with a view to the circumstances under which it was written. Letters to an author about his own work cannot always be candid; letters about the work of mutual friends or on subjects with which one's correspondent is preoccupied are liable to be influenced by personal feelings; letters to a publisher may justifiably emphasize a book's merits and ignore its defects [not if you want to keep the publisher's confidence]. Sometimes a letter may reflect a passing mood or a fleeting interest [*Men*, 9].

Nonetheless, Lawrence's comments on literary topics and people are so varied and voluminous, and directed to so many different persons over so many years—from 1908 to 1935, in this compilation—as to offer much insight into his character, opinions, and taste.

On the whole, their spontaneity, wit, irreverence, and candor contrast with his more tightly-worked writing for publication. However, his self-conscious mind always outraced his pen, so that parts of his letters exhibit some of the faults of his over-deliberated prose. Lawrence was "now [1923] taking immense care over the literary quality of his letters, which were sometimes redrafted more than once" (Wilson, 715). As Jean Villars (347), a perceptive early biographer, observes, "Lawrence's anxiety to be always brilliant does give to some of the letters a taut and irritating quality that often spoils them."

As for the relative honesty and frankness of private and public criticism: well, it all depends. Lawrence's introduction to *Arabia Deserta* is as flattering as his letters to Doughty, while his letters to Cockerell, Hogarth, and Edward Garnett grow increasingly critical of Doughty as a man, a poet, and a writer. His letters to Graves express open distaste for *I, Claudius*. Their friendship was under strain and Lawrence's criticism is not relieved by the humor, sympathy, and praise in his critical letters to Ede, Hanley, Schwartz, or Williamson. Frankness is a consequence of intent and feeling, not of the medium of expression; one can be as flattering, devious, or direct in private letters as in print.

Diffidence and self-mortification combined with an unattainable, indefinable literary perfectionism led Lawrence to only short bursts of critical writing. In this kind of writing, he had little of the perseverance he showed in *Seven Pillars* and in the *Odyssey* translation. However, he never abandoned his interest in books and writers and in corresponding and talking about them. By all accounts, his conversation was even more absorbing than his letters, suffering less from the self-consciousness that, when he was alone, seized his pen and paper, especially manuscript paper.

Of the possible ways of arranging these extracts, I have chosen those which highlight the nature and development of Lawrence's opinions about particular writers and certain broad themes that preoccupied him. Under each heading the arrangement is chronological. In some cases, a lengthy extract or entire letter is devoted to one writer or topic, but often only a paragraph or sentence, increasing the danger that the context and tone of a comment may be misconstrued. Appended notes may help to explain the context of some extracts.

To the charge that extracts, long or short, chop up the letters I necessarily plead guilty. Those who want a fuller and broader selection of Lawrence's wide-ranging, brilliant, kind, and unhappy letters should read the excellent volume edited by Malcolm Brown. However, Brown, David Garnett, and M. R. Lawrence, editors of earlier important volumes of Lawrence letters, give only long or expurgated extracts of too many letters. Almost sixty years after his death, no major collection of intact Lawrence letters has yet been published.[2]

Some extracts might, of course, be placed under different headings. The diligent reader of, say, Women Writers, should also read Lawrence's comments on Bell, Hall, Richardson, Sitwell, and Stark; the reader of Poetry and Poets, those on a dozen individual poets; readers interested in Lawrence's Likes and Dislikes or his views of Good and Great Writing should read the whole compilation.

4

On Writers

Introduction

Lawrence's castigation of **James Barrie** in his March 19, 1924 letter to Charlotte Shaw was prompted by her suggestion that Barrie write a preface to *Seven Pillars*. She did not think Barrie, her neighbor and friend, "a cozener & . . . a fraud" and reprimanded Lawrence. He apologized after repeating the charge in moderated form: Barrie was "a fine writer . . . [who] deliberately does the not-quite best." **Belloc**, Chesterton, and Graves (in *I, Claudius*) were guilty of similar offenses. All were talented men who, to sell their stuff, "aimed deliberately below the belt" (p. 256). "Belloc has real genius, but the necessity of keeping the pot boiling has strangled it."[1] His *The Path to Rome* (1902) is "like putting a fine sauce over diseased ill-cooked meat. Done for money" (p. 138).

Except for Graves, these strictures were directed at successful writers who did not really need the money; a needy writer must feed his family as best he can. ". . . you have a wife. . . . don't sacrifice to a theory every chance of profit," Lawrence counselled an RAF poet friend (p. 274). He also defended D. H. Lawrence's off-hand work against Wyndham Lewis's attack, terming *Mornings in Mexico* (1927) "just the snapshots of a literary artist, in the slack time while waiting for a subject" (p. 196).

He faults **Conrad's** good but less-than-best work for showing no development. "Did he try too hard? Did he write too much?" *Did he try too hard?!* Does that question Conrad or the intense years of labor on *Seven Pillars*? When Lawrence met Conrad, "he probed him on the methods of his craft," a characteristic interest he pursued with many writers. Conrad admitted "but little conscious design. Lawrence would say that he himself had over-studied his own craftsmanship,"[2] which was certainly true.

His comments on **Noel Coward** exemplify his disposition to over-rate writers that was evidently the opposite face of underrating his own writing. "[W]hen G. B. S[haw] goes, [Coward] will be the main

121

force in the English theatre" is not the only example of poor Lawrence prophecy. Lawrence and Coward enjoyed their occasional meetings and correspondence. The danger for Coward (as for many others) was not to be too effusive in showing how much he enjoyed them: indeed, in his letters to Lawrence, Coward speaks of being "over effusive" and "a trifle effusive" (*Letters*, 27–28). Years later, after reading Aldington's biography, Coward had second thoughts about Lawrence. Both second and first thoughts were (as Lawrence said of his first luncheon conversation) "not deep."

Lawrence was much impressed with **E. E. Cummings's** *The Enormous Room*, an account of the young Harvard graduate's mistaken wartime imprisonment in a French detention camp. He read the 1922 American edition, tried without success to promote an English edition, and was pleased when Cape finally brought it out in 1928. Lawrence is quick to deduce Cummings from his book: "a tiresomely silly american [*sic*]. . . . of an incomplete manhood, and ignorant of all that living is. . . . not all worm, nor all midge."

The Enormous Room and **Dostoevsky's** *The House of the Dead*, especially the latter, have obvious parallels with *The Mint*.[3] Like Lawrence, Dostoevsky was a gentleman's son living in barracks with lowly men; both explore the variety of men they encounter and the relation of officers to the ranks; both are respected by and also useful to their comrades because of their social standing, knowledge, and experience. Alfred Adler's discussion of Dostoevsky might have been written about Lawrence:

> [His] creations were to arise in the following way namely, that the act was to be regarded as futile, pernicious and criminal and that *salvation was to lie in submission as long as submission contained within itself the secret enjoyment of superiority over others.*[4]

Lawrence calls Dostoevsky "the greatest of the Russians"—"a great writer and a little soul." That is typical Lawrence, bowing down to genius and then rapping its clay foot. We have seen this turnabout with Homer, from "I love [the *Odyssey*]" and "Homer is very very great" to "The Odyssey disappoints me" and "A pot boiler." Tolstoy is "an enormous genius. . . . it is hopeless to grapple with [him]"— then *War and Peace* is "still good: very good: but not more-than-human, as I first thought." To think any human "more-than-human" is Nietzschean megalomania. Shakespeare is "the greatest poet"— but full of "shallow thinking" and "tiring euphemisms." On Melville, he remains laudatory. *White-Jacket* was a model for *The Mint*; *Moby Dick* is "a titan of a book"; his war poetry is "magnificent. Melville

was a great man." These are 1923–24 comments; it is unlikely
Lawrence would continue in this vein into the 1930s. As he aged,
he seemed to lose enthusiasms and those he kept seemed to lose lustre.

Lawrence's views of and helpfulness to **Charles Doughty** having
already been discussed (pp. 49–51 and 41–42), no more need be said
about that here. However, we may note the interaction of Doughty
with other figures in Lawrence's literary world. Wilfrid Scawen Blunt,
the prominent, wealthy Arabist and amorist, who had visited Hail
shortly after Doughty, introduced William Morris to *Arabia Deserta*
after its 1888 publication. The book became a favorite of Morris and
of his protege Sydney Cockerell, who then worked for both Blunt
and Morris. As Morris sought, and for a large coterie succeeded,
to revive the medieval world of crafts and sagas, he naturally admired
a work Doughty designed "to continue the older tradition of Chaucer
and Spenser, resisting to my power the decadence of the English
language"—that is, of "Victorian English."[5] Cockerell introduced
the book to Edward Garnett, who abridged it for Duckworth; this
1908 edition, *Wanderings in Arabia*, made Doughty more widely
known. Thus, William Morris, Lawrence's favorite writer, and
Doughty, author of the epic with which *Seven Pillars* was inevitably
compared, were linked in their effort to revive an old language, and
Lawrence was initially drawn to Cockerell and Garnett as keepers
of that quixotic flame. Cockerell also introduced Lawrence to G. B.
Shaw, a fellow socialist and friend of Morris, but not initially an
admirer of Doughty.[6]

Lawrence's amusing remarks on **T. S. Eliot** (which would not amuse
Eliot), together with those on Joyce and Pound, show where he stood
on the modernists. He read their work early and recognized their
importance but they were not his cup of tea.

Lawrence concedes Eliot's poetic imagination "a very high place"
but the poetry is "over-laboured in form" and "rather sparing." He
was not impressed with Eliot's "mock-profound" criticism,
"pompous" prose, "his cranky passion for the knuckle-end of the
Church of England," his essays, in which he "makes more mess of
a simple subject than any other conceived human being," or his
quarterly, *The Criterion*—"the Eliot-party seems to have dry rot in
their heads." "I shall believe him lost, if ever he makes a plain
statement," he tells F. V. Morley, Chairman of Faber & Faber, which
Eliot long served as reader, director, and literary lion. One Eliot piece
he likes unstintingly is his essay on Dante (1929), "a tribute of
understanding: so sensible and simple-minded and so wise."

Despite the perverse comedy of humbling himself to military
authority, Lawrence was a native anarchist and rebel against political,

social, intellectual, or cultural authority. That would be enough reason to poke fun at the priest of modernism and put him down as "An American, who missed an All Soul's Fellowship the other day . . . by my absence."

E. M. Forster met Lawrence in 1921 at a London lunch hosted by a member of Emir Feisal's staff. When he wrote "how glad, how proud, I had been to meet him," Lawrence did not reply (*Friends*, 282). In 1924, Forster wrote again after reading Siegfried Sassoon's copy of *Seven Pillars* (with Lawrence's consent). Astounded at its combination of "sensitiveness and introspection . . . heroism and largeness of vision," he had sent Sassoon "a fervent panegyric" (Furbank, 119–20). But, flattery having previously failed, he now took a different tack. "I thought it a masterpiece, but to have said so would have been fatal. I restricted myself to detail, and analysed particular sentences and paragraphs, chiefly from the point of view of style."[7]

This time Lawrence replied; in March, Forster visited him in Dorset, staying at an inn as his guest. They discussed *Seven Pillars* and Forster's unpublished stories on homosexual themes; Lawrence got Forster started on *Arabia Deserta*. Their friendship was launched and in June Forster stayed at Lawrence's cottage. In December 1926, just before sailing for India, Lawrence gave him "a gorgeous copy" of the subscribers edition of *Seven Pillars*; Forster was much moved. "I used to think him incapable of affection, but have changed my opinion, and think he has some for me."[8]

Lawrence was a shrewd detective (as an intelligence officer, he had been astute at interviewing captive soldiers) who tried to deduce an author's character and background from his work and to determine which elements were autobiographical and which, imaginative. That was one reason for his wish to meet authors. He was fascinated by the line between experience and imagination, between documentary and descriptive writing such as his own and the creative talent he saw in others.

Rereading Forster's novels in 1927 for the critical article he never finished, he was puzzled that "the portrait they make is not the least like you, as I've sat at tea with you" (p. 158). Forster offered to send him *Maurice*, his feeble heartfelt 1914 novel of homosexual love, first published in 1971, but Lawrence, who had declined to read it once before, declined again. Now Forster was puzzled, for Lawrence had read "The Life to Come," judged it fairly harshly, and thought it "quite fit to publish" (p. 155). "These ["The Life to Come," "Dr. Woolacott," and *Maurice*]," Forster wrote, are items which you must have in your mind if you want to sum me up. . . . I suppose I am elusive and difficult, but there are one or two people (and you're one of them) to whom I'd like to be clear. I haven't any secrets from you—that is to say there's no question you asked which I wouldn't answer. But this is not what you want, not what you want, alas.[9]

Lawrence responded, "I wanted to read your long novel, & was afraid to. It was like your last keep, I felt: and if I read it I had you: and supposing I hadn't liked it?" (p. 159).

There it was, put more explicitly than with other friends who wanted to approach closer: a certain emotional distance would be maintained. The distance was managed and defined by Lawrence, or kept undefined to keep it unfathomable even to so sensitive an observer as Forster. One arm of intimacy would be extended while the other was withdrawn.

With Forster, Lawrence was as open about his sexuality as with anyone: half-open. He confessed to his shattering rape by Turks at Deraa and his greater sympathy (openly stated in *Seven Pillars*) for homosexual than heterosexual love. Sympathy did *not* mean personal conduct: "I couldn't ever do it" (p. 160).

Having rebuffed Forster, virtually lampooning "The Life to Come," he praised "Dr. Woolacott" fulsomely. "It's the most powerful thing I ever read" "marvellous. . . . I did not know there could be such writing" (pp. 159–60). His fulsomeness was not confined to these pitiful stories. Forster's *Alexandria* was "great literature"; his watery, repetitious *Aspects of the Novel* was "superb"; *The Longest Journey*, "just great, without qualification." *A Passage to India* was worth praise, but "despairingly well done" and "you are a very great writer" were Lawrentian excesses. Writing Edward Garnett two months later, he questioned that judgment. "Forster: very good: but is he quite great?" (p. 157).

As has been seen, Lawrence could cut down great writers he did not know—Homer, Shakespeare, Joyce, Eliot—but, especially, talking and writing to them, tended to flatter great and less-than-great writers who were his friends. It was as if inflating their worth deflated his own, a point on which he brooked no other opinion—and whose judgment could be more authoritative?

Try as he did, Forster could not escape this trap. He wanted a good friend and got an adulator. "I had to figure as a great artist and he was a bungling amateur. This did not suit me in the least, but protests were useless" (*Friends*, 282). Forster insisted, "you are a 'greater genius than myself' . . . . Don't contradict me—only wastes time."[10] He dedicated *The Eternal Moment and Other Stories* (1928) "To T. E." The words and gesture were futile. "Truth is," Lawrence retaliated, "I'm not of the class fit to read your writing."[11] "I feel inclined to say Cher Maitre, and stop making a fool of myself trying to evalue what is so unutterably beyond my reach ["Dr. Woolacott"]. Don't laugh at my writing, by telling me that it's better than yours."[12] His armor was exasperating and impenetrable: a reverse paranoia, a fear of praise.

David Garnett's correspondence with Lawrence began in 1927 with a letter of thanks for the luxurious *Seven Pillars* he had given him via his father Edward. Lawrence had earlier discussed David's short novel *Lady into Fox* in several letters to Edward in which he visibly struggles: should he say he dislikes it or find something to praise? He twists and turns; writing David seven years later, his initial feeling returns: "I wish that you had not written *Lady into Fox*." (The title accurately summarizes the story: a young wife out for a stroll with her husband suddenly turns into a small, bright red fox; progressive adjustments are required in their loving and previously faithful marriage; the wife leaves for a home and litter in the fields but returns mauled by foxhounds, to die in her husband's arms.

David Garnett (1980, 194) writes with some astringency that

> [Lawrence's] opinions on art and literature fluctuated and were uncertain. On reading my book [*No Love*], he wrote that I was a symbolist and "every now and then one halts and says to oneself 'This is supremely important: this *matters*'." [p. 162] Two months later [in Lawrence's letter to Ede, p. 163] it did not.

Thereafter Lawrence's correspondence with David Garnett proceeded on a happier note; he liked *The Grasshoppers Come* (1931), calling it "a little masterpiece." (It is an admirable minor novel in which social commentary, character, plot, flying, and grasshoppers come together impeccably.)

Lawrence's letters on **Robert Graves's** work—his early poems, two books on poetry, memoir *Goodbye to All That* (1929), and *I, Claudius* (1934)—are a fraction of his 15-year correspondence. The larger portion deals with Lawrence's own writing, Graves's work on *Lawrence and the Arabs* (1927), and the tension between the two formerly close friends whose lives were diverging: one, self-consigned to "mind-suicide" in the military; the other, to poetry, every other possible kind of writing, wild flights of imagination, and Laura Riding in Majorca. It ends with his own obituary, which, three months before his death, Lawrence wrote for Graves to pass on to *The Times* as his own.[13]

At Oxford in 1920, Graves and Lawrence were both veterans trying to overcome the war, to write, and to decide how to live. Much under Lawrence's spell, Graves showed him his manuscripts, heeded his criticism, and dedicated several poems and books to him. "Lawrence was for years the only person to whom I could turn for practical criticism of my poems" (Graves, 10). Lawrence's July 21, 1920 letter itemizing his reactions to specific words, rhymes, expressions, images, and ideas is typical of the minuscule critiques (often, in minuscule handwriting) he sent many writers. As Graves matured and grew more confident, this kind of poetic criticism affected him less and Lawrence, ever sensitive, no longer offered it.[14]

"Writers & painters aren't like other men. The meeting them intoxicates me with a strangeness which shows me how very far from being one of them I am," Lawrence tells E. M. Forster in 1924 (Brown, 256). In 1929, he tells Graves, "It is a great thing to have the power of words: but it does not make one man different from another in kind" (p. 169). The years in barracks were changing him, changing his literary judgment and taste. He still valued the artist's talents but, having come also to value ordinary men, his comrades, he was less disposed to set artists above them as a light, guide, and preacher on how to live or as a rarefied class of aesthetes worthy of homage because of their exotic taste.

Meeting Lawrence in September 1930, Graves (165) noted "his speaking intonation had changed: from Oxford University to garage-English. . . . I do not mean that he spoke ungrammatically, but the accent was that . . . one associates with men who drive lorries. . . . [As the conversation continued] he gradually returned in accent . . . to the old Lawrence." When, in 1932, Graves, Laura Riding, or both (Graves's account is vague) sent Lawrence "a sample of some critical work that Laura Riding, myself and some others were engaged in" his reply annoyed Graves. Unfortunately, the letter is lost; Graves (169) says only, "His reaction as of low-brow to high-brows surprised me." Subsequent letters displaying mutual annoyance set the stage for Lawrence's attack on *I, Claudius* (p. 170) which Graves had asked him to read in proof to correct factual errors. Graves responded,

I wrote the most popular book I could write . . . within the limits of personal integrity. . . . I agree it is a pity that *Claudius* books have to be written because people won't pay a living wage for the essential works but at present it is so. The essential is always going on. Claudius is only the most stupid side-activity, like eating and dressing. [*Letters*, 111]

A comparison of Lawrence's reaction to *I, Claudius* and, for example, *Salammbo*, a work of unceasing cruelty and atrocity, which he much admired, or Hanley's merciless *Boy* shows that something was amiss between him and Graves. "I like [*Boy*] . . . ," Lawrence said, "because I like men, and ships and Alexandria!" (p. 175).

In an author's note to *I, Claudius*, Graves thanks "Aircraftman T. E. Shaw . . . for his careful reading of these proofs." He explains at some length why, despite Shaw's objection, he calls the German weapon *framea* "assegai."

James Hanley, born 1901 in Dublin, "sailor [at thirteen], stoker, cook, journalist, baker, butcher, clerk, porter, postman and runner,"[15] published his first novel, *Drift*, in 1930 and, thereafter, a stream of stories, novels, plays, and autobiography until his death in 1985. *The House in the Valley* (American title, *Against the Stream*), one of his best novels, appeared in 1981.

Lawrence evidently learned of Hanley's work through his bookseller friend K. W. Marshall and through C. J. Greenwood, head of the small publishing firm Boriswood. Lawrence had a special interest in emerging writers, as if watching their literary birthing pains yielded special insight into their creative processes. No sooner had he read *Drift* and several succeeding Hanley stories than he wanted to meet him. "I'd like to run into Hanley somehow. Would he resent being looked at admiringly?" (p. 174). He must have written Hanley, who sent him a partial typescript of *Sheila Moynihan*. Extracts from Lawrence's July 7, 1931 reply were later used as a preface to *La Maison Sans Issues* (p. 116). Lawrence met Hanley a few months later and several subsequent times. As he had a family and was quite poor, Lawrence tried to get him books to review; two newspapers "politely turned me down."[16]

Boy is the story of a bright, sensitive working-class boy of thirteen whose harsh father beats him and takes him from school to work scaling a ship's boilers in a Midland dock. Beaten by the other boys, he stows away on a ship and is roughly treated by crew members. In Alexandria, he leaves the ship, against the captain's kindly order, to visit a brothel. On the return voyage, beset again by several men and thinking he has syphilis, he flees to the captain for protection and, subjected to his loving assault, leaps overboard to his death.

The novel was published first by Boriswood in 1931 and, thereafter, in several expurgated and unexpurgated editions in London, New York, and Paris. The U.S. edition by Alfred Knopf in 1932, has no improper word or detail; it is emotionally brutal, not erotic.

"I hope you are not riding for a row with the Home Office," Lawrence wrote Greenwood in July 1931. His concern proved to be warranted. "If a book like *Boy* is publicly permitted here," Hugh

Walpole wrote, "we shall soon be at the mercy of every neurotic who wishes to startle his fellows by a public exhibition of his neuroticism."[17] In 1934, Lancashire police seized a copy of the book in a local lending library; in March 1935, Boriswood was prosecuted, pled guilty, and was convicted of publishing an obscene work. The firm was fined £250, the two directors and the librarian, £50 each; the prosecution was largely responsible for the firm's demise.[18]

Lawrence's approach to the danger and reality of prosecution is plain in his letters. He disliked a public confrontation, was not a political activist, and shrank from publicity; he believed in candor but not in politics or government; he cared for friends but not for the unknown "public." He preferred to operate behind the scenes, as invisibly as possible. His defense of homosexuality in *Seven Pillars* was privately published and excised from *Revolt in the Desert* (1927); the obscenities in *The Mint* were not widely published until 1973. "I far prefer censorship by the publisher to censorship by the police. . . . keep Hanley out of the Courts" was his unheeded advice to Greenwood (p. 176).

Hanley thought Lawrence "a most extraordinary man. . . . a wonderful person," but did not worship him. In an article on Lawrence, he says, "The besetting sin of this twentieth century is that it has a tendency to expect from its heroes an infallibility of judgment on subjects other than those that have contributed to their greatness. He was expected to give the final word on these subjects."[19] One of the subjects Hanley must refer to is literary criticism.

Lawrence calls **Thomas Hardy** "a proper poet & a fair novelist" (p. 181). In one of his more extravagant literary judgments, he declares that *The Dynasts*, "without any memorable phrase, or any perfect line, can by the mere bigness of its sweep outpass every other poem in the language" (p. 281). In contrast, the best two Hardy admirers can say about that laborious product of shallow philosophy is "burdensome" and "a museum piece."[20] It is hard to discern grounds for Lawrence's judgment other than a love of largeness; he read so fast that perhaps he could feel fully immersed only in the largest works. The idea can hardly be advanced seriously, though Lawrence did once claim "there are few bad epics" (p. 267).

On Hardy the man, Lawrence is sensitive and compassionate; he notes only what is fine in Hardy's character and outlook. His depiction of Hardy in his eighties has none of the lacerating lines in his portrait of Queen Alexandra that offended Bernard Shaw.[21] Though "a film seems to slip over his mind at times," Hardy's old age is serene, "envious," a "peace which passeth all understanding." From Lawrence's accounts, one would not know that Max Gate was a cold place because Hardy was too miserly to permit good fires or that the food was "absolutely minimal" or that local children would chant "Miser Hardy, miser Hardy."[22]

Anyone who has tried knows how hard it is to write a meaningful letter about the death of a friend. Lawrence's letter to Hardy's widow is extraordinary. Regardless of his own troubles, death and illness evoked in him marked sympathy, insight, and the right words.[23]

"He's the yet-unfollowed master of what will be the next school," Lawrence said of **James Joyce** in 1921. He had all four of Joyce's books then published and, later that year, subscribed to the limited first edition of *Ulysses* announced by Shakespeare & Co. in Paris.[24]

Lawrence was impressed by Joyce's verbal wizardry but not by his artistry. Joyce, he felt, had no architectural sense; his "mind has a leer in it"; neither his poetry nor prose conveyed genuine feeling; *Ulysses* was repulsively dull. He had little tolerance for the early extracts from *Finnegans Wake* or for the expatriate writers in Paris. "Not necessary, I feel, that urge to renew English. [But he liked the efforts of Morris and Doughty to revive antique English.] The language is . . . fresher than ever, in people's *mouths*. Only poor Joyce lives abroad, and doesn't talk to cabmen." Lawrence also rebuked Graves and Pound for living too long in Europe, away from the living sources of English. He stood with ordinary Englishmen, their language, and their land against literati who saw only the bad taste of the English masses and bourgeoisie.

Nonetheless, Joyce changed the way Lawrence wrote. "[T]o bring it [*Seven Pillars*] out after *Ulysses* is an insult to modern letters." *Ulysses* may be "dreary," "even worse to read than I had hoped," yet the prose is "superb," the first chapter "dazzling" and "as fine a piece of writing as the English language contains." "Joyce is a genius." *The Mint* has been termed Joycean. Lawrence wrote it "pell-mell, as the spirit took me, on one sheet of paper or another. Then I cut them into their sections, & shuffled them, as Joyce is supposed to have shuffled Ulysses."[25]

Lawrence had twenty-six volumes of **D. H. Lawrence** at Clouds Hill, reading each as it appeared. D. H. Lawrence represented to him a model of the earnest, impassioned writer absorbed in his work, developing, and serving only his artistic conscience: ". . . all the time growth, growth, growth. He never tries to please another judgment than his own . . . never re-treads the easy track of an earlier success" (p. 75). T. E. ceded to him use of the name he had abandoned. "Lawrence, for this generation, is D. H. L., an infinitely greater man than all of us rolled together."[26]

Lawrence is "a very great but very strange man," "a master of English prose" though the prose "stammers often" and he is "always losing control of his pen." Lawrence is "big" and writes with "power enough for six men." The words *big, great, power, strength,* and *force* recur in Lawrence's depiction of writers he puts in the first class.[27] All have a prolific natural (not carefully cultivated) talent, which overflows the normal bounds of literature. "People chasing anything big have no use for rules" (p. 270).

Lawrence did not care for *Lady Chatterley's Lover* (in which, at one point, Mellors, the gamekeeper, is compared to "Colonel C. E. Florence").[28] While admitting that passionate sex was "outside my particular experience," the novel "puzzled and hurt" him. "I've met only a handful of people who really cared a biscuit for it [sex]," he informs Edward Marsh. That does not square with his letters about the "cat-calling carnality seething up and down the hut" (Brown, 233) or the "apex" of his comrades' lives being "the coming together in sex of a man and a woman" (p. 218).

David Garnett (652) states that, though it "went so much against the grain, Lawrence was able [in his March 25, 1930 letter to Henry Williamson] to make the best criticism I have read of *Lady Chatterley*: one which shows complete sympathy and understanding of its author." Lawrence indeed had an unusual ability to put himself in someone else's shoes. The only thing wrong with Garnett's analysis is that Williamson, not Lawrence, wrote this letter, which, through a series of mishaps, appeared as Lawrence's in Garnett's collection.[29]

Lawrence esteemed **Wyndham Lewis** as an artist and commissioned some drawings for *Seven Pillars*, but Lewis, whose finances were often precarious, took £50 and never did the drawings. Lawrence's views of Lewis as a writer resemble his views of Pound and, to a lesser extent, Joyce: he was brilliant, needlessly and deliberately difficult, and eventually "unhinged." Lewis gave him *The Art of Being Ruled* (1926); Charlotte Shaw sent him (at his request) *The Lion and the Fox* (1927); William Rothenstein sent the first two issues of Lewis's journal, *Enemy* (1927; it expired with the third).

Lawrence did not like Lewis's "brazenly" puffing his own work. (Jeffrey Meyers describes the *Enemy* as "Lewis' virtually single-handed attempt to attract attention to his books and enhance his reputation.")[30] Lawrence's eventual conclusion, "I am not going to read him any more," was the same he came to with Joyce. No doubt he checked periodically to see if their course continued downward into incomprehensibility.

Frederic Manning, an Australian transplanted to England in 1930, was highly regarded by Lawrence as a writer and, in their last five years (they died three months apart), as a friend. In 1933, he named Manning first of "the three I most care for, since [D. G.] Hogarth died."[31] Manning is no longer listed in the *Oxford Companion to English Literature* (1985) or *The Cambridge Guide to Literature in English* (1988); his biographer Jonathan Marwil (304) concludes, "Any niche . . . Manning occupies in English (or Australian) letters will be small."

Manning's *Scenes and Portraits* (1909) consists of six carefully composed sketches and conversations set in periods ranging from Biblical and classical times to the Renaissance and heaven; a seventh, dedicated to "T. E. Shaw," was added in the 1930 edition. The discussions are philosophical, ironic, learned, spare, tolerant. Published when he was twenty-seven, the book sold little but Manning was hailed as "undoubtedly a new force in English letters"[32] and much admired by Pound, Eliot, Aldington, and (later) Forster.

Lawrence read *Scenes and Portraits* at the time (in 1930, he said he had read it "at least 50 times"); he also read Manning's poetry and even an obscure little 1940 sketch "of life seen through the eyes of an organ grinder's ape" (p. 201; Marwil, 79). In 1920, he called Manning one of his favourite authors (p. 255), and, in 1923, he thought of writing "a psychological study of [Nebuchadnezzar in] the Frederic Manning manner" (Garnett, 410).

Lawrence and Manning met once or twice, probably late in 1921,[33] but the acquaintanceship lapsed until the appearance of the war novel *Her Privates We* (1930), whose anonymous author Lawrence guessed from the stylistic resemblance of its preface to *Scenes and Portraits*. The hint that the author's name began with an "M" scarcely diminishes this feat, since the language, substance, and, to ordinary readers, style of the two works seem so different. In its way, the contrast resembles that between *Seven Pillars* and *The Mint*; and there are other similarities. Manning, too, was a gentleman private at ease with neither comrades nor officers. "I wonder how he really got on in the ranks," Lawrence mused (not, in fact, that well).[34] Yet beneath the men's cursing and the foulness, horror, and futility of trench warfare, Manning's common soldiers exhibit uncommon courage, comradeship, endurance, even nobility. Lawrence thought it "more of a love-book than a war-book."

Like Lawrence, Manning was shy and lonely, "possessed a deep reserve, a secretiveness, and preferred to guard against too much closeness" (Coleman, 65); Jeffrey Meyers states, while Marwil (326) disputes that he was homosexual. A classicist and a scholar, he lived in a Lincolnshire village one hundred miles from London. Aside from

Scenes and *Privates*, he wrote little, painfully, with "a sometimes cloying fastidiousness" (Marwil, 131), and never completed a novel he labored on for decades. A sickly man, he cannot have been happy. "An Unfinished Life," the subtitle of Marwil's biography, evidently derived from Lawrence's last letter to Rothenstein ("it is hateful to see him go out, unfinished"), is also applicable to Lawrence, who died two weeks after writing it.

The references to **Ezra Pound** in Lawrence's letters from Syria may have induced his brother William to invite him to talk at Oxford in February 1913. Pound later sent Will "a wonderful letter [with] . . . a lot of strange new poems" and invited him to his wedding in 1914.[35]

Lawrence's April 1920 letter to Pound (p. 208) was a reply to his invitation to submit something to *The Dial*, the American literary review for which he was a correspondent. This exchange shows more good humor than their later correspondence. In 1920, Lawrence congratulates Pound on his forthcoming departure for Italy; in 1934, he notes, "there are six shits in your letter. . . . More peace to your stomach! . . . . Will you never come back? The States, England . . . ? This is the same note he sounds in rebuking Graves—"you ought to come home, at least for a while. . . . You are losing your englishry" (p. 171): a note of allegiance to a land and culture the two poets had left behind. To Frere-Reeves, Lawrence speaks of Pound simply as "the silly ass" who has abandoned poetry for "financial theory."

Lawrence's previously unpublished letter to Jacob Schwartz, presumably an agent or publisher who had sent him a signed limited edition of *Two Studies* by the Australian woman novelist **H. H. Richardson**, is characteristically frustrating. He often replied at length to inquiries from strangers—for example, Lincoln Kirstein (Garnett, 796) or Walter Williams (p. 262)—to insist that he was ordinary, his fame was unwarranted, and his Middle East knowledge was dated. Sometimes he invited a visit, as if to say, "Come and see I am no circus freak."

In this case, he insists, "I'm no critic, nor a wide reader [untrue], nor primarily interested in books [true only if *primarily* is heavily emphasized]." He proceeds to detailed comments on Richardson's prose and background, and he closes with, "You were very kind to send me this book" and a remark that, while perhaps honest, belies its purpose: "If you will quickly forget this letter you will add to your kindness."

Siegfried Sassoon and Lawrence formed a mutual admiration society. "Damn you, how long do you expect me to go on reassuring you about your bloody masterpiece? It is a GREAT BOOK, blast you," Sassoon wrote of *Seven Pillars*; of *The Mint*, he said, "you are an extraordinary writer."[36] Lawrence countered with equal praise. He admired Sassoon's wartime antiwar poems and *Memoirs of a Fox-hunting Man* (1928), which won the Hawthornden Prize in 1929 (though he declined Edward Marsh's request to make the presentation, p. 214). In December 1933, he attended Sassoon's wedding. His 1934 letter extolling *Vigils* (1935)—he read the proofs engraved by Geoffrey Keynes—led Sassoon to say, "Every window . . . has been lit up by your letter" (*Letters*, 159).

George Bernard and **Charlotte Shaw** were too good friends and too kind and parental for Lawrence to be too critical of Shaw's work. To Frederic Manning he might say Shaw "never bothers to go underskin. His characters . . . have only the one mind amongst them." But to Charlotte Shaw, he says that *Saint Joan* (1923), whose heroine resembled him in many ways (Weintraub 1965), is "magnificent," "pure genius," despite flaws in her dying off stage, her dialect, and Shaw's misconception of soldiers' camaraderie. *Heartbreak House* (1920), he tells Charlotte Shaw and William Rothenstein in identical words, is "the most blazing bit of genius in English literature."

His praise of *Too True to Be Good* (1932), where he appears as Private Napoleon Alexander Trotsky Meek, is the most overstated. Not just good fun, it is "magnificent," "priceless," "devastating," "terrific," "a great work," "beats the Tempest into fits," "the finest acting thing G. B. S. has ever made." After reading the play in proof, he offered a series of technical corrections, which Shaw adopted.[37]

There has been so much poorly grounded speculation about Lawrence's politics, including charges that he might or would have led a fascist movement, that it would be instructive to know what he really thought of *The Intelligent Woman's Guide to Socialism and Capitalism* (1928). G. B. S. had a copy made with a specially printed title page: THE FOUNDATION OF THE SEVEN PILLARS, BEING THE WORD OF A WESTERN PROPHET TO THE DELIVERER OF DAMASCUS: SHAW BORN SHAW TO SHAW THAT TOOK THAT NAME UPON HIM (*Fifty*, 24). Charlotte Shaw sent it to Lawrence in advance of the June 1, 1928 publication date and asked his opinion.

He called it "above controversy"!, "a great book," and "*decent*" but said nothing substantive. Did it bore him? Politics and economics did not much interest him, particularly not the management of large governmental and corporate bureaucracies. When H. S. Ede (61) sent him Colbourne's *Economic Nationalism*, he returned it, saying, "I can't settle to it. . . . Sorry to be unhelpful."

It was not the socialist Lawrence admired in William Morris but the writer, craftsman, and medievalist. Likewise, it was not the socialist or didacticist he admired in Shaw but the writer, actor, wit, raconteur, the man who could verbally outrage every accepted social and political idea or convention and yet retain his respectability (unlike Pound, Wyndham Lewis, or Henry Williamson, who stepped over the line of respectability into ostracism, exile, or madness).

Lawrence was neither a fascist nor socialist but an anarchist-individualist—"a philosophic anarchist" he once said (p. 227)—who disliked authority, industrialism, government, and convention. When Shaw, visiting Russia, pronounced communism wonderful, all Lawrence would say was, "I am sure its end is right: but the means might spoil my faith" (p. 222). He told C. Day Lewis, then a communist, "The trouble with Communism is that it accepts too much of today's furniture. I hate furniture" (p. 287).

The long letter on *Tarka the Otter* (p. 105) was addressed to Edward Garnett. All but one of Lawrence's later comments on **Henry Williamson's** work went directly to him and are more charitable than critical. In February 1929 (before they had met) Williamson had asked Lawrence to be his literary executor—"I'd feel safer with you than anyone else I know of"—and he agreed—"I will do it. . . . But you must be generations younger than me [in fact, seven years], and I should ask you to be mine."[38]

The exception is Lawrence's defense of *The Gold Falcon* (1933), an anonymous novel in which he is a minor character. John Brophy, who reviewed it, rightly ascribed it to Williamson. A comparison of Lawrence's letters to Williamson and Brophy, one obviously written right after the other, shows how few words are needed to color a literary judgment: "grinning," "astonishing," and "preened" to Williamson; "laughing," "authentic," "favourably" to Brophy.

Williamson thought Lawrence's writing "Everest to my Snowden," but "Lawrence thought I was a better writer" (*Friends*, 452). Lawrence was impressed by his fecundity. "I would like to write like you . . . copiously . . . with a catching intimate easy speech, like a man in slippers" (p. 234). In fact, writing was not that easy for Williamson (74): it was "an unnatural practice of sitting still several hours out of the sun, forcing his vitality into his brain and striving to imagine things, to be turned into words, words, words: for money."

In September 1932, **William Butler Yeats** invited Lawrence to accept membership in the Irish Academy of Letters then being formed. As his name went to George Bernard Shaw, who had proposed it (Holroyd, 197), Charlotte Shaw became involved and Lawrence asked her to accept for him. "I should be troubled in writing to him [Yeats]: for I have regarded him always as an exquisite and unattainable poet" (p. 236). Nonetheless, when Yeats acknowledged his acceptance—

"you are among my chief of men, being one of the few charming and gallant figures of our time" (*Letters*, 213)—Lawrence wrote "how much I have appreciated this compliment of nomination by you. I am Irish, and it has been a chance to admit it publicly" (p. 236).

This was one of the few honors, perhaps the only one, Lawrence accepted; no one could have predicted the acceptance. His father, Sir Thomas Chapman, was Anglo-Irish, and Lawrence once told his solicitor, "There is a lot of land [in Ireland] in that name [Chapman] knocking about: and I don't want to chuck it away, as Walter Raleigh . . . gave it to my father's first Irish ancestor" (Brown, 333). However, Lawrence never visited Ireland; "he had always regarded England as his home, and at one time had taken pains to point out that his father's family had never inter-married with the Irish" (Wilson, 896). He was known as an English, not Irish, hero, and to advertise his Irish family connections might advertise his illegitimacy. But the only predictable thing about Lawrence was his unpredictability.

James Barrie

To Charlotte Shaw   19 March 1924
[Barrie is] a man who writes so vilely. . . . He's everything that Mr Shaw is not: a cozener & deceiver, a soft-sayer, a sentimentalist, a fraud: one who plays deep tricks with the real stuff of literature, in order to flatter people whose tastes are already beast-low. Has he a single redeeming work or feature? I don't want to be harsh, but he seems to me as vile as Belloc.

To Charlotte Shaw   Clouds Hill, 26 March 1924
Barrie. You justify him as a man. My attack is upon the artist. He writes with an eye upon the box-office, with an ear to please the very many. He succeeds: but must pay the price of annoying the few. It infuriates me when a fine writer (or painter) deliberately does the not-quite best. I don't mind dead silence. I can't stand Peter Panning or Arnold Bennetting. . . .[39]
Contempt. . . . A man gets carried away and says brave things. . . . . but if you take him away into a quiet place and lend him your pocket mirror he will recant. . . . We can indulge it only of ourselves. . . . I'm sorry to have overstepped.

To Mrs. Thomas Hardy   Clouds Hill, 12 November 1924
Once I met Barrie. He was very silent, & rather simple. Mrs. Shaw says he's very nice, as a human being. I think him detestable as an

artist. She won't say yes or no to that. I haven't told him my view . . . . . and won't. So we will not fight on the hearthrug.

To Charlotte Shaw   19 February 1930
I do not respect Barrie. He is not a great man. . . . I think it is his dishonesty as an artist which frightens me. To be insincere, in writing, is hardly to be forgiven.

To G. W. M. Dunn   Plymouth, 9 November 1932
Barrie is too grim and hard. There are claws under his fur, obviously. Old, of course, and not strong. He is not forthcoming.

Gertrude Bell

To J. G. Wilson   Karachi, 4 October 1927
    Gertrude's *Letters* came to me, and I read them with delight. They are very good, and well display her eagerness and emotion. I do not think that much of importance was edited out of these particular letters. Gertrude was not a good judge of men or situations: and was always the slave of some momentary power: at one time Hogarth, at another Wilson, at another me, at last Sir Percy Cox. She changed her direction each time like a weathercock: because she had no great depth of mind. But depth and strength of emotion—Oh Lord yes. Her life had crisis after crisis of that sort: and they are all missing from the book. Very probably they were missing from her letters home. A wonderful person. Not very like a woman. . . .

To F. G. Peake   Karachi, 20 October 1927
By the way, do read Gertrude Bell's letters. They are splendid.

To Hugh Bell   India, 4 November 1927
I've just been reading the 'Letters' which Mrs. Bernard Shaw sent me, and they have been so great a pleasure to me that I felt I must write to you and thank you for letting them come out. Until they were announced I hadn't realised that Gertrude was dead. . . .[40]
    Her letters are exactly herself—eager, interested, almost excited, always about her company and the day's events. She kept an everlasting freshness; or at least, however tired she was, she could always get up enough interest to match that of anyone who came to see her. I don't think I ever met anyone more entirely civilised, in the sense of her width of intellectual sympathy. And she was exciting too, for you never knew how far she would leap out in any direction, under the stimulus

of some powerful expert who had engaged her mind in his direction. She and I used to have a private laugh over that:—because I kept two of her letters, one describing me as an angel, and the other accusing me of being possessed by the devil,—and I'd show her first one and then another, begging her to be charitable towards her present objects of dislike.

To William Rothenstein   Karachi, 8 December 1927
    Miss Gertrude Bell's letters . . . are very good—but so on the surface as to be impalpably unsatisfying. Only twice did I feel that she had got actually down to anything. She was born too gifted, perhaps.

To F. L. Lucas   9 December 1927
. . . the letters of Gertrude Bell . . . were just the exact surface of Gertrude Bell: not once (yes, once perhaps,) did she touch ground in them: and so they disappointed me. I used to gaze at her, in life, wondering what there was really there. She was either very secret, or very shallow: but I liked her so much, for her goodness and eagerness. Let's hope she was very secret, too.

Hilaire Belloc

To Edward Garnett   [London], 26 August 1922
If I'd aimed low [in *Seven Pillars of Wisdom*] I could have hit my target as squarely as Max Beerbohm or Belloc hits it: but their works are only a horrid example. . . .

To Charlotte Shaw   Clouds Hill, 26 March 1924
    Belloc. Great Gifts: [*The*] *Path to Rome* [1902] a delightful saucy book. His historical work impudence. Half-truths or calculated lies, served out to the public brilliantly. It's like putting a fine sauce over diseased ill-cooked meat. Done for money. Caddish, I call that.

To Charlotte Shaw   [Karachi], 29 September 1927
Belloc is an unjust man, and a man who deceives others with his gifts: he is so clever that he can get his effect by being showy. Thus his work deteriorates. The path to Rome: and some of the poems were so good; and now he is all ruinous. A great pity. Belloc, Chesterton, & Barrie, could all have written well, if they had had the purity in them to try. H .G. [Wells]'s sincerity shines by comparison with them; and even, I think [Arnold] Bennett: because A. B. writes, like Compton Mackenzie, mainly to amuse himself.

To Charlotte Shaw   [Karachi], 8 May 1928
Belloc *is* very nearly a great man: he is also, as nearly, a bad man.

It is so hard for a Catholic to be honest: and Belloc is anti-Semitic, in the continental sense, and polyglot. He worships secular Rome, as well as spiritual Rome. Oh, he is very dangerous. The most able pen-for-hire in England. His history is interesting, as special pleading all the way. His feud against Henry VII delights me. If so great an enemy can find so little fault, then indeed H. VII was a great ruler, though a mean fellow. . . .

Belloc's best things are written in verse, I fancy: the Road to Rome is delicious. His praise of wine reads well: but have you ever seen his paunch? Wine and food have made him disgusting, and the need to earn enough to slake his greed has led him to do unworthy work. And this he would not have fallen to, unless he had a cheap streak in him. Nobler, many times is poor Ernest Dowson, or poor Francis Thompson, in the gutter. A least they were drunkards. Belloc is a tippler.

To Charlotte Shaw   [Miranshah], 27 November 1928
Belloc's extravaganza amused me. He does amuse me, & I'm ashamed to laugh. I want to hate him, for having all the divine gifts, & deliberately wilfully, misusing them. He writes so often below his best, I feel he writes for money: that he says "that'll do", ever so much before he has uttered his best, just because he is in a hurry to earn. Then, too, he is dishonest: inevitably and not by his fault, for no Catholic can be scientifically straight. An artist;—yes Catholics can be, generally are, fine artists. Look at Belloc's poems, how good they are. But a Catholic cannot write history, or sociology, or criticism.

To Siegfried Sassoon   Southampton, 6 September 1934
The Belloc [*An Heroic Poem in Praise of Wine*] gave me some fun. I was sorry he had not pulled it together and shaped it into one tight poem before printing it: and as a water-drinker I incline to smile at these wine-palates. They deprive themselves of the faculty of judging between waters, by coarsening their throats with fermented drinks— and that is a loss to their tastes. But H. B. writes with such bragging ferocity that I love him. What a man. I wish I felt as strongly about something.

Joseph Conrad

To F. N. Doubleday   20 March 1920
You know, publishing Conrad must be a rare pleasure. He's

absolutely the most haunting thing in prose that ever was: I wish I knew how every paragraph he writes (do you notice they are all paragraphs: he seldom writes a single sentence?) goes on sounding in waves, like the note of a tenor bell, after it stops. It's not built on the rhythm of ordinary prose, but on something existing only in his head, and as he can never say what it is he wants to say, all his things end in a kind of hunger, a suggestion of something he can't say or do or think. So his books always look bigger than they are. He's as much a giant of the subjective as Kipling is of the objective. Do they hate one another?

To Sydney Cockerell   Clouds Hill, 25 December 1923
   The Rover—many many thanks. What a fine effort for a man who has written all he wants and is carried only by the momentum of old effort. Magnificent. He could write in his sleep. . . .

To Sydney Cockerell   Clouds Hill, 13 January 1924
   Did I ever thank you for *The Rover*? A very good book; but not better than the other Conrad's. Don't you think a man would strain himself each time to surpass the last mark? There is no strain in this.

To F. L. Lucas   [Karachi], 9 December 1927
   . . . the Conrad letters. They show a real agony of effort. I wonder what the end was in his case. The Mirror of the Sea [1906] I feel is unqualified beauty; and I liked the Arrow of Gold [1919] and Nostromo [1904], and parts of the Rescue [1920], and the personal recollections. The other books wearied me a little. There seemed no development of Joseph Conrad in them: and one does not wish to know an unchanging personality very well. Did he try too hard? Did he write too much? The output was enormous in those few years.˙

Noel Coward

To Charlotte Shaw   15 August 1930
On Wednesday I lunched with Philip Sassoon, with whom came Noel Coward. He is not deep but remarkable. A hasty kind of genius. I wonder what his origin is? His prose is quick, balanced, alive: like Congreve's probably, in its day. He dignifies slang when he admits it. I liked him: and suspected that you probably do not. Both of us are right.

To F. N. Doubleday   Plymouth, 2 September 1930
I say, have you considered acquiring all the rights to Noel
Coward? He is not vividly published in England, or pushed by his
publisher. . . . He writes English like Congreve, and when G. B. S.
goes, will be the main force in the English theatre. I should nobble
him, if nobbleable, on both sides the Atlantic. . . .

To Noel Coward   Plymouth, 6 September 1930
Your work is like sword-play; as quick as light. Mine a slow painful
mosaic of hard words stiffly cemented together.

To Noel Coward   5 October 1930
I was at the second night [of *Private Lives*], and wondered to see
how perfectly the finished product went. . . .
The play reads astonishing well. It gets thicker, in print, and has
bones and muscles. On the stage you played with it and puffed your
fancies up and about like swansdown. And one can't help laughing
all the time: whereas over the book one does not do worse than chuckle
or smile. For fun I took some pages and tried to strike redundant words
out of your phrases. Only there were none. That's what I felt when
I told you it was superb prose.

To Noel Coward   Plymouth, 10 June 1931
I have read your play (which? why your war one, of course [*Post-
Mortem*]) twice and want to admire you. It's a fine effort, a really
fine effort.
. . . You have something far more important to say than usual, and
I fancy that in saying it you let the box-office and the stalls go hang.
As argument it is first rate. As imagination magnificent: and it does
you great honour as a human being. It's for that reason that I liked
it so much. . . . People won't like you better for being quite so serious
as you are in this: but it does you honour, as I said, and gave me a
thrill to read it.
Incidentally the press-man-magnate-son scene was horrifying. That
would 'act', surely? Only most of the rest was far above playing to
any gallery.
I think it was very good of you to have done this so plainly and
well. I needn't say that it's written with your usual spare exactness
and skill. You deny yourself every unnecessary word.

E. E. Cummings

To Curtis Brown   Clouds' Hill, 12 November 1924

After our talk it struck me that your organisation might place an English edition of Cummings' "Enormous Room", in which he relates his experiences as a suspect in a French war-time detention camp.

You probably know Cummings' poetry—well, his verse-practice has given atmosphere to his prose, and balance and rhythm to the construction of his book—while there is a surprising sense of character, and an almost terrifying actuality of imagination in his descriptions.

I went through "The Enormous Room" again, after I enlisted, while yet fresh to living in such enormous rooms, and from it knew, more keenly than from my own senses, the tang of herded men, and their smell. The reading is as sharp as being in prison, for all but that crazed drumming against the door which comes of solitary confinement. Cummings' party suffered common compulsion, with its abandonment of spirit, to make them as supine as the planks in their prison floor.

I've remembered the book for years, and other people who've read it have been similarly impressed. So I don't think you'd regret pushing it vigorously.

Don't think it will be a best-seller. It's too rare for that: and hasn't passion or laughter (or not much) and its excitements are mainly mental. But to produce it in England will be an honourable adventure for a decent publisher (it's a strong book) and if Boni and Liveright can supply it in sheets there should be money in the deal. It would be bought by writers in the first place, because it's an exceedingly good book: and by those interested in life and its materials, served up raw . . . . . and people who are particular will savour its occasional stylistic strangenesses. He uses some new alloys of words, and has rare passages as irridescent as decay in meat. The book is modern in feeling, and new-world in pedigree, and all the more exciting on this side in consequence. It seems to me so much the best American war-period book.

To Robert Graves   Karachi, 24 December 1927

I am reading the book of criticism [*A Survey of Modernist Poetry*] by L[aura] R[iding] and yourself. Cummings will be pleased at the place he takes in your thoughts; to see so much of himself in your mirror will help him write. I liked his prose, more, in the days when I read books. Indeed, I once tried hard to get his "Enormous room" published in England. Cape wouldn't touch it; nor could Curtis Brown, who touted it round with a very cautious little note from me, place it anywhere. I call it one of the very best of the war-books. . . . The last Cummings verse I saw was called 40 poems, and was held in a marvellous gold outer wrapper—but the inside was more like Oxo than the normal flesh of poetry. It struck me that in his refusal of phrases with a past there lay as much irritation as power. Power does not get ruffled to such assertions, readily. Unless he had special cause, he should not let the worn condition of words hamper his re-use of them. In my own tiny case, I actually looked for the traditional words. They seem richer to my taught senses. I suppose he is naturally rebellious, and that his treatment in France inflamed him, and that he belongs to some clique which worships reaction more than action. A pity, for I think his gifts are too good to be wrapped up in shorthand. Modern historians have put history on the shelf (or rather handed her over to non-historians) by being so scientific that their writing is only for themselves. Hence I like a poet to put a little sugar with his strength. I cannot remember by heart any of Cummings poetry, because of its tightness of texture.

To Jonathan Cape   [Karachi], 28 March 1928
    You decision upon the Enormous Room delights me. . . . It will do the firm good to published a book which all writing people cannot but respect . . . . the emotion and the incisiveness and particularity of the description of his internment camp do him every credit. Don't let them black out the word "Shit" in your edition. It is good Anglo-Saxon.

To F. N. Doubleday   [Karachi], 13 April 1928
    Cape has pleased me very much, by accepting "the Enormous Room", at last. Eight years ago it was a wonderful book. I suspect that Cummings could have written very good novels, if he'd wished. American poets are probably, though, as much in cliques as English ones. Something has Cummings by the leg. Do you know him? Lives in New York, I fancy.

To Robert Graves   Miranshah, 5 August 1928
    Cape sent me the *Enormous Room*. I read it all again, after the years. And I feel sure that it is worth while. There is stuff in it which I have seen nowhere else. And a taste of reality. And it is not yet out of date. If a book can get over its first ten years, it must be really original, I think. I suppose Cummings regards it as one of his deadliest sins, now: but I feel delighted that it's having another go at the public.

To Charlotte Shaw   [Miranshah], 18 August 1928
    Oh, the Enormous Room, by Cummings. He is an American of great

gifts, who has tried to express himself in paint, and in poetry, and, here, in prose. He has never quite succeeded, in any medium. I am able by my experience to sympathise and feel with a man like that. He was rather a tiresomely silly american, narrow and ignorant, when the French shut him up in a concentration camp of suspects, in the mad days of the war. He took the experiences of the camp as well as could be expected of him, and learnt a good deal out of it. This he tells naively and unconsciously, in the book. Its form, or its bad form, or its formlessness, whichever it is, may disgust you. . . . But it is real, so far as it goes. There are classes of people like this american. . . . They are silly souls, of an incomplete manhood, and ignorant of all that living is. . . . Poor little wretch. He shows himself not all worm, nor all midge. A very good book.

To Charlotte Shaw   [Miranshah], 16 October 1928
Did you like the Enormous Room? Or did the antics of the American-who-wanted-to-write-differently screen from you the very goodness of his eyesight. He really saw good in everything oppressed. If he could have seen good in his oppressors, too, he would have been a greater man than me.

To Edward Garnett   Southampton, 1 August 1933
Eimi [1933] by Cummings. Not so good as *The Enormous Room*, for his style disintegrates and not integrates, this time. Too pointillé. But the best thing I've ever read on modern Russia, all the same.

To A. S. Frere-Reeves   Bridlington, 7 January 1935
. . . Heinemann's should publish [*Eimi*] in England. Sell 500 copies, I think, and lose £50, but what a credit to your taste. . . . The book as a whole and in all its parts is ravishing.

Fyodor Dostoevsky

To J. B. Acres   15 January 1926
I've always believed him the greatest of the Russians: though he never achieved an epic like *War and Peace*. He never aimed at the epic manner. When I'm forced to describe *The Karamazov* in a word I say 'A fifth gospel'. It is that intense preoccupation with supra-moral goodness, Christ-like-ness, which marks him so strongly. An epileptic and ex-convict, he drew always from his own experience and feelings. That's why his books are full of neuroses: and his characters so often criminal. There is a sameness too: for D. lived over-much within

himself. Not many people are happy enough to strike the balance between inside and outside, and achieve a harmony.

André Gide's book on Dostoevsky [1925] was not good. He tried to make him into a Protestant (Gide is a French Protestant) and didn't get to grips with his real powers and depths. Few Frenchmen could. They are too dapper to feel as untidily and recklessly as the Russians.

To David Garnett   Miranshah, 14 June 1928
The House of the Dead is fine, strong, wonderful: but D. had not a crisp side or word in him: so it lacks the particularity of reported notes (*Mint*) or the subsequent rationalisation of experience (*Seven Pillars*). That's my memory of [C. J.] Hogarth's translation, read 10 years ago and not since.[41]

To Charlotte Shaw   [Miranshah], 18 August 1928
[*The Enormous Room*] and Dostoevski's House of the Dead, and the Mint are essays in the same level of man. Dostoevski wins, of course, being a great writer and a little soul.

Charles Doughty

To his family   Jerablus, 31 March 1911
. . . the probabilities are that I will bring home . . . enough camel-hide to bind my Doughty, when I get him. The book will be necessary, for I must know it by more than library use, if ever I am to do something of the sort.

To Mrs. Rieder   [Oxford], 26 September 1911
. . . if it [*Adam Cast Forth*] is a failure, it is a big one, & not unworthy of the man. . . . I like it:—but I would never venture to maintain its cause too openly. *I* think it's the best thing he's done:—and no one will ever agree about that. I'm sure. . . .

The Cliffs [1909]. A patriotic drama: invasion of Britain by aeroplane, & eventual victory of ourselves, chastened into a national frame of mind. I haven't read it: and I don't think I want to: I should be too much afraid of bathos: and the author of *Adam & Arabia* can't afford to fail.

Dawn in Britain [1907]. I have read this. . . . Behold an epic in 6 volumes:—a stage from Greece to the North Pole:—a period of 500 years, from the sack of Rome by Brennus, to the siege of Jerusalem, and the departing this life of Joseph of Arimathea.

You'll see that the 'epic' has no unity: there is no hero; plenty of characters: heaps of incidents told all in 'great' style. There is very little in the book which is less than magnificent: but do you want so much magnificence? . . . . It could be read in sections, for there is little coherence in the whole: you get Cassivelaunus, Caractacus, Boadicea: most Romans: a few Greeks, Tyrians, water nymphs: some *perfect* 'songs', semi-lyrical narratives in blank verse of twenty or thirty pages: these have nothing to do with the book and I mean to print them: they are perfect.

Do you want this book: I would like to send it you; immensely: but I am afraid it will only irritate you: remember Doughty goes his whole way along as he pleases: there is not the least concession to use or custom or authority: he *calls* it an 'epic' and presumably one has to do the same: but it is rather an imaginative history: of course it is meant to glorify things English, which with Doughty means not the Empire and *The Times* and the House of Lords but the language and 'Spenser & Chaucer traditions'.

To his family   Carchemish, 11 May 1912
I am not trying to rival Doughty. You remember that passage that he who has once seen palm-trees and the goat-hair tents is never the same as he had been: that I feel very strongly, and I feel also that Doughty's two years wandering in untainted places made him the man he is, more than all his careful preparation before & since. My books would be the better, if I had been for a time in open country: and the Arab life is the only one that still holds the early poetry which is the easiest to read. . . . the Soleyb have no touch of Gypsy blood in them . . . nobody but Doughty has met the real ones: (and Zwiemer, but he is hopelessly untrustworthy). Burton's were pinchbeck.

To his family   Carchemish, 12 September 1912
The Clouds [1912] is unequal—though in parts magnificent. I wish he would desert the pulpit. The poet's place is at the altar.

To Charles Doughty   [London?], 5 January 1920
I fear you will have thought me remiss in not answering you before, but I have been away, and when I got back at last decided that it was so old now, that I had better read *Mansoul* [1920] before replying.

I finished it today, in London, and I think I like it better than *Adam* and next to *Arabia Deserta*, of your books. Of course nothing can replace *Arabia*, to me, but *Mansoul* is very nearly doing so, in parts, though not as a whole. The *Arabia* is a complete picture of the life of the best sort of Arabs in the desert, & in the markets about the desert, and no picture of one people, by a stranger, has ever been painted like it, in my experience of books.

Did I ever tell you of your lunch with Mr. Balfour when the table voted on the best books of travel . . . . . five for you, and two for Marco Polo?

There are some things about *Mansoul* which I want to ask you about, but I will keep them till I see you. I want to contest one point . . . . . perhaps because I'm 30 and you 70!

To F. N. Doubleday   14 May 1920

What I really wanted to write about was Doughty's *Arabia Deserta*. It's a long book in two volumes (some 500,000 words, I should think) published by the Cambridge Press thirty years ago: full of little cuts and very wise. They printed 240 copies, and broke up the type. A copy now costs £30 in England, and is very hard to find. Duckworth (a publisher in London) produced an abridgement about 10 years ago, and has reprinted it three or four times since: the abridgement was of about $\frac{2}{3}$ of the original. The whole book is a necessity to any student of Arabia, but is more than that. It's one of the greatest prose works in the English language, and the best travel book in the world. Unfortunately it's solidly written (not dull at all, but in a queer style which demands care at first), and because of its rarity is far too little known.

Now I'd like to get it out again. I hoped to do it at the Cairo Press: but then Egypt became riotous, and they are vastly in arrears. To do it in England would cost £1,500 for type setting only, and Duckworth won't do it, because it would kill his abridgement. Doughty owns the copyright, and is willing to let it out again for nothing or thereabouts. Do you think any wise man in America would undertake it? I think I could get about 500 subscribers at 2 or 3 guineas a copy—perhaps more: but it would mean a lot of correspondence, and I'm a lazy person by nature. So I thought I'd ask your advice, as a publisher: it's a very great work, and it's a shame it should be so rare: and I like it better than almost any other book. It has of course an immense reputation amongst the elect.

To Charles Doughty   Oxford, 7 November 1920

I quite understand your saying about your neglect of *Arabia Deserta*: and I'm entirely of your opinion that it is less than *Dawn in Britain*, Mansoul, & *Adam*: but it is easier than these others, & so it's the best wedge to drive into the public. They will all read *Arabia Deserta*, & those who are seized with it will go on to the poems afterwards. I advise

those who ask me, to read *Adam* second, *Mansoul* third, & then
Dawn—because *Dawn* has to be read whole, and it takes courage to
start so long a book. Those who have taken my advice have all become
partisans of yours: and the clan is getting a large one. Still, it may
be years yet before you sweep the board, and meanwhile the best
weapon is *Arabia*. It's exceedingly good to have it out again. . . .

To Sydney Cockerell   Bovington, 22 October 1923
   My view of Doughty? But I like him too much (or his books, rather)
to start an analysis: you see the analysis proceeds always on its own
rails, beyond your control, except to set a bound to: and my instinct
forewarns me that in my sketch of Doughty would be much criticism.
His greatness is achieved by limiting himself and his judgement, so
that he is few-sided and confident in himself. A fuller man would be
more modest in attempted performance. D's moral pride is betrayed
by the scale of his works' designs. It is the man less than great who
dares to write greatly. D. holds no multiplication of characters in him:
he is a man rather than a universe.

To Sydney Cockerell   Bovington, 27 October 1923
   Of course I admire him [Doughty] enormously, but I'd admire
his simplicity more if it was artificial, a laborious surface covering
thousands of facets & phases, than now, when it is natural to him.
A bigger man would not read the *Morning Post*.

To E. M. Forster   6 April 1924
To me it['']s artistry [*Arabia Deserta*], with a capital A, in its point
of view, its style, its framing. The only unhappiness is the formless
length & redundancy of the episodes:—but then I like packed writing.

To David Hogarth   [Karachi], 21 April 1927
   Your Doughty discoveries are interesting. Where did he learn his
geology, & his survey work? His map was surprisingly good, all things
considered: and he laid a sort of foundation of our knowledge of the
Arabian watersheds. There was much more of the scientist in the old
man's intention, when he went down with the Haj (of his *secondary*
intention, anyhow) than of the poet.

To Charlotte Shaw   [Karachi], 4 May 1927
[Doughty's] ''style'' isn't Elizabethan in any sense. It is Scandinavian,
pure & simple, in its syntax (the inversions, the queer verbs, the broken
directness [?]) and very eclectic in vocabulary. He used words from
any language, Saxon, Latin, Arabic, Greek, where his sense demanded
them: and had an exquisite sense of the right word. Many of his

adjectives are final, so far as fitness goes, if my judgement is worth anything: and some of these adjectives I've used, because no better ones will ever be found to fill their place.

In that sense I've copied Doughty: but I don't like his style, his syntactical style, any more than I like his recondite vocabulary, or his point of view. . . . He was like a well—very deep, of course, but small in the bore. . . .

People who call Doughty's book a perfect and polished whole have not read it. He had less sense of design even than myself: his book is invertebrate, shapeless, horrific: a brick-yard rather than a building.

. . . He was a real & tremendous poet. . . . His faults are big: due to too much power of mind. . . .

Doughty was a very curious person, who took his politics and feelings about politics direct from the Morning Post. He had no personal friends, and no bonds or nerves uniting him to his own generation, or his fellow-men. His hardness of eye closed him up, apart from life. That led to the inhuman arrogance of his work—himself being the meekest & gentlest of men. It takes a saint to judge the whole world wrong: a god to cast it into hell.

To Charlotte Shaw [Karachi], 16 June 1927

Doughty's mind. Surely that unshakeable conviction of his own rightness is a proof of deep roots? Doughty really believed in his superiority to the Arabs. It was this pride which made him meek in oppression. He really believed that he held a knowledge of the truth, and that they were ignorant: that this thing was better than that thing: in fact, he did really believe in something. That's what I call an absolute. Doughty, somewhere, if only in the supremacy of Spenser, had a fixed point in his universe, & from one fixed point a moralist will, like a paleontologist, build up the whole scheme of creation. Consequently Doughty's whole book is rooted: definitive: assured. That makes his outlines as hard as iron, as sharp as photographs: as amateur's photographs. . . .

I don't find vast plains in Doughty: only a thin pencil of illumination shining very brightly for the time and place: a spotlight. Doughty sees through his eyes, and not through the eyes of his companions. He was devoid of sympathy: a solitary isolated freak of a mind. To see the real man you must look at the Cliffs, the Titans, Mansoul. They give me creeps. Such fanatic love & hatred ought not to be. Who are we to judge? I don't believe even God can.

To Edward Garnett Karachi, 7 July 1927

That Barker Fairley book on Doughty[42] spoiled itself, by trying to do too much. He maintained that the *form* of *A.D.* [*Arabia Deserta*] and of *Dawn in Britain* was subtle, and designed, and balanced, and cumulative. I think it was accident: and a bad accident. Doughty seems wholly to have lacked the strategic eye which plans a campaign, as the sub-commander plans a battle, or the company officer a trench raid, or the soldier a bayonet-thrust. *A.D.* is hampered by its lack of form, less only than *Dawn*, because there was a basis of fact to follow, and life isn't as shapeless as unassisted and undisciplined art. Why, I think *The Seven Pillars*, that untidy general-provider, is better planned than *A.D.*! That's saying nothing much, either. Both are rotten bad: but *A.D.* has the merits of magnificence in its materials, its vision, its attitude, its prose, its poetry, its author. Whereas the poor *S.P.*!

To David Hogarth   Karachi, 27 August 1927

I've been through much of Doughty, of late, and checked Fairley's book on him. *Adam Cast Forth* is splendid. Its goodness defies the lack of form which would have ruined a less great work: but otherwise I cannot see more than great effort and great failure in his poetic work. Doughty's imagination was weak: his sense of scale faulty: and he had no sense of design.

Arabia Deserta remains wonderful, because there his weak imagination had only to select from an array of thronging facts; his sense of scale had a whole desert for its province: his sense of design could express itself only in the aimlessness of his wanderings, and not in confusing the record of his wanderings. *Dawn in Britain* is like the trace of Doughty's journeys in N. Western Arabia, with Arabia left out.[43]

So I conclude that the parts of your book[44] which will matter most are i) Any further light his letters throw on the making of him before he settled in Italy to write *A.D.*

ii) Your dissection of his notebooks.

and '2' is infinitely the more important of these efforts. If you can set side by side parts of the notes, & parts of the finished text, and indicate how the notes were made, & how far they *all* went into the text, or if there was abridgement, or selection, & where the padding is . . . . . then you will be doing a very great thing. *A.D.* is one of the mystery-masterpieces of the world: and people who ever write will always be grateful to you for making plain how it grew. There is no impiety in studying the works. I should have liked to have had a cut at that part of it, myself . . . . . but it was out of the question that I should ever write anything again.

To David Garnett   [Karachi], 30 November 1927

. . . I regret Doughty's style, and find it unjustifiable; not that his skill in using it does not justify him, as a verbal artist, in using it, but because the difficulty of it has barred so many readers from what is, after all, much more than a piece of verbal art. Philologically, too, he is all wrong; why should we borrow our syntax from the Sweden or Denmark of 80 years ago?

. . . . Doughty's lack of form sank his epic, but sank it rather nobly, I think. One reads it with pride at the effort.

To Charlotte Shaw   [Karachi], 2 February 1928
I am not a "fanatical adherent" of Doughty's poetry. He was a great poet, and wrote one fine thing "Adam cast forth". He was also crankily obsessed with unworthy theories of form and idea: and his other work is, much of it, horrible.

To Edward Garnett   Karachi, 2 February 1928
   I can't write to you about Doughty's style. All the arguments are on your side: but a sediment of dissatisfaction remains in the bottom of my mind: agreed it served his purpose, and helped to convey an idea of a strange country and new-old way of living to those who did read his book. But you say 'Could he have done this any other way?' Yes, in a dozen other ways, being a very great writer. He could have put all the strength and bitterness of Arabia into two-syllabled words, had his name been John Bunyan: or into plain words, had his name been Shaw or Swift. Oh, there are as many ways as there are artists. Doughty's way was only just simply Doughty's way: and you would admit, if you lived here with me, that he had thereby much circumscribed his audience. To like Doughty you must be somewhat educated, and a little scholarly, and have a bias for Scandinavian. After that you can begin to relish his style. I lend *Arabia Deserta* to man after man of the crowd in camp, decent fellows, who enjoy books, and have a hungering after good ones: they struggle through a few pages, and then lay it down in despair, not being able to get one visually-sharp image for it. I think it was a pity that he become so learned. Once I said that the best writer was the man who asked most from his readers: but by that I meant a fair asking. To use foreign constructions, and an archaic vocabulary, and hundreds, literally hundreds of Arabic words which have serviceable English equivalents . . . . . no, it was great skill, but was not necessary. Simplicity is as often the mark of first-class work as complexity is of second-class work. Doughty's book mirrored Doughty as much as it mirrored Arabia.

To Sydney Cockerell   Karachi, 22 March 1928
I do not see what a biography has to do with criticism. The biographer's job is to present the facts of the man's life and work, so far as they

have a bearing on the shape of a man's character or person or output; not to appraise him critically. In the case of Doughty the important things would seem to be the collation of the notes on Arabia with the text of *Arabia Deserta*: and the discovery of the roots of Doughty's style (I think they are ultimately pure Swedish: but it may be older: Icelandic even) and the motives which led him to tackle *Dawn in Britain*, *Adam*, and the *Cliffs*, *Clouds*, *Titans*, *Mansoul* subjects.

These lines would show the man: and the goodness of the poetry (very great, I think, despite the superficial affectations) would be left for the taste of the future to read or reject, as it pleased.

To Charlotte Shaw   [Miranshah], 11 November 1928
I have been reading Hogarth's book on Doughty. Between the lines he gives you the truth. Doughty says in one place "They accuse me of having copied the book of a Mr Hardy, the Dynasts. I do not know his name or work, and propose to continue in that state". I know the sequel, which D. G. H. didn't: when Doughty got his honorary degree, Hardy lent him the Doctor's gown for it. Hardy smaller than me, Doughty much taller than G. B. S.! But isn't it a deplorable ignorance, to be proud of being ignorant?

To Charlotte Shaw   [Miranshah], 27 November 1928
The D. G. H. Doughty life is so *good*: just that adjective. It makes me proud of D. G. H. I couldn't have been good to Doughty all through, like that. It shows you how catholic and kind he was. A man of real understanding. Doughty was the easiest man to laugh at anyone ever came across: and so noble and splendid an old man. I couldn't ever make clear to anybody how or why he was so great an old man. But I feel that not till he got old did he justify himself. He was not a pleasant young man, I'm sure.

T. S. Eliot

To Sydney Cockerell   Cranwell, 29 December 1925
I . . . passed my spare time reading T. S. Eliot's collected poems (he is the most important poet alive). . . . It's odd, you know, to be reading these poems, so full of the future, so far ahead of our time; and then to turn back to my book [*Seven Pillars*], whose prose stinks of coffins and ancestors & armorial hatchments.

To Charlotte Shaw   [Karachi], 15 September 1927
. . . don't be led away by the adoration of his [Eliot's] disciples. They

call him the most significant poet of modern Europe. He has immense influence, critically; and produces a little original work, over-laboured in form. An American, who missed an All Soul's Fellowship the other day by the skin of his teeth: or should I say, by my absence?

To Edward Garnett   Karachi, 22 September 1927
Eliot must be a strong fellow: he dominates all a group, and writes hardly anything.

To Robert Graves   Karachi, 26 January 1928
The *Criterion*—the Eliot-party seems to have dry rot in their heads. They word-spin in the most fatuous way, trying to be intellects (4th rate) instead of imaginations, in which T. S. E., anyway, took a very high place. His thinking seems to me almost like tosh for tosh's sake.[45]

To Charlotte Shaw   2 January 1930
. . . Eliot's Dante . . . is a tribute of understanding: so sensible and simple-minded and so wise. I did not think Eliot had such human kindness in him. (I think kindness there means "of like kind", and not "charity". I hope it does: better so.) He would not be lonely in a barrack-room, if he were always straight-forward and open-eyed, like this.

To Sir William Rothenstein   Plymouth, 20 October 1932
. . . everybody criticises books. The plain man criticises them better than the expert. Your T. S. Eliot is the worst of critics. Arnold Bennett almost the best.

To Frank V. Morley   Plymouth, 21 October 1932
God, what a labour that man [Eliot] makes of criticism. I get some joy out of reading.

To G. W. M. Dunn   Plymouth, 9 November 1932
T. S. Eliot I have not met. His poetry is good, if rather sparing. His prose is pompous. His criticism mock-profound. His range of interests very queer and spotty. Yes, I'd like to meet him; shall we hunt him out, some day? He is in U.S.A. now.

To G. W. M. Dunn   Plymouth, 15 December 1932
. . . the Eliot essays . . . . went to you because they are interesting, I think. I did not read them all, because many of them have already passed my eye in other publications. He writes freely for the *Criterion*

and other papers, you know. His *Dante* I have as a small book. It is excellent.

Many of the other essays are not good. He has a confused and knotty mind, and makes more mess of a simple subject than any other conceived human being. I don't know any critic who more darkens the merits[46] and confuses the faults of his authors. After an hour of Eliot I thank God for Arnold Bennett!

To F. V. Morley   Southampton, 16 April 1934
I hope Eliot goes along well, and still avoids the categorical. I shall believe him lost, if ever he makes a plain statement. However, last I read of him, he was still a long way off being lost. O si sic lectores! [Oh, if this could be said of his readers!]

To C. Day Lewis   Bridlington, 16 November 1934
Why does your period stress so much those few thought-ridden poets, Donne, Vaughan, Crashaw—not Herbert, I think? I suspect a little fashion in it, started perhaps by T. S. Eliot[47] with his cranky passion for the knuckle-end of the Church of England: and that's a consequence, probably, of his being an American. A parvenu longing for roots.

E. M. Forster

To E. M. Forster   20 February 1924
Of your work I only know *Howards End* & [*The Story of the*] *Siren* & *Pharos* [*and Pharillon*]: but that's enough to put you among the elect. . .

To E. M. Forster   Clouds Hill, 6 April 1924
Your coming here[48] was a very great pleasure to myself: and a very great profit, I hope, to that difficult book I'm engaged in. You, being by nature a writer, won't realise how lost I feel in attempting to see whole, & improve what was more an experience than a creation of my seeking. The compulsion of circumstance upon me to write it removed it from the normal category of welten things. . . .

I'd like, very much indeed, to see the unpublishable stuff: any of it you feel able to show me. It shall be safely kept, & returned quickly.

'Unpublishable' is a relative, even a passing qualification. *The Seven Pillars* earned it two or three years ago: and have lost it in that little time.

To E. M. Forster   30 April 1924

Comment [on "The Life to Come"]? Oh, it's very difficult. How
much you will see by my confessing that in my first avid reading of
it I ended it, & laughed & laughed. It seemed to me, in the first instance,
one of the funniest things I'd ever come across.

It's abrupt, beyond grace & art: but at my second reading what came
out of it strongest was a feeling of pity for the African man. You cogged
the whole of life against him . . . . . and he was no good to wait all
that while. None the less his illness was overdone, or his sudden spasm
of strength at the end of it. It was too unexpected. Couldn't you have
led up to it by some careful hints of force & sinew in the last pages?

Then there were things that grated on me. "Of god-like beauty"
a hateful careless worn-out phrase. The tale itself is too rare to be
spoiled by a gash like that across it: and across its most beautiful
opening too. The passionate & the pathetic are beautifully done; but
the two main figures, while very complete in character, are only
shadow-drawn physically. Can't you make them flesh & blood.
V[ithobai] only came to shape lying on his roof just dying naked.
Before that he'd not been embodied. And the missionary never, except
in that hacked phrase of the first page.

The thing is too short. The passage of time doesn't make itself felt
naturally. Perhaps paragraphing might bring this out.

Is breaking the neck necessary? It is brutal, snatching, a spasm of
agony. I'd rather have had a slower clutching killing. However you
are the artist, & the emotion charged in it all makes me feel that it's
very uncommon art. Contrary to your opinion I incline to consider
it quite fit to publish. Perhaps other people's improprieties come a
little less sharply upon one? It doesn't feel to me nearly as bad as my
true story. Incidentally we're different, aren't we. I make an awful
fuss about what happened to me:[49] & you invent a voluntary parallel,
about which the two victims make no bones at all. Funny the way
people work.

To E. M. Forster   9 May 1924

I don't seem to have put my remarks on your story ["The Life to
Come"] very well. That's good, because my mind has never cleared
upon it. I agree with S. S. [Siegfried Sassoon] as to its excellence: my
memory is still concerned, not with its parts, but with its general
impression: for anything to last with me three weeks is unusual:
and this preoccupation is a daily one, almost. You have conveyed
something, very powerfully: but it feels like a something quite foreign
from the impression of the details, which I criticised. As though your

two and two, put together, had made not four, but a prime number of some sort.

Technically, as writing, as a story, I don't think it quite so good as very much else of your writing: but what comes through is very strong. To try another metaphor . . . . . as if it were a fine stone, finer than most, but your cutting of it were not quite finished . . . . . or quite exact, anyway.

Why make it over-ripe? or cynical? That seems to me grievous; the thing is so healthy as it stands, in its meaning, that it seems a pity to taint any detail of it.

. . . Your efforts are always so patent, that no one could ever be troubled by them. It isn't a subject which can give offence, but its treatment. . . .

Don't take my criticisms seriously. I have dabbled in writing, but have no vocation, & therefore no technical standard on which to base a judgement. Only I thought you might be interested to know that my absorption in the stream of your main idea was broken into sometimes by a detail, whose foreignness I took to be unessential to the story: but which quite probably you inserted deliberately. It's these conscious variations, flaws, in the rhythm of ideas which mark the artist . . . . . like the irregularities in Shakespeare's blank verse, I suppose.

To E. M. Forster   24 July 1924

I've long ago finished the India book [*A Passage to India*]. Half-through I laid it aside for a while, saying 'The sensation is finished. India, a continent, is on the canvas complete.' Afterwards a remorse for the interrupted action took me, & I went on. Then the characters asserted themselves, & became so lively that the continent faded (till near the end) & the book became breathlessly exciting. It's a three or four-sided thing, more like sculpture, therefore, than painting. Extraordinarily satisfying, to the reader, in the multiplicity of its effects & cross-lights & bearings. . . . You can shape so spare & trim a thing out of an innumerable heap of impressions and materials.

The scene in the Club: from p. 180 onwards: wicked: but very nobly done. Did you know that was a possible combination? It's a most punishing chapter for anyone who has, like me, the Englishman's reaction to other people's tragedies. Just before it comes the Godbole conversation, miles away from our mind, but just as present to you. And then chap XIV: the landscape of the caves. Oh, it's despairingly well done.

The truth is of course that you are a very great writer, & that it's irredeemably weak of me to envy you. ' . . .

If excellence of materials meant anything, my book would have been as good as yours: but it stinks of me: whereas yours is universal: the bitter terrible hopeless picture a cloud might have painted, of man in India. You surpass the Englishman & surpass the Indian, & are neither: and yet there is nothing inhuman (like Moby Dick) in your picture. One feels all the while the weight of the climate, the shape of the land, the immovable immensity of the crowd behind . . . . . all that is felt, with the ordinary fine human senses.

A marvellous book. My final hope is that you never do worse than this again.

To Edward Garnett   16 September 1924
E. M. Forster: very good; but is he quite great? I like him, but a little shamefacedly.

To E. M. Forster   Clouds Hills, 17 June 1925
Did I ever tell you how very much I liked *The Longest Journey* [1907]? It struck me as more from the heart than any other of your work: and the characters were all three-dimensional, that rarest of (unintentional) creations. They keep on coming back to me, as people; not in virtue of any particular thing they say.

To Robert Graves   21 October 1925
E. M. Forster's guide book to Alexandria [*Alexandria: A History and a Guide*, 1922], published there by Whitehead Morris Co., is great literature, and a good guide. Boost it.

To E. M. Forster   26 April 1926
It's my opinion that you will yet write (or have written & not yet shown) something very big: bigger than the *Passage*, which deliberately was bigger than any of the previous novels. Greatness lies in the eye that contemplates not in the subject: & your eye has grown very slowly. All the more lasting, thereby. Of course it's a bore being famous. You have cracked the crib, & the swag isn't any longer up to your standard. Consequently you feel empty, for the while: as if the profession was exhausted. But it isn't. Just wait a bit. Ten more years if necessary. You aren't wasting your time: everybody likes seeing you. Your present emotions span themselves into articles for the *Labour Leader*. Very well. There are sparks & flames: affairs of degree. Yours are the most sporting & fiery sparks. They are so good that someone will some day collect a shower of them. You needn't do that. Let the *Passage* represent you for the moment.

To E. S. Palmer   [Karachi], 15 March 1927
Do you know, he [Forster] is the most civilised person I've ever met?
I dally continually with my memory of him and his books, trying to
find out for myself something of their secrets. There was never anything
so elusive, so subtle, so delicate, so robust . . . as his way of thinking.

To Charlotte Shaw   [Karachi], 30 June 1927
He [Forster] has the power of saying what he thinks: or at least
characters do. Look at Ansell and Stephen Wonham in the Longest
Journey . . . . . a terrible book. He is acute, too, almost to in-
humanity. I too, feel that the epilogue is more like a picture of me
than myself.

To E. M. Forster   [Karachi], 14 July 1927
I've read all your books, except the *Passage to India*, several times
lately.[50] They beat me. All over them are sayings (generally terrible)
which I feel are bursting out from your heart, and represent yourself:
but when I put together a sheet of these, the portrait they make is
not the least like you, as I've sat at tea with you. Tea, of course, is
your drink, as water is mine and beer is Chesterton's and Burgundy
is Belloc's.

To Francis Yeats-Brown   Karachi, 6 September 1927
E. M. Forster has taken the last shine out of my hopes as a judge,
by producing that splendidly far-seeing little set of lectures on the
Novel. Have you read them? Are they out? I've studied them again
and again, lately, without exhausting their value.

To E. M. Forster   Karachi, 8 September 1927
   Your booklet (such a little one!) on [*Aspects of*] *The Novel* is superb.
No other word fits it, because there's a complete lack of superbity
about the manner & matter of it. So that the total effect is superb
shows that the novel really belongs to you. It's like sitting at the feet
of Adam, while he lectures to a University Extension Society about
the growth and development of gardens. As soon as it came I rolled
it out flat, and galloped through it: the names of some of the books
& people I liked or disliked were in it, all right. Two days later I
galloped across it again, seeing more of them: and this week, if my
stretching and shrinking eyes will hold themselves to a page for an
hour—this week I'm going to begin to digest it. There's a curious
difference in tone, between you and [Percy] Lubbock [*The Craft of
Fiction*, 1920]. One treats the novel rather like the glazed un-
approachable pictures in a public gallery. The other talks of novels

as though they were things one writes. I expect you will find it one of the best-selling of your works. . . .

I'm sorry your short story isn't publishable. As you said, the other one wouldn't do for general circulation. Not that there was a wrong thing in it: but the wrong people would run about enlarging their mouths over you. It is a pity such creatures must exist. The *Royal Geographical Journal*, and *Journal of the Central Asian Society*, two learned societies, both found *Revolt in the Desert* indecent. It seems almost incredible.

I wanted to read your long novel [the unpublished *Maurice*], & was afraid to. It was like your last keep, I felt: and if I read it I had you: and supposing I hadn't liked it? I'm so funnily made up, sensually. At present you are in all respects right, in my eyes: that's because you reserve so very much, as I do. If you knew all about me (perhaps you do: your subtlety is very great: shall I put it 'if I knew that you knew . . . . . '?) you'd think very little of me. And I wouldn't like to feel that I was on the way to being able to know about you. However perhaps the unpublished novel isn't all that. You may have kept ever so much out of it. Everywhere else you write far within your strength.

. . . I suppose the new stories date from *The [Celestial] Omnibus* [1911] & *[The Longest] Journey* period. If so they will be very helpful. There is a chasm, technically, between *The Journey* & the other books. The deaths in *The Journey* all happen in a half-line, off-stage, looking back over your shoulder, as you write. Nothing of the sort anywhere else in your writings.

To E. M. Forster   Karachi, 27 October 1927
Now I have your short story ["Dr. Woolacott"]. It's the most powerful thing I ever read. Nearly made me ill: and I haven't yet summoned up the courage to read it again. Someday I'll write you properly about it. A great privilege, it is, to get a thing like that.

Virginia [Woolf] obviously hadn't seen it: or she wouldn't have put so much piffle in her note on you.[51] Which note also holds some very good stuff. I liked it: but she has only met the public side of you, apparently. Or else she doesn't know the difference between skin and bone.

I say, I hope you know what a wonderful thing *Dr. Woolacott* is. It is more charged with the real high explosive than anything I've ever me yet. . . .

It is also very beautiful. I nearly cried, too.

To E. M. Forster   [Karachi], 21 December 1927
I got your note about *Dr. Woolacott*, and am going to read it page by page, and send you my untouched commentary: . . . .[52]

The car lights are wonderful. I'd got frightened here, wondering how you would get out of it, and beginning to doubt you had skill to end what you had begun.

The rest is marvellous. There is no other word for it. It bruises my spirit. I did not know there could be such writing.

Is the mechanism of the ring necessary?

There is a strange cleansing beauty about the whole piece of writing. So passionate, of course; so indecent, some people might say: but I must confess that it has made me change my point of view. I had not before believed that such a thing could be so presented—and so credited. I suppose you will not print it? Not that it anywhere says too much: but it shows far more than it says: and these things are mysteries. The Turks, as you probably know (or have guessed, through the reticences of the *Seven Pillars*) did it to me, by force: and since then I have gone about whimpering to myself Unclean, unclean. Now I don't know. Perhaps there is another side, your side, to the story. I couldn't ever do it, I believe. . . .

Meanwhile I am in your debt for an experience of such strength & sweetness and bitterness and hope as seldom comes to anyone. I wish my account of it were not so vaguely inadequate: and I cannot suggest 'more when we meet' for it will be hard to speak of these things without dragging our own conduct and bodies into the argument: and that's too late, in my case.

To David Garnett   [Karachi], 16 February 1928

E. M. F.'s crises are the crises of a super-sensitive mind: storms in teacups, I called 'em once:[53] that is except the Pan solutions:[54] and Pan to him means physical excitement, I fancy. His best Pan-stuff is unwriteable, I fancy: but in his mind, very surely and succinctly. His social work (*The Longest Journey*, most significant of all) seems to me great . . . . . just great, without qualification. It hangs permanently in my memory, as if it were stuck there: it's like rolling on a fly-paper, which I've seen a hairy lap-dog do. E. M. F.'s stuff clings.

To E. M. Forster   [Karachi], 16 April 1928

Don't cut me off from anything you may write in future, because you've sent me one supremely good thing. I've liked everything you've written: some of it very much, some of it less: but liked it all.

To James Hanley   28 December 1931

I found Forster a very subtle & helpful critic, over my *Seven Pillars*. hardly anybody else (of the dozens of critics who dealt with that or

Revolt in the Desert) said anything that wasn't just useless pap. All Forster's notes on books or writing seem to me workmanlike. After all, he writes, & so knows what authors are up against. In himself he is a very witty, pointed, shy, emancipated person. I like him.

To E. M. Forster   Southampton, 24 May 1934
. . . I have just finished your life of G. L. D. [*Goldsworthy Lowes Dickinson*], upon which I have been quietly happy for many evenings. . . .
   Your book has been quite precious. The restraint, the beautiful tidiness of it, the subtlety, and its commonsense . . . . . your glorification of quiet and care for the average man . . . . . all these points lift it far above ordinary biography. It must have been hard to do, but seldom can an artist have so surely and confidently achieved his aim. The very care to avoid the unattainable is wisdom.[55] Full marks to you.

David Garnett

To Edward Garnett   [Farnborough], 6 November 1922
Lady into Fox [by David Garnett] is very remarkable. I sandwiched it between Flecker's *Hassan*, and the *Religio Medici* [Sir Thomas Browne, 1642]: and it kept its character. So there is more than skill to it. It's what I mean by style: but I'm sorry for the sophisticated simplicity. That's decadence. If a man is not simple by nature he cannot be simple by art, and if he tries he only achieves a falseness. You can only (if complex) get simplicity by my 'third degree': by distilling a scene into quintessential action.

To Edward Garnett   [Farnborough], 12 November 1922
   I withdraw my words about *Lady into Fox*: but it's the line of thought which couldn't ever cut my track—the fantastic. Everything of mine is dry.

To Edward Garnett   [Farnborough], 20 November 1922
   I recant my judgment of *Lady into Fox*. It's remarkable. By the way isn't it unusual that literary power should carry on from generation to generation like that. He's the third, isn't he?[56] Yet, to my scholar's taste, *The Twilight of the Gods* is more attractive.

To David Garnett   [Karachi], 30 November 1927
You seem to me too correct, usually. I like rough edges, and broken rules, and wastefulness . . . . . profusion, perhaps, and the exact way

you do what you set out to do makes me feel I should keep off the grass.

To David Garnett   Plymouth, 4 May 1929

What took me at once in *No Love* was the reality of the people: more especially of the minor people. The Admiral was best of all. It was a most vivid study of several admirals I have known. The scene in the bakery, where he comes in and reads a poem, for which faculty nothing in anything you had said had prepared us, is altogether admirable. It struck me like a ballet. There was something so deliberate in its orchestration and arrangement, and the balance of art and life most beautifully kept. You realise, probably, that you stand wholly outside the realist movement. Your work is symbolist, through and through. Everything of yours which comes off does so by virtue of some significance carried in the acts or words: a significance not stated anywhere, nor possible to state, nor implicit nor concerned with anything the people you create may be doing or saying. It just happens, every now and then, that one halts and says to oneself 'This is tremendously important: this *matters*'. How or why God knows.

. . . Roger is better than Benedick:[57] at least I think so. Do not ask me to qualify every phrase in this letter by 'I think so'. I do. Simon was very real as a boy (incidentally your children are all good) but he was faint towards the end. Did you get exasperated with the bunch of them? I did, rather. They seemed to lose their way in life, and to stray a bit aimlessly. Of course that is real too: but an author's characters should be better than life, or it's hardly worth our mind's while to invent them. If all we did was to invent people who were passably real, it would be easier and more realistic yet to go and procreate real children on any woman. . . .

Wherefore I did grow angry with Simon, and Cynthia (she is a bit of a ghost all the time) and Benedick, after the elders were dead. You see, the elders were the better drawn, and the riper people. Your young ones never got grown up at all: only the shine of youth seemed to rub off.

Last book of yours I read left me with an abiding sense of a low country: fennish or next door to fens: water and willows or poplars, and an air that was moist. In this book there is no landscape at all: or only one old tree arching over the sleeping kids on the shore. Otherwise a void in which these astonishingly real people gyrate and hover. London does not appear, nor the bombardment, convincingly. The people, Benedick and Cynthia, are alive in it. They wake up astonishingly, during that London leave. It is their final kick before they die on you: but London remains only a back-curtain. I suspect

you meant this too. One is always pulling up at some astounding simple
line or move on your part, and saying 'Is this the simplicity of a child
or of someone so grown up that he can be childish?' There is a feeling
as of superb skill and deliberation about the progress of your novel.
This limpidity is too good to be true. . . . Your first three books were
resonant with echoes of other men's styles and work. Not this. It is
independent.

However, as I say, I'm sorry that you denied yourself landscape.
It is nice stuff. You do it well, too. Perhaps you do not know that
side of the Hayling-Portsmouth area well enough to let yourself go?
Another time I hope you will put your people in a non-geographical
place, and let yourself go, descriptively. If you can get walking and
talking people, you have got one third of what the novelist wants. The
other third is something keener seen than the earth of our eyes, to
set them in: and the last third is something for them to say better and
richer and riper than the stuff we say ourselves. You have put each
of the ingredients into one or other of your books. Now I want you
to stir them together into one pudding.

So much for *No Love*. Forgive the crudity of my criticism. I have
no theory or notion of art: but I do like to read novels. And there
are so many almost good enough: and so few that are quite good
enough to be better, like yours. You are growing all the time. Yet I
wish that you had not written *Lady into Fox*. Everybody will urge
you all the rest of your life to make them more toys of the spirit.

To H. S. Ede   [Plymouth?], 29 July 1929
Another and another letter from you turns up, unanswered. I'm afraid
I'm a beast. One holds an admirable summation and demolition of
the thesis of 'No Love': I am entirely with you. Such titillations of
the spirit are prostitution, and nasty Maddox St. prostitution at that.
Better to be like a healthy bull and cow in a field.

. . . Do not worry about David Garnett's criticism. The man is over-
educated, too good a craftsman, and so short-sighted.[58]

To David Garnett   19 November 1930
I send back your flying notes [amplified and published as *A
Rabbit in the Air*, 1932]. They are uncommonly well done, and have
pretensions—or at least they achieve effects, and such things seldom
come unawares. I think they are the beginnings of a most excellent
(and widely sold) handbook on the art of amateur flying. Keep them
going till the solo day has come, and after it for any out-of-the-way-
yet-communicable flights: and the result will be a joy to everyone who
likes the air. They feel so real and direct and modestly true. Very good.

. . . It is nervous and exacting prose. . . . They give the actual feel of being in the cockpit and looking out. So few people are qualified both in foreground and background; that makes them so satisfyingly true.

To David Garnett   Plymouth, 10 June 1931
The Grasshoppers [*Come*, 1931] is . . . imperative need for a letter. In it you have suddenly broken, I think, into sincerity. The flying is real. For the first time, in all that you have written, I feel a *necessity* of utterance, a fusion of matter and manner so complete that the manner is almost absorbed. Only one precious word I saw—'sighed' for the prop-tip—and what a good word!
You told me about the tale long months ago, and it frightened me that one with no sense of the air should touch it. There are so many bad flying books. Then you went flying, and qualified yourself superbly, and this little masterpiece is it. . . .
The book has pleased me quite beyond what I had thought possible. It is the first account of real flying by a real writer who can really fly: and it gave me a very great sense of long distance, and of that incommunicable cradle-dandling which is a cockpit in flight.

To John Brophy   Plymouth, 13 February 1933
It seems ever so hard to write books to order—witness Pocohontas [1933]. By that I don't mean that anyone ordered it, but David Garnett feels it's up to him to find a subject for his next book, within six months of his last—and that's a pity. E. M. Forster chooses the better way.

Robert Graves

To Robert Graves   21 July 1920
You have fairly got me now: I have the *Gnat* volume and have read it many times, and frankly I don't know about it. I like it so much: it is so masculine, so much deeper than the others write—and yet there seems a conflict in it, as though you were not sure yourself which sort they ought to be. That's where the rhymed ones score, for the music is an end in itself, and thought follows it. I am not in the least qualified to talk like this, but it won't do any harm, because you will take no notice (or at least no polite notice).
Incubus—splendid: isn't "Smiles for freedom, blinks an eye" too earthly an exit from such a night? It seems to me to jerk us rather violently down from the general to the private. Also "nothing wrong" grates on my degraded ear.

Return—not "blank" thirst: surely. Thirst is an agony, tearing distracting pain that gapes a man's black mouth open, and makes him stagger drunkenly. You are all shredded out of your balance with horror. Also stone doesn't go ragged with heat, but with rain. Heat polishes, splits, blackens it, often warps it crooked. These are pettifogging points, which would only occur to one who had nearly died of thirst. Don't attend to them.

Drinking Song—That is yours. I don't get loud with other people, and loudness in them makes me shut up. No doubt it is a good poem: but I'd rather be a prig than be sociable.

The Gnat—Of course this is the crux of the whole matter, and I feel myself hopelessly unable to pick a hole in it. Only isn't it a sort of criticism to say that I feel there is a flaw somewhere? The stuff should, I think, be fused once more before you publish it. It seems to me again a conflict between the frankly dream-stuff and the realist school. There are legends—introduced scientifically as quotes from Josephus. A mystic beast—which bumps the furniture after flying out of his mouth. Of course its strangeness, and the little fear it puts in you when you read it, may come from this very mixture of world and other-world. I'm not a poet, or I'd know how you get effects. Let's get back to verbal details. I don't like "Prepare: be ready". They are very close together. The standard of style for minor voices should be high: surely. I don't like "tyrants use": it's become a phrase now: not crisp enough: also the rhyme of "fare" and "hair" is rather wanton, I think. Your blank verse is strong, irregular and musical enough without endings of this sort. I don't also know if I like the isolated "agony", though I haven't the least idea if any change could be made. It's the hardest word to put in the whole poem, I suspect, for it must be a climax of the previous very fast-moving, high coloured verse—and you have gone up so high in the picture of the beast straining itself to get out, that a climax has to be some climax. I pity you here. The end strikes me as the goods: though I'd like something less exact than the catalogue of the new shepherd and his dog: one line or three perhaps: it does seem to me you show a perverse pleasure in using the common adjective, where one a little less usual would maintain the illusion which to me is the power of the poem.

The Magical Picture is fancy, not vision of course, and like the drinking song is not my sort.

The Pier-Glass. This is metaphysic, and your music and happy words only look out of place, about this thought. (I mean "magic" curtain, "dismal" bellrope, "sullen" pier-glass.) The last two sections do entirely without subjective furniture: couldn't you show the mood of the mind that came in on its problem-pilgrimage, less directly? A suggestion that it saw sullenness and dismality in the mouldering place, without point-blank catalogue of adjectives? I think the last two sections right up to level again, and the second, as I said, in a different key. But it's impertinence in me to discuss what only you can do.

Distant Smoke. I'll go through it to the bitter end, for perhaps you feel annoyed with a baby or something, and this will be a counter irritant. "Yesterday" to "Adam" is splendid: but I don't like "Summoned . . . . . up": and "Defining . . . . . journey" strikes me as your nearest approach to a bad line. Please remember "A Mr. Wilkinson, a clergyman" produced in a moment of absorption by a great man. I don't like "God's curse" and "Father's blessing" side by side later on. However it's only an association. The wit of the thing is simply great: but "pity" seems to me hardly the note to end on. After all these were primitive men, and pity is too soft a motive for the desert.

Look here: It's a shame to treat you this way, for my babblings are only the meannesses of a Philistine. I have enjoyed the booklet immensely. Must I send it back?

To Robert Graves   Cairo, 22 April 1921

I've just seen a review by Square in the *Mercury* of your last book [*The Pier-Glass*?]: but it's rot. I know you won't care much, but things people say about one generally stick in a little, in spite of denials: and the man has the face to call the book "promise". You know it isn't: it's fruit, ripe and splendid and as good as you can do. And while of course it isn't your last, yet it's easily your best to date, and something whose line you won't pass, as with time you'll change, and this earlier feeling will be out of your reach, backwards; so please don't try to be dramatic,[59] or anything else: all's well.

To Robert Graves   London, 21 May 1921

Your great fit of writing sounds exciting: I'll look forward greatly seeing it. . . . I'm glad the "Tangled in Thought" has gone forward: army captains are fruitful things (why not full colonels: still fruitier?) metaphysics, songs dreams, sleeps and royalties: it sounds a new volume: and all in rhyme, and all in editors' offices. I hope the said editors will do their part. Some day you should write a poem about an editor: (or rather you shouldn't, but Pope should have: it doesn't matter what Pope writes about).

To Rees   [London?], 20 February 1922

There's a young poet I know, called Robert Graves, a man of some standing in his class, because he shows grey stuff in among his lines. His early work being of the nursery type was much read. His later work is psychological: his next book [*On English Poetry*, 1922] is a prose study, provocative in character, of the nature of the poetic excitement. It will annoy the poets, as it tries to find physical reasons for their emotions.

However the point is that he's hard up. In similar case Robert Nichols was cured by being able to write regularly for the Observer. I know the Sunday Times uses Gorse: but the world is rather tired of too much Gorse, and so you may be. In that case would you consider Graves? He might be worth a trial either for casual or for regular stuff, and if he showed aptitude would do you very well. I only suggest it as an experiment, for poets aren't, like bricks, good or certain building material.

To Robert Graves   18 January 1923
I'm glad you're feeling easier. In mechanical jargon you've been "revving" yourself too high for the last eighteen months. Such forced running means a very heavy fuel consumption, & is not true economy. Your "philosopher" period as a poet is worth taking care for, since its product will surpass your lyrical.

To Robert Graves   Clouds Hill, 9 May 1924
How do your ways lie? . . . . You are writing more than usual: reviews, articles, all sorts of prose. It seems to me a good arm to put forth. The poems were getting too tight to breathe easily; & the exercise of ad hoc prose will loosen your spiritual arms.

To Robert Graves   Cloud's Hill, 5 December 1924
Alexander, God bless him, is V.V.V.V.G.[60] Of course I laughed, laughed enormously, as I read him in bed in the hut. The troops stared. I showed one excellent one . . . the MS. cause-of-laughter, and he laughed as loudly, and has called me Alexander sometimes since.

It isn't the whole story, though. There was an old Alexander which survived in part, and a bit of an actor, and a sorry fellow, and many other fellows. . .

To Robert Graves   [May?] 1925
The Presence. Very moving. It reads like a first draft, too charged with passion for its form. The metre isn't common, and does not always fit the thought perfectly. I've underlined two phrases. The first didn't please me: and you repeat it (its grammatical form is what I'm talking about) four lines lower.

Also "abuse" and "use" feel as if brought in just to match one another. I may be wrong. They seem like bubbles in the mixture. "Accusingly enforcing her too sharp identity". That strikes me as a bit mannered. Bad-mannered, like the Sitwells' over-punctilious ceremony of phrase. Pernickety: Max-beerbombish.

I'd like to transpose some of the opening lines: the "of whom" etc. down to "on memory" aren't, intellectually, greater, louder, or in complement of "dead is gone . . . . . underground": indeed I fancy they come before it: and I'm old-fashioned in liking my climax last . . . . . or in liking the poem to open crescendo and not diminuendo.

This is not to be taken as a denigration of *The Presence*. The power of the whole comes through its parts . . . . . transcends its parts: so that you wonder after having come down that uneven stairway of rhymes, to find yourself possessed of a place entirely new.

On third thoughts I wouldn't alter it. The spontaneity is one of its strengths.

To Robert Graves   25 June 1925

You underestimate *Poetic Unreason*. It isn't a bit over-worked: au contraire: one of the freshest things ever written on poetics. And the matter is as good as the manner. The only place where I cavilled was the treatment of *The Tempest*.

To Robert Graves   [November?] 1926

I've had the L. R. book [Laura Riding, *The Close Chaplet*]. It puzzles me. Either she is very deep or very different-minded—another way for saying that her poems slide out of my grip. I cannot remember them, after I have read them. This is not criticism, but a personal statement. Your work affects some people that way: whereas my mind seems tuned exactly to them, so that what you say is what I'd say, if I had your power.

To Robert Graves   [Karachi], 19 May 1928

In the way up to the Office my gratitude switched over from the personal obligation of the Jupiter,[61] to the general obligation, which everybody owes you for that volume of collected poetry. . . . There isn't any of that wriggle in them as though they'd been pried, unwillingly, from the spiral depths of some shell, with a pin and great pain. I wonder how you do it? One's sober judgement sees how hard worked they are, and how many words of felicity have come as afterthoughts: but it's the first breath, still alive in them, which makes them priceless. (One feels your poetry in the hollow diaphragm, just under the cage of ribs.)

Alas, that word "priceless" has been deflowered, in English, and also in French. However, time gives back their virginity to languages.

So let's let it stand. The ink will be three weeks old before you see
it. One could write the *Iliad* in 3 weeks.

To Robert Graves   Miranshah, 5 August 1928
   You are a queer mixture. You scold the world like a slutty Joan
Keel-the-pot, in one line, and append a poem like *To the Galleys* a
minute later. The galley-slave applies to yourself, you say. It applies
also to half your generation, (and mine) and to S. S. [Siegfried Sassoon]
and H. G. Wells, and Arnold Bennett and Barrie and God knows
how many more. You are a psychologist in one eye, and jaundiced
in the other. Thereby you have the advantage over so many of us,
who are scathing upon the subject of humanity, whenever we are
not talking forpublication. Goodwordthatforpublication.
   Are there no just men in Sodom? Well, that depends on the point
of view, I suppose. For them and for you . . . . . I am delighted that
you are still writing poems. You have never turned backward to a mood
after leaving it. Perhaps you were made without a reverse gear. As
your studies of man happen generally to put me on the track of
something I'd not thought of, but had been growing to unconsciously
suspect—(O Muse, help me to get out of this sentence)—therefore
your stuff is good for me.

To Robert Graves   Plymouth, 5 May 1929
Honestly R. G., hasn't the scale of your judgement been out, lately?
It is not my business, and I cherish my own freedom to do as I like
too much to dream of interfering: but you have been so drastic in your
condemnations of ordinary people, of late, that I've been afraid to
stay near you. You see, I know by the best of all proof (continguity
with ordinary men in barracks) how ordinary I am; and because
ordinariness is not wholly a flattering feeling, I have been led to look
for my own likes in ordinary people: and from that I have grown to
see the ordinariness in nearly everyone. But whereas that makes you
rage and condemn, it makes me feel akin and friendly. I like your
stuff, because so often you seem to me to say clearly something that
all our generation is trying to say. There is no monopoly of feeling:
lots of people are feeling like you: but only an occasional man can
say it decently. It is a great thing to have the power of words: but
it does not make one man different from another in kind, as something
that L. R. [Laura Riding] said when we last met half-implied.

To Robert Graves   Plymouth, 13 September 1929
   This [*Goodbye to All That*] is very good. The war is the best part
(terrible idea: is the war always going to be the thing we do best?)

and completely carries on & up the excitement of the opening chapters. Most excellent. Your pictures of wounds & nerves are exactly as they should be: sane, decent, *right*. . . .

I'm glad, too, that there is so much humour, so little unalloyed spleen, in the book. You have had enough lately to embitter a saint— and the saint laughs, a little wryly.

No corrections or changes to make, on the point of taste or prose. It's very good writing, and the characters are so alive. A very good book. The rise & fall is noticeably planned, & excellent.

To H. S. Ede   Plymouth, 8 February 1930
Graves 'Goodbye' presented a vigorous mind and spirit, very simply and plainly. It was good, without being noble.

To Robert Graves   Clouds Hill, 12 November 1933
I have now to write you about [*I*,] Claudius, after going through the proof from Arthur Barker and marking it and returning it to him. . . .

Practically I was useless for the Claudius job. Even in my schooldays I was no classic, and today I am twenty-five years rusty. You have made your scenes your own, and there is little parade of research: the tone is deliberately modern, and I like that. Two trifles jarred on me for some reason, your use of French and France, which seemed a pity when everybody knew of Gaul and Gallic: and your calling the German spears, in the story of Arminius, always "assegais". Assegai is bastard Bantu, I think. It was a very broad-bladed paddle-like stabbing spear. The early German spears were throwing-spears, I think, with leaf-shaped blades: not very like assegais. I'd have said javelins for them: and *not* javelins for the pilum of the legionaries. The pilum was a weapon on its own. Bothered if I know what to call it.

Also you make too much use of paper, to the entire exclusion of parchment and papyrus. You should have at least winked at the commoner materials.

And were the vine-shoots of the Roman N.C.O's really the rods that killed? I envisage them as light cane-like minor punishments.

About the book—and there I am in a difficulty. It is long, and not brisk: the middle section is crowded with figures and moves too slowly. It is a chamber of Roman horrors, too. In every direction you take the way of crime, so that your chronicle becomes more scandalous than the most hostile Roman story. There may be chapter and verse— the amount of study you must have done for the book is appalling— but there is hardly average on your side. In so much human nature there would have been some good specimens, surely? Your Germanicus is a lay-figure.

It gripped me, against my will. I couldn't help reading at it, long after bed-time, with the bed-room of my lodging here in Southampton growing deadly cold—and an early call in the morning facing me. The writing is superb: the aloof and cold-blooded narration masterly: the possibility of Claudius' having written it always borne in mind, and always made possible. I give you very high marks for the sustained effort. And yet—and yet—quo vadis, Domine [whither goest thou, Lord]? I have an uneasy feeling that it will be valued and collected and talked about for its vices, rather than for its force. It is not an essential book.

You have gone a long way from your beginnings, now: and I have a feeling that you ought to come home, at least for a while, and meet people who don't care enormously about your subjects and don't value your work—and who aren't as foreign to you as the Mallorcans. You are losing your englishry—and not taking on another habit. It is loss.

I expect money is very difficult. Claudius may make the difference there: I hope so. It is an extraordinary book, and will raise your publisher-value, at any rate. The man who can do it can do anything. Yet I fancy it will not be a very great success—except for the wrong reasons. You'll think me very Victorian: but I want books to have a compelling reason—and Claudius has none, for me. Horrific: elemental; ungarnished: but not essential. I can't say why, exactly, but I feel unsatisfied.

To Robert Graves   Southampton, 17 December 1933
Yes, your prefatory note to Claudius helps it much. It saves us from having to find out your intentions as we go: and that forestalls criticism.

I still feel that the assegai, whatever its pedigree, is now too localised a word for classical use. Words die, as words are born. For instance "pictures" now mean cinema performances: and one couldn't describe Claudius as "broadcasting" news through Rome. "Blooming" died because the cockneys fell in love with it. Kipling murdered his infant "far-flung". Morris overlaid "wan". Perhaps you will bring back assegai to broader use.

As Claudius recedes from my memory, it leaves on me more and more the impression of unrelieved crime and horror. As you rightly say, there are normal characters: but in relation to normal life these are as rare as criminals.

This mild sense of having been shocked is likely to be personal to me, I think; for in daily life crime leaves me cold. I skip all the innumerable columns of the papers which deal with yesterday's murder. I have never finished a detective yarn—nor for years begun one. I know that many people read them: more, even, seem to write them. It is perhaps a need of the age which has passed me by. There are so many thousand cares of the generations of yesterday and today which seem to have missed me. If you ever do come home you will find me haunting Dorset like an aurochs. Remote enough, I hope, to be interesting to you.

Good wishes for poor Claudius.

To Robert Graves   Southampton, 4 May 1934

Barker sent me a very early copy of *Claudius* and I have taken the chance to read it through much more easily and fluently than was possible in his huge galley-bundle.

You know, it's a grim tale. You will say that so was the epoch: yet if Blunden had written it, it would have been a bucolic lyric! I think we must be subjective animals.

I hope Claudius pays. It seems to me too grim: but then as you discovered, I do not read crime books, and I skip the court news in the papers. So I'm a bad judge.

To Arthur Barker   Felixstowe, 4 May 1934

...I found it [*I, Claudius*] hard as a stone, and cruel. The humour that used to be R. G's seems to have taken flight: and the book goes on deadly serious, from horror to horror. The only parts when I could relax at all were with the later Caligula, whose Dawn Dance, for example, was farce, and good farce.

To Frederic Manning   Southampton, 25 July 1934

"I Claudius" shrivelled me up. Robert Graves asked me to read the proofs (for archaeological reasons) and the tone and subject of the book were sickening. I told him so, and he replied that it was a good "crime book". Away with crime books, then: but I believe they are all the rage today.

To Eric Kennington   Bridlington, 3 January 1935

I hated "I, Claudius", for the scandal and the perverse misreading of history: but in Claudius the God he justifies himself and creates on a grand scale.

To Robert Graves   Bridlington, 13 January 1935

I, Claudius, which I shrank from when I read it, you described as a crime-book, and I was confirmed in my dislike of crime. But *Claudius the God* [1934] is utterly different—the sun has risen. I put much of my pleasure in it to your sympathetic picture of Herod. In the other volume there was nobody (not even battered Cassius Chaerea) whom one could like. Herod is charming: and even Claudius wins a battle.

I am glad the gamble came off, for a historical novel is a desperate gamble, I think . . . . . unless, perhaps, it is translated from German! . . . .

I think the public now expect you to write a life of Nero. I would like you to spend some imagination, instead, in early Galilee: those Greek-Syrians have been overlooked.

Radclyffe Hall

To Charlotte Shaw   [Miranshah], 6 November 1928
   The Well of Loneliness is certainly not indecent:[62] at least I do not see what annoyed James Douglas: or does he think that all attractions are cross-sexed? They are certainly not. I've seen lots of man-&-man loves: very lovely and fortunate some of them were. I take it women can be the same. And if our minds go so, why not our bodies? There's only a wall between the farm and the farm-yard.

To Charlotte Shaw   [Miranshah], 11 December 1928
   Miss R. Hall is not one of my admirations. Her book is not big: clever & right enough: but deserves no extremity of praise or blame. James Douglas, silly ass, did her too much honour.

To E. M. Forster   Miranshah, 12 December 1928
   I read *The Well of Loneliness*: and was just a little bored. Much ado about nothing.

James Hanley

To K. W. Marshall   Plymouth, 29 January 1931
   The Hanley story interested me. . . .
   He must be a queer fellow. Young, I take it, and probably not in the war at all. It reads like imagination. I don't encourage my imagination to wander off the rails. If my body, blowing about, comes across a horror I can study it and record it, exactly: but I don't give my mind the same freedom of adventure. So I would not like to have written this: nor another story of his I have, about the last hours of a man about to hang. Both are repulsive, in the real sense. Yet I see the power in them which Drift had not. Then who (bar Joyce) cared ever for the interactions of scholastic catholicism and ignorance?
   Let me know about it. . . . If more Hanley comes out, chuck it my way. . .

To K. W. Marshall   9 March 1931
I call this a fine thing: it is really three-dimensional and excellent.
If it was lately written then Hanley is growing fast. . . . It is seldom
one is lucky enough to find a thing that can be eagerly read twice off
the reel.

His teutonic construction tickled me, making the verb 'to be' in its
various conjugations the most emphatic word in the sentence. That
gave me a sense of time passing, of stages of action or thought. He
used the trick so often that its vigour wore off. He also missed out
so many the s [sic] and his's that I failed to feel their want!

But why, in God's name, an introduction by Richard Aldington?
Honestly, that's low. Hanley writes a damn sight better than R. A.
and doesn't pule in print. Why not an intro. by Sir A. Quiller Couch?
Why not let it rip without any chaperon?

To K. W. Marshall   Plymouth, 9 April 1931
The bitterness you complain of in Hanley is not, I think, the result
of his suffering, but its cause: and the same with D. H. L[awrence].
They were born to feel like toads under the wheels of their own
circumstances. With time these miseries mellow, or at least they do
occasionally, with special people. Theodore Powys now writes happily,
after 50 years of black hate. Hardy reached his Dynasts later yet. Poor
D. H. might have got through his pains, and I hope Hanley will.

Have you ever read "Children of Earth" [1918] by Darrell Figgis?
It is long and formless, but big in its way. He had reason to be unhappy,
poor wretch, and yet there is no complaining in his pages.

I'd like to run into Hanley somehow. Would he resent being looked
at admiringly?

To James Hanley   Plymouth, 2 July 1931[63]
I'm not a reviewer, and my notions of a book take time, like muddy
water, to settle down and clarify. It [Sheila Moynihan] is hot writing,
like all of yours. It goes rather higher and further, in Fr Hooley's long
soliloquy: there is real thought in that, and the torrent of idea flows
well and brilliantly. This seems to me bigger than any other of your
writing I have yet seen. But it is unfinished, and how plain & poor
the Venus of Melos would seem, with her arms! Work that is not ended
is so hard to judge: but you should take it as a good sign that I badly
want to read more of it—all there is.

You must work very fast: yet your writing is all good, clear & fitting,
and when necessary beautiful. Yet all your own. You have been
delivered from the cliché: if the 'viols' on page 10 are real. I heard
the Dolmetsch crowd once playing what they called viols, and thought

them pretty foul. Also your cataracts puzzled me. There were three of them, quite close together, once as a verb, once an adjective and once a noun. I fancy you overdid 'em. Otherwise your writing is just a transparent medium, through which what you want to say slips invisibly and silently into my mind. I like that: it seems to me the essence of style.

I don't find the development of *Sheila Moynihan* as yet fulfils your MS. note above the title. Priests—yes. Innocence—yes: grasping greedy—fathers, rather than mothers, so far. Poor Mrs. M. was baby-racked, and couldn't care, surely? 'Cold-ice-cold and hungry English mistresses'—not yet: not in the first 130 pages! Something cold wouldn't be out of place, after the hotness you have given us.

Your character-drawing is superb, here & in *Boy* and in *The Last Voyage*, and *Drift*, and in the story of the two soldiers worrying their prisoner. You can draw characters as and when you please, with an almost blistering vividness. . . .

You need not bother about the Latin Quarter, or about schools & cliques. They will bother more about you: and if you don't pay attention they will fall to praising everything you do. Whereas praise is always waste of time to hear, and harmful, in overdose. After years of it you look for it and credit it, and then are soiled. . . .

I will not throw *Boy* away. I propose to read it more. It is good. I like it better than *Sheila* (while seeing that it is less) for subjective reasons, because I like men, and ships and Alexandria!

I will try & find something not pimpish of me in Arab kit, for you. It was long ago, and a scabby episode in my life, I think. Politically the thing was so dirty that I grew to hate it all before it came out more-or-less honestly in the end. So when I see pictures of myself in Arab kit I get a little impatient—silly of me, for it was long ago, and did really happen.

Your sanity and general wholesomeness stick up out of your books a mile high: people with dirty patches in them skirt round and round them, alluding but never speaking right out. They are afraid of giving their spots away—and you can map them, just by outlining the blanks. Whereas, God almighty, you leave nothing unsaid or undone, do you? I can't understand how you find brave men to publish you!

To Edward Marsh   Plymouth, 7 July 1931
The only chicken I can find who writes well (about forbidden things, usually and alas) is Hanley.

To James Hanley   Plymouth, 14 July 1931
Now comes this question of Greenwood and "Boy". Do you think

it is good tactics?[64] Somebody said once that every tub should stand on its own bottom; and if it can't, then it had better not be a tub, I fancy. Publishers are always after introductions and reviews and critical opinions, and I doubt whether in the long run these do more than limit a man's reputation. *In the long run*, of course, for they tell me that praise by Arnold Bennett in the Evening Standard used to sell 2000 copies of anything.

I don't care, personally: so long as I'm not accused with reason of setting up as a critic, which I am not qualified to be. Only if he does print something, make it clear that it is from a private letter, & let it be a fair sentence: by taking the wrong one and putting it alone you could make the book sound quite different to what I was trying to say. Hang it all, a fellow does not write judicial letters!

To C. J. Greenwood   Plymouth, 17 July 1931
I think Hanley a very good, if not always gay, writer. *Boy* is very remarkable, in the draft I read. I have not seen your revised text. He is profuse, various, and vigorous.

I hope you are not riding for a row with the Home Office. That sort of thing usually gives the author a kink against decency, and makes him bought by all the wrong people, for all the nasty reasons. Hanley is too good to be labelled by them. Of the evils, I far prefer censorship by the publisher to censorship by the police. If you publish *anything* a fellow writes, you only give the police an easy entry. So do outrage your love of liberty so far as to keep Hanley out of the Courts.

Of the two sentences you quote, nothing (on the score of fairness) can be said against the first.

The second is not so fair. I told him that nobody but a sane and decent person could write so freely about—well, filth. As you put it, people in search of a sane and wholesome book for their sons and daughters might blindly buy *Boy*—and be indignant. Can't you even it out?

To James Hanley   Plymouth, 21 August 1931
Lately in London in one day I re-read the new book right through. Its writing is white-hot and terrific, but as a piece of work it has not the force of *Boy*. For one thing, I suppose, you have never been a maid-servant in Liverpool: nor, I think, was the village-fisherman life of the first pages yours. At least I did not feel (except by fits and starts) the strangeness of the Moynihan family on which you laid stress, to carry the book into rational experiences. Both father & mother were interestingly drawn, & their priest magnificent: but the

inevitable element is missing in the tragedy. I think it overlabours the disaster of being seduced: I could bear it with some fortitude, personally! I think it over-states the proportion in which sex inhabits our minds. Sheila meets two priests—one rapes her. She meets two bus-conductors—both have a shot at it. Now, honestly, you overdo the lechery of bus-conductors. A decent, wearied, cynical and rather hasty-tempered class of men. Also the final coincidence, though perhaps the only way of ending a book keyed so high, is rather a coincidence, isn't it?

The quibble that the priest's performance on the cross might be technically difficult you could rebut, because I judge only by report.

Are you laughing now? I doubt it: yet you will find that others besides me will take refuge in laughter against your over-dose of terror. I think the book is keyed too high. It is amazing: ingenious: unusual: and carries itself off. I do not think anybody but yourself could have conceived it, or would have attempted it, or could have gripped me, as I was gripped while I read it: but it is a criticism, surely, that I kept on crying out 'NO, no' to myself even while I read. You held me, but did not carry me away: and the only justification for extravagance is that it should be wholly successful.

I'll tell you the part of the book I shall never forget; what struck me as perhaps the finest scene (bar the man & wife in *The Last Voyage*) of all your writing—and that was the priest & his churchwarden fellow over the bottle of whisky, while the priest sophisticated upon his intended rape. It was unearthly and yet entirely real: really three-dimensional. I could feel all round and about the two creatures while they talked. You can make queerness come to life. Will you rave to hear that I said 'Dickens' as I read it, though Dickens is a man I cannot bear to read?

You see, not being a conscious critic, I cannot tell you what I really thought & felt about the book, nor can I explain what it really was that made me think & feel: but I did imagine that your cause, and your effect, were both of them disproportionate (too trivial) for the vast tone of your treatment. A big thing should, I fancy, be quietly treated, for it states itself: and a small thing has to be underlined and picked out. Your tragedy does not feel inevitable, or typical: it is individual, perhaps accidental. I think what you wanted to describe was the unhealthiness of a celibate priesthood, and that the victim was introduced as illustration. I don't know: but I feel that as an imagination the book lacks the complete appearance of life.

How I fumble! It is astonishing, as writing; whole pages of sustained eloquence such as I've never read in you before.

To Frederic Manning   Plymouth, I September 1931
   In this year I have read . . . two or three books of Hanley, an eager
and lusty Irishman who has vigour enough to pardon his being
unfair. . .

To Henry Williamson   1 September 1931
. . . James Hanley, a thunderous young Irishman from Wales. Unfair,
morbid even: But gusty with life.

To Lady Astor   Plymouth, [1931 or 1932?]
   James Hanley lives at la Cranley Gardens, London S.W.7. If the
Observer[65] can find him something he could sign, and draw signed-
rates for, it would be useful money & exercise for him: But I do not
guarantee Hanley. He is too forceful, sometimes, for true strength,
to my niggling mind.

To James Hanley   [Southampton?], 28 December 1931
   [Stoker] Haslett is good. It lines up with the other short stories of
yours, and holds it own with, for example, The Last Voyage. It is not
so terrible as your higher tides: nor does it take us any further than
the rest. I am pinning my hopes on your new novel, as likely to develop
your writing beyond the point reached by Boy & the rest.
   By the way Marshall told me that Boy is being reprinted, with the
asterisks cut or replaced by words. That is very good. In its cheap
form it reads worse (as regards indecency!) than the limited edition.
I think it would have gone much better if you had made the cheap
edition a new book, rather than a mutilation.

To Frederic Manning   Southampton, 2 January 1932
Hanley, a wild Irishman whose books so far have said one thing with
great emphasis. . .

To C. J. Greenwood   Plymouth, 12 October 1932
   Have just read Hanley's Ebb and Flood. A very fine effort. He has
definitely enlarged his range, in it. There are good books coming from
him. I hope he keeps his head above water, too.

To C. J. Greenwood   Plymouth, 26 October 1932
   I shall be glad, very glad, to have the Hanley. The book isn't
artistically necessary, I thought. Hanley was only getting something
phlegm-like off his chest. If I knew his life-history probably I would
know that. Accordingly for all the terrific power of it, I cannot regard
it as a child of his daylight hours. No doubt I am wrong: but there

is too much feeling in it for an extravagance, too much extravagance for cold fury. I shall value my copy, permanently.

To James Hanley   Plymouth, 7 December 1932
   Your Ebb & Flood I enjoyed. It had more reasonableness in it than usual. So many of your characters are suddenly angry for little cause: and I prefer stable beings. So the slowness of the Ebb & Flood people was good. . . . You are immensely fertile, aren't you? Book after book. . . . your Dom. resurrexit. That's rather like printed dynamite.

To H. S. Ede   Southampton, 2 January 1932
   'Boy' is unfair: yet so emphatic one must respect the chap's honesty.

To G. W. M. Dunn   Bridlington, 26 January 1935
I expect you do not wish to read the home life of the Liverpool Irish poor [Hanley, *The Furies*]. . . . It is good: but its people lack quietness. Exasperation palls in long doses, as a substitute for character.

To K. W. Marshall   Bridlington, 27 January 1935
   I received an advance copy of Hanley's new book, and delayed writing to you until I had finished it. It's a big affair; not so proportioned and polished a work of art as the D.R. [Resurrexit Dominus] but of great power and achievement. He is certainly a man to reckon with. I begin to fear, however, that he is never going to carry me away. There is such conviction in him, but it is not conveyed. I think he lacks wisdom. Or is it detachment? There is something I wish the Gods had added to his eagerness.
   Will you tell Greenwood how exceedingly sorry I am for this entanglement at Bury?[65] It is intolerable that *any* Bench in the kingdom should be able to arrogate to itself the power of judgement. I cannot believe that an isolated action will necessitate, or justify, his withdrawing the book. I would offer to refuse all further orders of copies from Bury booksellers, and beg them not to hinder the rest of the world from enjoying what it finds good. I shall anxiously look to hear what happens.

To K. W. Marshall   Bridlington, 1 February 1935
   It is certainly awkward, and prolongs the uncertainty. On the other hand, at the Assizes you come before a professional Judge, with a possibility of cultivated judgement.
   I cannot advise, for my experience of English Courts, or Law, is nil. G. B. S. is an insecure guide, too, I should say; and besides Mrs. Shaw is desperately ill. She didn't like *Boy*, however.

My inclination would be to say 'This book was published in 1932 and has been continuously on sale, in England and the Colonies, ever since, passing through four editions. It was never challenged, or described as indecent, till last month at Bury, in Lancashire. Here is a book of all the reviews it has had, in the British Press. You will notice that no reviewer appears to have perceived any moral objection to the subject or the treatment, and I will confess that no such notion had occurred to myself, until the Bury Police action. I then examined the book again, and perceived that the challenged passages could be charged with an offensive significance, by a trained mind.'

'While the case has been sub judice I have suspended the further circulation of the book, but in justice to the author (who has written many novels of very high critical reputation) I am hoping that your decision will permit the edition again to be released. Naturally I am willing to do all in my power to prevent further copies being supplied to booksellers in the Bury neighbourhood.'

But in cold fact, you'll be in the hands of your counsel. I should go to Chatto & Windus and ask them for advice, pointing out that the case is likely to react on the future of *The Furys*—and they will probably tell you who is a likely lawyer to brief. . . .

It is very hard luck. If you can find out who at Bury initiated the prosecution, and send me his name and address, I will try and get him sent from Paris, by post, a regular supply of really indecent literature: something that will show him the difference between pornography and works of art.

To C. J. Greenwood   Clouds Hill, 5 April 1935

Now about your case. It seems to me monstrous. To say that every publisher is at the mercy of the discretion of any Police Chief, at any time—why, it makes publication almost an impossibility. This altogether apart from the personal question of penalties assessed upon your firm and yourselves. They seem wholly disproportionate to Boriswood, but would be a fleabite to Macmillan, for example. What evidence had the Judge as to your means?

It does not seem to me that the Authors' Society has much right of entry. Hanley has not been involved (and will not savour being dragged in!) and that rather cuts E. M. F. [Forster] out of it.[67] It would be a new thing for the body of authors to rush to the defence of a publisher: unless the body of publishers was also active in your defence and should call upon the body of authors to help. What chance is there of concerted protest by the governing body of Publishers? Not much, I gather. The big ones disregard the little ones.

I saw E. M. F. while the case was pending and talked to him about it. He is one of the few writers who might dare lead an attempt at help. Most of them are afraid of the word sodomy. I wonder why?

I thought it would be more effective if I tackled E. M. F. before rather than after judgement. A subtle mind, that one. You are seeing him, you say: he likes Hanley's work (but not *The Furys*) and will help, if he can. I do not know how much he weighs with the Authors' Society.

. . . your case is a dangerous one, an inroad on book-security. It ought to be the publishers' move, all the same. I wish Cape was not abroad. He can mobilise the young ones and compel the old stodgers to move. Without him there is no courage in their ranks: and many of them resent your rise.

To K. W. Marshall   Clouds Hill, 7 May 1935

I couldn't do just as you suggested: it is very dangerous to come between a carnivore and its prey. But I have made guarded enquiries. My friend knew nothing about the "drive": and after he had sniffed round to find out, he knew there was no drive, so far as his minions were concerned. Nor is there any connection between Bury and London. They regard Lancashire as rather foolish to have done what it did.

Apparently a gentleman named Inship [?] is the real nigger in the pile. He would like to do a good deal. Two of his colleagues have been talked to, and agree that he might thus lose them votes next time. They will try to make this generally believed amongst their friends: and if so the nigger will be reined in.

Don't expect any immediate effect from these hidden strings being pulled. As I say, it's dangerous to attempt to do anything direct. At the least hint of influence, all the underlings take their bits in their teeths, and go awkward; for they know that the would-be influencer is afraid and cannot hurt them afterwards. Eddie Marsh is the only man I know who has squared the Home Office for a friend and got away with it.

I hope Boriswood is unbowed and bloody, under these stresses. it is the right mixture. . . .

Commend me to Greenwood, and say that I'm sure my interventions have not harmed him: and hope they may help. But they were very indirectly done.

Thomas Hardy

To Robert Graves   London, 20 March 1923

I wanted to ask you . . . do you think old Hardy would let me look at him?[68] He's a proper poet & a fair novelist, in my judgment, &

it would give me a feeling of another mile-stone passed if I might meet him. Yet to blow in upon him in khaki would not be an introduction. You know the old thing, don't you? What are my hopes?

To Mrs. Thomas Hardy   Bovington, 25 March 1923
   A letter from Robert Graves (to whom I had written) tells me that I'm to get into communication with you. It feels rather barefaced, because I haven't any qualifications to justify my seeing Mr. Hardy: only I'd very much like to. *The Dynasts* & the other poems are so wholly good to my taste.

To Robert Graves   8 September 1923
Hardy is so pale, so quiet, so refined into an essence. . . . When I come back I feel as if I'd woken up from a sleep: not an exciting sleep, but a restful one. There is an unbelievable dignity and ripeness about Hardy: he is waiting so tranquilly for death, without a desire or ambition left in his spirit, as far as I can feel it: and yet he entertains so many illusions, and hopes for the world, things which I, in my disillusioned middle-age, feel to be illusory. They used to call this man a pessimist. While really he is full of fancy expectations.
   Then he is so far-away. Napoleon is a real man to him, and the country of Dorsetshire echoes that name everywhere in Hardy's ears. He lives in his period, and thinks of it as the great war; whereas to me that nightmare through the fringe of which I passed has dwarfed all memories of other wars, so that they seem trivial, half-amusing incidents.
   Also he is so assured. I said something a little reflecting on Homer: and he took me up at once, saying it was not to be despised: that it was very kin to *Marmion* [by Walter Scott, 1808]. . . . saying this not with a grimace, as I would say it, a feeling smart and original and modern, but with the most tolerant kindness in the world. Conceive a man to whom Homer and Scott are companions: who feels easy in such presences.
   And the standards of the man! He feels interest in everyone, and veneration for no-one. I've not found in him any bowing-down, moral or material or spiritual.
   . . . to him every person starts scratch in the life-race, and Hardy has no preferences: and I think no dislikes, except for the people who betray his confidence and publish him to the world.
   . . . It is strange to pass . . . from a barrack of hollow senseless bustle to the cheerful calm of T. H. thinking aloud about life to two or three of us. . . . The peace which passeth all understanding;—but it can be felt, and is nearly unbearable. How envious such an old age is.
   However, here is enough of trying to write about something which

is so precious that I grudge writing about it. T. H. is an experience
that a man must keep to himself.

To Mrs. Thomas Hardy   2 December 1923
What took away my mind, so that I could only stammer to you
in the hall, was the beauty & power of the verse [Hardy's *The Famous
Tragedy of the Queen of Cornwall*, performed at Dorchester]. The
phrases preserved their full force in that artless limpid speech of the
actors: and I've never heard finer English spoken. That's the profit
of the simple acting. . . . Your people had no technique, no arts
and graces, to put between their 'book' and us. It took my breath
away. . . . it is great [tragedy] & very greatly put. The 'O Jan' was
like a benediction after a very stormy sermon: a blessed piece of foolery
to give our poise back to us.

To Charlotte Shaw   30 August 1924
Hardy is artist enough to fall out of rhythm when he rages. The
climaxes of "Iseult" are nearly banal, in the plainness of their prose.
In great strained moments simple words are vehicle enough for the
weight & thrill of men's voices. Most of their sayings at such a time
are very plain . . . . . too plain for dignity when the event which
enriched them is become history.

To Edward Marsh   Clouds Hill, 12 April 1925
I waited till I'd seen old T. H. again (yesterday): to revive my
memories of what he said. The old man never gives judgements upon
live writers: so don't quote it. He would not talk to me if he thought
I made notes. . . .
He said '*The Fables* [La Fontaine's, translated by Marsh] . . . . . oh
yes . . . . . I thought they were excellent reading. Good.' Then he went
on to talk of the rat which found oysters upon the sea-shore, & thought
they were ships. . . . and then this old hen butted in: & when she had
stopped, & I asked again, he had forgotten that he had read the fables.
The truth is that a film seems to slip over his mind at times now: and
the present is then obscured by events of his childhood. He talked next
of seeing Scots Greys in a public house in Dorchester drinking strong
ale, whose fumes made him (aet. 6) drunken.

To Mrs. Thomas Hardy   Karachi, 15 January 1928
This is a Sunday, and an hour ago I was on my bed, listening to
Beethoven's last quartet: when one of the fellows came in and said
that T. H. is dead. We finished the quartet, because all at once it felt
like him. . . .
And now, when I should grieve, for him and for you, almost it feels

like a triumph.[69] That day we reached Damascus, I cried, against all
my control, for the triumphant thing achieved at last, fitly: and so
the passing of T. H. touches me. He had finished and was so full a
man. Each time I left Max Gate, having seen that, I used to blame
myself for intruding upon a presence which had done with things like
me and mine. I would half-determine not to trouble his peace again.

. . . T. H. was infinitely bigger than the man who died three
days back—and you were one of the architects. In the years since
The Dynasts the Hardy of stress has faded, and T. H. took his
unchallenged—unchallengeable—place. Though as once I told you,
after a year of adulation the pack will run over where he stood, crying
'There is no T. H. and never was'. A generation will pass before the
sky will be perfectly clear of clouds for his shining. However, what's
a generation to a sun? He is secure. How little that word meant to him.

This is not the letter I'd like to write. You saw, though, how I looked
on him, and guessed, perhaps, how I'd have tried to think of him,
if my thinking had had the compass to contain his image.

To Sydney Cockerell   [Karachi], 2 February 1928
For T. H. none of us can have great regrets. His life was a triumph,
just because it was prolonged for that last, unexpected, twenty years.
It must be restfuller, too, to be certainly dead, than to be precariously
alive.

To Mrs. Thomas Hardy   [Karachi], 16 February 1928
. . . I've been reading *The Dynasts*, and I can feel that there is a
very great thing gone from my reach. T. H. was the most honourable
stopping place I've ever found, and I shall miss him more and more.

To Sydney Cockerell   [Karachi], 22 March 1928
Somebody said there was another volume of T. H. poetry to appear;
yet the old man told me once that he thought everything worth while
had been printed. I wonder if there was stuff he kept back for any
reason except that of insufficient goodness. However you are safe to
destroy anything of his which does not come up to your standard and
his.[70] He was so generously large a poet that his individual lines are
of small value.

To William Rothenstein   [Karachi], 14 April 1928
Yes, I was a sudden loser when Hardy went. Not that I could be
a friend of his: the difference in size and age and performance between
us was too overwhelming: but because I'd seen a good deal of him,
& he was so by himself, so characteristic a man, that each contact

with him was an experience. I went each time, nervously: and came away gladly, saying "It's all right". . . .

I regret Hardy's funeral service. Mrs Shaw sent me a copy.[71] So little of it suited the old man's nature. He would have smiled, tolerantly, at it all: but I grow indignant for him, knowing that these sleek Deans and Canons were acting a lie behind his name. Hardy was too great to be suffered as an enemy of their faith: so he must be redeemed. . . .

I wish these black-suited apes could once see the light with which they shine.

To Mrs. Thomas Hardy   [Karachi], 16 April 1928
. . . you say you have failed him at every turn. Of course you did: everybody did. He was T. H. and if you'd met him or sufficed him at every turn you'd have been as good as T. H. which is absurd: though perhaps some people might think it should be put happier than that. But you know my feeling (worth something perhaps, because I've met so many thousands of what are estimated great men) that T. H. was above and beyond all men living, as a person. I used to go to Max Gate afraid, & half-unwillingly, for fear that perhaps it would no longer seem true to me: but always it was. Ordinary people like us can't hope (mustn't presume to hope) that we could ever have been enough for T. H. . . .

The biography is a very difficult thing. . . . What he told you, on November 28, that he'd done all he meant to do, absolves you from infinite toil.[72] He will defend himself, very very completely, when people listen to him again. As you know, there will be a wave of detraction, and none of the highbrows will defend him, for quite a long time: and then the bright young critics will rediscover him, & it will be lawful for a person in the know to speak well of him: and all this nonsense will enrage me, because I'm small enough to care. Whereas all that's needful is to forget the fuss for fifty years, and then wake up and see him no longer a battle-field, but part of the ordinary man's heritage.

To Charlotte Shaw   [Plymouth], 5 December 1930
Cakes & Ale, that Somerset Maugham,[73] made my flesh creep: It was wrong to do that. Those who did not know him will see Hardy there.

To Mrs. Thomas Hardy   Clouds Hill, 22 April 1935
The *Indiscretion* [Hardy's *An Indiscretion in the Life of an Heiress*][74] proved charming. I like the appealing simplicity of the prose . . . . . like, and yet a very poor relation of, the sweeping sentences that make

up *Jude*. I understand why he kept it unprinted, yet it is not a thing
to be ashamed of. If only T. H. had found time and will to follow
up *Jude* with yet one more work, it would have linked his prose, in
power, with his poetry.

You have made a beautiful little book of it. I have enjoyed the
reading, and enjoy the possession.

Homer

To Ralph Isham   Karachi, 2 January 1928
When your letter came I took the *Odyssey* down from the shelf (it
goes with me, always, to every camp, for I love it), and tried to see
myself translating it, freely, into English. Honestly, it would be most
difficult to do. I have the rhythm of the Greek so in my mind that
it would not come readily into straight English. Nor am I a scholar;
I read it only for pleasure, and have to keep a dictionary within reach.
I thought of the other translators, and agreed that there was not a
first-rate one. Butcher & Lang—too antique. Samuel Butler—too little
dignified, tho' better. Morris—too literary. That only shows the job
it is. Why should my doing be any better than these efforts of the
bigger men?

To Bruce Rogers   Karachi, 16 April 1928
Something about this *Odyssey* effort frightens me. It's too big: Homer
is very very great: and so far away. It seems only a sort of game, to
try and bring him down to the ordinary speech of my mouth. Yet that
is what a translation ought to mean. I do it, tacitly, every time I read
him: but that is for my own belly. Isn't there a presumption in putting
my version abroad?

To Charlotte Shaw   [Miranshah], 25 June 1928
. . . that poor fish Telemachus, and his horrible mother. A woman
wrote it, did she?[75] Well, she wanted kicking, that's all. Really, I
think better of women. There's precious little poetry, too, in book
I: only four lines, about old Laertes. The rest is a novel in metre. A
good but queer novel, very much improved by its age. Not primitive
at all: archaistic, rather than primitive. More like Morris than like
Beowulf, I mean.

To Bruce Rogers   Miranshah, 30 June 1928
He is baffling. Not simple, in education; not primitive, socially. Rather
a William Morris of his day, I fancy.

There's a queer naivety in every other line: and at our remove of thought and language we can't say if he is smiling or not. . . . Homer compels respect. I confess he has me beaten to my knees. . . . The work has been very difficult. . .

To E. M. Forster   [Miranshah], 30 October 1928
. . . I wish Homer had not been quite so matter of fact, in his first few books. As bad as an opening by Walter Scott.

To Charlotte Shaw   [Miranshah], 11 December 1928
The original Odyssey is, as I see it, a clever historical reconstruction and essay in the (then extinct) epic mode. I feel that the book is written with immense art, and an entire lack of simplicity. Therefore I feel that Butler is too good for it. He makes it real, whereas it is artificial.

To E. M. Forster   Miranshah, 12 December 1928
    I think the *Odyssey* is mock-heroic: a sort of Selfridge-Epic: more like *Sigurd the Volsung* [by William Morris, 1876] than *Marmion*. It's awfully well written: clever as seven devils: and very hard to put into clear English. It's Wardour Street, itself, in Greek & all rings false. But gorgeous. I wish I had written the *Odyssey* & not *The Seven Pillars*.

To Emery Walker   Miranshah, 25 December 1928
    The Odyssey is very difficult. It is clever, in the real sense, which held no derogatory meaning. A very skilful *literary* performance, not simple, not primitive: very, very artful and artificial. It's full of tags out of the Iliad, but is not epic at all. It's a narrative, and all its persons have character. That in itself would save it from epic, for the persons of an epic should be on the stupid scale and the grandeur of it come from a relentless march of events.
    Nor is there much poetry about the story, so far as it has gone. The author writes in metre, as that was the consecrated form of the early novel, or chanson de geste. He was a poet—oh yes, a great poet, I fancy: but this was a story he was telling.
    He was also an antiquarian and filled in his background with lots of quaint furniture, to give it the antique feel. Quite Wardour Street, as I said before, with the modern bones showing through the fancy fleshings.
    His naivety is sham, too: he laughs in his sleeve at his puppets. Line after line is ironical, as if he wasn't sure if it should be Sir Topas or not. Perhaps the first part of Don Quixote is a nearer parallel. I said "Sigurd" before: only Morris was more of a man than this writer: and Morris didn't snigger, as the Odyssey does. Also Sigurd sings. Orlando giocondo, perhaps.
    I think my version is richer, on the whole, than the original: as

Samuel Butler's version is balder. Butler was the realist, telling a tale. Thereby I think he did the Odyssey too much honour. The author was picking flowers, on the way, also.

He or she? Honestly I don't care. No great sexualist, either way: no great lover of mankind. Could have been written by a snipped great ape. A marvellous crafty tale, mixed just to the right point with all the ingredients which would mix in. The translators aren't catholic, like their master. Each of us leans towards his private fancy.

To Bruce Rogers   30 July 1929
The feminine authorship is a possibility: either an unsexed woman or an unsexed man. My feelings are for the second, as I can't see a woman drawing Penelope so meanly.

To Charlotte Shaw   4 December 1929
He (or she) [Homer] does describe every cup of wine, every man, every wave, of the world. Intolerably slow, and yet so delicate, so subtle, so sophisticated, so civilised. Hoots:

To Charlotte Shaw   Plymouth, 19 January 1930
I have been Homering all morning and afternoon, and must not delay for long...: first of all thanks for reading that XIth Book.[76] I am afraid it is very difficult. I have been over it three or four times since it came back, and have managed about 100 minor alterations. That is for the good. I changed, so far as I could, all the places you had marked. It is very difficult.

What you say about it is about what I feel: a sense of effort, of hard work: of course there must be this. I never wrote (for printing) an easy line in my life. All my stuff is tenth-thoughts or twentieth-thoughts, before it gets out. Nice phrases in letters to you? Perhaps: only the difference between nice phrases in a letter (where one nice phrase will carry the thing) and an *Odyssey* where one phrase not-nice will spoil it all, is too great to carry a comparison.

To E. M. Forster   Plymouth, 23 January 1930
    The Odyssey disappoints me. It is not really good stuff. How does it go on being praised?

To Bruce Rogers   29 January 1930
The underworld is the only place, if there, where the Odyssey becomes great. Everywhere it seems to prefer grace and smoothness and subtlety and skill to largeness. The Italian word 'terribilita':—that is the main lack of this particular Homer: whereas the owner of the Iliad had it almost in excess.

To Henry Williamson   3 May 1930

These *Odyssey* pages aren't sent for criticism: but to show you that no one can help in them. Translations aren't books, for in them there is no inevitable word: the whole is approximation, a feeling towards what the author would have said: and as Homer wasn't like me the version goes wrong whenever I let myself into it. Consequently the thing is a pot-boiler only, a second-best . . . .

The work is not meant to interest you: the Homer who wrote the *Odyssey* was an antiquarian, a tame-cat, a book-worm: not a great poet, but a most charming novelist. A Thornton Wilder of his time. My version, and every version, is inevitably small.

To L. M. P. Black   [Plymouth?], 25 November 1930

. . .I am so tired of the smug Odysseus and his priggish son and sly wife. A horrible family. Don't get to know them well!

To Edward Garnett   5 December 1930

I am tired of all Homer's namby-pamby men and women.

To Bruce Rogers   3 January 1931

You may have thought me cavalier in preferring my own way to W.'s[77] professional suggestions, sometimes: not his verbal suggestions, but his archaeology. Yet, actually, I'm in as strong a position vis-à-vis Homer as most of his translators. For years we were digging up a city of roughly the Odysseus period. I have handled the weapons, armour, utensils of those times, explored their homes, planned their cities. I have hunted wild boars and watched wild lions, sailed the Aegean (and sailed ships) bent bows, lived with pastoral peoples, woven textiles, built boats and killed many men. So I have odd knowledges that qualify me to understand the *Odyssey*, and odd experiences that interpret it to me. Therefore a certain headiness in rejecting help.

To Bruce Rogers   Plymouth, 20 August 1931

When I read Book XXI on its coming from you, I felt it had movement, and suspense: it was like a prelude to catastrophe: and XXII has done its best to be grim and bloody: or at least to be grimmer and bloodier than Homer. In parts the Greek is poor melodrama, and stinks of unreality: and I am hoping that you (and others) may find my version more credible, as tragedy.

Just before my leave ended I finished off XXIII and XXIV and sent them to London last Saturday. They have been confronting me in the rough, as you know, for months: and are very difficult books. After the slaughter of XXII some quiet finish was artistically necessary: and there were all manner of loose strings flapping from the poem. So Homer (*Odyssey*-Homer, should we say?) started out to tidy everything; and hopelessly lost his way. These 'little' artists, to use little as a term of sheltering affection, find a theme so hard to end. His last movement drools on and on like one of Schubert's everybody (author included) dying to end it, but mellifluously unable.

I've been wrestling with it intermittently for all these months, trying to get shape into it, in my mind: for if I could have seen it in one piece, then shape would have somehow marvellously appeared. And it did improve: though it will remain a failure, always. You can help, in XXIV, by leaving a space where the author's cunning deserted him or he tried his skill too high. At any rate he failed to darn over his gaps and transitions.

Mind you, these books are authentic stuff. It will not do, as they said in Alexandria, to end the *Odyssey* where he and Penelope get into bed. This is not a comic opera: but I fancy that poor *O*-Homer threw his hand in at the end, rather as I did, after trying very hard. He has lavished on these two books some of his loveliest intimacies—only the need was for one or two big things, and he couldn't write big.

Eurycleia stumbling upstairs; the entry of Penelope upon Odysseus; her comment upon his death-story; the funeral of Achilles, where Thetis comes; Agamemnon's praise of the Odyssey; Laertes in his garden; the babbling childhood of Odysseus amid the trees; the welcome of Dolius; the wrangle upon valour between O., Telemachus and Laertes—all these are in the best manner, perfect touches which only imperfectly conceal the need for good construction. It is most true and genuine *O*-Homer. Even another comic lion, another shipwreck, and more birds arrive, worked in unhandily to cover climaxes he couldn't deal with, straightly.

So when you are disappointed with these two books, blame *O*-Homer as well as me. I have worked on them till I went blind and stupid.

To Sir William Rothenstein   Southampton, 22 April 1932

Homer? A pot boiler, long ago done with. When, or if, it will be published is not my concern. The Greek isn't very good, I fancy: and my version is frankly poor. Thin, arty, self-conscious stuff, the Odyssey. I believe the Iliad to be a great poem—or to have fragments of a great poem embedded in it, rather. But the Odyssey is pastiche & face powder.

To Sir William Rothenstein   Plymouth, 20 October 1932

About the Odyssey. I fully agree with you. My version is fustian: but so is Homer, I think. The more I dwelt on the Greek and struggled with it and its story, the more possessed I became with the view that here was something too artfull for decency. It tried by surpassing pains and skill to simulate the rule-leaping flood of authentic greatness. All the talent in the world never approaches genius: the two things are incompatible. The Odyssey is a creeping work. Its author was Maurice-something, Baring + Hewlett + William [Morris]—. He was out to construct an epic, on the Iliad's model: and it all smells forced. The style is booky, too.

So it is hopeless to make a pawky novel of it, as Samuel Butler did. It isn't. A great man could make a great poem or a great novel out of its material (how much better [Morris's] Sigurd is than the Siegfried legends in Norse or German) but a translator can only expose the fraud. I am a translator, definitely, in my version: and you can see through it, I hope, easily: as a mawkish fraud....

What's really wrong with the Odyssey is Homer.

To Mrs. Thomas Hardy   Plymouth, 3 December 1932
It [the *Odyssey*] is not in any way a remarkable work. As translation it is faithful, within the limits I lay down in a little postscript to the book. The English is very schoolmastery—by which I mean that relative clauses, prepositions and particles are correctly placed. There is too much inversion—twisting of sentences to compress the English into little more space than the much more concise Greek. There are some colloquialisms: no slang, I hope; if we call slang those colloquialisms which not everybody yet understands and uses.

. . . Everybody dislikes his last book, of course: but this is only a pot-boiler, and little intensity went to it. I did it as well as I could, of course, but did not feel like signing it.

To Harley Granville-Barker   Plymouth, 23 December 1932
Don't read the *Odyssey* aloud to Mrs. G. B., please. She would die of it, and both of us suffer a sense of loss, as Homer would say. It must have been nice to live in a literary period when even a platitude was a discovery, and clichés were waiting to be made. He was very successful in both these ways, I think.

To Henry Williamson   Plymouth, 13 February 1933
I thought old Homer duplicated too often. Tricks in books feel sharper than in real life.

To H. G. Andrews   6 March 1935
The Iliad is a poem and as untranslatable as Paradise Lost. No great poem has ever been translated—yet. The poor little Odyssey is a mere novel, and need not lose...in the process.

W. H. Hudson

To Edward Garnett   Bovington, 4 October 1923
  The Hudsons are sumptuous. How well the old man reads in them.
The *Shepherd* [*A Shepherd's Life*, 1910] has found two friendly readers
already: yet I like better, much better, the memories of his childhood
[*Far Away and Long Ago*, 1918].
  Wonderful that one man should have written that, and [*Idle Days
in*] *Patagonia* [1893], and *The Purple Land* [1885], and *Green Mansions*
[1904]: and I go about thinking that into his first book anyone not
a born writer can put all that his spirit holds.
  Hudson is hardly a born writer, either. Not for him that frenzied
aching delight in a pattern of words which happen to run true.

To Edward Garnett   Clouds Hill, 3 December 1923
  The Hudson letters. I determined not to write to you till I had ended
them: & that was last night. They are very Hudson & you know how
high that is. The reading them has been a pure pleasure. He was a
splendid critic.....and his mind seems as limpid as his prose.
  Probably it will not be a very popular book.....but the loss if it
didn't exist would be very real. There is more of Hudson in those easy
letters than in all other of his work—the old Hudson, I mean, for
the young man in his exuberance is preserved for ever in the Purple
Land.
  I've been reading the Purple Land, & the Far Away & liking them
just as hotly as ever: and the Wiltshire book [*A Shepherd's Life*] is
so true & good & wholesome.

James Joyce

To Winifred Fontana   [December 1920?][78]
How it [Joyce's *Portrait of the Artist as a Young Man*] savours of
a rather dull and sunless entourage in which the young man's soul
cannot find the colour it gropes after. Evidently he had not taken up
Greek or he would have been happier, and he would have known where
to go when he finally broke aimlessly away. Like Irish genius, the book
ends unachieved, but anyhow it is very far above the ordinary even
thoughtful work.

To Robert Graves   London, 9 January 1921
  Have you read any Joyce? Portrait of Artist
                         Dubliners
                         Exiles
                         Poems

They should be in All Souls, if not borrowed from me. He's the yet-unfollowed master of what will be the next school.

To Sydney Cockerell   Cranwell, 29 December 1925
Yet people have the nerve to tell me it's [*Seven Pillars*] a good book! It would have been, if written a hundred years ago: but to bring it out after *Ulysses* is an insult to modern letters. . .

To Charlotte Shaw   4 January 1926
It [*Dubliners*] shows more mastery than the Portrait of an Artist, or Ulysses: for the pieces are short, & Joyce's lack of the constructive (architectonic) sense can't become glaring. Of course Joyce's mind has a leer in it. . . . Joyce being not a great writer, has got more complicated, more stylised, as he gets older.

To Eric Kennington   Karachi, 25 March 1927
Years ago I lent him [Frank Dobson] a copy of Ulysses, by James Joyce. This is a book hard to get. I'd like to re-read it. . . . would you recover it, wrap it up, & send it me *book-post*? . . . . Ulysses is a compendium of literary technique, which every man concerned in books should study occasionally. . . . Bennett (Arnold) said that Ulysses reduced novel reading to penal servitude.

To Eric Kennington   Karachi, 19 May 1927
    Somebody, Celandine [Mrs. Kennington] probably, sent me the *Ulysses* I craved for. These long dreary slow-marching books are invaluable friends in Drigh Road.

To Charlotte Shaw   Karachi, 19 May 1927
. . . I settled down to another fillet of Ulysses. Mrs. Kennington sent me out my copy of Joyce's book, & I'm ploughing section by section, through its repulsive dullness. The technical skill of that first chapter is as dazzling as anything I've ever met: & the later ones fall right away. You don't "feel" in them: you are conscious all the while of the effort and virtuosity of the author; and his straining muscles are so palpable that you have no admiration to spare for the puppets.

To Eric Kennington   Karachi, 16 June 1927
    Many thanks for *Ulysses*. It is even worse to read than I had hoped. Months: and such dull stuff. Joyce is a genius, but an unlucky one. His writing has the architectural merit of Balham. It goes on for ever, and needn't ever vary in spirit.

To Charlotte Shaw   Karachi, 30 June 1927
    Joyce in "transition" rather stumps me. Is life long enough to spend

in learning new languages, when English is not worn out? No. I won't
be bothered with him.

To Robert Graves   [Karachi], 26 January 1928
   No, please don't send Transition.[79] If Joyce's new book is in
English I shall read it gratefully. But I don't want to read any foreign
stuff, just now. Too hard work.

To Charlotte Shaw   [Miranshah], 15 August 1928
Joyce's Ulysses is the text-book, the Bible or Polite letter-writer of
the age. It shows how to write in every mode, and often, too, how
not to write. It shows every possible style, and eighty four imposible
styles. As prose it is superb. As character it is null. That opening chapter
of early morning in the Dublin Martello Tower is as fine a piece of
writing as the English language contains. The rest of the book is an
uncommercial traveller's sample-case.

To W. M. M. Hurley   Plymouth, 1 April 1929
   I enclose you some sample pages of Joyce's latest (not yet ready
for publication in book-form) and remarks by A.E. on Joyce and his
poetry. There is this colony of dispossessed English and American and
Irish writers living rather intensely in one another's cheap lodgings
in Paris and writing desperately hard. I fancy, for myself, that they
are rather out of touch with reality; by reality I mean shops like
Selfridges, and motor busses, and the *Daily Express*. At least there
is a hot-house flavour about their work, which makes me wonder if
it's a wholesome day-to-day food. Remarkable, certainly, but a bit
funny. However people who do not practise writing aren't really
qualified to judge of it.

To H. S. Ede   Plymouth, 2 January 1930
   Those 'poems' of Joyce's are queerly good. He want to write 'em
as sentimental cough-droppy things, (like chamber music) and is afraid
of the public and his reputation. So he wraps 'em up in a smile, as
if they were not quite meant. They are, however, one of the realities
of Joyce.

To E. M. Forster   8 February 1930
Joyce has passed rather beyond my ken now. Not necessary, I feel,
that urge to renew English. The language is more flexible, stronger,
fresher than ever, in people's *mouths*. Only poor Joyce lives abroad,
& doesn't talk to cabmen.

To Jacob Schwartz   Southampton, 26 April 1932
Joyce, too, is very learned, they say*....
*I've added "they say" for I found the learning of Ulysses rather
a pretence.[80] "A genbite of inwit"—that sort of silly cleverness,
marring a great effort.

Rudyard Kipling

To F. N. Doubleday   [Miranshah], 16 October 1928
The pirate Kipling is too convenient to be missed. I am adding it
to my Library: that is a very select body of books: very select indeed.
It is full of misprints: but easy to read. Indeed, I've read it all. That
is a hard test for Kipling: he comes through it: not without damage,
but certainly an immortal. The "Light that Failed" and the "City of
Dreadful Night", the prose account of Calcutta, held me more than
the more skilled short stories. I see now that his India isn't very deep:
and that his natives are not individualised, & his scenery only very
limited. "Properties" you might call them. What remains to him
is a swiftness of phrase, a perfection of style which gets there
marvellously, in the most finished way, and knocks you all of a heap.
An incredible fencer-in-words.
The collected volume of his poetry is being read, cover to cover.
Why? For the same reason: to try & surfeit myself. Vain hope. The
man is too great to be cured of.

D. H. Lawrence

To Charlotte Shaw   Edinburgh, 22 August 1926
... there is a very great but very strange man writing book after book
as D. H. L. I can smell the genius in him: excess of genius makes his
last book [*The Plumed Serpent*] sickening: and perhaps some day the
genius will burst through the darkness of his prose and take the world
by the throat. He is very violent, is D. H. L.: violent and dark, with
a darkness which only grows deeper as he writes on. The revelation
of his greatness, if it comes, will be because the public grow able to
see through his dark thinking.....because the public begin to be dark-
thoughted themselves. D. H. L. can't make himself clear: he can't
use the idiom of you and me. So often you find men like that, and
sometimes the world grows up to them and salutes them as 'kings-
before-their-time'.....and sometimes nobody ever bothers about
them at all, afterwards.

To William Rothenstein   Karachi, 8 December 1927
Then he [Wyndham Lewis] goes for D. H. Lawrence, who's [*sic*] boots
he is not big enough to wear. He does not seem to have read much
Lawrence, so far as I can see. He criticises only some pages of his
little Mornings in Mexico, which are just the snapshots of a literary
artist, in the slack time while waiting for a subject—the same way
as a barber snips his empty scissors all the time he is moving the comb,
and preparing a new grip on an uncut lock of hair. Just the maintenance
of a vital rhythm. I'd like, immensely, to see W. Lewis tackling such
a thing as D. H. L.'s Plumed Serpent, an immense and significant
book.

To his mother   Karachi, 4 January 1928
    Italy, you have chosen: and Rome, of all places in Italy. Now I could
have understood some little village in the hills. Did you ever read
D. H. Lawrence's marvellous novel *The Lost Girl* [1920]. . . . . with
its pictures of country life, very high up, in Italy? One of the most
beautiful of modern stories, told by a master of English prose. You
can get a 3/6 edition of it, published by Martin Secker. In such a house
as that you might be quiet.

To David Garnett   [Karachi], 16 February 1928
    We seem to differ about. . .D. H. L. I call the form of *The Plumed
Serpent* very shapely and satisfying: and the architecture of most of
his novels excellent. Of course his prose stammers often. Somebody
said he was trying to make the solar plexus talk plain English.[81]

To Charlotte Shaw   [Karachi], 23 July 1928
The story "Glad ghosts" in that [D. H. Lawrence's *The Woman Who
Rode Away*] stunned me. Such unexpected common sense and logic,
for him; and power enough for six men. Amazing.

To Charlotte Shaw   [Miranshah], 11 September 1928
D. H. L. is obviously a strange being, & must have dark corners: but
he has kept them to himself for 20 books, and the idea of a terrible
21st. leaves me cold.

To Charlotte Shaw   [Miranshah], 18 September 1928
D. H. L. You say he is dying of consumption. Sorry for that. But
he has written 20 novels. A rather febrile creature, always losing control
of his pen. I was upset once, when he wrote a memoir of a poor little
rat, called Maurice Magnus, & prefaced it to Magnus' Memoirs of
the Foreign Legion. It was a marvellous character-study. . . . but

Magnus was ground-game: and D. H. L. showed meanness in chasing him beyond the grave. Yet I doubt the...tale of his "beastly" novel. I do not think D. H. L. would actually unbridle himself in public.

To Edward Garnett   London, 28 February 1929
Lady Chatterley is not very good, I think. Part of the power of D. H. L. may have come from the effort to say something, by implication, which the law would not let him say directly.

To Edward Garnett   Plymouth, 14 March 1929
I could not deliver *Lady Chatterley* to you, though I tried twice: and I didn't post it, not feeling sure of the little mountebank.[81] You may be evil-seen by him.
So eventually I dumped it on Garnett III [David Garnett], who has promised to return it you. I liked spots of it: but the whole hadn't very much meaning for me. Of course it is outside my particular experience—thank the Lord.

To Edward Marsh   Plymouth, 18 April 1929
Yours wasn't a letter but something very magnificent: *Lady Chatterley*.[83] I'm re-reading it with a slow deliberate carelessness: going to fancy that I've never read a D. H. L. before, and that it's up to me to appraise this new man and manner. D. H. L. has always been so rich and ripe a writer to me, before, that I'm deeply puzzled and hurt by this *Lady Chatterley* of his. Surely the sex business isn't worth all this damned fuss? I've met only a handful of people who really cared a biscuit for it.

To Edward Marsh   3 June 1929
I've re-read Lady Chatterley: three times that is. Poor D. H. I'm dreadfully sorry for a man who's gone right through life and found that it means no more than that at the end.

To Henry Williamson?   [Plymouth?], 25 March 1930[84]
What D. H. Lawrence means by *Lady Chatterley's Lover* is that the idea of sex, & the whole strong vital instinct, being considered indecent causes men to lose what might be their vital strength and pride of life—their integrity. Conversely, the idea of 'genitals being beauty' in the Blakian sense would free humanity from its lowering and disintegrating immorality of deed and thought.
Lawrence wilted & was made writhen by the 'miners-chapel-dirty little boy, you' environment: he was ruined by it: and in most of his work he is striving to straighten himself, and to become beautiful.

Ironically, or paradoxically, in a humanity where 'genitals are beauty' there would be a minimum of 'sex' and a maximum of beauty, or Art. This is what Lawrence means, surely.

To Charlotte Shaw   Plymouth, 4 April 1930
   The Rainbow [1915] I read years & years ago: during the war. It wasn't anything much, I fancy, but I have forgotten most of it. Of course, D. H. got all his values wrong. We all do, probably: but for me his values are hopeless, and his world utterly remote from mine. That's the great thing about a [sic] artist: by his means you can (dimly perhaps) apprehend other worlds & values. One's own worlds & values are the theme of all ordinary books. . . . The rarer a man's world the more he is worth while, to us.

To Charlotte Shaw   Plymouth, 6 August 1930
There was a great core of instinct and strength under that fretful impatient surface. I do not think he was a thinker: and his life was, in its way, superficial. Only he wrote with power and was sincere and did his very best. That would make a nice epitaph for a writer who had not wholly succeeded, would it not? And D. H. L. for all his gifts, failed somewhat.

To Charlotte Shaw   [Plymouth?], 24 October 1930
   "The Virgin and the Gipsy" is very good. D. H. L. never revised it, and so the stuttering paragraphs in which he tried to emphasise the uncommunicable are absent from it. I have a fancy that he wrote simply and D H Lled it afterwards. As I fancy that Doughty thought in English & then twisted his words after they were cold. I may be wrong. This story is poignantly strong and lively. So unlike "Lady Chatterley".

To Edward Garnett   Plymouth, 12 October 1932
. . . I am going through D. H. L's Letters. The first 100 pages (my progress so far) are mostly to you. Good letters.

To K. W. Marshall   Plymouth, 20 October 1932
. . . read the D. H. Lawrence letters. Gosh, what an ungenerous soul. It's all very well to put instinct above intelligence. . . . . but see to what weathercockery it leads.

To Frank V. Morley   Plymouth, 21 October 1932
Did you try the D. H. L. letters. It must be rare to find 800 pages without one sentence of generosity: but it is interesting to find that

the deliberate rejection of the intellect makes the rejector like a centre-board boat that refuses to let the board down, in cross winds. How he wobbles.

To F. N. Doubleday   Plymouth, 2 December 1932
Frere-Reeves gave me the D. H. Lawrence *Letters*. I read them all, in daily doses extending over a fortnight. A sad reading, rather because D. H. wrote some lovely novels, and all of them came to me as they appeared, and I had a regard for the silly angry creature. And his letters lack generosity so sadly: couldn't he have said one decent thing about some other man of his profession? Also he was too much on the make. However, I should have been very sorry not to have seen and read those letters.

To John Brophy   Plymouth, 7 February 1933
    Books? . . . . The letters & last poems of D. H. L. (Letters revealing & lowering; poems very fine: uncommonly fine, with bad spots. What a poor character and big writer!)

To C. J. Greenwood   Southampton, 16 April 1934
D. H. L. threw away his reason—but it harmed him. It is all very well *feeling* hard and quick and hot—but feeling cannot be put on paper convincingly except to the already converted (and who wants to talk to his disciples) without brain and logic and argument to back it up.

Wyndham Lewis

To Wyndham Lewis   Clouds Hill, 11 May 1924
    Mr. Zagreus[85] is a very knuckly part of the leg of mutton which your new book must be. Huitzopochli & Quetzacoatl!!!!! and all the other symbols of man's thought in all the ages & places. Help! Joyce seemed recondite. I found fault with Eliot for being so subtle. Do you intend to be both subtle + abstruse, and universal? Have some pity on us. Not so long ago novels were written for our diversion on a railway journey.
    Which scream mustn't drown the truth that I liked not merely the inventions, but the manner of them. Throughout the extract I dropped on even single words which gave me a shock of pleasure, for their fitness*. At the same time the man who could judge of the forthcoming book from this extract of it would be either very discerning or very

brazen-sure of himself. As an amateur I'm left hoping (gasping too)
for more.
  *malicious diffidence
   thrilling charm
   croupier-like
   sultry covetousness
   and all the picture of the candle-flame[86]

To Charlotte Shaw   [Karachi], 4 May 1927
   Lewis is a queer soft-voiced, unhealthy-looking, podgy white-handed
white-faced man, who lives with his windows shut in stuffy rooms,
& is vain, & much courted. Glasses, long-hair, effeminate. Yet he wrote
Tarr: and the Caliph's heritage [*The Caliph's Design*], & the Art of
Being Ruled: and dominated artistic theory for two years. How? I
can't tell you. Somewhere behind that cushioned exterior must be a
core of mind and character. Yet he poses so. I give him up. He owes
me £50![87]

To William Rothenstein   Karachi, 12 May 1927
   Hot foot by the next mail appeared the Enemy! Wyndham Lewis
has done it very well: much better than the Lion into Fox,[88] which
was a falling short after the Art of Being Ruled. I thought D. B. W-L
[Dominic Bevan Wyndham Lewis] rather small game for him to gun
at. D. B. will be forgotten five years hence: and he can't help his name:
indeed if I was him I'd go for W-L, and curse him for being an
uncousinly disgrace![89]
   But on people like Pound, & Gertrude Stein, & Joyce he's extraordinarily interesting. I wish he would let himself go properly over
the whole area of modern letters, & tell us where he places D. H.
Lawrence, & Forster, & Graves & Sassoon and all the rest of the people
who write. There is so much being written, & so few guides to help
occasional visitors to books through the masses of them.
   However perhaps he will carry it on. If the Enemy is successful it
may encourage him to branch out into criticism. I take it his creative
side, which produced Tarr so long ago, has dropped off withered.
   It was very good of you to send it out. Don't you think the cover-
design, the Tartar horseman, very beautiful?

To Charlotte Shaw   [Karachi], 26 May 1927
"Tarr", his novel, meant a great deal when it came out, years &
years ago. The "Caliph's heritage" was good criticism. Some of his
magazines had good writing in them, and his "Art of being ruled"
was strange and individual and acute: though the man's judgement

does not impress me. He locks himself away, & is seen only by precious men and women. So he has a "London" mind, like T. S. Eliot and the Sitwells: and London isn't as good for matter as it is for manner.

To William Rothenstein   Karachi, 8 December 1927
   Many thanks for the second Enemy. He digresses too much, in it; so that there is almost no main argument. If he would send his ideas one by one to the weekly press as they occur to him—then what a critic he would be. The background of a general idea, some vague bogey of a time-spirit, would then give depth and strength to his writing. . . .
   Yet Lewis is a first rate brain, and a very good artist, surely? His drawings impress me with their power. They are really fine, I fancy. Isn't it odd to like all that a man does, and to dislike, almost vehemently, all that he likes? Or is that a natural consequence of living in his generation.

To Robert Graves   Karachi, 24 December 1927
   I have been trying to keep up with Wyndham Lewis in his philosophy, and his "Enemy" and in his stories; and must confess that I cannot see where he wants everybody to go. Behind so many words there must be something to say. . . . but he cannot convey it to me. If he wants to change the spirit of the age? but that is done by invention, not by criticism . . . . . give it up.

To Robert Graves   8 November 1930
[Wyndham Lewis] did not write.[90] His conscience is still alive, I suppose. It must be giving him a time, too. Nothing less dignified than his antics over this new book of his can be imagined. He puffs it brazenly, poor worm. I am not going to read him any more.

To William Rothenstein   Plymouth, 20 October 1932
Lewis is a challenging mind: but it is an unhinged mind. He jazzles me.

Frederic Manning

To E. M. Forster   Karachi, 8 September 1927
Your portrait-purchase I find very subtle of you. Now Frederic Manning always spells it 'subtile'. Do you like F. M.? *Scenes & Portraits* [1909] is all of him I know: though also he wrote a life of Sir Wm. White [*The Life of Sir William White*, 1923]: and a picture of life seen through the eye of an organ-grinder's ape.[91] *Scenes & Portraits* was good. That first picture of the court of the king of Uruk,

& of Adam & Eve in the watermelon field, sticks in my very inaccurate memory. Also the picture of Machiavelli: and the long sermon which Paul preached.

To Charlotte Shaw   6 February 1930
[I] finished on Saturday at noon, just in time to see [J. G.] Wilson in the [Bumpus book] shop before it shut. I said to him 'who wrote *Her Privates We* [by "Private 19022," published Janaury 1930]— (that being a superb lovable book, what *The Mint* ought to have been)—for I know his touch?'. He said 'I think it begins with M. . . . .' and rang up Peter Davies [the publisher]. That let a flood of light in: So to P. D. I said 'You haven't heard of me, my name is Shaw: but perhaps you've read a thing called *Revolt in the Desert* which I published as Lawrence. Did the author of *Scenes & Portraits* write *He Privates We*?' He was flabbergasted, having promised not to give it away.[92] In the sequel Peter Davies, Wilson and your servant lunched at Barrie's and talked much shop. . . .
   Scenes & Portraits, which John Murray probably published, has been one of my friends since undergraduate days, so of course *Her Privates We* is bound to make me happy. I wonder if you will like it. It is a war book, of course, but with a difference. The troops in its are real, at last. Manning is a very exquisite person. So queer.

To Peter Davies   [early February 1930][93]
No praise could be too sheer for this book [*Her Privates We*;] I'm sure it is the book of books so far as the British Army-in-the-War is concerned. (The writing might be taken for granted, since Manning wrote it.) I always told everyone that he could, if he would, write greatly, but I never dreamed that time and the man would produce anything like this . . . so loving, exact, delightful, inwardly and outwardly true, so generous, politically and morally and militarily. . . .
How admirable are its restraint, and humour, and vividness, the lovely weather, the lights and darknesses—there are too many sides to the book for it ever to be forgotten. . . . anyone would be proud to have written it. It justifies every heat of praise. Its virtues will be recognised more and more as time goes on.

To John Brophy   Plymouth, 8 February 1930
Lately I read with delight and astonishment a book called "Her privates we" and thought it much the best picture of the English soldier ever produced. So humorous, so finely discriminating, so truthful. A very delicate, though hurried, bit of writing by a man for whose prose I have had admiration ever since he published his first book of imaginary

portraits. I never dared, though, to hope that so essentially delicate
a man could write so robustly about real people. He was bookish before
the war.

To H. S. Ede   Plymouth, 8 February 1930
. . . 'Her privates we' published by Peter Davies is so wise and fine
and humorous and truthful. I seem, in it, to see at last the present
generation of enlisted men. Its author loved Pater, when he was young,
and wrote very preciously. In this last book he has written hurriedly
and nobly, yet with astounding sympathy and liveliness.

To E. M. Forster   [Plymouth], 8 February 1930
    If you want to read a noble, truthful, humorous, sane and subtle
book upon the common man, read "Her privates we". The present
generation of soldier is alive in its pages. Peter Davies publishes. It
is superb. . . . the best war-book yet, and I love it.

To E. M. Forster   17 February 1930
    The charity of Her Privates We is very astonishing. The fellows are
never bitter, you know, and bear no grudge. . . . [Manning is] a good
queer thing. I had no idea that he could be like Bourne.[94] Yet it's
clearly him. . . . Manning was very precious, very posh, very well
dressed, rather exquisite.[95]
    It is a wonderful book.

To Frederic Manning   Plymouth, 25 February 1930
    No it wasn't Rothenstein.[96] . . . As for the authorship of the
book—the preface gives it away.[97] It is pure *Scenes & Portraits*. How
long, I wonder, before everybody knows? You need not worry at their
knowing. It is a book everyone would have been proud and happy
to have written.
    Of course I'm ridiculously partial to it, for since 1922 my home has
been in the ranks, and Bourne says and thinks lots of things I wanted
to have said. But don't imagine that I'm anything like so much of
a lad as he was. . . .
    I have read too many war books. They are like drams, and I cannot
leave them alone, though I think I really hate them. Yours, however,
and Cummings' *Enormous Room* and *War Birds* [by Elliott Springs]
seem to me worth while. *War Birds* is not literature but a raw sharp
life. You and Cummings have produced love-poems of a sort, and
yours is the most wonderful, because there is no strain anywhere in
the writing. Just sometimes you seem to mix up the 'one's' and 'his's':
but for that, it is classically perfect stuff. The picture about 2/3 through

of the fellows sliding down the bank and falling in preparatory to going up for the attack, with the C.O.'s voice and the mist—that is the best of writing.

I have read *Her Privates We* twice, and *The Middle Parts of Fortune*[98] once, and am now deliberately leaving them alone for a while, before reading them again. The airmen are reading the *Privates*, avidly: and E. M. Forster (who sent me a paean about the *Privates*) has *The Middle Parts*. Everyone to whom I write is loudly delighted with the *Privates*. I hope the sales will do you good.

Peter Davies is trying to use my dregs of reputation as one more lever in the sales.[99] Do not let that worry you. Adventitious sales and adventitious advertisements are very soon forgotten: the cash will remain with you, and your book be famous for as long as the war is cared for—and perhaps longer, for there is more than soldiering in it. You have been exactly fair to everyone, of all ranks: and all your people are alive.

. . . I owed it to you to thank you for the best book I have read for a very long time. I shall hope to meet you some day and say more— and bore you by saying it—for what is so dead as a book one has written?

To Charlotte Shaw   Plymouth, 25 February 1930
I am a little sad that you do not like *Her Privates We*. In that is the reality of the common Englishman: and Bourne, the educated little cock-sparrow, is the commonest and most human-like of them all. I think it more of a love-book than a war-book, and have read it three times, without satisfying myself.

I agree with your weariness against all ordinary war books: but for those who fought they are like dram-drinking, and cannot be refused, however one may hate them. Books about ourselves, you know. I cannot help scanning (even if it is always in disgust) anything that appears in print about myself. There is a fascination—a longing to get it over and *know*. *Her Privates We*, however, did not disgust me. I liked it.

To B. H. Liddell Hart   Plymouth, 5 March 1930
"Her Privates We" is by Frederic Manning, son of a Colonial Office official (overseas): an exquisite, and an exquisite writer. I wonder how he really got on in the ranks. Too fine a mind, I think, for real contact: but he has drawn a wonderful picture of the other ranks as I know them.

To Frederic Manning   Plymouth, 21 March 1930
The worst thing about fame, I think, is that in a few years steady

experience of it the victim begins to believe it, against the sure and certain knowledge of his own heart. And then he's a living lie.

But cheer up. Your next book, if it is an introduction to Epicurus[100] or Epictetus or Epaminondas will not sell fourteen editions or increase your fame. . . . The fame was won altogether honestly and on the square, too, by an anonymous book. I envy you the cleanliness of your scoop. . . .

I think your book, because of its hastiness of form and maturity of design will live a very long time. One gets impatient with the signs of too much work in e.g. George Moore, and says "If the blighter was any good he'd get on with something else and stop fidgeting with this." Whereas your book couldn't have had 10 minutes less spent on it without losing. And your dialogue and sense of character is very fine. It's by what your people say that they live.

I have read it once more since last time, and everybody in the hut seems to have read it. Bad for royalties, that: but I enjoy lending a good thing.

To Frederic Manning   Plymouth, 15 May 1930
Your prose has a very definite and deliberate manner, which appeals to me, as most 'airs' do. Your poems have helped you to that concision and force. The best of peotry is all the clauses it leaves out, and that is why poets so often write such tough and nervy prose—or so I fancy.

To Frederic Manning   24 June 1930
I am glad you are revising Scenes & Portraits: That means for the new edition, which someone said was to have one more scene or portrait, or both.[101] I shall look forward to reading it for the n.th time. You do not.

To William Rothenstein   Plymouth, 18 October 1930
Wasn't it delightful to find Manning coming out so suddenly as a real flesh-and-blood figure. Beautiful as are Scenes & Epicurus, ever so much more worth while is "Her Privates We".

To Frederic Manning   Plymouth, 1 September 1931
. . . I have been reading some of you. I tried the Privates: but it was too fresh in my mind. So I read the Poems of the war [*Eidola*, 1917] and then the Scenes again: and then the Epicurus introduction, twice. As I have done "God" three times you will see that your old power, to make me repeat you again and again, endures. As soon as I finish a new work of yours I turn again to its first page and do it all over again. One misses so much the first time of reading: and even the second. Some queer difference in mind between you and me makes

you as satisfying a writer, to me, as anyone who has ever written. Therefore I call you very good, though it seems a slender and individual ground for appraisal. Why should you be very good because you please a quirk of a creature, like me?....

The perfect fitness of God for its place, to sum up, end, draw together and transcend all the Scenes & Portraits (alas: not a scene: only a portrait) amazes me. Nothing but that unrelieved stretch of abstraction could have carried it off to a climax. The Devil begins by sounding and behaving like me: only he gets over my head instantly and soars away. I am a concrete image.

As for Epicurus, your introduction makes the poor book so thin. I don't think old and famous books bear introducing: it is like rattling an aged three-decker to death by an auxiliary motor. Yours is a very fine little motor: full of stuff, gutty, smooth-running, and fast. Only Epicurus was before the age of internal-combustions.

I can't keep my metaphor in the air any longer. So here flops this letter.

To Sir William Rothenstein   Southampton, 6 September 1932
I was an older reader of Manning than you thought. A review in the Time Lit. Sup. [*Times Literary Supplement*] sent me to his "Scenes & Portraits".....it said "while we have Mr. Manning to write prose for us there is no need to despair of English style"! That must have been 1909 or so.

I am a shameful correspondent, and have not even written to poor F. M. for months.

To Frederic Manning   Bridlington, 16 November 1934
Peter Davies wrote to me that you were still consumed with a longing to write that old book which has so often refused to come to you.[102] I beg of you, don't. Copy the poise and equal mind of E. M. Forster, whose every book is acclaimed by the highbrowed as a masterpiece, and who yet refrains successfully from ever deliberately achieving another. There are so many books and you have written two of the best of them. To covet a third is greedy. Don't be a book-hog.

To Peter Davies   28 February 1935
On Tuesday I took my discharge from the R.A.F. and started southward by road, meaning to call at Bourne and see Manning: but to-day I turned eastward, instead, hearing that he was dead.

It seems queer news, for the *books**[103] are so much more intense than ever he was, and his dying doesn't, cannot affect them. Therefore what has died really? Our hopes of having more from him—but that is greed. The writing them was such pain—and pains—to him. Of late I had devoutly wished him to cease trying to write. He had done enough: *two wonderful works*,* full-sized: four lesser things. A man who can produce one decent book is a fortunate man, surely?

Some friends of mine, in dying, have robbed me; Hogarth and Aubrey Herbert are two empty places which no one and nothing can ever fill. Whereas Doughty and Hardy and Manning had earned their release. Yet his going takes away a person of great kindness, exquisite and pathetic. It means one rare thing less in our setting. You will be very sad.

. . . Strange to think how Manning, sick, poor, fastidious, worked like a slave for year after year, not on the concrete and palpable boats or engines of my ambition, but on stringing words together to shape his ideas and reasonings. That's what being a born writer means, I suppose. And to-day it is all over and nobody ever heard of him. If he had been famous in his day he would have liked it, I think; liked it deprecatingly. As for fame-after-death, it's a thing to spit at; the only minds worth winning are the warm ones about us. If we miss those we are failures. I suppose his being not really English, and so generally ill, barred him from his fellows. Only not in *Her Privates We* which is hot-blooded and familiar. How I wish, for my own sake, that he hadn't slipped away in this fashion; but how like him. He was too shy to let anyone tell him how good he was.[104]

To Sir William Rothenstein   Clouds Hill, 5 May 1935
   Manning died as I was on my way to Bourne, to visit him. I turned off and rode down here. . . .

As for Manning, I cannot say how sad the news made me. He was a lovely person, and it is hateful to see him go out, unfinished. But gone he very definitely is. It makes one feel as though nothing can matter very much.

Herman Melville

To A. E. Chambers   10 March 1923
   You will have thought me slow in sending you this: [Melville's *White-Jacket*][105] but I am contented only to have remembered it. I go seldom to Chingford, where my books lie idle. . . .

I hope you like it: had it not been meant to improve the American Navy it would have been a better book: but at least that is an honourable fault, & the particular aim was achieved. I would willingly have done something in this manner upon the R.A.F.—a much finer show than the States' Navy of 1820:—but that's another of the undone things.

To Sydney Cockerell   Clouds Hill, 19 March 1924
   Moby Dick.....ah, there's a titan of a book. Do you know *Redburn*, and *Pierre*, two of the less common ones? *White-jacket* very good: *Mardi* dull: two early S. Sea adventures (*Omoo* and *Typee*) fair. One of his finest works is *Clarel*, in verse: but it isn't as fine verse as his War Stuff. That's mangificent. Melville was a great man.
   I got £20 for my *Piazza Tales* the other day. Someone is working a Melville boom, and I've sold all my early editions profitably.

To Jonathan Cape [?]   30 March 1923
White Jacket is V.G. [very good] Mardi rather dull. . . . "Redburn" would sell somewhat in Liverpool, as a local curiosity. . .

To A. E. Chambers   Clouds Hill, 5 December 1924
   Melville was always pondering the end & reason of life, & profound things—and couldn't write a line without thinking of them. Wherefore he runs very far into symbols, which meant more to him than they can to any reader.

Ezra Pound

To his family   Aleppo, 20 February 1912
   Pound has a very common American affectation of immense learning in strange things.

To his family   Carchemish, 12 September 1912
The great risk of Pound's poetry is the symbolic for its own sake: He has educated himself on old books and never correlated them. A good poet though.

To his family   Carchemish, 6 March 1913
   I am glad Will got Ezra Pound: & that he was a success:[106] sounds a very curious person: I think the *Goodly Fere* is by far his best thing.....though some of the Provencal canzoni run it very close indeed. Indeed the *Yearly Slain* may be better.....No matter.

To Ezra Pound   Oxford, April 1920
   . . . I haven't even a wish to feel the existence of a vortex—if I had one I'd try to get it cut out:—and so I fear that my writing would

not be to your standard. Of course *The Dial* may be ordinary, but I haven't seen it, and so it is likely to resemble *Blast*. . . .

Congratulations on going to Italy. You'll be a millionaire there on small outgoings, and it's going to be beautifully warm. I wish I could leave England for a long spell. No such luck.

To Ezra Pound   Oxford, 20 August 1920

For twenty days I have been faced by your letter: each day I read a new name of a contributor to *The Dial*: but there is surely no place for me in that galaxy? . . . .do you see the point? I'm academic idyllic, romantic: you breathe commas and exclamation marks. We ought not to exist together on one earth, but the earth is so broad-minded that she doesn't care.

To William Rothenstein   Karachi, 8 December 1927

[Wyndham] Lewis is vastly entertaining on poor Ezra Pound [in *The Enemy*].[107] The poor worm. I wouldn't have the heart. You know both of them are flabby-faced and soft-handed, and pant when going up flights of stairs. Of course this is not really criticism of their heads. . . . .or is it? I should begin to respect them if I felt that either of them was wholesome flesh. But a meal off them would be poison.

To Ezra Pound   Bridlington, 7 December 1934

I laughed over your letter. You were so hot about something. Now in England (good) the most telling style is understatement. To say that 'you fear some of your adversary's premises may be not well-founded' is damaging. To call him a canting nit-wit only provokes a smile. You'd say 'cunting', I fear; there are six shits in your letter. If that happens to me more than once a day, I know that some recent meal is disagreeing with me. More peace to your stomach! . . . .

I think many of us go wrong by being too exclusively cerebral. I've spent the last twelve years in the ranks of the Air Force; and nobody so in daily contact with people who work at crafts could get so heated as the *N.E.* [*New English Weekly*] does about the regimentation of the world. My own job has been producing motor boats: and I fancy that each concrete thing I launched took away some of my bile. Whereas the uttering of a poem only increases it. Old Gandhi would prescribe for you a daily wrestle with the spinning wheel, to grow contentment. The English working men are another creation from us. Abstract ideas are another name for maggots of the brain. Heads are happy when they employ hands, not when they earn idleness for them. . . .

Will you never come back? The States, England, even Paris? . . .

Rapallo is years away from Texas, as Texas from Rapallo. Who dare put one before the other?

To A. S. Frere-Reeves   Bridlington, 7 January 1935
Lately I've had a letter or two from Pound who (misled perhaps by his name into thinking himself a born economist) seems to have run off on a new hobby-horse of financial theory. I think perhaps my art of boat-building is now the only one the silly ass has not tried and done fairly well. It wouldn't matter, but that all the time we are missing a full-sized poet, thereby. Still, he might have died young, and that would have come to the same thing, except to himself. Always angry, is Ezra P.

Erich Maria Remarque

To Herbert Read   Plymouth, 26 March 1929
All Quiet is a most interesting work.[108] Your judgment 'distilled bitterness of the generation shot to pieces by the war' is exactly fitting. Incidentally it would have been a bigger book without that bias. The railing against our elders of p. 19 is not worthy of a man.[109] Our elders are only ourselves: there is no difference between one generation & another—nor, in war (or in that war) between class & class. The war-fever in England rose from bottom to top, & forced our unwilling government's hand. It was the young (youth) & the ignorant (age) who, as usual, made the war. Wars are made in hot blood, not in cold blood. Of course Cramer[110] suffered so much that one must excuse him. Lots of people lose their balance when they have suffered painfully. Yet the war was all our faults.

It's surely well written—and I expect the goodness is in the German, as well as in the translation. . . . It is over-written sometimes, the killing of Duval in the crater—that should have been short: so should the shelling in the graveyard. He squeezed his orange too dry there.

He does his pathos wonderfully—the death of Kemmerich: the wounded horses (one of the highlights of the book): the chapter of going home on leave (the highest light of all, I think). Only the pathetic stop is like the organ's vox humana. It's too easy. That point also makes me think Cramer not so much strong as sensitive. . . . He revolts too much, usually, against his horrors: but he was only a lad, & it's quite likely he has some Jew in him. The point of view is hardly that of a German amongst Germans. The care with which he inserts the daily coarseness & carnality of army life feels foreign too. I suspect him of not being pure German. Not that it matters what he is. The book is international.

I've seen nothing in English war novels so good as this, and I have read very many of them.

To Edward Garnett   Plymouth, 10 April 1929
It [*All Quiet on the Western Front*] is very good yet I think the writer is not a good writer. Only he was moved by the war. Too moved, to be a great man.

To Henry Williamson   10 July 1929
"All Quiet" is the screaming of a feeble man.[111] It will not last as long as Tarka [*the Otter* by Williamson], except as a document.

H. H. Richardson

To Jacob Schwartz   Southampton, 26 April 1932
The H. H. Richardson book followed me here from Plymouth, and I have liked reading it.[112] She has lavished great pains upon these two stories, I fancy. Parts of her Australian trilogy[113] were quite careless, as prose, and those 3 volumes are all of her that I know. It is surprising to find one who can write so much and so freely in the open style taking pains upon the smaller scale, too. Usually it is one or the other.

I write to you with some diffidence. I do not practice as a writer, but because I got some reputation during the war in quite another field, my name has a certain publicity value, and publishers have an inclination to use any praise I may incautiously utter upon a book as a advert—which is unfortunate, because I'm no critic, nor a wide reader, nor primarily interested in books, and I resent my casual judgments gaining the force of print. Will you please keep this letter private, therefore?

It's one thing to try and boost an unknown man; but for me to praise H. H. R. would be an impertinence. What you tell me about her small sales astonishes me. I should have thought Australia and England good for many thousand copies of the Richard Mahoney books. After all, they were very widely talked about. Everybody knows that she is one of the people to count. Nobody can say more than that. It is not for contemporaries to place Richardsons in order of merit. We are too near to see plain.

The worst of writing too hard is that one attains the tableland of excellence, to which all good authors come, and from which there is no absolute ascent. It is common ground. Take Mary Christina, for instance. I read with soothed delight as far as page 18: then I came to "time and again" and "little by little" on successive lines. Too close. I wanted to put "slowly" for "little by little, however" and purge my lines of the assonance. On page 20 I fell foul of the comma after sky. It tripped me as I read, and tried to relate the bulbous clouds to the knocker. The "English" also shocked me. The rest of the story was unplaced: universal. Pity to tie it down. Also the quotation from Jacobsen had made me think of the north. Sweden rather than Denmark, oddly enough. It was so good of her to quote from N. Lynne. On page 21 "too big for such frolics" they rebuked her. Without the quotes it is they that were big. On page 24 I do not like eating her heart out while pressing a dress to her face. Concrete and cliche.....they jar together, rather. On page 25 perdurable reminded me of Swinburne. It is almost a dead word. The wonders had been a chimera. I don't know off-hand what the plural of chimera was: if there was more than one of the beast. "Unsubstantial pageant" is a pity too. Shelley that was: and patented for him exclusively, I think. "Impossibly distinguish." Her rhythm insisted on that: but I don't like my sound leading me through a bog of words. You get mirages, too, by staring, not by glancing. On page 29 I was puzzled by the word "unblessed". The Sister of Mercy should have warned the priest. Or is the story just a bit of something longer, with a story to it? It is very beautiful, and so exquisitely wrought that one can imagine such tiny blemishes as those I have picked upon above. It is only the finest stuff that shows specks. For the beauty of the whole and of its parts I have no words worth putting down. If she could write a book like this it would best her Thule books[114] out of court, fine and large though they were. . . .

Knowing 15 languages must be a daunting thing. She will be sure, as she reads, that never could she write as well as Werner or Merner or Turner. . . .

The Australian strain? Whence does that come? You say half Irish and English. What about the other half? Or is it half Irish and half English, and Australia an accident? There was not a great deal of earth in the Mahoney books: and none in this, except for the lightly-touched in Rhine valley life in Peterle. Why, oh why, does she call the Minister[115] of Strasburg "Immortal"? That is a bad adjective. These Gothic spires have no endurance, in ages.

You were very kind to send me this book. I have greatly liked it. If you will quickly forget this letter you will add to your kindness.

Arthur Rimbaud

To Laura Riding   [1932?][116]
I carried his poems with me for many years. They are quite by

themselves, I think: very raw, very explosive, very over-spoken, violent rather than beautiful. This sort of loudness in beginning so often is proof rather of youth than of strength. Roy Campbell, for instance, is sick not strong. Rimbaud would not have gone on writing anyhow, I think. And he showed his sense by cutting it right off and working himself out in the Red Sea instead. I am sure he had no more wish to write after he left the Paris group. It was more Verlaine than Rimbaud, probably. Also he was not truthfully homosexual, I fancy. There is not much passion in his poetry, but much feeling for visual impressions and a love of twisting words. He had not the power of writing simple phrases: he twisted everything, and so sometimes he hides his bare passages and so sometimes he hides his beauties. Untranslatable, I think: many of his verses are very hard to understand and very uncertain in meaning anyhow. Probably he didn't mean anything in particular by them. Also he gave words his own ordinary signification. A lost sheep, but a miracle among Frenchmen.

Siegfried Sassoon

To Robert Graves   1924?
What's the cause that you, and S. S. and I (from the S. S. to the ridiculous!) can't get away from the War? Here are you riddled with thought like any old table-leg with worms: S. S. yawing about like a ship aback: me in the ranks, finding squalor and maltreatment the only permitted existence: what's the matter with us all? It's like the malarial bugs in the blood, coming out months and years after in recurrent attacks.

To Robert Graves   Cranwell, 29 August 1925
I'm very glad to hear that S. S. is all right. He is rather like a Miltonic archangel: no doubt all right in the archangels' mess: but rather terrifying to the rank and file.

To Robert Graves   [Karachi], 19 May 1928
Do you see S. S.? or is he amongst the suits you have worn out? I'm afraid of S. S.: but I'm sure he is a great man. Regard me to him, if ever you meet, unexpectedly, on some neutral pavement.

To Robert Graves   Miranshah, 6 November 1928
Look at the *Memoirs of a Foxhunting Man* to see how magically simple things, like birds, come to life again, on paper,...without any twisting of words, or strange words.

To Edward Marsh   Plymouth, 19 March 1929
I can't do that.[117] It would be to arrogate to myself a claim to
literary judgement, on the strength of one book produced under stress
of external circumstances. . . .

I hope S. S. will understand. I enjoy his work, because it touches
nearer to my own train of mind than the work of anyone else
publishing. Every verse of his makes me say 'I wish to God I'd said
that': and his fox-hunting gave me a shock of astonishment that he
was so different and so good to know. If I was trying to export the
ideal Englishman to an international exhibition, I think I'd like to
choose S. S. for chief exhibit. Only I wouldn't dare, really, to give
him a prize.

To Henry Williamson   10 July 1929
. . . if you see Sassoon to speak to,[118] tell him that his book (novel)
pleased me: but I'd lose it all for his worst poem.

To Robert Graves   Plymouth, 13 September 1929
S. S. comes out very well [in Graves's *Goodbye to All That*]. I'm
glad of that, for I like him: homosex and all. He's a fighting man,
& generous. Hates his family millionaires.

To William Rothenstein   Plymouth, 18 October 1930
Sassoon comes out on top of all us war-timers, I think. More vigour,
more grace and swiftness of movement, more fire & heat—that's in
his poetry—and more tranquil charm, in his prose. S. S. strikes me
as probably a great writer, all in all.

To Robert Graves   Southampton, 17 December 1933
But tomorrow I have an interlude that would amuse you—S. S. is
being married in the morning, at Christchurch near here, and I have
promised to go over and see the deed done. I hope, about him, without
feeling too sure. He is restless, over-strung, very tired of feeding on
himself: she is younger and wise, I think, and knows what she is
undertaking. If any of my generation has earned harbour after storm,
it is S. S. and I am hoping for him, as I said.

To Geoffrey Keynes   Southampton, 10 February 1934
I return the S. S. proof-pulls [of *Vigils*]. Thank you for the sight
of them. . . . These script engravings are very beautiful, very delicate.
Slow to read and impossible to glance over in one blink of the eye,
the way one usually swallows short poems the first time, to see if they

taste good. These have to be read word for word, and one of them, 'Degrees of groping thought,' didn't stand up, in my mind, to such syllabic treatment. I like the others, and shall like the book, if I ever get it!....

I think they seem to go a little ahead of *The Heart's Journey*.....at least 'Vigils' does. A very lovely poem, technically done. . . .

If he does, as we hope, 'go on' now, after his marriage, we shall be fortunate. But if the poor man turns happy instead and writes no more—why, he has deserved it, surely.

To Geoffrey Keynes   Southampton, 6 August 1934
I intended to tell you of my raid upon Heytesbury. . . .[119]

S. S. looked abnormally happy. Much of his hesitant diction has been forgotten. He speaks easily, and is full of private jests. He looks so well, too. . . .

Whether it will last I cannot say. The barometer cannot always stand so high. . . .

We spread out on the floor all the proofs of your engravings, with the lovely title-page, and gloated over them. It [*Vigils*] will be a gracious and estimable book. . . . The pages are clean and legible. However they yet have to be read slowly, almost word for word. Type has grown so instinctive to our eyes that we swallow printed books a line, if not a paragraph, at once. That is all right, for things currently written, like *The Times*; but these chiselled and balancing verses of S. S. deserve to be read almost as minutely as they were made. What an iconic stillness there is about his images, now! He has progressed from flesh-and-blood (in *Counter Attack* [1918]) to bronze. As for *The Old Huntsman* [1917], it is difficult for me often to trace the connection between that early man and S. S. now. At Heytesbury he showed me his first published poems, the cricket verses. They seemed an age away. One of the good things about S. S. is that he changes freely and completely. . . .

The price of the book worries me. Two guineas is so much. I have not, as yet, even brought myself to order a copy. S. S. is one of the few poets that keep step with their generation and I would have him generally read. . . . Can you contemplate a plain edition afterwards, which I can send to my friends?

To Siegfried Sassoon   Clouds Hill, 17 December 1934
Written, this is, from Bridlington: but I have been reading your *Vigils*, and I felt I could not write about them from the 'Ozone Hotel'[120]. My cottage is where they should be read.

They have deeply moved me. They are so . . . . . gentle, I think I want
to say. To be read slowly and in sequence. The rather conscious script
helps them, by delaying the eye. These poems are like wood-violets
and could easily be passed over by a man in a hurry. When I came
to the war-poem I checked for a moment, sorry: but soon saw that
it was right. Not if you had never written before; but here in its place
among your poems it helps, by translating into quietude the fierce
moods that held you for *Counter Attack* and the Satires [*Satirical
Poems*, 1926]. Every other one of the 22 looks forward. I can feel
the solidity of the war-anger and the peace-bitterness under the feet,
as it were, of these poems: they are all the better for it, but so far
from it: so far above and beyond.

Sometimes, in a lyrical phrase or an adjective of accumulated beauty,
I can link them to your earlier work: but only thus, externally, by a
common ornament. . . . You are not ashamed of 'suddenly burst out
singing' but growing shy of it. Just a word or two hint at happiness,
and then your blotting paper comes down.

I will try to write you again about them when I have grown into
them a little. They aren't like Shakespeare, at all. They are human
and very careful and faint and solitary. Each seemed to me to shut
one more door of your gigantic house. There are heaps more doors
yet; and of course you might one day open one. By their implications
I date the first drafts of all of them from before that day at Christchurch,[121] and I feel that you, yourself, have changed colour somewhat since the writing. You have more colour now, I think, and more
colours too.

But these are exquisite poems, exquisite. First reading was like sitting
under an autumn tree, and seeing its early leaves falling one by one.
I shouldn't like you to go on writing *Vigils*, world without end. They
are seasonal fruits, but lovely. You can dare them because of your
past fighting: and those of us who have deserved a rest will feel them
and be grateful to you.

That last little volume of political poems [*The Road to Ruin*] had
frightened me a little, for you seemed to look back. Here you go a
full stride forward. Cheers, and long life to your pen. It is doing us
good—and proud.

I've read this through and see that I've forgotten to say that these
things are streets ahead, in power and beauty and calmness, of anything
of yours I've ever before seen. You presumably know that: but when,
I ask you, are you going to reach your prime? Near fifty and still a
growing poet. It's like T. H. [Thomas Hardy] isn't it? He grew till
seventy. Don't answer this rot!

William Shakespeare

To his family   Carchemish, 11 May 1912
   Will [his brother] may like Galsworthy's book (I/–) on Shakespeare: it is written from a very fresh standpoint, though he rather obscures the merits of the plays by considering them as dramatic works. It always seemed to me that the rather unworthy humour was Shakespeare's concession to theatrical demands. The poetry, if anything, unfits them for presentation, since one cannot find a man worthy to do anything more than think of it.
   I have been reading a good deal of Shakespeare lately. . . . The Rabelais will be a consoler: one wants something o' nights with a little more thought in it than Shakespeare.

To Edward Garnett   1 December 1922
   I didn't call Shakespeare 2nd rate: only his intellect. He's the most consummate master of vowels and consonants: and the greatest poet. As a philosopher and moralist I have no abnormal respect for him: but the Elizabethan age was tempered rather than forged steel.

To Robert Graves   25 June 1925
God knows we each of us have our own fancy pictures of W. S. . . . . . and my fancy is to have no picture of him. There was a man who hid behind his works, with great pains and consistency. *Ergo*, he had something to hide: some privy reason for hiding. He being a most admirable fellow, I hope he hides successfully.

To Charlotte Shaw   5 November 1925
There is more word-music in W. S. mouth than in all human mouths since. He couldn't say an absolutely ugly thing: though granted that the sound far surpasses the sense.

To E. M. Forster   [Karachi], 11 January 1927
It's no good to put shallow thinking into mellifluous words. That is how Shakespeare has been able so long to reign alone.

To David Garnett   10 February 1930
The present discovery is of his [Shakespeare's] badness, here and there. He can write page after page of the most tiring euphemisms. It astonishes me to see how much "of his time" he was. How he tried to be a posh author and write like the others: and the reason we like him is because here and there he didn't—couldn't—manage it.

To David Garnett   19 November 1930
...I am still reading Shakespeare II,[122] having taken the chance of
what I hope is the slow production of your edition to read him all
through again. Parts are very heavy and very bad: and then the next
page will take one's breath. What a queer great man. Dimly I feel
that something went so wrong with his life that he lost heart, foreswore
London, and abandoned his work. I wonder. It could only be some
internal vice, for nothing from outside could hurt such a one.

George Bernard Shaw

To G. B. Shaw   7 December 1922
Your picture of him [Julius Caesar in *Caesar and Cleopatra*, 1907]
is one of the few of great men with any life in them: and to it
and *Heartbreak* [*House*, 1920] are due my sending you *The Seven
Pillars*.[123]

To G. B. Shaw   Clouds Hill, 20 December 1923
I want to talk to you some day about [*Back to*] *Methuselah* [1922].
We aren't going that way, if the fellows here are an indication, and
I suppose they are extracts of the widest English class. Their only
criteria are the physical: they judge, speak, think, enjoy, only in terms
of the senses. There is nothing abstract in their lives, no ideas for them
independent of an external form: and their apex, their sublimation,
is the coming together in sex of a man and a woman.

To David Hogarth   Clouds Hill, 21 January 1924
Shaw (the genuine one) was here lately....very bracing, though such
sureness of success has closed his pores.

To Charlotte Shaw   6 March 1924
Methusaleh [*sic*]—in its lines—is "so": one understands it with
the brain, & it's a very subtly-proportioned & planned edifice. But
the sight & hearing of it[124] build quite another picture inside me:
something far more significant. It's as though Mr Shaw had felt at
last that he had something to convey, in which no skill & power of
his would avail: and so he made us feel it too. Anyway, there was
something unearthly. It wasn't a play, but a declaration of faith.

To Charlotte Shaw   Clouds Hill, 16 March 1924
I've read *Joan, St. Joan* [1923].....and want to say straight out
that it is one of his best writings. Don't take me as a play-judge. I

know nothing of the stage, and don't care very much for it: a play to me is only a particularly art-form like a sonnet: but as writing *Joan* is magnificent.

Some sea-change has come over G. B. S. in the last ten years. Perhaps it isn't new that he should be on the side of the angles—even when they are undisguised angels—but surely it's new that every one of his characters should be honest and kindly and even-minded? I like it, and find it essentially true, the more I see of men (almost I'm able to think gently of some sergeants.....they mean less than appears. . . . their official style has to be subtracted before you measure the manner and matter of their delivery): but people don't usually feel fair towards humanity till they are old and successful and ready to retire.....and G. B. S. isn't the third, and probably will never be the first.....just as I'll never be the second.

Seriously, it's done his art and heart good to get the doctrine of *Methuselah* off his breathing-works: and the poet in him is now going to have a little dance. Did you note the balance of prose in the fighting parts of *Joan*? Take care: he may yet write an epic of blood-lust. All things are possible with a delivered evangelical.

Wonderful lines in *Joan* were on p. 26, where the Archb[ishop] rebukes the lap-dogs. Oh, I'd like to hear de Rais stamp out his desperate sane-face from that!

I shrink from Joan's very little dialect. It seems to me a literary manner, like italics: unworthy of an artist with Mr. Shaw's cut and sweep of spoken word. He gives Joan a loud simplicity without it.....and I'm a detester & despiser of bumpkins. The best men in the ranks aren't the bumpkin-spoken. A fellow worth listening to isn't the tyro, but the man who is trying once more, on top of ten thousand failures, to phrase precisely what his mind feels.

Page 31 where the Dauphin snaps his fingers in La Tremouille's face. Excellent.

Page 35 Who was Dunois' second wife? The jape about 'Staff Officers' lower down is a real deep thrust. It lightens up this scene, which to my mind doesn't hold quite as much metal as the preceding one.

The next pages, where Warwick and Cauchon & the ancestor of the diehard play together is a delight in its sheer skill of character-work. The three men stand out & live solidly & separately.

Pp. 53–65: they are adequate: but Mr. Shaw doesn't know how men who have fought together stand in relation to one another (when there has been recognisable personal relations in the fighting line) afterwards. They understand so deeply that they never hesitate to differ fundamentally. The word 'pet' should come out of the last line of

p. 53. They have a half section, a pal, a chum: not more than one, either comrade, or no comrade: there aren't degrees in fellowship. The development of the tragedy grows fast through this scene.

I found pp. 66–95 intolerable. The shadow of the tragedy at the end lay over the first pages, & made the so-accurate historical 'placing' of the men a horror. Over these pages I galloped, to reach the crisis. Joan came in, & held her own, indeed increased her nobility. It was good to make her sign that confession.....and then she died, 'off'. I have a prejudice against the writer who leaves the reader to make his top-scene for him. *Hounds of Banba* [by Daniel Corkery, 1920] does it, in the story of the burning of the village.....but faces the struggle in the story of the man's funeral. I funked it, in the death of Farraj, my man: faced it, in the plain narrative of my mishaps in Deraa the night I was captured.[125] Here in *St. Joan* the climax will be a red light shining from the fire into the courtyard. Authors feel they aren't up to writing about so tremendous a thing, & so they put a row of dots,.....or swallow silently & leave the poor reader to stuff up their gap with his cherished & grudged emotion. It's indirect art & direct shirking.

Of course if he'd dipped his pen in all his strength & written straight forward the play could never have been presented: but the more honour so. It would have cleaned us all to have *seen* Joan die.

The fifth act is pure genius. I wouldn't have thought of it otherwise than written: I'm most thankful to you for letting me read it.

. . . I've only just finished Joan, after five days spent in reading her twice.

To Charlotte Shaw   Clouds Hill, 26 March 1924
O dear. I've gone and done it. Very very sorry. This 'to-be-envied' camp-life makes me rebound too high at times. Explanations.

. . . The trial scene in *Joan*. Poor Joan. I was thinking of her as a person, not as a moral lesson. The pain meant more to her than the example. . . .

The sting of the burning was very big in *Joan*: and G. B. S. would have made his play impossible by portraying it. Yet if the play was to be not a morality but life itself, he would have given the physical its place above the moral.

In Methuselah his human-kind ended in the supremacy of mind. The army has taught me that our race is running towards a supremacy of body.

To Charlotte Shaw   3 May 1925
C. & C. [*Caesar and Cleopatra*] is much superior to Joan in

everything except musical rhythm of prose. More fire: more light: sharper. Yet it does not hang together so well: & it hasn't a supreme moment, such as the Dauphin's bedroom at the end of all. Of course the trouble with Joan was the woman chief-part. There hasn't ever yet been a woman of genius (at least I don't think there has) and so it's rather running deliberately upon a rock to put her first in a play. G. B. S. couldn't put a conviction in her mouth, because he wrote her speeches intentionally in character . . . . . not straight from the pen: and the sense of balance wouldn't let him give any of the minor characters anything "terrible" to say. Consequently they could only gossip about things like nationality & authority, pasteboard scenery amid which we breakfast.

Of course Caesar was a great part: it represents almost the ideally-great man . . . . . he bulges with mind, & is so cheery at doing things. Yet I wondered as I listened . . . whether that tiny strain of cleverness-of-the-wrong-sort (pertness) isn't incompatible with greatness. To be very great a man must be pretty stupid . . . . . otherwise inevitably he will catch sight of himself, & burst out laughing.

To Charlotte Shaw [Karachi], 12 April 1928
 That first act of Heartbreak House. . . . The most blazing bit of genius in English literature. There is not one decent sentence. The stuff is all lit by lightning, & there's a devil's kitchen in the background, & a chorus of hyaenas, I'd rather have produced that than anything in the English language. I wonder why you don't like it. Of course it is wicked in its way; worse than the 5th chapter of Gulliver: but the characters of Shotover & his family are super-human: even Hector.

To William Rothenstein [Karachi], 14 April 1928
 It is interesting that G.B.S. sits again to you. He is beclouded, like Hardy and Kipling, with works which tend to live more intensely than their creator. I doubt whether you can now see him. You know too much. His best chance would be to find some foreign artist who did not know his face; and to be painted by him as "Sir George Bernard". So perhaps we would know what he would have been if he had not written. Lately I've been studying Heartbreak House: whose first act strikes me as metallic, inhuman, supernatural: the most blazing bit of genius in English literature. I'd have written that first, if I had choice.

To Charlotte Shaw [Miranshah], 23 July 1928
 It [*The Intelligent Woman's Guide to Socialism and Capitalism*] is a very great book. I rejoice at his having successfully conquered a new

province. It is like the aged Hardy writing poetry. Only the pity is that only a handful of people will be fibrous enough to read him as he should be read, and digest him, and do him proper honour. For the rest of us, who are not Bertrand Russells or Bagehots, can only guess at the book's standard.

To Charlotte Shaw   [Miranshah], 4 August 1928
. . . I turn to G.B.S. and read a page or two . . . of his lovely Socialism, in which without greatness or condescension from greatness he sits down at the bedside by me, and talks just straight, like one honest man to another.
. . . . I do not think that he has, finally, written it for anyone but himself.

To Charlotte Shaw   [Miranshah], 27 November 1928
That Socialism book is shot through with quiet sunshine. Don't tell him: he'd like it to be fervent, soap-box and street corner hot gospel. It is more like a testament. It unrolls itself so surely, & securely. It is safe. There is a sense of being above controversy.

To Charlotte Shaw   [Miranshah], 18 December 1928
No, I have not finished Socialism. I read ten or fifteen pages whenever my brain is not grinding something Odyssean in its mills. Rarer & rarer, now. It is a great book. He makes himself no bigger than us, all through. It would be so easy for him to use his strength, & force the thing on us. Instead he tries to make it grow up in us. The first thing I should call it is *decent*.

To Charlotte Shaw   [Plymouth], 10 July 1929
I told her [Lady Astor] she was a cocktail of a woman, and about as companionable as a typhoon. That shocked her: so I explained that G. B. S. was a cocktail too, and that you were not. . . . Did I tell her that the blend of you and G. B. S. was a symphony of smooth and sharp, like bacon and eggs? Possibly. Conjoined you would be complete humanity.

To Charlotte Shaw   29 April 1931
I am glad G. B. S. upholds the virtues of the Soviet experiment.[126] I am sure its end is right: but the means might spoil my faith if I encountered them.

To Charlotte Shaw   26 June 1931
A point about Pte Meek occurred to me last night, driving back

from Torquay as guide to an R.A.F. car (or is it Meake?): He wouldn't have told the Colonel that he was his *Intelligence Officer*. He might have said, "I do the Intelligence work" or more likely "I am also your Intelligence Staff, Sir,". . . to which the Colonel would have responded by dwelling on the Staff, probably, and forgetting the Intelligence. The Meeks of the world are shy of describing themselves as officers.

It is so hard to judge by just one act of a play. Who could deduce the Apple Cart from its 2nd Act? But I liked this new thing. It should get home.

Rifles at the ready: stand by with the maroons: sights up to 2000, over their heads, no hitting: contact. Charge your magazines (or cutouts open; if magazines were already charged). Ten rounds rapid fire. . . . Something like that.

Meek wouldn't have said illiterate. . . . at least he doesn't. His difficulty is having not passed the educational exam. for promotion. He would probably have said that he hadn't got his educational certificate. "Not educationally qualified" is written on my half-yearly return for promotion!

These squalid inaccuracies should not affect G. B. S. He must write so that audiences will comprehend.

To James Hanley   Plymouth, 2 July 1931
Take poor G. B. S. who must have been wonderful when he was your age, fifty years ago. Now he is pedestalled, and not so good as you are. Whereas 50 years hence you may be rotten.

To Frederic Manning   Southampton, 2 January 1932
As for persons in his [Shaw's] plays, I regret to report (with a horrid grinning pleasure, too) that I appear in an indecently thin disguise as Private Meek in his new play, "too true to be good". Only a minor part: but evidently not a type. I should say. My criticism of G. B. S. would be that he finds it so easy to be brilliant-surfaced that he never bothers to go under-skin. His characters are characters, all right, but have only the one mind among them. However I do not set up to be a critic.

To Charlotte Shaw   Southampton, 9 January 1932
Miss Patch has sent me the proof of "Too True" and I have read it three times. It makes a superb impression on me. . . . "Too True" by virtue of its last act ranges with Heartbreak House and is magnificent. . . . I know you do not think of Heartbreak House as I do: it fits my mind and moods as nothing else . . . until this "Too True."

It varies more than Heartbreak House, and gains by the contrast between its movements. The first act is Mozart-Shaw, by which I mean that he has written it, and its themes, before. The doctor—the mother: they are nearly extinct creatures. He has laughed them to death. When the existing species have gone there will be no successors. Also the fresh air school is triumphant over them, and the present women are not hypochondriac. The microbe is good: and the curtain to the act brought me down in a heap. . . . It is a wonderful curtain, and the act does its bit in making these impossible three young people possible. Only ramping lunacy, of this sort, could have achieved it. I did really feel, after it, as if the play was over, now.

The second act is priceless. . . . If anyone from the moon wanted to know what comedy meant a scrap of this, or a scrap of Sheridan, would answer him. Its reality makes a perfect foil to the classicism of Act I. At the end of Act II, I felt that no conceivable third act could be any other than an anti-climax. The play had been keyed too high for any final movement.

Not true: for the IIIrd. act swept me off my feet, as it ended. That final speech of Aubrey's beats the Tempest into fits. I do not know if it will play: but as reading it transcends the great speech of Methuselah. The whole long act leads up to it splendidly, too: and gives us time to admire the stagework: the way the figures enter and (especially) leave. G. B. S. told me once that plays do not end with a big bang, climaxes being put in Act 3 and softened by Act IV. Only this time the bang really comes, and is devastating. The play is terrific, when you look back on it. No single part of it is, but the collocation of three such diverse movements overwhelmed me.

Of course I know nothing about the theatre: but I think that "Too True" is probably the finest acting thing G. B. S. has ever made. I'm afraid, only, that Hardwicke will let my conception of Aubrey frantically down.[127] He will never understand what he represents. I shall dread seeing the play acted, for fear it does not come up to what it is. . . .

Only at one point did my nature want to say "no" to G. B. S.: where he said that the war had spoiled the Services. It did alter them profoundly, for the time. After troops had left England for one of the fronts there was no brotherhood remaining. It was fighting spoilt it. But after real peace came, the pre-war mood returned. Relative to civil life the service today is more serene than it was of old. . . . Partly we feel eternal. The army is always aged about 20. . . . the peace-time soldiering is still the best lay brotherhood.

Here enclosed is a sheet of unimportant details for G. B. S. to consider if he has time. . . . I have not so enjoyed a printed thing since "Her privates we" of years ago.[128] It is much more important than the Apple Cart. . . .

p. 14. Actually, to have had them once is no defence against *German* measles.

p. 21. "Hell I will" is usually "Will I hell!"

p. 25. Ignition switches on motor bikes are almost unheard of. I race my engine on stopping as I pull out the clutch or put her into neutral—not to fill the cylinders (two!) but because I take off the lead suddenly.

p. 27. "The fact is, Colonel." It would outrage the Colonel to be called Colonel by an "other rank." It is a style reserved for fellow-officers—or civilians.

p. 28. Last line. Ditto. (It is all right later where Meek gets Tallboys educated up to him!)

p. 31. 32. We only half-salute ladies. Just raise the hand to the front (not the side) of the forehead. The Col. does the right thing on p. 35.

p. 38. "the same old priest . . . for centuries." I expect this is intentional?

p. 42. "influenza" Perhaps malaria in that climate?

p. 43. Is hanging "bumps off"? I fancied it was a term for murder or illegal execution.

p. 81. "Ten rounds rapid—go." Last word should be "fire." Orders are never ambiguous. "Go" might mean charge or run.

p. 89. "Subalterns" An officer's word. The Sergeant would say "loo-tenants."

p. 91. "Nuder than unshorn lambs." I fail to see this very clearly. Lambs would be nuder shorn: but seldom are worth shearing!

To Charlotte Shaw   Southampton, 27 January 1932
. . . the first act [of *Too True to Be Good*] is so-so. I suspend judgement. G. B. S. has done it before. It does not develop. . . . Act II . . . . is mainly farce: excellent farce. Very delightfully foolish & foolishly delightful. Is the play just entertainment, I ask. Act III gets quickly to grips, and then relaxes for the Colonel to hit Mrs. Mopply over the head. The crowd laughs with relief, and before they can recover from the shock of surprise comes the overwhelming end. Until the last speech the play is all loose threads. That speech knits it all together and makes it terrible. . . . It is a great work. The people will not like it so well as the Applecart, I think: but it is far finer.

I regret to see that, probably by my fault in being too exclusively an engine-monger these days, on page 51 the rifles here have "cut-outs." These should be "cut-offs," of course. I am also not sure if Meek should twice "double" or "trot" out (pp. 32 and 53). In the R.A.F. and Navy other ranks double *to* an order. In the Army progress is always at the march. Perhaps I pettifog? I suppose, too, that Articles of War is correct for the Army Act? We always called it the Army Act, officially.

"Too True" is the only bright spot in my existence this winter. It gave me inexpressible pleasure. I went about for days with a feeling that some great unknown benefit to me had happened. And that does *not* mean Pte. Meek!

To Walter Hudd   London, 3 September 1932
As you can imagine, the first seeing was rather an occasion for me. The part you play is obviously a hit at me, and I felt very nervous, until all was over, lest something in it should hurt.

Actually I thoroughly enjoyed it—or rather I should say that I hope to come one night in London and see it again, for enjoyment's sake. The first time my stomach felt a bit hollow all through.

I thought you did the part admirably. You looked decent (I am always as correct as I can be, regimentally speaking) and I only wish nature had let me look half as smart and efficient as yourself. Only I get more gaiety out of my position. It's comic really, and I often see that, whereas you looked grim.

I hope you find the part a comfortable one. Acting and plays aren't much in my line—but I thought G. B. S. had really given you some pretty good chances, which you fully took. The house wriggled with delight over some of your quips and business.

. . . I have written only to thank you for a very rare and peculiar kindness you are doing my reputation, nightly.

To Richard Warner   Plymouth, 18 October 1932
That *Too True* play of G. B. S. was, I thought, very good. The counterfeit me was unfortunately much nicer than the original.

To Sir William Rothenstein   Plymouth, 20 October 1932
I found this last G. B. S. play [*Too True to Be Good*] magnificent. Tempest-like, almost, as a valediction.

To G. W. M. Dunn   Plymouth, 9 November 1932
G. B. S. is not a vast electric discharge. He is more like a cocktail. Very beneficent and plain to read. Slightly hard of hearing and short

of sight—by which I mean, prone to imagine the whole from an incomplete part.

Upton Sinclair

To Charlotte Shaw   [Karachi], 26 May 1927
I am, as you know, very left-wing: a philosophic anarchist, if you need a label. After Oil [1927], I rose up a capitalist, sympathising so utterly with the victims of Upton Sinclair's attack that there seemed no two sides to the question. Whereas of course there are, and after I've forgotten Oil all will be well again. But for the moment I'm like an Irish pig whom someone has tried to drive down a particular road. And yet his book is good, with sound material in it. If his bias had been hidden it would have been a convincing book. Is he, do you think, secretly an ally of the "big business" men? I suspect his sincerity. This is not the flaming earnestness of the Jungle [1906]. Old and rich, perhaps.

Edith Sitwell

To Charlotte Shaw   [Karachi], 4 May 1927
Mrs. Sitwell's book about India—well, you know, she is one of these restless people, who must tease something, either with their fingers or their wits, out of sheer inability to be still & simple for a moment. If ever she became quiet she would give away herself as an empty vessel, whose stillness was vacuum, not fullness—or that is her fear, & she hasn't yet gained enough courage to be quiet for a moment, & risk the failure. It is therefore not a book. No more are the books of the three Sitwells[129]...books, either. They have no life in themselves. Sometimes they are shadows of things we know, looking odd & twisted because the screen which catches them isn't true: (these perverted, artificial, fancy-dress minds are curses which the richly-born cannot throw off except they forget their Angevin ancestry, & become like babes) and sometimes they are just the retchings of a fine imagination which is queasy in itself, & strains to bring something up, and cannot! You perhaps have felt (as I did once) that worst wretchedness of sea-sickness upon an empty stomach. The Sitwells are always struggling to write, poor devils, and never will, till they stop striving, if ever they do. I don't suppose they will. I don't suppose they can. They are slaves of their time and generation. You should be very sorry for them.

"Frustrated artists", someone called the artful educated classes of today. There's an awful lot of rightness in the words.

Freya Stark

To Sydney Cockerell   Bridlington, 28 November 1934
   Well, I read *The Valleys of the Assassins*. I am grateful to you for the chance. She unfolds herself as a remarkable person. It is astonishing how the book takes life whenever she or anyone else speaks in it. Subtract the characters and the journeys fall dead. She uses far too many names, and hasn't the faculty to express places as she does people. A gallant creature. I hope she does not meet mishaps in Yemen or Hadhramaut. I suppose it is this Sheba myth that she pursues. Better that, anyway, than an uncrossed desert which when crossed proved to be empty. . . . Press her, some day, to care far more than she does for the communication of landscape to her readers. She fails to 'see' it.

Tolstoy

To E. M. Forster   20 February 1924
   War and Peace is almost the largest book in the world. I've carried it whenever I had the transport, and ever wished it longer. But then Tolstoi was an enormous genius. While I was trying to write I analysed most of you, and found out, so far as it was within my fineness to see, what were your tricks of effect, the little reserves & omissions which gave you power to convey more than the print says. But it is hopeless to grapple with Tolstoi. The man is like yesterday's east wind, which brought tears when you faced it and numbed you meanwhile.

To Charlotte Shaw   Karachi, 11 January 1927
   On the road out I read *War and Peace* (still good: very good: but not more-than-human, as I first thought). . .

H. G. Wells

To V. W. Richards   27 February 1920
   I haven't read [Wells's] *Boon*: and I don't like Wells. He has written eighty books.

To Charlotte Shaw   5 November 1925
   . . . H. G. neglects the beauty of writing so cavalierly that he must

know something about it. I've always respected his straightness, his speed of mind, his generous width. He has all the vulgar side which Sir H. S. [Herbert Samuel] wouldn't show. . . . H. G. W. shows it so broadly that clearly he isn't really vulgar. . . .

To Charlotte Shaw   3 June 1926
H. G. converted me to like him when he stopped writing about grocers, & published "The new Machiavelli [1911]." You perhaps thought it poor. I like it next best, after "[*The Island of*] Dr. Moreau" [1896] and the "[*Outline of*] History" [1920].

To Robert Graves   [Karachi], 29 March 1928
I'm losing my cutting edge, and therefore understand better, sympathise with, people like Wells and [Arnold] Bennett and the rest, who slide down the easy slope into fatuity.

To F. N. Doubleday   [Collieston, Scotland], 18 September 1930
. . . I eat pounds of peppermints. . . or read H. G. Wells' *History* in a dollar edition lately produced, as you may have heard, by a young and pushing publisher in the States. I wish I had a dozen copies to give away: but only one ran the customs gauntlet to do Cassells out of his English rights. Believe me, it's a good book.

To Charlotte Shaw   Southampton, 23 August 1933
   I met H. G. Wells in the train three weeks ago. 'You' I said rashly 'probably want to write no more stories now'. He replied 'I dare not: my reputation is too great to risk a failure: and one writes a good story only by writing three or four bad ones, and till the public has read them the good does not appear from the bad. So I can only afford to write histories and things'. There is something behind that: probably an excuse for having grown up.

Thornton Wilder

To Charlotte Shaw   [Karachi], 25 February 1928
   St. Luis Rey: Bridge of. I have finished it: too quickly, I think. The good little man who wrote it with such care and kindness worked himself a little too hard. So there is a thinness about it, after all. The first chapter, where he struck me new, was a knock out: and all the development of the letter-writing great Countess was superb: also her hill journey, & conversion to a sane mind: and upon that her death. I call all of it wonderful: there I should have liked the book to stop. It was tempting providence to dare that bridge again, after he had

once leaped it: and I do not think he got better each later time. Probably any one of the after chapters would have read well first: but the great dame is surely his mistress-portait. Pepita, & the Abbess.....all wonderful. A very great pleasure the reading of that Bridge of S. Luis Rey.

To Charlotte Shaw   [Karachi], 26 April 1928
    The Cabala by Wilder. I liked this, in some ways, better than the Bridge. There was more observation, and less theoretical character-making. Wilder's inventions aren't as good as his eyesight, I fancy: though I'd like to know him before being sure. His work isn't big, & never will be:...yet I felt reality behind some of those absurd Romans. How he can dare put his tongue so constantly into his cheek, I can't imagine. I'd have laughed first. . . .

To Lady Astor   Plymouth, 8 January 1930
His "Bridge" was a performance that made one like him. Not a great writer: not perhaps essentially a writer at all: but a very decent fellow, and an artist in souls.
    I sent him a line. Why? Lord knows. Why not?

Henry Williamson

To Henry Williamson   Karachi, March? 1928
    Had I known you were so established a writer I'd never have had the cheek to write down my 'prentice ideas about the book.[130] By the care and passion of the text I'd assumed you were a beginner, half in love with his first effort, and probably now heart-broken at its failure to come anywhere near the perfection dreamed of:—I'll never forget the despair with which I read my Seven Pillars in 1923, after forgetting it for two years. It was incredibly unlike what I'd thought my talents (of which I'd had too good an opinion) would bring forth, that I then and there swore I'd never try again. If there'd been any redeemable feature.....but the whole thing was unwholesome.
    Back to Tarka: the worst thing about the war-generation of introspects is that they can't keep off their blooming selves. As you saw, I'm glad to say, by the length and elaboration of my remarks, the book did move me, and gratify me, profoundly. It was the real stuff. I shouldn't, if I were you, attempt to re-do it; the non-successes, the gritty stuff, of real people, are altogether topping as examples of how things come and grow; it's like sculpture: the brokenness of the

Venus de Milo is the main virtue of that sentimental but very lovely work. I like best of all the books in which fallible men have burst themselves trying to do better than they can be. Tarka, to anyone who's tried to write, is a technical delight, all the more perfect for being imperfect, here and there. If you write it out again, and make a rounded and gracious thing of it, you'll rob us of the object lesson, and deprive us of what might have been a new and lovely book, on another subject.

I wonder what you'll do about money. Tarka will not have made much, and the more carefully you write the less you are likely to earn. Do you notice how the writers who are very widely sold are so often careless writers? Dickens, I'm thinking of, and Tolstoi, and Balzac: though Balzac rewrote all his novels in proof, but he wasn't thinking about their form, so much as of the forms of the characters in them. I wish I could think clearly enough about all the writers of the world, and see if it's more than blind chance which makes one seem good and another bad: if only there was an absolute somewhere: the final standard by which everything could be measured. At present we have ever so many surveys of literature: but they aren't so much surveys as sentimental journeys across it. For a survey you must have a measured base: and instead of that we have just opinions and opinions.

...You say the Pathway[131] is unhappy stuff. Well, so is all my writing. Let not us impotents be shy of our impotencies, behind the licked envelopes of letters.

To Edward Garnett   Karachi, 22 March 1928
Williamson has sent me a book of his, *The Old Stag*: stories. He seems pleased over what I said of *Tarka*. But he has written a great deal. If I'd known he was so practised I wouldn't have dared write him.

To Henry Williamson   Karachi, 1928
You'll laugh to hear that I still pick up Tarka often, read a few pages, and lay it down. I find it holds more than I thought, even at first: and what I said the first time was "pemmican": a variety, I'm told, of pressed beef.

The public pressure on you to write another book before you feel inclined to think of a pen seriously, must be horrid.

To Henry Williamson   [Plymouth?], 1930
I have been too long, perhaps, over the Patriot's Progress: but after my first reading of it everybody in the Hut got hold of it, and I only saw it again yesterday, when I read it for the second time.

It is all right: that is the first thing to say. To do a war-book is very hard now, after all that has been written, but yours survives as a thing of its own. I heaved a great sigh of relief when it was safely over. I like it all.

Your writing scope grows on me. This book is a tapestry, a decoration: the almost-null John Bullock set against a marvellous background. It is the most completely two-dimensional thing possible —and on the other hand you give us your cycle of novels (about yourself, I dare say) which are as completely three-dimensional, full of characters as a Christmas Pudding of almonds, with the background only occasional, and only occasionally significant. I am convinced, by both Tarka and the P.P. that you have many other books to write before you repeat yourself and become a classic.

I sandwiched the P.P. between readings of "Her Privates We". The P.P. is natural man, making no great eyes at his sudden crisis: whereas "Her Privates We" shows the adventures of Bourne, a queer dilettante, at grips with normal man in abnormal circumstances. The two books complement each other so well. Yours is the first quite unsentimental war-book—except perhaps for its last page, and nobody could have resisted that kick of farewell. I should have thought less well of you without that touch of irony here and there.

The incidental beauties of the book—the dewdrops on its leaves—are so common as hardly to be seen. That, I feel, is right in a book whose restraint is so strong. You seem to be able to pen a good phrase in simple words almost as and when you please. You beat Bunyan there, for he got to the end of his P.P. without throwing in a deliberately fine phrase. . . .

I begin to suspect that you may be one of those comparatively rare authors who write best about people or things other than themselves. I hope so, because it is the sort that lasts longest, unless one is a very deep man, like Dostoevsky, and can keep on digging down into oneself. I hope you aren't that, because it means misery for the artist, and the two roads happiness and misery, seem to be equally within our choice, and it's more common sense to be happy.

Tarka and this P.P. are better than your novels, I think, because you get further outside the horrific convolutions of your brain in each. The objective, as someone would probably say, which is the classic rather than the romantic manner.

I have enjoyed the P.P. very much. The Hut fellows say it isn't properly named, it being not a "bloody bind" like that Bunyan chap's stuff. "Bind" is a lovely word: mental constipation.

To Henry Williamson   1931?
    . . . a full-blooded book of men and women [*The Dream of Fair Women*], very hot, rushing, and life-like. The characters so good; the

places so good. Your Rats-Castle, was it?—a creation. Folkestone in Armistice year—the reality itself. Your men so good: all of them. The chief woman feels like a living being... You have, in it, come wholly out of your ivory tower. Only in the tower could you have written Tarka: but life is better outside the tower than in.

Does the Dream finish the Maddison books? I suppose so. New York will have prompted you to interests so far from your dead self. Only take my assurance that the Dream is very rare and fine and strong.

To Henry Williamson   Plymouth, 13 February 1933
   I've been grinning through the week-end over the Falcon [*The Gold Falcon*], of which a vellum and gold copy reached me from Faber on Saturday.

By the same post arrived a plain copy, sent me from an indignant reviewer,[132] demanding to know why I had fathered this decadent bilge upon an innocent world. It's a queer world, my mistresses!

The Falcon has that jumpy, nervous, stippled technique that you were developing in the Dream of [Fair] Women. It fits a jazzy subject, and conveys an astonishing sense of movement, all through the tale.

. . . There are several astonishing bits of characterisation. The climax was perhaps your only way out of a difficulty. . . . All right in life, but too coloured for a tale.

Wrink I didn't recognize: but all your contemporaries (except Priestley, perhaps) will recognize themselves preeningly. I preened. Are my letters real extracts, or have you polished?

To write the day after is not wise. I can't say how I really regard the book. You are a long way from the chiselled and rather static prose of your beginning: and it is always good to go on, and bad to repeat. Only I sometimes wonder where you are going.

They'll all call Manfred a self-portrait: but somehow I remember you as much more solid than that.

To John Brophy   Plymouth, 13 February 1933
   Thanks for the Gold Falcon[133]—and this morning a copy of it arrives from Faber & Faber, a luxury book, in vellum & gold! So H. W. is *not* ashamed of it.

Nor, candidly, am I. Let me confess that I got a good deal of laughing pleasure out of it. You will think me very decadent, but this disintegrated, exclamatory style fits its subject, and keeps the whole book in movement. It is not as good as "Dream of Fair Women", H. W.'s remarkable study of the armistic rot. . . . . but it is probably a not-too-wild picture of the literary New York that he knows.

As for his contemporaries, he is hot against Priestley—but all high brow writers are: and he praises all the others, including me, if I am a writer & contemporary. Admittedly he has quoted letters of mine, but such harmless plain phrases. My memory has forgotten them: yet they are likely to be authentic. No room for objection, from me.

So on the whole I sum up favourably. There is no growth in the book: and the climax is a surrender to an impossible dilemma: a weakness: but there is much activity, some good pictures of town & country, two (at least) characters. Pros and cons. Not a favourite book, nor a well-selling book, but not despicable. You are over-harsh, I think.

To Henry Williamson   Southampton, 14 May 1934
Sorry about the book—or, rather, about the U.S.A. verdict upon its prospects. I expect the *Falcon* has frightened the publishers over there. You handled them too freely, perhaps.

If you can become objective again, for a spell, it will give us something deeper and more exciting than what you have written before, I hope. The subjective stuff is wonderful exercise, but temporary in its value: or temporal, rather, for its significance seems to ebb and flow with the times. Good for now, rotten in 20 years, interesting again after sixty years. Whereas the objective stuff does not date.

However you have the gift of twisting surprises out of ordinary words and situations and happenings: so none of your writing can fail to give at least technical pleasure. Sometimes I would wish you at least one skin more, for daily wear, however. Your writing costs you too much.

To Henry Williamson   Bridlington, 11 December 1934
I have so much the better of you: for when I want a talk, it is just putting out an arm and taking a book from my shelves. . . . but . . . for a word with you yesterday I had to go to York and lay out three days' pay on The Linhay [*on the Downs*]. . . . .which I have been dipping into, with satisfaction. . . .

What a sentence for No. I! Do you find it hard to begin books? Let me take down your hackles by two quotes from the Linhay: bad sentences P. 67 "how heat and the floating algae. . .takes". . .P. 36 "many old bucks are caught in gins which otherwise would eat young rabbits".

It isn't fair, for I would like to write like you, easily or grudgingly but copiously, able to make a sentence of all you see and do, with a catching intimate easy speech, like a man in slippers. For a mannered writer, you have the best manners in the world.

Don't vex yourself over Walpole or Shanks or Hanks or Banks: or vex yourself only because they discourage your book-buyers. Or do they? The best way to sell a novel was to persuade the Bishop of

London to preach against it. I can conceive Hugh Walpole being second-best. I fancy writers get so wrapped up in their own sort of writing, that they find all variations from it bad. At least, they seem to me to make poor critics of contemporary stuff. You write almost disarmingly well. You write better than Richard Jefferies, splendid fellow though he was: better for me, that is: I feel more heart and see less eye, in you. You look for the unusual, he for the average. Of course he had an awful life. No Alvis, no country contentment, or comfort, anyhow. Few concerns aside from earning, and no war to light his background. We learned a lot in those years, which makes us immemorially older and wiser than the old or the young.

W. B. Yeats

To Ezra Pound   Oxford, 20 August 1920
. . . surely R. Aldington and W. B. Yeats are no good?

To Charlotte Shaw   [Karachi], 21 April 1927
Yeats is a dismal poet. Very good: oh very good: with, like Wordsworth a congenital inability to write a good poem. He lacks vulgarity, in him, and consequently lacks the sense to avoid vulgarity, and sentiment, which is the female of vulgarity. . . . Of all the Irish movement it's only G. B. S. who has a hearty laugh. Moore and Joyce snigger: and A E and W. B. Y. smile: with a faint and far off smile.

To Charlotte Shaw   [Miranshah], 23 July 1928
For Yeats' critical judgement I should not give one bean. His prose is awful. His verse magnificent.

To James Hanley   Plymouth, 2 July 1931
Yeats, I think, suffered in his middle years from Lady Gregory and others: but his later poems have been wonderful. Of course he's a great poet, and alive. I think the second quality the better!

To Charlotte Shaw   Plymouth, 16 September 1932
About W. B. Yeats' letter. You know, it staggers me that I should seriously be considered in such company. All the best Irish, except A E, I fancy: and many of the not-so-good, too. I don't think any other country of the size would produce such a list.
I would like it, because it is a gesture on my part, that I am Irish: and I would like to think that. My work from the *Seven Pillars* onward, probably does not justify my joining that company. My reputation

probably does. So on the whole I ought to say Yes to W. B. and to thank him for an unexpected and extraordinary compliment. Will you write for me? I should be troubled in writing to him: for I have regarded him always as an exquisite and unattainable poet. He passes the test of the bigger people that his later work is more interesting, if less melodious, than his early work. Those *Tower* poems were splendid.

To W. B. Yeats   Plymouth, 12 October 1932
Your letter is dated 'Feb 26th'. . . . I have been away from Camp. . . . Otherwise I would have tried to say at once how much I have appreciated this compliment of nomination by you. I am Irish, and it has been a chance to admit it publicly—but it touches me very deeply that you should think anything I have done or been to justify this honour.
. . . It is very good of you, and touches me particularly, for I have been reading your work for years. You got your compliment in first, so I will not try to butter back: but you must see how valuable to a flash-in-the-pan is praise from one who has almost a lifetime of growing work behind his judgement.
I set eyes on you once, in Oxford, many years ago, and wanted then to call the street to attention (for lack of power to make the sun blaze out appropriately, instead!) but fortunately did nothing. I hope that you are going further yet, in poetry, for our benefit. That sounds greedy; but you never repeat yourself, and so everything matters.

To Siegfried Sassoon   Clouds Hill, 17 December 1934
His [Yeats's] *Tower* poems are like the ash of poetry. People offended his taste by putting *Innisfree* into all the anthologies, because they liked it not for the poetry but for the green sap running through it.

5

Literary Themes

Introduction

Lawrence never set forth his ideas on good writing in essay form; his mind focussed on individuals, books, events, places, or periods rather than general ideas (a reason it is so easy to catch him in evident contradictions, for what seemed appropriate in a letter to one person was the opposite of what was appropriate to another), and he would not foist his taste on others (though his enthusiasm for Doughty, Day Lewis, Hanley, or Manning helped to sell their books). He never claimed and often disclaimed to be a "critic."

Nonetheless, certain ideas and preferences inescapably recur in his correspondence, as do expressions like "I fancy" and "have you noticed." They might be called his critical signature, a reflection of his character, his own writing experience, and the nature and range of his literary insight and tolerance.

His letters **On Reading** show a bookish young man of twenty-two who could be absorbed in plays and knightly French romances on a long summer bicycling trip and, seven years later, in Aristophanes or Malory on long desert treks. One would not expect a man who "does not like things [books and scenery] if there are other people about" (p. 237) to be a natural leader of other men and reader of their minds and moods.

Despite his many friends and many more acquaintances, Lawrence was a loner, a man who loved no one (except, perhaps, Dahoum, a young Arab) and bound himself to no thing (except, perhaps, his motorcycle). Thus, reading and corresponding were of unusual importance to him, providing some of the intimacy he otherwise lacked.

His **Spelling**, especially of names, most especially Arabic names, is too entertaining to be subjected to analysis. Poor Charlotte Shaw, to whom he confided so much, had to fathom which confessions were genuine, which were aspirations, and which, inventions: "he is such an INFERNAL liar" she once expostulated (Shaw 1977, 40). "I don't want to use a large vocabulary" was a singularly futile aspiration. "I've never been stable enough to own a dictionary" was a condition repaired with the two-volume 1933 edition of the *Shorter Oxford English Dictionary*.

The double sense of past and present evoked in Lawrence's account of his walk through Athens to the Parthenon (p. 251) he doubtless also felt in his walk through Palestine and Syria, the ruins along the Euphrates, and Doughty's tracks in Arabia.

His remarks on **Greek** literature are characteristically contradictory. One year, Noël Rieder should prefer Greek to Latin; another year, "There is not a great deal of good Greek to read"; then "There seem to be ten good Greek books to every Latin one." Whatever his judgment of Greek literature, he is definitely down on Latin.

In his comments on **French Writers**, the theme of "power" and "strength" reappears; likewise in his discussion of **Rimbaud** (p. 212). ". . . there went something out of France after the Fronde [1648–52]: what I call strength" (p. 254). That Montesquieu was "more of a man" (whatever that may mean) than "Old Montaigne" (who died younger than Montesquieu) is odd. Is wisdom unmanly?

The books Lawrences **Likes and Dislikes** tell us as much about his character as chapter 103, "Myself," in *Seven Pillars*, and more about how it changed as he aged. Some favorites in his early twenties and later are adventure stories and fantasies boys read in their teens. At twenty-three and again at forty-two he commends Algernon Blackwood's *The Centaur*. There are, of course, other signs that, despite his remarkable talents and achievements, Lawrence remained a permanent adolescent.

The Centaur (1911), reprinted in the Arno Supernatural and Occult Fiction collection (1976), is a peculiar tale of a young Irishman's encounter with mystic spirits on a ship to Batoum. The spirits inhabit a strangely primitive, silent Russian "Urmensch" and his son, who disappears over the ship's rail like a spirit taking flight. In the high Caucasus, the Irishman, "a wanderer . . . . never quite growing up . . . . in a state of perpetual astonishment at the mystery of things," meets the Russian again, sees a large troop of prancing centaurlike spirits, and discovers (as the reader is assisted to believe by quotations from Fechner, William James, and Oliver Lodge) that the earth itself is a great "living, conscious Being." Returning to London to impart these transcendent truths to the unbelieving English, he can write only a fragmentary, inadequate manuscript and dies of a lack of interest in living and eating in the dispiriting world.

"I'd rather have written the Well at the World's End [and several other Morris stories] . . . than anything of the 19th Cent. except War & Peace or Moby Dick," Lawrence told Charlotte Shaw in 1927 when he was thirty-eight. "I suppose everybody loves one writer, unreasonably. I'd rather Morris than the world." And two years later: "My reason tells me that he isn't a very great writer: but then, he wrote just the stuff I like."

The Well at the World's End (1896), reprinted in Ballantine's science fiction series (1975), tells of twenty-one-year-old Ralph, youngest son of good King Peter of the happy little kingdom Upmeads, who rides forth in knightly armor to seek the well that "saveth from weariness and wounding and sickness; . . . winneth love from all," quenches sorrow, clears the eyes, and (like Morris's *Glittering Plain*) makes old people "as young folk for a long while again." There are contests and battles with spear and sword, battle ax and bow, fields and forests, villages and castles, kingdoms fifty or one-hundred miles across, lords, yeomen, slaves, fighting men "waged," women captured and sold.

Goodness and badness are visible in a stranger's features. Oaths and bonds are honored, beads and tokens pledge the help of a tribe, loyalty and love are frankly declared and unswerving, prophecies are fulfilled, sorcery is overcome by wise old men. Ralph and his love Ursula escape an evil king and bandits, cross woods and fields, mountains and lava beds, deserts, a great ampitheater filled with the bodies of those who died in the quest. At a distant, rocky shore they find the well; a drink heals scars and wounds and makes them blemishless, strong, and youthful for generations.

After writing this, I was astonished to read the glowing praise of H. G. Wells, Swinburne, and Yeats in their 1896 reviews of this novel. Wells, who knew the socialist Morris, dismisses "those absurd younger days, when one seriously imagined we were to be led anywhere but backward by this fine old scholar." Yet Morris's prose is "a purification"; his book, full of "naked beauty . . . . stout oaken stuff that must needs endure." To Swinburne, *The Well* is "a perfect and unique masterpiece," a "magically beautiful tale." To Yeats, Morris was "a prophet" who conveyed a vision of the "perfect life" with "pictures of beautiful things and beautiful moments."[1] Writing shortly after Morris's death, all praised a man surely worthy of praise by praising a work less surely so praiseworthy. Or has the passage of a century so overturned our judgment that the passage of another will turn it round again?

Morris, extraordinarily energetic and productive, wrote his fantasies in intervals between his countless crafts and businesses, his poetry, friends, and socialist preaching. He took them less seriously than Lawrence:[2] but how seriously *did* Lawrence take them? He did not, apparently, go to the movies, did not read detective stories, did little light reading of any kind, did not smoke, drink alcohol, or indulge in any known form of normal sex. He did indulge in Morris's boyish fictions.

Lawrence's literary taste was conservative. Among his contemporaries, he preferred Conrad, Kipling, Wells, Forster, and D. H. Lawrence to Joyce, Wyndham Lewis, Gertrude Stein, or Aldous Huxley. He disliked verbal high jinks and fol-de-rol (though, to judge from his appreciation of Pound and Roy Campbell, he might indulge some in poetry). As Sidney Cockerell told Hardy, "He is not an upholder of anarchy or eccentricity—and his opinion of some of the noisier writers of the young generation is no higher than your own."[3]

Two modes Lawrence frequently extolled, the profuse epic (*Moby Dick, War and Peace, Arabia Deserta*) and the carefully composed work without a hair misplaced (*Salammbô, Eothen, Scenes and Portraits*) are in conflict. It is hard to be both relaxed and controlled at the same time; if *Seven Pillars* tries, it fails since sheer length and profuse detail cannot replace free feeling or what Lawrence called "rough texture." In his later years, Lawrence gradually turned against the controlled stylists. "I now like H. G. Wells better than Norman Douglas: and call Kipling better than Crackanthorpe: just because their carelessness gives me a sense of power. . . . The stylists are too miserly. Agreed I am a bad example of the too-careful type" (p. 258). "It is not a merit to write . . . for the very few. The very few are not so useful as the very many" (p. 282).

Lawrence objects to art as preaching or propaganda. The artist is less qualified for this than the preacher or politician, and preaching disturbs the faithful rendition of his vision. So, "had it [*White-Jacket*] not been meant to improve the American Navy it would have been a better book" (p. 207); *The Well of Loneliness* (p. 173) (like *Maurice*) is a poorer novel because of its propagandistic purpose (though it might also be poor without the propaganda). Upton Sinclair's diatribe against "capitalists" elicits Lawrence's sympathy for them; Remarque's screaming against "war" shows how little he (unlike Graves, Sassoon, or Manning) knows about it; if, in *The Enormous Room*, Cummings "could have seen good in his oppressors . . . he would have been a greater man than me" (p. 144).

The Clouds suffers from Doughty's preaching: "I wish he would desert the pulpit. The poet's place is at the altar" (p. 146). "Poets hope too much, and their politics, like their sciences, usually stink after twenty years" (p. 283).

Simone Weil and Victoria Ocampo loved Lawrence, vicariously, to be sure, for neither knew him or noted (or, if they did, took seriously) his disaparagement of **Women Writers.** "There hasn't ever yet been a woman of genius."[4] . . . all the women who ever wrote . . . could

have been strangled at birth, and the history of English literature . . .
would be unchanged" (p. 261).

Robert Graves (9) reports Lawrence's opinion "that women were,
historically, incapable of writing or painting anything first-class. He
had little opinion of Emily Brontë, and held that there was not enough
of Sappho's poetry extant to warrant his revising his opinion on her
account." A few kind words for George Eliot, Willa Cather, and
H. H. Richardson all but exhaust his stock of praise. To his mind,
the emancipation of women had gone far enough by 1928. "Perhaps
in the days [of yore] . . . women were oppressed: but I see little traces
of it today. . . . [I fear] the boot will soon be on the other foot."[5]
Lawrence fled seduction other men would welcome, including, it seems,
seduction by prose.

Lawrence's complaint to University of Missouri President Walter
Williams that the books selected as the "best and most important"
of 1932–34 excluded too many **Writers Ahead of The Time** shows
the uncertainty of such judgment. He commends the inclusion of
Halper, Housman, MacLeish, Shaw, and Tomlinson, but overlooks
Blunden, Eliot, Graves, Huxley, and Wells, who were also on it, not
to mention Bennett, Buchan, Galsworthy, and many American writers
whose location ahead, behind, or just abreast of the time may be
uncertain. Of the seventeen names he cites as worthy of addition,
four (Richardson, Roberts, Stein, Woolf) were women.

The list was not so bad as Lawrence suggests. Emphasizing American
writers and embracing history, biography, politics, economics, religion,
travel, and science, its choice in literature was necessarily limited.[6]

Reflecting on what makes for **Good and Great Writing**, Lawrence
is preoccupied with the issue of deliberateness. He himself was too
conscious too constantly. "Lawrence's chief curse is that he cannot
stop thinking," Robert Graves (1927, 49) observed. Excessive thinking
cursed his living (as an obstacle to loving, relaxing, and enjoying many
things) and writing; he wondered what part it played in great and good
writing.

"Do . . . people ever write *consciously* well?" he asks; he wants
to say "yes," but for great writers the answer is "no." "Most of us
have to plough and harrow the upper mind, deliberately. . . . If you
can put your subconscious mind to work . . . , then you write without
apparent effort, and are a genius" (p. 269). Too deliberate writing
can become mannered writing, which Lawrence long esteemed but later
depreciated. ". . . I come to value the manner less and the matter
more. Once I scorned any prose that was not mannered" (p. 273).

C. Day Lewis rightly notes "the fascination which the imperfect
held for him" (*Minorities*, 15). " . . . the charm and comfort of

imperfection," Lawrence suggests, "makes up for most of the failures of the world" (p. 270). "The goodness of artists lies very much in their reticences: the little things they do not say:—as the beauty of the Venus of Melos lies in the loss of her arms" (p. 266).[7] He makes the same point about poetry, revisions, misprints, and even book bindings. "Art . . . is avoidance as much as it is presentation" (p. 278). "The blemishes he [the artist] does not see are remarked by the world" (p. 274). " . . . you'll find your heart going out to the blemishes" in a leather binding (p. 275), he tells Charlotte Shaw, whose heart probably did no such thing.

Beside Lawrence the perfectionist, Lawrence the realist is here discernible, the scoffer at other people's orderliness, the scruffy officer who would not wear his hair or uniform right, who saw the flaws and failures in all things human and sought, but failed to accept them in himself. Lawrence's interest in archeology may have stemmed in part from the same fascination with wear and tear, with the imaginative reconstruction of a once-whole world from its worn and shattered fragments.

The worst writing, regardless of style, is "manufactured writing" which has nothing to say. The Sitwells and "the artful educated classes" who write like that "must tease something, either with their fingers or their wits" (p. 227). When *he* had nothing to say (he often felt that way in later life), he did not try.

The genius, who writes abundantly and effortlessly, is at the opposite pole from two kinds of writers: 1) Those whose work is a physical necessity, "like discharging the matter of a boil" (p. 267). "A book should burst out of a man, against his will, like a vomit into the sea" (p. 271). This is art as emotional seizure à la Van Gogh, for which the artist hardly deserves credit, since he is the powerless instrument, not controlling power, of its creation. 2) Those who "burst themselves" trying. John Davidson is a poorer poet than Ernest Dowson but "worthier, because he tried his hardest, and burst in the effort " (p. 279). "I like best of all the books in which fallible men have burst themselves trying to do better than they can be" (p. 257).

However, effort is futile without talent; talent and effort together cannot rival genius. Inspiration is central; conscious effort, peripheral. The **First Draft** is everything **and Revision**, of minor value. "No revision makes an incomplete thing into a creation. Life comes either at once, or not at all" (p. 273). "All the talent in the world never approaches genius" (p. 191). In creative work there isn't any place or hope for good intention, for the second best; it's the least democratic thing imaginable" (p. 266). Genius does not burst itself striving; it is relaxed, even careless. "The big men (of the Balzac, Tolstoi, Dostoevski,

Dickens stamp) are incredibly careless. . . . There's a lavish ease about their stuff" (p. 267).

Ordinary writers have the consolation of appealing to ordinary people. "It feels more homelike. That's the reward of secondary writers. They don't knock-out: but by their very smallness, or middle-size, they become good companions for ordinary people" (p. 268). "We admire the very great, but love the less" (p. 270).

Where once he put artists above other men, Lawrence came to attach less importance to both artists and art. "I don't think publishing or reading are very valuable activities" (p. 268). A special gift did not make a man different, in other respects, from his fellow men, or better *as a man*. "Your precious artist . . . comes second to the common man" (p. 271).

Of the **Critics and Criticism** of his day Lawrence likes Graves on poetry, Wyndham Lewis on the modernists, Forster on the novel, Edward Garnett and Arnold Bennett on almost everyone but T. E. Lawrence. He derides Eliot: "mock profound"; "I don't know any critic who more darkens the merits and confuses the faults of his authors" (p. 154).

Needless to say, his views were not shared universally. Lawrence himself gave up on Wyndham Lewis ("I am not going to read him any more"), whose special talent was making enemies. F. R. Leavis held Forster's *Aspects of the Novel* to be "intellectually null"; Charlotte Shaw thought little of Edward Garnett's critical judgment;[8] while Robert Graves, Wyndham Lewis, and J. Middleton Murry, among others, castigated Arnold Bennett as mendacious.[9]

Lawrence places **Poetry** above prose **and Poets** above other writers. Is it because he could not write poetry—"I have never yet written a line of poetry in my life" (Garnett, 589)—could not let go his feelings? Only three Lawrence poems have come to light[10] and the best-known, the dedicatory poem "To S. A." in *Seven Pillars*, was rewritten by Robert Graves.

When Lawrence tells a fellow airman who had begun to write poetry that he is "unsure of the capacity you have for more" (p. 281), he is politely trying to separate the amateur talent from the professional. Volume of output is the simplest way; often he seems to make too much of it. "I like profusion. . . . the small thing is suspect, as the writer may have been himself small" (p. 257)—as was Lawrence: a mere five-feet-five. Does bulk explain his inexplicable rating of *The Dynasts* above "every other poem in the language" (p. 281)? His own anthology, *Minorities*, singles out "minor poems": "good poems by small poets, or small poems by good poets."[11]

Kingsley Widmer finds Lawrence's taste in poetry "sentimental and paltry" (Meyers, 30); the publishers at Cape, which issued *Minorities* in 1971, privately called it the worst anthology they had seen. Striving to commend Lawrence's taste, C. Day Lewis must nonetheless observe that *Minorities* (15–16) includes "a good many . . . flowery and shallow" poems and that Lawrence's "dislikes can seem as unwarrantable and violent as some of his enthusiasms."

Lawrence's kindness can at times vitiate his judgment, as when he tells a friend, "there is no good or bad poetry: just poetry" (p. 281)—or is that the *reductio ad absurdum* of his growing faith in simple writing for simple people?

His attempts to console Forster and Manning for the inconsolable loss of their creative power faintly resemble his letters to bereaved friends. To Forster, he says, "you feel empty, . . . as if the profession was exhausted. But it isn't. Just wait a bit. Ten more years if necessary" (p. 157). To Manning, he adds a touch of humor. "Copy the poise . . . of E. M. Forster whose every book is acclaimed . . . a masterpiece, and who yet refrains successfully from ever deliberately achieving another" (p. 206).

The case of Ernest Altounyan discloses the gentle personal motives Lawrence's criticism of a friend's work can serve. In 1933, Lawrence named Altounyan, a surgeon and poet, one of "the three [with Manning and Forster] I most care for" (Graves, 170); after Lawrence's death, Altounyan published a long poem extolling him.[12] In 1933 and 1934, emotionally sick and disturbed, Altounyan was under a doctor's care; his letters effusively declare his love of Lawrence.

Lawrence's criticism of the manuscript poems Altounyan sent him (pp. 282, 284) can be better understood from several letters to Geoffrey Keynes, a mutual friend. "Yes, Ernest is in a bad way," Lawrence writes Keynes January 28, 1934. "I asked [Altounyan's doctor] for directions, and he told me not to dash his hopes or beliefs abruptly, but to distract him. They [the poems] are very wild, argumentative, ejaculatory, interjectory. . . . All very spasmodic. . . . They record more rapture than they convey. . . . I have suggested interspersing the poems with prose notes." On February 10: "There is . . . much incoherence" in Altounyan's new poems. "I am telling him so, gently". On August 6: "I am beginning to praise his poems now, to check his tendency to lose heart over them" *(Bodleian)*. It is a plain case of criticism as therapy.

The Mint "got David rather badly—& after his wife had read it, you, the idol, fell off your pedestal, but was picked up quickly & wiped & replaced there," Edward Garnett informed Lawrence in July 1928 (*Letters*, 101). A few days later, David Garnett spoke for himself:

My first impression is that you are a queerer man than I took you to be from The Seven Pillars: (you have probably become queerer) queerer & less intellectual. You don't strike me from the Mint as intellectual at all: I see you as much more a man with the gift of words, a poet, an orator, a preacher, than a man of ideas or thinker. (*Letters*, 83)

A man who wrote three poems and delivered no orations is scarcely a poet or orator, yet Lawrence could hold an audience silent with his soft, penetrating, word-perfect talk and something in this analysis rings true. Lawrence did change after *Seven Pillars*. In it, he preached the Arab cause; in *The Mint*, the cause of the air force and the men who served it, to the displeasure of David Garnett (a conscientious objector in World War I), E. M. Forster, H. M. Tomlinson, and others to whom the RAF was a satanic instrument of destruction—until the Battle of Britain.

The contention that Lawrence had grown less "intellectual," less "a man of ideas or thinker" is more problematic. It is justifiable if "intellectual" signifies a believer in and proponent of large ideas and generalizations, preferably scholarly or scientific ideas established by empirical evidence. But few literary men would then be "intellectual." Probably Garnett merely means neither scientists nor professional scholars but intelligent, cultivated men who discourse on the issues of their circle and time.

In that sense, Lawrence, an intellectual in his political and early literary days, subsequently thought less of intellectual activity and more of the skilled and unskilled labor of common men. "The genius raids, but the common people occupy and possess," he said in his own obituary (Graves, 181–82).

However, his attacks on **This Frenzy to Know** show he never had much faith in grand ideas or the virtues of knowledge (as against the practical usefulness of specific ideas and information). Seeing Chartres—"the sight of a lifetime"—in 1908, soon after his twentieth birthday, he says, "the truth doesn't matter a straw if men only believe what they say or . . . believe something" (p. 284). Of course, he means "doesn't matter" to how we should live and behave.

That feeling persists throughout the years. ". . . the more I tried my head . . . on ideas, . . . the less they meant" (p. 284). "We know too much, and use too little knowledge" (p. 286). "The curse of our age is this thought-maggoty caries of the head from which the high-brows suffer" (p. 286). "I think an established land . . . can do with 1% . . . nihilists. That leaves room for me" (p. 287).

Nihilism is where Lawrence came out. Once he escaped his fundamentalist home, he believed in no god, no political ideology, no intellectual creed, no literary school; he joined no party, organization, or association (not even a motorcycle association whose invitation he spurned). A hero who sought and failed to escape fame, a writer who wrote a great book but felt he had not, a great reader, he began by idolizing literary artists and ended by questioning their importance. An intellectual—if a penetrating, independent mind, encyclopedic knowledge, the power of incisive analysis, exposition, and persuasion, of getting to the heart of the matter make one—he came to question the importance of intellect, especially the "highbrow" literary intellect.

His literary criticism, like his character, was incisive, provocative, inclined to hyperbole, kind, wide-ranging, tolerant, funny, rather old-fashioned, contradictory, changeable, at times incomprehensible.

In both life and letters, he was unusually kind, perhaps excessively generous, to his friends and far too harsh on himself. The imbalance was unjust and self-destructive. He had himself whipped literally and whipped himself mentally. Loved by many, he could not love in return and hence was lonely and unhappy. His life is the tragedy of an extraordinary man who despised himself.

On Reading

To his mother   Le Petit Andelys, August 1910
The book I had was *Petit Jehan de Saintré* [by Antoine de la Sale], a XV Cent. novel of knightly manners—very good:—I have wanted to read it for a long time, but the Union copy was so badly printed that I had not the heart for it. Now I have found (for I f. 25) a series quite nicely typed on fairly good paper. So far I have only got 4 volumes, because they are rather much to carry: it is altogether glorious to have found good French books at last. I can read Molière & Racine & Corneille & Voltaire now:—a whole new world. You know, I think, the joy of getting into a strange country in a book: at home when I have shut my door & the town is in bed—and I know that nothing, not even the dawn—can disturb me in my curtains: only the slow crumbling of the coals in the fire: they get so red & throw such splendid glimmerings on the Hypnos & the brass-work. And it is lovely too, after you have been wandering for hours in the forest with Percivale or Sagramors le desirons, to open the door, & from over the Cherwell to look at the sun glowering through the valley-mists. Why does one not like things if there are other people about? Why cannot one make one's books live except in the night, after hours of straining? and you know they have to be your own books too, & you have to read them

more than once. I think they take in something of your personality,
& your environment also—you know a second hand book sometimes
is so much more flesh & blood than a new one.—and it is almost
terrible to think that your ideas, yourself in your books may be giving
life to generations of readers after you are forgotten. It is that specially
which makes one need good books: books that will be worthy of what
you are going to put into them. What would you think of a great
sculptor who flung away his gifts on modelling clay or sand?
Imagination should be put into the most precious caskets, & that is
why one can only live in the future or the past, in Utopia, or the Wood
beyond the World [by William Morris, 1895]. Father won't know all
this—but if you can get the right book at the right time you taste
joys—not only bodily, physical, but spiritual also, which pass one out
above and beyond one's miserable self, as it were through a huge air,
following the light of another man's thought. And you can never be
quite the old self again. You have forgotten a little bit: or rather pushed
it out with a little of the inspiration of what is immortal in someone
who has gone before you.

To his family   Carchemish, 10 December 1913
The librarian of the Royal library of Munich . . . . called when we
were out . . . and finding a fire and books and a decent chair . . . sat
down and read till we came back in the afternoon. He said ours was
the best (in quality) of any small library he had ever seen, and that
it showed on the face of it natural genius in selection: he would not
go away! indeed in the end we had to lend him four books for his
night's reading in the German camp: one German, one English, one
Greek, and one French: he wanted to take a latin one, but feared he
would be greedy. We heard from the bridge engineer that he sang our
praises all night over there. . . . my new Heredia[13] was the crowning
virtue of our shelves. He borrowed one of the new Meredith's Mother
sent out this season: and has promised us three or four rare editions
of mediaeval German poetry from his own collection: the amusing
part about it is that we only have about 150 books, which have to
represent eight languages!

To A. E. Chambers   Clouds Hill, 3 August 1924
   You are in the book-hungry stage, reading for the sheer joy of it:
and I envy you, since my memory of myself then is a rich one. I was
at Oxford, aged 20 or so, and ravenous in six languages.

To Robert Graves   [Karachi], 1927
. . . I read every book which interested me in the Library of the Oxford
Union . . . in 6 years. My father used to get me the books while I was

at School: afterwards I borrowed always 6 vols. a day, in his name and my own. For 3 years I read day and night, on a hearthrug which was a mattress, so that I could fall asleep as I read. Often 18 hours reading in a day, and so good at the job, by practice, that I could tear the heart out of the soberest book in half an hour.

To Winifred Fontana   [Karachi], 2 May 1928
My habit is to read once: forget: and read again. Somehow my mind is a very dense one. It can read fifty times, & yet find more that is to be learnt in the fifty- first reading.

To A. Pugh   Miranshah, 6 September 1928
If Mrs Shaw and the others send me out, to here, as many books as they used to send to Cranwell, why then the local library will not hold them all, and I shall have to go round the departing Flights, saying 'Please do not go without helping yourself to at least two books'. It got like that at Karachi, where I received over 250 books, and mustered only 100 of them, when I left. That hundred were what the irks called the 'Binders', but which to my odd taste, included most of the attractive books to arrive. So I am pleased at the course of natural selection, and so (let's hope) were they. . . . I'll get those 100 sent up in a case by rail.

To F. N. Doubleday   Plymouth, 28 June 1929
Just I have half an hour in the morning, before breakfast, which I keep for my own reading. I make the half-hour, by getting up before reveille. One can't *read* in odd half-hours: reading is to soak oneself hour after hour all day in a single real book, until the book is realler than one's chair or world . . .

To F. L. Lucas   3 May 1930
    I have now read [Lucas's] *Cecile*, for a first time. After I have read it again I will feel more sure of what I think about it. That is the worst of my slug-like mind. It delays its impressions far beyond most men's.

To Edward Garnett   Southampton, 15 September 1933
    I have now collected all my surviving books in my cottage: and am rather saddened at the gaps that declare themselves.*
*all Hudson, most Conrad, some Doughty.
They have been in London, with friends, for 12 years, and open to [Hart] Cranes, only one S. Reynolds: no early D. H. L.! Fortunately all the poems remain; only the prose has gone; and I like reading— re-reading—poetry better than prose, I feel, as I get older. I have six

volumes of D. H. L. poetry: and bit by bit I shall restore the missing prose books. There are about 1,000 books surviving: so that 200 or 300 alone need be replaced. If I have such a shelf-full, my old age will be provided for.

To Winifred Fontana   17 May 1934
There are 1200 books there [at Clouds Hill] . . . all read once at least, and worth reading again. . . . 'No books before 1850 and no music since' I say at rash moments: but it isn't true.

Spelling

To Dr. W. B. Adams   Carchemish, 19 April 1913
In the matter of spelling;[14] why follow Carnegie, whose ideas of literature seem to be free-libraries? If you want something simple, and beginning with a C, take Chaucer as your guide and spell as you please: in fact spell on each occasion in the manner most fitting to your emphasis and meaning:—for example, if you mean terrible, very terrible, make it erririribble, and everybody knows how it comes off your teeth . . . . . And otherwise, if you find it too difficult to make a language for the Saxon world upon your own, speak and write in French, wherein spelling is neither simplified nor simple. Incidentally, my own spelling is considered admirable by most judges.

To Mrs. Rieder   Carchemish, 24 April 1914
Did you hear that that horror Dr. Adams sent me a letter misspelt? . . . . . I returned it corrected in blue pencil: since then peace: he only sends verbal messages now.

To Charlotte Shaw   31 August 1924
My spelling is good, originally, & any errors in it [*Seven Pillars* proofs], or in the grammar, will be frank misprints . . .

To Robin Buxton   Clouds Hill, 25 June 1925
The misprints [in sample pages for *Seven Pillars* subscribers] don't matter. There are two intentional ones, & one accident.

To Charlotte Shaw   30 July 1925
I've never been stable enough to own a dictionary, & never use one, since spelling comes to me naturally, & I don't want to use a large vocabulary. A few words are enough, if you try to make the few fit your scanty impressions.

To Charlotte Shaw   26 December 1925
You offered to do it [the *Seven Pillars* proofs] for "literals": but I
don't care enough for that. A misprint is a trifle: not a fault like a
crooked sentence, a too-long paragraph, an unbalanced page. It will
not worry me if there is a misprint per page in the finished article.
It's sense, not form, which comes first.

To the Proof-reader of *Revolt in the Desert*   late 1926?
Arabic names won't go into English, exactly, for their consonants are
not the same as ours, and their vowels, like ours, vary from district
to district. There are some 'scientific systems' of transliteration, helpful
to people who know enough Arabic not to need helping, but a wash-
out for the world. I spell my names anyhow, to show what rot the
systems are.

To Bruce Rogers   Miranshah, 30 June 1928
   You will realize, on the minor points of name-spelling, punctuating,
paragraphing etc, that I don't care the least little bit what changes
you make, to please yourself, to please your audience, to fit your type
or page. The printer should use the MS of a *new* book (not a reprint)
as raw materials to be cooked into decency.

To Bruce Rogers   Miranshah, 4 January 1929
   As for the spelling of proper names: I have left them half-Latinised.
I mean, I write MENELAUS: Homer wrote MENELAOS. I write
ALCMENE: Homer, ALKMENE. . . .
   There is no need for consistency. . . . Spell everybody as you please.
I am, as you know, personally indifferent to—or at least a very loose
user of—people's names (beginning with my own.)

To Bruce Rogers   10 February 1930
   Also I saw some misprints [in *Odyssey* page-proofs]. Here they are,
on a slip. I have marked them in my sheets. Too late, I think to do
anything else. I do not care. Misprints are trifles and take nothing
from the goodness of a printed page.

To Bruce Rogers   12 February 1930
   As I said, I shouldn't bother to correct any misprints. They are
accidents, obviously, and not intentions.

To G. Wren Howard   1932
   I write (and wrote) this [introduction to *Arabia Felix*] in lodgings,
away from books. Will you please check the spellings of

Wilfrid Blunt
Shakespear
Leachman
Burckhardt
Baunkeier

[Lawrence spelled his cottage Clouds Hill, Cloud's Hill, or Clouds'
Hill. Captions in the 1926 edition of *Seven Pillars* spell the port Jeddah,
Jiddah, and Jedda.]

Greece, Greek, and Latin

To his family,   Shipboard, December 1910
Of course I got ashore at once, & plunged into the intolerable cesspit
of the Piraêus: the place is a filthy drain for all the dregs of the capital,
its only virtue that it saves it from being a port. Before you reach Athens
you pass through green fields & over small streams, that effectually
wash away the taste & smell of the sea. The rail lands you in the midst
of a very modern looking town of squares & gardens, with a character
partly French but not wholly European or Asiatic; too bright for the
one & too clean for the other. It was above all things quiet, the quietest
town imaginable, with few trams, & those slow ones, no motors or
bicycles & very few carts. The streets are usually asphalt-paved, & there
seemed hardly any dogs to bark and fight. Even the vegetable-hawkers
shouted like men, not like jackals or fog horns. Everywhere were palm
trees & mimosa, with green lawns. I had to go back through the town
to reach the Acropolis, & chose therefore to wander into by-streets,
that I might come out at the Theseion; and the further I went the
stronger became a curious sense of unreality, almost of nightmare. Here
was a town full of people speaking the same tongue & writing the same
character as the old inhabitants of 3000 years before. Some of them
looked like what we know & hope the old Greeks were, others of them
are visibly of the class of metirs or βαναυσοι or freedmen, whom
Aristotle so loudly scorned. The Athenians to whom he appealed were
never more than a handful, a little party who held by themselves walking
in the gardens, & looking out dispassionately upon the world around
them: they had heard (as I did) tousled black-haired women calling
loudly for their children Gorgs or Aristomenes, & they had seen (as
I saw) the two women up the street hurrying breathlessly along, tiring
their hair, to meet the procession, of priests in vestments this time, but
still the same undercurrent of back-biting and slander, and ill-natured
comment of the neighbours. A cabbage-seller passed me, before just

such a sausage-stall as one had looked for in the street of Victory that leads to the Temple of Theseus, driving his ass, & chaffering with Demosthenes, a fisherman. It was all out of Aristophanes or Juvenal, all in keeping, so that it seemed quite natural when I walked up a little hill, & passed under the pillars of the temple. It stands today as perfect as ever it was, with the added beauty of the stains & hollows with which Time has endowed its stones. . . . There were no porters, no guides, no visitors, & I walked through the doorway of the Parthenon, and on into the inner part of it, without really remembering where or who I was. A heaviness in the air made my eyes swim, & wrapped up my senses: I only knew that I, a stranger, was walking on the floor of the place I had most desired to see, the greatest temple of Athene, the palace of art, and that I was counting her columns, and finding them what I already knew. The building was familiar, not cold as in the drawings, but complex, irregular, alive with curve and subtlety and perfectly preserved. Every line of the mouldings, every minutest refinement in the sculptures were evident in that light, and inevitable in their place. The Parthenon is the protocathedral of the Hellenes. . . . then I came down again into the town, & found it modern and a little different. It was as though one had turned from the shades of the ancestors, to mix in the daily vocations of their sons: and so only this about Athens, that there is an intoxication, a power of possession in its ruins, & the memories that inhabit them, which entirely prevents anyone attempting to describe or to estimate them. There will never be a great book on Athens unless it is one by an enemy: no one who knew it could resist its spell, except by a violent attack upon its spirit, and who can attack it now of artists, when Tolstoy is dead? He, and he alone, could have uprooted Greek culture in the world. I am coming back by Athens I think next year to stay a little time. For the present I am only confused with it: I do not know how much was Athens, and how much the colouring of my imagination upon it.

To Mrs. Rieder   Carchemish, 12 September 1912
I am exceedingly sorry to hear that Noël's[15] glands have proved themselves not gentlemen. . . . You are very wise to look after them before bothering about schools . . . you know a year or two doesn't matter in the end. I was reading (chiefly police news) at four, and learning Latin at 5, and at 17 I was no more forward than the rest of the school, beginning Latin only at $8\frac{1}{2}$. · · ·

And don't bother about Latin. I take it Noël is more likely to be Modern than Classical in his tastes, and if one doesn't want to write Latin verse, and knows French, one can read the Latin one needs in a six-month, and other than that he will only have to write Latin prose, which is a mechanical stupidity, ground out of a Grammar and Dictionary, and to be handled at will. If he reaches 10 (an extreme age, probably) without Latin, he will merely be set to occupy his French hours in the older language. And a school is such a slow business that a little special training will overtake its standard in no time. Latin is a very important thing: but there are lots of Latin languages, and if he knows one it will make his way easy for the rest, (e.g. I can read Italian prose, & even poetry not incorrectly: never having learnt them).

To his family   Carchemish, 12 September 1912
Of late I have been reading a lot of Spenser, Catullus, Marot, the *Koran*, Simonides, and Meleager. Parts of Simonides are very splendid: also Antipater of Sidon, Tyrtaeus, and Hipponax: all in Bergk and the Anthology. I got a Greek dictionary from Mr. (now Canon) Parfit in Beyrout, and have made great play with it. There is one very splendid Meleager, beginning Ενφορτοι ναες πελαγιτιδες [richly loaded ocean ships] . . . . . Ant. xii. 53 and another Ειχονα μεν Παριην ζωογλνφος [statue in Parian marble] xii.56, and his elegy on Antipater is splendid: also that verse of Leonidas of Tarentum, when the old man, without his fellows on earth, turns about to join the greater company: or Meleager's epitaph ό τον γλυχνδαχρυν Ερωτα, χαι Μουσας ίλαραις συστολισας χαρισιν [He who, uniting sweet-teared Love and the Muses with cheerful charms]. You have most of the man there, and he wrote it himself: there is a great deal of the Syrian in Meleager: far more than one would suspect from his Greek clothes and habits and turns of speech. Clement Marot has many excellent things, though it is rather a silly jest to talk of him after Meleager and Antipater of Sidon.

To Mrs. Rieder   Carchemish, 8 March 1914
Latin is an awfully dull language: you know when you have after many years of tribulation learned it, you find out to your horror that there are only two or three little books in it worth the re-reading: and to think that with a little of that labour one might be proficient in Greek! The excuse made for Latin is that scientific books and philosophy demand a knowledge of it: but if I had my way I would build a causeway to America with all such productions.

To David Garnett   [Karachi], 16 February 1928
A fellow must pick and choose in foreign literature. For instance I loathe Horace and love Virgil: a remark which would discredit a Roman's judgement: but is only a foible with an Englishman.

To Harley Granville-Barker   Plymouth, 23 December 1932
  You ask about my Greek. It is rusted and patchy. I can just read
enough (that is without a dictionary) to get the meaning and enjoyment
out of familiar books—parts of Aristophanes, and the Anthology,
the Iliad, Anabasis and Aeschylus. I cannot read a strange Greek book
without a crib to help me. There is not a great deal of good Greek
to read. I would like to add Herodotus to my repertoire, but am too
lazy, or too engrossed with mechanics.

To C. Day Lewis   Bridlington, 20 December 1934
  My Latin wasn't ever much good, so that I have never enjoyed
Catullus. I suppose that means that I have never justified the time
I spent trying to learn the beastly language? There seem to be ten good
Greek books to every Latin one.

French Writers

To David Garnett   [Karachi], 16 February 1928
Bovary . . . . yes: she's all right: but I own that Salammbo [by
Flaubert, 1862] takes me as almost the best thing in French. . . .
there's Rabelais the best of all: and yes, probably Salammbo
second, with Bovary and Balzac's twenty-volumed novel, and some
Miserables near by. . . . I weary of Proust: and Paul Fort over-did
it: and their war books were a little wearisome. Their old prose: their
mediaeval poetry: of that I've read more than most people: Belloy:
yes, fine. Old Montaigne less so: Montesquieu was more of a man.
Racine: I have read all his work . . . and re-read very much of it. I
wish he had written on for ever. Molière no good, and the memoir-
people and Taines and Voltaires and Thiers all a wash out. I refuse
to read Crebillon fils. Lamartine I like, the prose of him: but the next
great group are the de Nerval Rimbaud (a demi-god) Verlaine, Leconte
de Lisle, Heredia crowd, with Mallarmé, perhaps, though often he
is too dry to fit an Anglo-Saxon mouth. Baudelaire wrote fine
prose. . . . my reading stopped in 1914: since then I have only met
a chance book. . . . What disappoints me in French prose is its lack
of power: and in poetry its smoothness. . . .
  I should never have thought I'd have written about French, and
left out Merimée: but I haven't put in half the people I like. Yet
. . . . . there went something out of France after the Fronde: what
I call strength.

To Charlotte Shaw   [Miranshah], 25 September 1928
   I like Daudet: have liked him, the stories, for long. Not the long
novels. Daudet, Merimée, Gautier, <u>Flaubert,</u> Maupassant, Hugo; yes,
they have had some recent writers. Not Proust, I think; nor Barres
nor Loti nor France.

Likes and Dislikes

To his family   Cairo, 31 January 1912
Read it if it falls in your way, *The Centaur* by Algernon Blackwood.
I have read it three times with profit, and have left it behind me, of
intention, literally and metaphorically: incomplete, that's what it is.

To his family   Aleppo, 20 February 1912
By the way how does the family like [William Morris's] *Sigurd* [*the
Volsung*, 1876]? Has it wooed father yet?—for it will—. Read *Richard
Yea and Nay* [by Maurice Hewlett, 1900] in Egypt for the ninth time.
It is a masterpiece.

To his family   Carchemish, 12 September 1912
   . . . I have re-read for about the sixth time [Henry] Baerlein's novel
of the Crusade of children [*On the Forgotten Road*, 1909], that you[16]
criticised in Oxford. It is very good, very vivid: I don't think the man
could do better with his talents and occasions. In Beyrout I read
Renny[17] by Hewlett: one smells the craftsman too much: I think
Hewlett is finished.

To Ezra Pound   Oxford, 20 August 1920
Of course Joyce can write (and does, just occasionally): you can write
(and do): T. S. Eliot . . . . . perhaps: but the people I like are so
different, Hodgson; Sassoon: D. H. Lawrence: Manning: Conrad.
[blot] I suppose that blot means you fainted, so I won't go on. . . .

To Edward Garnett   [London?], 26 August 1922
   . . . I collected a shelf of 'Titanic' books (those distinguished by
greatness of spirit, 'sublimity' as Longinus would call it): . . . they
were *The Karamazovs*, *Zarathustra*, and *Moby Dick*.

To Edward Garnett   [Uxbridge], 23 October 1922
My mind on literature is not yet crisp. . . . Failing poetry I chased
my fancied meal through prose, and found everywhere good little stuff,

and only a few men who had honestly tried to be greater than mankind:
and only their strainings and wrestlings really fill my stomach.

To Vyvyan Richards [early 1923]
The stillness of absolute works of art. You admire these most.[18]
. . . But honestly I doubt whether stillness is an 'absolute' element
in works of supreme art. It seems to me a manner like another. My
big books Rabelais, *Moby Dick*, *Karamazov*, leave their readers in
a sweat. *Zarathustra* has his stillness. Of the poems there's no stillness
in the *Cenci* (exhaustion rather) or in the *Oresteia*: or in *Lear*. Of the
priests who serve one stands still, & eight move about & work for him:
and there are religions full of movement. I think you are mistaking
a preference for a principle.

To A. P. Wavell Bovington, 11 May 1923
. . . among my favourite books are the . . . great failures—*Moby
Dick*, *Also sprach Zarathustra*, *Pantagruel*,—books where the authors
went up like a shoot of rockets, and burst.

To E. M. Forster 9 May 1924
The writing which disgusts me is stuff aimed deliberately below the
belt: Barrie: Belloc: much of Chesterton: they could write so well, &
are too cheap in grain to wish to try.

To Edward Garnett 16 September 1924
Hudson gone.
Conrad gone.
Hardy very old: G. Moore gaga: D. H. L. ditto; whom have we
to welcome year by year?
(Not Aldous Huxley, not a Sitwell, not J. Joyce, not Wyndham
Lewis: somebody lovable).

To Charlotte Shaw 29 November 1924
. . . the Swallow Book of Ernst Toller's. It is most moving & excellent.
I've been through it about six times, gladly: and am so grateful you
sent it me.

To Charlotte Shaw 4 January 1926
More & more I come to hunger after the swift running writers: the
Dean Swift first of all: G. B. S. very near him: two Irishmen. . . .

To Charlotte Shaw [Karachi], 23 March 1927
Morris was a great poet: and I'd rather have written the Well at the
World's End or the Roots of the Mountains or John Ball or the Hollow

Land than anything of the 19th Cent. except War & Peace or Moby
Dick. Sigurd & the Dynasts & Paradise Lost & Samson & Adam Cast
Forth are the best long poems in English. And Morris wrote fifty
perfect short poems. Why the man is among the very great! I suppose
everybody loves one writer, unreasonably. I'd rather Morris than the
world.

To Robert Graves   Karachi, 28 June 1927
    As a bookman you may be amused to know that I carried with me
during the desert war 1) a Morte d'Arthur, 2) Aristophanes, 3) Oxford
Book of English Verse, and no other books. They say I carried
Doughty, but it's not true.

To Charlotte Shaw   [Karachi], 14 July 1927
I'm reading . . . the early prose stories of that master man [Morris].
They are glorious.

To Charlotte Shaw   [Karachi], 21 July 1927
The Well at the World's end came. I sleep for two or three hours at
a time in its pages.

To David Garnett   [Karachi], 30 November 1927
. . . there aren't many creators about . . . . . Tolstoi, of course, and
I think Defoe and Dickens and Melville and D. H. Lawrence in
English. . . .

To Charlotte Shaw   [Karachi], 8 December 1927
. . . I like profusion, in Letters. For me, books are seldom too long,
and the small thing is supect, as the writer may have been himself small.
I run praisingly after Rabelais, and the Brothers Karamazoff, and War
& Peace, and Moby Dick, because they are large, and in them the
authors have burst themselves, and the canons of art, in trying to do
things beyond human capacity. It is very good to fall short of the
impossible by just a little.

To Robert Graves   Karachi, 24 December 1927
    My judgement inclines my reading more & more to the easy men.
I prefer Bennett & Wells & Galsworthy & Tomlinson & Kipling &
Forster to [Wyndham] Lewis and Joyce & Stein. Is that mental fatigue,
or the ossification of age beginning?

To David Garnett   [Karachi], 16 February 1928
    Sorry you don't like Caesar's *Gallic War*. I call it a miracle of self-
suppression: one of the most impressive things in print. My *Seven*

Pillars is nearer Xenophon, a much less ambitious ancient. Hats off to Caesar, though, for really pulling off the impersonal thing, and yet leaving his stuff palpitant with excitement.

Rough edges my preference? I like a rough texture, which is not the same thing.

To Robert Graves   [Karachi], 29 March 1928
We must be travelling different ways. You are getting exasperated, hating the dullness and stupidness of mankind, and especially of writing mankind. I'm losing my cutting edge, and therefore understand better. . . .

To Edward Garnett   [Karachi], 14 April 1928
Opinions are not worth much: they are too subjective. There is no absolute, and therefore no criticism. As you say, I tend to go Tolstoyan with years: I now like H. G. Wells better than Norman Douglas: and call Kipling better than Crackanthorpe: just because their carelessness gives me a sense of power. They feel they have gold to throw away. The stylists are too miserly. Agreed I am a bad example of the too-careful type.

To Edward Garnett   [Karachi], 2 May 1928
I'm so glad the *Poor Man's House* has got into the Travellers Library: Cape must add *Alongshore*, and *The Holy Mountain*, and some Crane (*Jenny*[19] is right out of print, and unprocurable). The airmen here have adopted the Travellers Library as a hobby. Many of them buy one a week, just for fun. It is an uncommonly good series. I recommend a novel of Henry Baerlein, about the Children's Crusade: don't know its name.[20] Very good stuff. And why not do *Marie Grubbe* [by Jens Jacobsen, 1876]? Or must they all be English.

My Heart and My Flesh. Admirable, but too anxious: too dry: a little Steinish. Not as wholesomely flesh-like as *The Time of Man*.[21]

To Robert Graves   Miranshah, 5 August 1928
It is an odd feeling to be satisfied. I think that makes me content to like Bennett's books, and Wells' stories and John Buchan. Williamson, the *Tarka* merchant, has good stuff to come, I think. Also I like and look forward to more D. H. L., more E. M. Forster, more S. S [Siegfried Sassoon]. That makes seven or eight producing people who enlarge my wits. Not bad for a single age. There aren't seven yet-alive Elizabethans. . . .

To Jonathan Cape   [Miranshah], 23 October 1928
. . . I like the Confessions [of Rousseau]: or at least I am interested
in them. What a queer fish R. was.

To Robert Graves   Miranshah, 6 November 1928
You have a standard, & it enables you to be censorious. I only see
what's better than my *performance* (quite different to a mental
standard, that) and so I admire & enjoy Wells, & Bennett, & Forster,
& Sir Thomas Browne, & Rossetti, and Morris and everybody who
deliberately tries to better his every-day speech (which is my definition
of style). Not a bettering of speech, mind you: but an effort to better
it. It's the trace of effort which warms my diaphragm:—beg pardon,
cockles of my heart—whatever are cockles?

To H. S. Ede   Miranshah, 12 November 1928
I have studied Ulysses, and read all D. H. Lawrence: and worked as
well as I could at all the modern schools of writing, without actually
wishing ever to belong to any of them. I don't see the high seriousness
and purpose of literary art, in the way they do. . . . Everything seems
to me well done, or nearly everything; from W. J. Locke to Sacheverell
Sitwell: from Surtees to Doughty. Graves curses me for liking Bennett.
Shaw thinks I'm all wrong to like Hardy: Bunyan is good stuff, so
is Jules Laforgue. So catholic a taste isn't a taste: it's an appetite:
and I suppose my style can't very well have a date worked into it,
because my taste hasn't any rejections, except raw oysters and boiled
parsnips. My dislikes in books aren't much more than that, in number.

To Charlotte Shaw   [Miranshah], 31 December 1928
I stare at Gertrude Stein & Cummings & the rest of them: and can't
understand. All my likes are the old: I like nearly everything that's
been done up to the present: barring Wilkie Collins, & Jane Austen
& the Brontes: but George Eliot could write.

To H. S. Ede   1 April 1929
One's taste gets hardened and prejudiced so that the new stuff doesn't
appeal. . . . It may be that I'm getting out of date. In letters, for
instance, I do not enjoy Gertrude Stein. Interesting, she is, and curious:
but I fail to envy her work: I wonder why.

To Charlotte Shaw   London, 4 October 1929
. . . I would choose to live with the works of William Morris, if I had
to make a single choice. My reason tells me that he isn't a very great
writer: but then, he wrote just the stuff I like.

To A. S. Frere-Reeves   Plymouth, 19 February 1930
"Like to have" the new Tomlinson! What a way to put it. Tomlinson
is one of my entirely uncritical admirations, as man and nature and
mind—and particularly pen. If he took over Bradshaw and edited it
monthly, I should subscribe.

I am a pluralist, a whole-hogger, in all his words and works: and
All our Yesterdays [1930] is a big thing among them. The biggest thing?
How should I know? Can one say that a man's one hand is bigger
than his other hand? These things put together make our Tomlinson.
[I do so hope that All our Yesterdays will make our Tomlinson rich,
too. He deserves it, for the honourable little man he has always
been.][22] I have just written to him, about the book, which I feel very
unfit to appraise.

To William Rothenstein   Plymouth, 18 October 1930
Have you read *Other Man's Saucer* [by Keith Winter]? . . . . If its
characters are imagined, then he's a coming author. If they are his
own circle, then he's not. It is as striking, in its way, as *The White
Peacock* of 1912, was it? . . . .

In the other direction I commend Algernon Blackwood's *Dudley
and Gilderoy*. Yes, I know that normally he is no good: but this and
his Autobiography [*Episodes before Thirty*] and *The Centaur* are
different. This is much the best. Very distinguished indeed.

. . . The poor old war creatures bore everybody so much that we
give them too little credit, I fancy. Yet Sassoon's books; Manning's;
War Birds [by Elliott Springs]; *Ermytage and the Curate* [by A. M.
Cogswell]; all those stuck in my mind: and so will *Salute to [of] Guns*
[by Donald Boyd], I fancy, though I read it too lately to say for sure.

To Frederic Manning   Plymouth, 1 September 1931
Others, like Geoffrey [of Monmouth?] and Herman Melville and
Chaucer and Shelley and Spenser and Virgil (but not Homer of the
Odyssey!) also pleased me yesterday or today: but tomorrow perhaps
all of you may be dethroned by Edgar Wallace, so fickle and veering
is the human eye.

To Frederic Manning   Southampton, 2 January 1932
As for [Emil] Ludwig, I read his Napoleon, and thought it a brainy
and skilful fact-assembly and selection: but entirely without urge. Then
I saw some later books by him (or later-translated) and they were utterly
unnecessary. . . .

Wasserman is good, so far as my slight knowledge of him goes.
Hanley . . . thinks him the best writer in Europe. For my part there

are ten English writers (one to whom I now write, and nine others whose names momently lie in the back of my mind, out of reach) whom I should inevitably prefer. I cannot enjoy any language but my own, for reading. The effort to apprehend becomes too great, if the tongue, as well as the mind, is strange.

To G. W. M. Dunn   Southampton, 19 July 1934
I don't think much of private letters, as an art form. Not even Fitzgerald's, or Keats': or D. H. L's or Gertrude Bell's. They always have something ragged, domestic, undressed, about them.

Women Writers

To Sydney Cockerell   Clouds Hill, 13 January 1924
    Haven't heard of Charlotte Mew:[23] but all the women who ever wrote original stuff could have been strangled at birth, & the history of English literature (& my bookshelves) would be unchanged.

To Sydney Cockerell   Clouds Hills, 19 March 1924
    Miss Mew: too much emotion for her art, for her intellect, for her will. Such intensity of feeling is a sign of weakness. She is a real poet . . . . . but a little one, for the incoherency, the violence of overwrought nerves does much harm to her powers of expression.
    It's good stuff . . . . . *Beside the Bed*: *On the Asylum Road*: *I have been through the Gates*: *On the Road to the Sea*: these are four excellent things . . . . . but only the passion is molten: the form, the thought, the music, these are unresolved, to be guessed at, or worse, to be supplied by the reader if his passion is set burning by sympathy with hers. I'm frigid towards woman so that I can withstand her: so that I want to withstand her.

To Charlotte Shaw   3 June 1926
    Women writers: "no good plain stuff"!!! Heavens. Jane Austen, Katharine Mansfield, the Bronte family, Dorothy Richardson, May Sinclair, Virginia Woolf. Plain as pikestaves. Foully plain. What woman lacks, in literature, is the power of writing adornedly. There are plenty of woman writers: no artificial-prose-artists.

To William Rothenstein   Karachi, 14 April 1928
    I wonder if Max [Beerbohm] is right in saying that women write good letters: good for their men perhaps: but Byron & Keats & Horace Walpole & Chesterfield are not to be matched by any four women's

letter writing I've read. Perhaps he means of unpublished letters: the sort that do not get into print. But even there I think he would be wrong.

To Charlotte Shaw   [Karachi], 17 May 1928
    Last week I read Ethel Smythe's latest.[24] I confess she slightly jars me. Perhaps, in the days she remembers, women were oppressed: but I see little traces of it today. If many of them feel like her, the boot will soon be on the other foot . . . . . The other book was Rose Macaulay's. I wonder how autobiographical it was? A queer queer book . . . . . you say G. B. S. reads her particularly. That is extraordinary.

To William Rothenstein   Plymouth, 20 October 1932
    Willa Cather is exquisite, in her range. There are several such U.S.A. women. Did you ever read any "Elizabeth Roberts"? Cape publishes. She uses a broader pen than Willa Cather.

Writers Ahead of the Time

                                    Felixstone, 24 November 1934
To Walter Williams (President, University of Missouri)
    I failed to answer your first request for my autograph out of politeness. It seemed to me hardly consonant with the reputation of a great University; and therefore I glanced through the list of selected books which accompanied your letter. That completed my astonishment, for I found (besides the inevitable names of Shaw, Housman and Tomlinson) only two names, Archibald MacLeish and Halper, that stood in any way for the considerable body of people trying to write ahead of this time, today.
    Your list contained no Faulkner, no Yeats, no Day Lewis, no Hanley, no Houghton, no Auden, no Stein, no Biggus, no Jewett, no Cummings, no Elizabeth Roberts, no Joyce, no Jeffers, no Richardson, no Pound, no V. Woolf, no Dos Passos. I live in barracks, and make no pretence to keep astride of the generations as they develop—but it is not flattering to find one's work included in a collection from which nearly everything one cares for is shut out.
    I hope the University of Missouri is not infected with the safety play that has so often made European universities lose touch with reality.
    I am aware that you are only the unfortunate recipient of this avalanche of dead books, and hope the readers in the Library that must eventually house them will (like yourself) treat them as decora-

tions or as scalps, and not as incitements towards thinking; but it does seem to throw a lurid reflection upon the state of mind of your selectors. I should change them.

To Bruce Rogers   Bridlington, 24 November 1934
. . . I've been the victim of a strange incident . . . . . repeated letters from the "President of the University of Missouri, Columbia", your side somewhere, enclosing me a list of their "best and most important" books of 1932–1934, (among them our Odyssey) with a request for my autograph in the shape of a letter to insert in it.

. . . the request tickled me. But then I examined the list of books judged worthy of inclusion in this selected library—and I was amazed. Words fail me (as Odysseus would say) to describe the junk that kept our poor effort company.

So I replied to the gentleman that his compliment of inclusion was a doubtful one. . . .

You never saw such an outrageous list in your life. I've shown my opinion of it, I hope; but I fear inadequately. Incidentally I hinted with some politeness that it perhaps isn't the place of a President to tout for autographs. A Mr. Walter Williams: what is the standing of the University of Missouri, if it does stand? I suspect it of lying!

A Common Thread

To William Rothenstein   Karachi, 8 December 1927
Your work will be exactly dateable to your epoch, in the eyes of the future: as will the work of all your contemporaries. The most academic of them, and the most fiercely revolutionary, will all be 1880–1930 . . . . . isn't that odd? What are these 50 years of a man's production, if his own time takes such possession of him? I think, mainly, that it means that any search or endeavour after *difference*, (as an end in itself) is wasted effort.

To H. S. Ede   [Karachi], 16 April 1928
It makes me smile, sometimes, to think that all the varying pictures produced in 1928 will all date themselves, by some subtlety of likeness to 1928, in the eyes of 2028. Yet today we are hardly on speaking terms.

Of pictures and sculpture I'm not talking, now, but of the writing gangs: the Joyces and the Kiplings, the Steins and Wells, the Forsters and D. H. Lawrences: they will all date within 20 years, by some yet-imperceptible solidarity. There will be a common thread between T. S. Eliot and Alfred Noyes.

To C. Day Lewis   Bridlington, 16 November 1934
We imagine such degrees between contemporaries, while we know in
our hearts that the Saintsbury of the future will see the affinities
between you and Noyes and Doughty and Housman and Herbert
Trench and Drinkwater and Humbert Wolfe and Hodgson and
Blunden and William Watson, and will wisely explain the common
impulse that led to all these similar blooms.

Good and Great Writing

To F. N. Doubleday   21 July 1920
Words are weapons: and when I get a good one I like to throw it like
a brick at someone, and hit them with it. This other man[25] teases his
sentences out into a woolly stifled mat like a blanket.

To Vyvyan Richards   August 1920
. . . prose depends on a music in one's head which involuntarily
chooses & balances the possible words to *keep tune* with the thought.
The best passages in English prose all deal with death or the vanity
of things, since that is a tune we all know, and the mind is set quite
free to think while writing about it. Only it can't be kept up very long,
because of mortal weakness and the wear & tear of things, & the
function of criticism, revision, & correction (polishing) seems to me
to be either.
   (i) *putting* a thing into thought
   (ii) [putting] thought into rhythm
   (iii) putting *expression* into meaning.
It seems to me that if you think too hard about the form, you forget
the matter, & if your brain is wrestling with the matter, you may not
have attention to spare for the manner. Only occasionally in things
constantly dwelt upon, do you get an unconscious balance, & then
you get a *spontaneous* and perfect arrangement of words to fit the
idea, *as the tune*. Polishing is an attempt, by stages, to get to what
should be a single combined stride.

To Eric Kennington   10 April 1922
   It's easier to do creative imaginative work under 30: though you
can go on doing it after, if you have
     (i) a memory of what youth was like
   or (ii) an incapacity for fixed ideas.
Very often after 40 the hardness of the thirties breaks down, and men
become artists again, till nearly 60. I personally at 33 notice very little
change in myself since about 1914.

To Edward Garnett   [London], 23 August 1922
It's no remedy or consolation for my lack of style to point to
Dostoevsky in the same dock: it's partly why people prefer to read
him in the English version. *War and Peace* I thought decently written
on the whole. Of course not a miracle of style like *Salammbo* or the
Moralités Légendaires: or like Doughty and *Eothen* and *Idle Days in
Patagonia*.[26] If mine had been simple stuff it wouldn't have mattered.
It could have gone into the Hakluyt category as a good yarn: but it's
elaborate and self-conscious: ambitious if you like: and that makes
failure a discredit. It doesn't matter missing if you don't aim: thereby
Lane's *Arabian Nights* is better than Burton's.

To Edward Garnett   [Farnborough], 7 December 1922
No, the born writer is the real fact, and without such ichor in his
veins a man only makes a journeyman's job of book-writing: and my
critical sense makes me not covet the creation (even while I enjoy it)
of those who do so, by pain, make literature.

To Vyvyan Richards   [early 1923]
*Written history has never yet so nearly approached the unity of a
work of art*. Written history is inevitably long & must be judged by
the standard of epic rather than lyric. The *Iliad* has only a fictitious
unity. Gibbon at least as much. I suppose the *Peloponnesian War* has
more unity than the average drama. Only perhaps you'd call it not
true. I'll admit that modern history has seldom been 'composed' in
the artistic sense. Trevelyan's Italian efforts perhaps.[27] But modern
history tries to be a science, not an art.

To Aubrey Herbert   March 1923?[28]
I don't know what to liken it [draft extracts of a travel book] to—
perhaps an Egyptian necklace of figured beads, whose string has
snapped:—it's beautiful stuff, . . . the best material for a book that
ever was, but it's not a book yet.
In your place I'd retire to a solitary place and have the stuff read
to me by a slave, again and again. Then I'd dismiss the slave and dream
over those times until all the adventures came together. Then I'd dictate
a slow story of my progress: avoiding so far as possible, what is here
put: then I'd use this as the bag of plums and sift them slowly into
the new cake, and stir them together with a third version, which would
be a book of books.

To Edward Garnett   [Bovington], 4 October 1923
. . . lately I have been finding my deepest satisfaction in the collocation
of words so ordinary and plain that they cannot mean anything to

a book-jaded mind: and out of some of such I can draw deep stuff.[29] Is it perhaps that certain sequences of vowels or consonants imply more than others: that writing of this sort has music in it? I don't want to affirm it, and yet I would not deny it: for if writing can have sense (and it has: this letter has) and sound why shouldn't it have something of pattern too? My sequences seem to be independent of ear . . . . . to impose themselves through the eye alone. I achieved a good many of them in *Le Gigantesque*: but fortuitously for the most part.

Do you think that people ever write *consciously* well? or does that imply an inordinate love for the material, and so ruin the art? I don't see that it should. A sculptor who petted his marbles from sheer joy in their grain and fineness would (pari passu) be better than a mere block-butcher.

To Charlotte Shaw   Clouds Hill, 26 March 1924
Style. I make it a tin god, because I'm in need of the help of that god. People like Belloc and G. B. S. despise him, since they are endowed with the utmost of his gifts.

To Charlotte Shaw   30 August 1924
In creative work there isn't any place for good intention, for the second best: it's the least democratic thing imaginable.

To Charlette Shaw   3 May 1925
To be very great a man must be pretty stupid . . . . . otherwise he will catch sight of himself, & burst out laughing.

To Edward Garnett   [Karachi], 1 December 1927
'Great books are written in moods of spiritual light and intellectual certainty'.[30]
I would maintain against him that these moods never produced an imaginative work the size of a mouse from any of the people sterile enough to feel certain. My notion of the world's big books are *War and Peace*, *The Brothers Karamazoff*, *Moby Dick*, Rabelais, *Don Quixote*. Of course we treat of prose. There's a fine set of cores of darkness!

To Charlotte Shaw   [Karachi], 9 February 1928
The goodness of artists lies very much in their last reticences: the little things they do not say:—as the beauty of the Venus of Melos . . . lies in the loss of her arms.

To William Rothenstein   [Karachi], 14 April 1928
There are few good letter writers, I fancy: as few as there are good

sonnetteers: for the same reason: that the form is too worn to be easy, & there are too many who try. It's a less crowded profession, is epic poetry: and that's why there are few bad epics.

To E. M. Forster   [Karachi], 16 April 1928
I've tried to write, myself, and know that a man doesn't ever succeed in mating sound and sense and expectation. We land, always, other than we meant to land. That's presumably the fun as wll as the vexation of writing. Your less-good work is very helpful to me, as an amateur of writing: for our minds are parallel enough for me to see your intention behind the expression, (or to flatter myself that I do partly and in some senses see it . . . . . oh shades of Henry James in this style of letter!) and just because it may not completely come off, so I may be able to see the works inside it more clearly.

And I don't expect you to be always at your best. Indeed I once said that it was the mark of a little writer to be very particular about his standard. The big men (of the Balzac, Tolstoi, Dostoevski, Dickens stamp) are incredibly careless, here & now. They seem to have said 'well, it doesn't matter. If the readers can't see what I mean, they needn't'. There's a lavish ease about their stuff: and an agony of carefulness about the Henry James & George Moore & Flaubert class. These are two points of view. I like both lots. But don't, please, stand on ceremony with me. The most beautiful parts of all the best Greek statues are their mutilations.

To H. S. Ede   [Karachi], 16 April 1928
'Clean and clear, hard and cold and BALD.' Yes: I think that's a good ambition. . . . In writing nearly everybody tries for hardness and clearness: but the unconscious drag all the while is to cover up. A negro might make quite uncovered things, if he and his people had never thought of clothes: but for a clothed race to be deliberately naked in art intention is to be ever so unnatural. We should not, in thought, pass the bounds we set ourselves in deed: or our ideas will not ring true. And to live bald and hard and clean: ah; that's beyond a fellow's power, except he be solitary. In the ranks of the R.A.F. we get very near it, for the oppression of discipline makes us unable to pretend, amongst ourselves, to be better than just ordered bodies: and our outward sameness of dress means that we wear no clothes at all: but not even here do you get a community of understanding.

To Edward Garnett   Miranshah, 17 July 1928
As for the Mint, let's forget it. Your temperament leads you to over-estimate the goodness of books. Writing them is, for the author, like discharging the matter of a boil: it is a process which gives relief. I

don't think publishing or reading are very valuable activities. They are more like vaccinations than like life.

To Robert Graves   Miranshah, 6 November 1928
    'Resides not in drill'. That, you say, is style, I like style, I fancy. The anticipation of an antithesis, which is not fulfilled is good. Old Asquith's speeches were intolerably boring because all the anticipations were bitterly fulfilled. 'All there is to be done is to write with ink on paper'. Alas, that is the last & easy stage. It's the balancing your subject before you begin on it: the scheming proportion for it, the adding wings and feathers to carry all your prepared ideas, fitly: and the spacing the few ornamental ideas each of us have, so as to relieve the monotony of the plainer surfaces:—that's all got to be done before the easy ink-on-paper stage.
    I know you didn't mean the remark to be taken so literally. You fell foul of my ornament [in *The Mint*], not because it is ornamental, but because it isn't: and you're sure right there. It comes in the wrong places, and it is clumsy. Yet the 'pencillings of light' were just as clear (are just as clear) to me as the sweat and swear-words. Only they are so much harder to put down. Anybody can catch the ugly to the life: but to make the smoothly beautiful at once beautiful and not sticky— aha, that's where the poet scores. . . . A man's a great writer when he can use plain words, without baldness. See how bald Theodore Powys is, despite all his power to write . . . . . It's because he's not big enough.
    If a fellow isn't big enough he must do the other thing:—what you call style:—surface his work. It is a mode, too. The *War-and-Peace* plainness is better, perhaps: but one is fonder, often, of the rather less big work. It feels more homelike. That's the reward of secondary writers. They don't knock-out: but by their very smallness, or middle-size, they become good companions for ordinary people.

To H. S. Ede   Miranshah, 25 December 1928
    Your letter says it puzzles you how a man should 'work' at style, or writing. Well, I find that my fifth writing (after perhaps fifteenth reading) of a sentence makes it more shapely, pithier, stranger than it was. Without that twist of strangeness no one would feel an individuality, a differentness, behind the phrase. Unless it stays long enough in your thinking box to catch your likeness, it will not be demonstrably yours: and if anybody else could have written it, then it's no good.
    Am I being drastic? I hope not. Admittedly it's taking pains, and

not genius, that I describe: but most work is taking pains. Genius, I sometimes fancy, is when the subconsciousness does the work in the darkness, without the mind's being aware, or sharing the labour. Most of us have to plough and harrow the upper mind, deliberately and of malice prepense. If you can put your subconscious mind to work, at will, then you write without apparent effort, and are a genius.

Shakespeare wasn't that, I fancy. Coleridge was. 'I am slain by a fair cruel maid'—yes, that's style. The thought has warped the phrase which came first to the mind. It came as 'cruel fair maid'—a fair maid being a cliché: and he twisted it, and made poetry. 'Nowadays there is in painting so little obvious craft.' Oh: Oh: so little else than an immense marvellous sleight of brush. They say nothing—but with an air! I'd say that the curse of this century is an overdose of style, so that you get Gertrude Steins, who are nothing but style.

The conversational is the thing to aim for. You should try and make your pen-work supple and intoned as your voice. That means trying each pen-phrase over and over in your unspoken voice, till it rings like something you'd have liked to have said. Then it's yours. Most peoples' sentences—even their spoken sentences—aren't really speakable. All language, bar the spoken word, is dead: there are marvellous, magnificent corpses—Arabia Deserta, Marius the Epicurean, Les Moralités Légendaires, Moby Dick—corpses better than any living dog. . . .

To H. S. Ede   Plymouth, 20 March 1929
About your Gaudier book [*Savage Messiah*]. It's really very good. Gaudier is quite clear, and so is she. They both come, very intensely, *through* what you have written. That means you have done it well, in the large sense. In the smaller sense, syntax and the power of paragraphing, you have not done so surely. I could pick holes in any page; but the little things can be learnt, and are learnt, by going on writing: whereas the big thing, which is right in this case, comes right by instinct. So you are fortunate, and will probably write another book, after this one, and it'll be better than this. Do not leave Garnett to correct anything you can achieve yourself, by taking pains. Your own work is better, the more thoroughly you do it, for nobody else will really care as much for this book as you do. That's the way, always.

To H. S. Ede   Plymouth, 28 March 1929
Syntax comes with thinking about it. It's not to be learned by outside study. If you know it, you can do without it: but you should know it, before you assume freedom.

To H. S. Ede   Plymouth, 9 May 1929
   Your difficulty of working or lazing, as the mood takes you, is
everyone's. I think the self settles the problem, without asking you
to take a hand. If you can work you can: when you have been lazy
and done nothing, then you could have done nothing well. Some
fellows have forced themselves into task-work: and to meritorious
work. But the work I find myself re-reading and enjoying holds some
zest, some might-fingered eagerness to get at something: and Trollope
and Scott and the praiseworthies don't ever catch this.

To F. N. Doubleday   Plymouth, 28 June 1929
   Do go on writing your memoirs. . . . Dictate quite a lot, for then
that dry sparkle will cling to the words. Pens are stiff things to hold,
and they make our words too mannered.

To Henry Williamson   10 July 1929
Do not distress yourself about "lasting": not even our bones do that,
except momentarily. I think that to last is only to be in doubt longer.

To H. S. Ede   [Plymouth], 29 July 1929
   Adeptly is a perfectly good word. There is, and there damned well
will be lots of them, if ever Eddie [Marsh][31] tells me there isn't or
aren't. Grammar and Syntax (English being yet a living language) are
the usages of you and me and him. I can't stop him saying 'sweet'
and he can't stop me saying adeptly. It's likelife. Words keep on being
born. Only dead ones are finally dead.
   In Cardiff is correct: and *at* Littlehampton. Cardiff being big enough
to contain several people at once. *In* a ship: *at* dinner. *In* London is
the only possible word. 'The fattest man *at* London'. Hoots.
   . . . People chasing anything big have no use for rules. Your Gaudier
is the goods.

To Charlotte Shaw   London, 4 October 1929
. . . the charm and comfort of imperfection makes up for most of
the failures of the world. We admire the very great, but love the
less. . . .

To John Brophy   Plymouth, 19 November 1929
I want a diary, or record of events to be as near slice-of-life as can
be. Imagination jars in such instances. In novels however slice-of-life
jars, because their province is the second-remove, the sublimation of
the theme. See the difference between Sgt. Bourgogne & War and

Peace: or between War Birds and the Return of the Brute. One is eye-witness or ear-witness, & the other creative mind. In the first the photograph cannot be too sharp, for it's the senses which record: in the second you need design. Any care for design renders the record infect.

To John Brophy   Plymouth, 8 February 1930
People shouldn't write unless they have something especial to say. It should be forced out, against the grain. These wanting-to-write authors are a nuisance.

To Ira Jones   London, 1930?[32]
   Read works by the classical authors—Hazlitt, Addison, Dryden, Johnson, Macaulay, etc. Read good class novels by such authors as Shaw, Dickens, Eliot, Meredith, Hardy, Conrad, etc. Try writing short essays on any subject that takes your fancy or interest in order to shape your thoughts and ideas, in neat, precise, plain English words. Knit your sentences by original metaphor and sparkling examples, such as description of places and scenery. Create your own style—do not copy. Avoid like the plague, cliches—tautologous phrasing—repetition of instances—using the same words in a sentence or paragraph—superlatives—trite and banal references—exaggeration or hyperbole.

To William Rothenstein   Plymouth, 18 October 1930
Anybody who writes a very good first book is doomed.
   . . . Often I ask people for the names of "under-30's," fellows whose 2nd. book is better than their first, and who are not yet thirty. Only they will so seldom tell me of one. There must be several promising things in the offing; for the war is, thank God, at last over and done with.

To F. N. Doubleday   27 January 1931
To-day there is nothing I want to write, and I will not try to write out of an empty mind. A book should burst out of a man, against his will, like a vomit into the sea.

To G. W. M. Dunn   11 March 1931
   Use the adjectives which seem to your senses best fitting: it will then depend on the sanity of your senses whether others find them significant or not. Don't forget that a strain of vulgarity, in the best sense, is indispensable in the greatest art. Your precious artist, however real, comes second to the common man.

To Edward Marsh   Plymouth, 7 July 1931
My soul is aching for decent work by people nearing thirty: not flashes
in the pan, but steady writers, attempting their third book or so. Are
there none such?

To L. M. P. Black   Plymouth, 2 September 1931
   Now the book.[33] I have read it twice, and I like it. You were too
ambitious, to draw early Britain & metropolitan Rome at once. . . .
   I think it rather a pity you did not go on. You had learned to write
vigorously, in doing that, and your next book would have profited
by more of your attention to the content, and less to the expression.
Every first book is over-careful of its manners, and freedom comes
only after it has been bought. Your second book would have been your
test. It is everybody's. . . .

To Ernest Altounyan   Plymouth, 9 January 1933
Words get richer every time they are deliberately used . . . . . but only
when deliberately used: and it is hard to be conscious of each single
word, and yet not at the same time self-conscious.
   I mustn't slip again into the technique of writing. Writing has been
my inmost self all my life, and I can never put my full strength into
anything else. Yet the same force, I know, put into action upon material
things would move them, make me famous and effective. The
everlasting effort to write is like trying to fight a feather-bed. In letters
there is no room for strength.

To John Brophy   Plymouth, 23 February 1923
Neurotics cannot write about themselves except with that sense of the
tragic that you deplore: and cannot write about others than themselves.
You would perhaps have them leave writing alone: but the literature
of disease is more interesting, to me, than all the healthy books.
Dostoevsky v. Galsworthy!
   . . . I can't understand the Irish fecundity in letters—unless it is
a feeling that it's time their country did something after the silence
of the Middle Ages! Also these infections are catching. When Yeats,
Moore and AE lived together in Dublin, no wonder the young took
fire. The old are an inspiration.
   . . . The secret of conveying feelings lies in the arrangement of
words, so often. You can get speed by economising in introductory
words, for instance: and pathos in a falling close.

To B. H. Liddell Hart   Isle of Wight, 23 May 1933
   Don't worry about your prose style, or mine. It's not how you say
it, but what you say. I only write well when excited.

To Edward Garnett   Southampton, 19 August 1933
  Bother . . . all manufactured writing. Only the necessary, the
inevitable, the high-pressure stuff is worth having. If the regiment of
authors agreed, how easily would readers keep abreast of output! By
your standard Buchan is nowhere: or rather he is with all but three
or four living names.
  Irishmen are disappointing men. They go so far, magnificently, and
cease to grow. They bring forth more promise and less fruition than
the rest of the English world massed against them. Give me the man
whose first book is not marvellous, whose second is better, and whose
third is different. Greatness in writing is a tree with many branches.
You do not see it till the tree is old.

To Alec Dixon   Clouds Hill, 9 November 1934
As time passes I come to value the manner less and the matter more.
Once I scorned any prose that was not mannered. Now I feel that so
long as the man is doing his best to say something, I can abide him.
Whereas those other better writers who write because they have an
itch to write, and marvellous technique, and yet say nothing—well,
they weary me.

To James Whittaker   6 March 1935
The old fluent sentences are those with which I grew up, and the flicking
or bombarding prose of today tires me, by never giving me a still place
on which to let up.

First Draft and Revision

To H. S. Ede   Miranshah, 12 November 1928
It's hard to drop a deep habit: and I did work my hardest, at writing,
for years and years. If I spent years more at the Mint it might grow
a shade slicker, superficially: but fundamentally it would never be
better. No revision makes an incomplete thing into a creation. Life
comes either at once, or not at all.

To Charlotte Shaw   Plymouth, 21 March 1930
Have you ever patted butter? My style is like butter. It must be worked
& worked to get smooth. I admit that smoothness is only a bore if
it hasn't a strong body & current running beneath it, and that can
only come from initial heat. Unless it goes well the first time no labour
will save it or redeem it. But if it goes well the first time no labour
will hurt it, or conceal that initial strength.

To Bruce Rogers   Plymouth, 20 August 1931
All the revision in the world will not save a bad first-draft: for the
architecture of the thing comes, or fails to come, in the conception,
and revision only affects the detail & ornament, alas!

To Bertram Thomas   Plymouth, 22 August 1931
No help, no revision, no pains taken, will make a poor draft into
a good book: everything lies on your first conception, upon the
excitement running into your hand as you write. . . .

To John Brophy   Plymouth, 23 February 1933
   Revision is a privilege of the artist, in which he has the pleasure
of improving his work. The blemishes he removes are those which only
his eyes see. The blemishes he does not see are remarked by the world
later. We can't help revising . . . . . I re-write all my stuff at least three
times in holograph, before typing . . . . . and it is all wasted work.
Gilding lilies or thorns, as the case is. The merit of a book lies in the
conception.

Tickling the Public

To H. S. Ede   Plymouth, 2 January 1930
   Title: 'A boy and a Woman' yes: with a sub-title 'Study in the
relations of H. G-B and Mlle. B.' or something about an artist,
and poverty and love and London.[34] Your popular edition must be
designed to catch the slightly-vulpine-amorous-gossip-loving-yet-
would-be-high-brow many of London. It is London that makes
books succeed in England. Look very closely after your American
and Continental rights: and try to serialise. If you feel nakedly
inexperienced before all the publishers in the world, then use an agent.
I paid one 10% of my takings, and profited myself about 20%. It's
a gamble, using an agent—you lose if the work is a huge success: and
profit, if it only just goes.

To Alec Dixon   Clouds Hill, 9 November 1934
To earn money by writing you must tickle the public below its
belt. . . . You have too high a standard for this, and I should be so
sorry to see you come down. Yet the other way is starvation and failure,
and you have a wife. . . . Go on doing what you best can—but don't
sacrifice to a theory every chance of profit that offers itself.

Books as Objects

To Charlotte Shaw   29 November 1924
Sorry you got the illustrated Twilight of the Gods. In the plain edition the stories read well. In that Christmassy garb they will feel callous and precious & thin.

To Robin Buxton   4 January 1926
I don't want to make the number [of *Seven Pillars* copies, Subscribers Edition] exactly a hundred, for one of my dislikes is the bibliophile, & that sort of man makes a fetish of number. To defeat him I am not numbering my copies, nor disclosing to anyone quite how many have been printed, nor making any two just alike.

To Charlotte Shaw   [Karachi], 30 June 1927
The very finest binding is no good till it has been well used. Only use will take the artificiality out of the surface of stretched and varnished morocco. In time you'll find your heart going out to the blemishes of the skin: the dark & light places, the veinings. . . . and also to the accidents of use—to the scratches made by the stains of butter, when you have moved it away from the teacup, to the round rings from which you have removed the spots of candle grease. A book-binding should have a history. . .

To Charlotte Shaw   [Karachi], 13 October 1927
There are about 40 of your (= my) books at the moment on loan in the camp. . . . I keep no record of loans . . . so I trust to their being returned: and they always are, in the end: but it may be months, & they may have been to 20 hands. . .

To H. S. Ede   29 July 1929
Next letter repeats the half-baked yapping of some idiot about my . . . living by selling the books decent people gave me. I have to my regret sold three books in my time. They were all deliberately bought for sale: Herman Melville's firsts: Galsworthy's Forsyte Saga, and Hudson's Purple Land.

To Judge   Plymouth, 11 January 1930
I agree entirely with you about the idiocy of collectors. They would rather treasure a washing-bill of Thomas Hardy's than read his Dynasts.

To John Brophy   Plymouth, 8 February 1930
India ink is the only stuff for proof-correcting, or indeed for any kind of correcting. I use it in a fountain-pen (sold only by Reeves of Charing Cross Road) and find it an unlimited blessing. You have to use a Bourgeois ink, then: but unless you are a communist, that will not hurt your feelings. It lasts for ever.

To K. W. Marshall   Southampton, 9 December 1931
It is my habit to celebrate events in my life by presenting myself with books. . .

To Wilfred Merton   Plymouth, 29 November 1932
I must have two more Odysseys, if the firm can spare them: preferably not too good, as copies! A blemish in a book makes it more friendly, I think.

To Edward Garnett   Southampton, 5 October 1933
. . . Some scruple makes me unable to sell books by people I like. I profiteered once on Galsworthy firsts—but that was different. He left me cold.

To Vincent Stuart   5 June 1934
I have grave doubts about the decency of hand-printing to-day; it feels archaistic. . . .
    The man who slightly improves the general level of commercial printing seems to me better than the artist who sets it an impossibly-precious example.

Critics and Criticism

To Vyvyan Richards   [early 1923]
More critic than artist. That's the analytic vein in me. Ineradicable. A critic in conscious creation is of course an artist. Ditto a blacksmith or a playwright. A critic is no more barred from creation than any other being. I'll say even that there's creative criticism: not literary nor artistic, but personal (biography) or ethical (Pater's *Imaginary Portraits*). To have an excess of creative over critical sense produces a Swinburne. To be excessively critical is to be like Rupert Brooke. The perfect artist is half-critic & half-creator.

To Charlotte Shaw   [Karachi], 19 May 1927
You sent me no end of a quaint cutting about me by Arnold Bennett.

He linked D. H. L. (a prodigious person) with TEL (a rat) as *stylists*!
My breathing ceased suddenly: then I laughed and with that laughter
went out the queer feeling of respect I've cherished for years at the
certainty of conviction Arnold Bennett puts into his critical writing.
He writes as if no person could ever conceivably, not overturn, but
challenge any one of his literary judgements. And now stylists! Hoot!
Hoot! Prose like Wagner & Schubert: . . . . Prose like Big Ben and
a muffin bell. Hoot Hoot Hoot.

To E. M. Forster   [Karachi], 14 July 1927
How hard critical work is. I wonder if I'll ever be able to write that
article I imagined before I left England.[35] It would be something
snatched from the shipwreck which is this visit to India. . . .
    And your critical lectures?[36] Aren't they to come out? I'm hoping
to add them to the novels, as part of the evidence against you. Do
realise that it's your duty to give the world a flag as guide to your
course (even a rabbit shows the white of its tail in flight): otherwise
the great hunters will never win your pelt: and how other can they
keep warm in wnter, except they dress in writers' skins? The keynote
of this age is critical.

To Robert Graves   [Karachi], 19 May 1928
    Incidentally, Arnold Bennett warmed me, in an article on the young
who write, by coming out handsomely on your side. There is something
quite peculiarly of the craft about Bennett's criticism. It does not allow
itself to get philosophical; or to speak of religions and ideals and
principles; it takes a book as something which somebody has written
(damn all readers, thinks A. B.: it's writing which is the job) and
considers it as that. Whenever I get hold of a bit of Bennett's criticial
stuff I push it into my belly with delight, and rise up hungry; for he
chops it into little bits, to fit newspaper columns, and is provokingly
patchy: but he writes like a Lord, as though he didn't care who read
him. No damned merit, no nonsense: yet such an admirable straight
scent. Oh yes, really good. (Yet he wrote those awful 5-towns, or was
it 7-towns, novels!)[37]

To H. S. Ede   Plymouth, 10 April 1929
After all, praise is no help to the poor brute who's trying to write.
He wants criticism: fault showing.

To G. W. M. Dunn   [Plymouth?], 11 March 1931
Detailed criticism is the only stuff worth having—plain praise being
the most useless and boring stuff in the world—but the only people

who can give you detailed criticism fit to help you are other craftsmen working themselves upon your job. Not being a poet I cannot venture towards you. . . . [38]

Heed no advice or criticism except from your peers.

To Jacob Schwartz   Southampton, 26 April 1932

Have you noticed that criticism never helps? I once wrote a book, and after it eagerly began to read its reviews, hoping that I was going to learn where I had been wrong. Only nothing concrete was ever said, and so I've not been able to do better. I suspect that is a common case.

To G. W. M. Dunn   Southampton, 26 September 1933

. . . do not expect detailed criticisms of me. I am not a critic, but a hard-working boat-overseer. Critics are confident men, able to weigh spirits. I only weigh anchors. . . .

I am very glad you are coming out. Only out of many minds, and after many days do judgements emerge. In time we shall know what the work is worth.

Poetry and Poets

To C. H. St. John Hornby   London, 26 January 1922

It's the best long poem in English [*The Faerie Queene*]; and I've read it again and again till I've been sick of it: and always returned to it with an appetite a day later.

To Edward Garnett   [Uxbridge], 23 October 1922

I have looked in poetry (the crown and head, the only essential branch of letters) everywhere for satisfaction: and haven't found it. Instead I have made that private collection of bonbons:[39] chocolate éclairs of the spirit: whereas I wanted a meal. . . .

I can't write poetry. . . .

To Vyvyan Richards   [early 1923]

I think Brooke's technique as good as Keats, but his sense of the taste of words was less fine: and his native irony restrained him from the sugary-pictures of Keats. It restrained him too much, so that it was seldom musical: whereas Keats when his self-criticism held back from the sugar, had almost no likely fault to avoid. Art Creation is avoidance as much as it is presentation. And it's interesting to see Keats's growth in force (& decline in sweetness) from *Endymion* to *Hyperion*.

To Sydney Cockerell   [Bovington], 22 October 1923
   It's a choice between Sassoon & Squire?[40]. . . . . Well, let the poet
win: I'd always put poets first, & men afterwards.

To Charlotte Shaw   31 May 1925
I . . . quarrel . . . with Burdett's book on the ninetys.[41] It
patronises . . . . . and the nineties were very rich, very strong, very
successful. They can do without his kind attention. [Ernest] Dowson
wrote some glorious poems. [John] Davidson was bigger but not as
good: worthier, because he tried his hardest, & burst in the effort.
However, bother Burdett. He hasn't burst himself.

To Robert Graves   Karachi, 24 December 1927
The whole of it [Graves's biography *Lawrence and the Arabs*] does
not carry so much meaning, to my judgement, as the single poem about
Alexander in your collection.[42] Not to call the Clipped Stater your
best poem—but it is related in subject to the long book. I put any
poem by you above any prose effort you attempt. . . . . just because
poetry is inevitably more tight in form, and because the reader can
put into it as much of his own subtlety and desire as he pleases. Look
for instance at how much more you get out of Shakespeare in the old
spelling.

To Bruce Rogers   Karachi, 16 April 1928
   The [Maurice] Hewlett pages you typed out for me are
fascinating.[43] The introduction says exactly what I'd like to say to
everybody who reads or writes translations; and the verse pages are
wonderful. I can't do anything like that. Hewlett was really a fine
poet: I have seen a trilogy (classical) and a volume of short pieces
(*Artemesia*?)[44] and an epic of peasant life . . . . . a sort of Georgic
. . . . . and they were all the real thing. He was also a good prose
writer and a charming critic. His monthly reviews in the *London
Mercury* were the best-reading criticisms of their time. So his *Iliad*
is, naturally, the best yet. I can see that, even from the fragment you
send. What a pity he never finished it.

To David Garnett   Miranshah, 14 June 1928
   Don't you like Rupert Brooke's sonnets? They are wonderful:
especially for a man who was not very good in anything he wrote.
Really, people are odd. They are writing apologetically of Rossetti,
in the papers, everywhere. He was a magnificent poet. Morris is half-
praised. Morris was a giant. Somebody said that Dowson wasn't a
great poet; or Flecker. God Almighty! Must everyone be as seven-

leagued as Milton and Byron and Hardy? The English world is full of wonderful writing, by live men and dead men. Look at *Mr. Weston's New Wine* [by T. F. Powys, 1927].

To Maurice Baring   Miranshah, 30 October 1928
    As you say, a man doesn't know what he has done in this job of writing: nor do I ever surely know what another man has done: but nearly sure, I do feel, sometimes: and I think that if ever a death-poem has been good it is yours. It takes me, each time I read it (even years after, as now, for I haven't seen it, certainly, since 1922 when I enlisted) absolutely by the throat. It is a lovely thing: and big, ever so big: and so simply sincere, and grievous, and splendid. I think Lucas[45] will live, thanks to you, for as long as your language.
    I stopped at the end of it, for I was quite full, and there would have been waste only in going on. Later I will read more, and see what I recognise and what I like. But there can't be any more upon the key and scale of the Lucas poem: people do not do their supremest more than once in life. Lucky if they do it once. I envy you the perfect welding of art, and feeling, and expression, and nobility of thought.
    Damn it all, what a slow and clumsy way of saying that you have lifted me right out of myself in happiness. It is a wonderful thing: makes me shiver.

To Maurice Baring   Miranshah, 18 December 1928
You have a gift—the great gift—of just putting out your finger, effortlessly, to touch us in the heart.
    Your poem on Lieut. Spencer is ever so queer; quite half its lines are plain prose, and the whole of it is poetry. Of course I know that bricks, bricks, bricks, build a house; and words, words, words make a poem. You, somehow, make prose upon prose become definitely poetic—and there's the touch of intimacy, given by this everyday language and half-slang phrase, which gets to its target (the heart, as I said above) more truly than grand words can do.
    Your exquisite ear for the syllables of grief. . . . .
    "I do not need you changed, dissolved in air
      Nor rarefied,
      I need you all imperfect as you were" . . . . .
But there's no need for me to quote your verses at you. The judgment that can choose these melting vowels knows better than the rest of us how seldom they have been as surely acheived.
    There isn't much of it under the hat, I expect. One, two, or three perfect things (the Lord Lucas first of them all): but how good it is to be perfect in one's way. Your novels interested me, held me, pleased

me: but those bits of poetry double me up and carry me away. Only by spending such pains to write well could you have caught that melody which lies behind the wording of the poems.

To F. L. Lucas   3 May 1930
. . . I'd give all the novels in the world for 1/1000th of its poetry. What is it that makes a tiny poem seem infinite, and a great novel too short?

To G. W. M. Dunn   Plymouth, 21 October 1931
I'm not yet ready to say exactly what I think of your poems. They are poems, of course, very real ones; and there is no good and bad poetry: just poetry. Only they leave me unsure of the capacity you have for more. Everybody can write poetry for a few weeks or for a few years of his life, if any intense emotional experience comes his way before he has settled into a groove. You seem to have done rather more than that minimum.

. . . In poetry quality and quantity are not just scale and sort—they intertwine, so that such a poem as the "Dynasts", without any memorable phrase, or any perfect line, can by the mere bigness of its sweep outpass every other poem in the language. Keats failed to write a great poem in Endymion, lovely though bits of Endymion are. One suspects he was a great poet, for the evidence of scale throughout his work; but I think he did not write a great poem.

I think your "O winds, have mercy on this summer night" altogether good. Yet in it I would have avoided the "tender" stars, the "limpid" eyes, and the dream of the acolyte. Choir boys are, in my experience, unmixed little devils. So I scoff, by instinct, at the acolyte's profession! . . . . If the acolyte stays in, then the nun of v.4 must go; and I prefer the nun. "Burning bright" is a memory; Of course I know that T. S. Eliot is full of memories; but can you take his liberties? Only yourself knows.

I call this poem awfully good, all the same. It is a real pleasure to try to pick a hole in it. . . .

"There shall be great winds blowing where I go" is very, very good. . . . Why not put it in the Prof's magazine?[46] It does a good poem good to print it, and see it in the new shape. Perhaps after that you might better it, still; though I see no need or fault.

. . . You have a heart-searching gift of phrase, so heart-searching that you needn't, ever again, deliberately seek out the pathetic things. It is hitting below the belt, in writing, to use the full pathetic stop. Also it is nearly always a merit of youth. . . . If the rank and file carry on cheerfully, so should we. They have few compensations for the load of existence: no music, no poems, no good books, no colours or forms to make them glad. . . .

Now I want to keep these poems, if I may. I have the notion that I ought to show them to someone. Exactly whom I do not know; but someone who is a practising poet, for only tradesmen are qualified to value goods.

To Geoffrey Keynes   28 January 1934
They [Altounyan's poems] are very wild, argumentative, ejaculatory, interjectory. . . . All very spasmodic. . . . They record more rapture than they convey. . . . I have suggested interspersing the poems with prose notes. . .

To Ernest Altounyan   7 April 1934
Your poem—essentially it is one, a poetic history—is so long, so interwoven, so exhausting, that it demands full attention. Don't be hurt by the word exhausting. I do not mean wearisome but wearying. It is a strenuous exercise to reach much of it. Like boxing, which is a severe art, whereas golf is easy. You are a muscular poet, and few readers will ever grapple with you competently.

This tax upon your readers is physical. It is possible that intellectually you may make an equal demand. Your metaphysic, your physiology, your philosophy may be as articulated and articulate as [the] forcefulness of your writing. My mind slides over what it fails to understand, and is not troubled at having such depths under its keel. So I do not weary my brain as I read your poems. If your subsequent readers do, why then more of them will fall by the wayside. Be merciful to the reading public! It is not a merit to write, like Blake in his prophetic books, for the very few. The very few are not so useful as the very many. To imagine ourselves—because we are freaks—to be therefore rare and admirable creations is to deceive ourselves. Two-headed chickens and Siamese twins are rare—and unfortunate. Generally they are bottled young.

To C. Day Lewis   Bridlington, 16 November 1934
It's an impertinence to write to a writer; but I cannot help it. Your book on poetry [A Hope for Poetry] is only half an argument. So long as you wrote poems I was content with reading them. Over Dick Willoughby I laughed. This, as I say, is different. . . .

When you talk of poetry being as hard to read as to write you must be thinking of the metaphysical poets. They are much harder to read than in the writing, for they weren't very good philosophers, or clear logicians or subtle metaphysicians. They were afraid of plain statement, and feared that their real minds were foolish. Poets of today feel often that their real feelings are foolish. So they splash something about shirt-sleeves or oysters quickly into every sentimental sentence, to prevent us laughing at them before they have laughed at themselves. But you must qualify that saying about poetry being difficult, either to write or to read. Some poetry! *Kubla Khan* took no writing, nor any of W. Morris' early verse, nor Chaucer's tales, nor most of Shakespeare's speeches. *Paradise Lost* is as easy to read as the *Aeneid* or *Don Juan*—yet these must have been hard to write. Dandyism in style revived with l'Isle Adam.

I hesitate also to attach great weight to the war. My age made me just ripe for it, and I went through it with as major consequence a great faculty for wasting time uncomplainingly: perhaps a sense that time and myself and you and things done or to do were not very significant. As a historian by training I shouldn't like to think that accidental participation in this one war of the infinite series past and to come had made me put it bigly in the foreground of any but its victims. Sassoon wasn't tough enough. It broke in him a good lyric writer. I was glad to see your sensible regard for D. H. L. and Owen. As for Hopkins, he would repay a closer study on the pathological side: the Jesuit at war with the sensualist. I think fear of giving himself away led to those inversions and syntactical quirks. A very fine poet!

I'm glad you concentrated on Auden, Spender and yourself. Auden makes me fear that he will not write much more. Spender might, on the other hand, write too much. You have given numbers of us the greatest pleasure—though for me *The Magnetic Mountain* was a qualified pleasure. In this book your suggestion that it may represent an approach to politics rejoiced me. It was not merely explanation but recantation, I thought. Poets are always (and have been always) savagely political: and the real politician, the politician-by-trade, always carts them properly. Poets hope too much, and their politics, like their sciences, usually stink after twenty years. I call our time very rich in poets, quantitatively and qualitatively.

To make your book invaluable you need to give us an exposure-meter by which we could pick out the one lighted window in the houses they build. Your quotations,—from yourself and the others—aren't those I (or anyone) would choose. Do you believe in a yardstick, or any solvent to divide even the very good from the very bad? . . . .

Thank you for an exciting and quite unsatisfying book: but if you want to make us really happy, you will expose yourself to the risk of writing some more poems: and for the ear, not the eye. These cheap typewriters do poets much harm.

To Winifred Fontana   Bridlington, 28 November 1934
  E. A. [Ernest Altounyan] is depressed. . . . and the flush has gone

from his writings. Poor E. I wish he could be helped. I read in the great poem-sequence often: it is and it isn't. How tell him?

To Ernest Altounyan   Bridlington, 9 December 1934
   Ah me, but I find you difficult. Your verses twist and turn like eels with your thought ever slipping away from me, and with never a stop. It moves and moves, and moves, until I find myself longing for somewhere to sit down and rest. Have you, in your re-reading of it after the heat of creation, noted its restlessness? All of you and it jigging non-stop?
   I think you'll have to make pauses, sometimes, for the readers to draw breath. Imagine it a song you had written, with never a blank half bar even, for the singer to refill her lungs. Now that I have more leisure and cool blood to confront the mass of it, I see that the prose headings and divisions and arguments for which I pleaded were not to explain it (it explains itself) but so many landings on which to halt a moment. Otherwise you'll kill your readers. Spenser killed them with his *Faery Queen*. I've read that, heaps and heaps of times. I lived on it till 1916 or so. Yet I know that nobody can really grapple with it because it runs on too fast.
   . . . Do felicitate yourself on having a real craft, a hand-craft, behind you. To be a writer and no more is to be misshapen, lop-sided, unstable. Solid poetry cannot be written by a shaky man. If you let yourself fall down easily you condemn *all* your work. I feel great power in these writings: everything except the power to stand still, and that can only come in a revise.

This Frenzy to Know!

To his mother   Laigle, 28 August 1908
Certainly Chartres is the sight of a lifetime, a place truly in which to worship God. The middle ages were truer that way than ourselves, in spite of their narrowness and hardness and ignorance of the truth as we complacently put it: the truth doesn't matter a straw, if men only believe what they say or are willing to show that they do believe something.

To Lionel Curtis   [Bovington], 27 March 1923
Can there be profit, or truth, in all these modes and sciences and arts of ours? The leisured world for hundreds, or perhaps thousands of years has been jealously working and recording the advance of each generation for the starting-point of the next—and here [in the Tank

Corps] these masses are as animal, as carnal as were their ancestors before Plato and Christ and Shelley and Dostoevsky taught and thought. In this crowd it's made startlingly clear how short is the range of knowledge, and what poor conductors of it ordinary humans are. You and I know: you have tried (Round Tabling[47] and by mouth) to tell all whom you can reach: and the end is here, a cimmerian darkness with bog-lights flitting wrongly through its gas.

  . . . Your mind is like a many-storied building, and you, its sole tenant, flit from floor to floor, from room to room, at the whim of your spirit's moment. . . . At will you can be gross, and enjoy coffee or a sardine, or rarefy yourself till the diaphancité [sic] of pure mathematics, or of a fluent design in line, is enough to feed you. Here—

  . . . Hut 12 shows me the truth behind Freud. . . . These fellows are the reality, and you and I, the selves who used to meet in London and talk of fleshless things, are only the outward wrappings of a core like these fellows. . . . our wrappings and bandages have stunted and deformed ourselves, and hardened them to an apparent insensitiveness. . . . but it's a callousness, a crippling, only to be yea-said by aesthetes who prefer clothes to bodies, surfaces to intentions.

  . . . the end of this is that man, or mankind, being organic, a natural growth, is unteachable: cannot depart from his first grain and colour, nor exceed flesh, nor put forth anything not mortal and fleshly.

To Vyvyan Richards   [Karachi], 15 March 1927
It seemed to me, the more I tried my head . . . on ideas, that the less they meant. To destroy a thing you have only got to think about it hard enough. . . . There is no distinction between mind and body, soul and spirit, god and man, matter and force, space and time, abstract and concrete, fact and idea, colour and beetroots, stones and smells. At the heart of everything I find a sameness, a unity of substance. . . .

  Ergo human speculations have about the value of human experience or acts or creations or excreta. . . . I have not dumped my gods overboard, because there are no gods, and no board, nor any me to dump anything.

To Eric Kennington   Karachi, 16 June 1927
. . . [I] go on learning because the more one learns the less one knows, & some day I may attain perfect ignorance, that way.

To Lionel Curtis   Karachi, 22 December 1927
You are retired to write your book about the Empire. Good. Remember that the manner is greater than the (?) matter, so far as modern history

is concerned.[48] One of the ominous signs of the time is that the public can no longer read history. The historian is retired into a shell to study the whole truth; which means that he learns to attach insensate importance to documents. The documents are liars. No man ever yet tried to write down the entire truth of any action in which he has been engaged. All narrative is parti pris. And to prefer an ancient written statement to the guiding of your instinct through the maze of related facts, is to encounter either banality or unreadableness. We know too much, and use too little knowledge. Cut away the top-hamper.

To K. W. Marshall   Plymouth, 9 April 1931
Without being intellectual or a scholar, I have mixed for many years with people of great learning and reputation—and have been slowly persuaded that there is nothing in all that. We apprehend with our instincts and senses: brains come into play later on, to rationalise what we already know through feeling: and a simply healthy person has little need of brains. The curse of our age is this thought-maggoty caries of the head from which the high-brows suffer; which spoils all they do.
Because of this I prefer Noel Coward to Aldous Huxley!

To Lewis Namier   Southampton, 6 September 1932
I liked your little book of essays [*Skyscrapers*]. The thinking ones wear well. Your "England . . . . . [in the Age of the American] Revolution" pleases me less. Your history is not digested enough for any public except historians to read. That puts a premium on the Omans, who re-hash for the general public. And I don't like re-hashes. . . . So there we are. All Souls was resentful when I offered a copy of Wells Outline of History to the Library.

To H. S. Ede   Plymouth, 18 October 1932
For the play,[49] I felt that it was a statement of the fact of three or four years ago: and that we had all already agreed that no answers to general questions of life or death are desired or desirable or possible: and so we carry on. What an impertinence, this frenzy to know!

To H. S. Ede   Southampton, 25 September 1933
Thank you for the Betjeman book.[50] He has some of the matter in him: but all generalisations or inferences are vain, unless they are drawn from the full body of evidence: and the full body of history is too full for our finity. Not to mention that the full body infers and deduces nothing. So J. B. if born 70 years ago would have dogmatically advanced the ideas he now combats: and 70 years hence would say—what? I don't know and don't much care.

To Ezra Pound   Bridlington, 7 December 1934

I'm sorry, as I said, about Orage.[51] He is a real loss. For another
to continue the *New Age* would not console me any more than if Henry
Newbolt (after your premature demise) should in pious memory utter
a Canto. It is Orage who mattered: not what he believed or bit. We
admire the spirit of the bull-terrier, without endorsing its action in
biting the postman's trousers. To my mind both Guild Socialism and
Social Credit were levities to engross the mind of Orage.

Your sheet of questions—they don't matter, either. I don't care a
hoot for economics, or our money system, or the organisation of
society. Such growths are like our stature; what time I have for thinking
(not enough, I agree) goes, or tries to go, upon themes within my
governance. A fig for financiers.

Of course I know that economics is the fashionable theme, today.
A fad almost. Everybody talks and writes about production and
exchange and distribution and consumption. Twenty years ago science
was *the* subject that we all let off hot air about. It was going to do
what the lads fancy political economy will do now. Ah well; I'm 46,
and if I live another 20 years there may be a prevalent fashion less
dull than economics, and perhaps I'll join in that.

. . . some instinct tells me that the people who fuss about the money
of the world are on the wrong tack. Money only serves to keep us
alive: and people like you and me wouldn't impair the usefulness of
the world if we went down. I incline to resent our presuming to tell
our physical betters what ought to be done. Disposing other people's
minds is an infectious activity.

To C. Day Lewis   Bridlington, 20 December 1934

Perhaps I don't read them [the metaphysical poets] because the sciences
are closed books to me. I can't feel that knowledge matters at all. There
must be theories, apparently: but one can spend the few active years
one has so much more enjoyably out of doors on practicalities—like
my R.A.F. boat-building. So I try not to want to think.

. . . I hoped you were getting bored with politics. The ideals of
a policy are entrancing, heady things: the translating them into terms
of compromise with the social structure as it has evolved is pretty
second-rate work. I have never met people more honest and devoted
than our politicians—but I'd rather be a dustman. A decent nihilism
is what I hope for, generally. I think an established land, like ours,
can do with 1% monists or nihilists. That leaves room for me. The
trouble with Communism is that it accepts too much of today's
furniture. I hate furniture.

Notes

Preface

1. Thomas Mann, Introduction, *The Short Novels of Dostoevsky* (New York: Dial Press, 1945), xviii.

Introduction: Booklover, Writer, Literary Cognoscente

1. Austen H. Layard, *Ninevah and Its Remains* (1848–49) and *The Ruins of Ninevah and Babylon* (1853).
2. E.g., "I walked to Sidon, along the coast-road: seeing very little of importance, except the Arab site of Jonah's coming ashore from his fish"; "Banias Mother will remember from Matthew XVI or Mark VIII. . . . it may be that the Transfiguration took place on one of the neighbouring spurs of Mt. Hermon"; "Tell-el-Kadi. . . . is the Laish of Judges XVIII, & subsequently Dan"; "the site of Abel-Beth-Maachah, where Sheba was finally run to earth by Joab" (July 17 and August 2, 1909 letters, *Home*).
3. August 6, 1934 letter to Geoffrey Keynes (Garnett).
4. "When I like a book I always read it twice" (Wrench, 144). Cf. Virginia Woolf, who "believed in reading a book twice. The first time she abandoned herself to the author unreservedly. The second time she treated him with severity and allowed him to get away with nothing he could not justify. After these two readings she felt qualified to discuss the book" (E. M. Forster, *Two Cheers for Democracy* [New York: Harcourt, Brace, 1951], 119).
5. As when he told Robert Graves (64), "I read every book which interested me in the Library of the Oxford Union (best part of 50,000 vols. I expect) in 6 years," six a day. Richard Aldington's venemous biography (31) correctly notes, "6 books a day for 6 years doesn't make much more than 13,000"—not that that, or a fifth as many, is insignificant.
6. Yeats-Brown in Wrench, 144; elsewhere he says Lawrence read the book the three hours (Yeats-Brown, 444). *Lives of a Bengal Lancer* (1930) is some 68,000 very readable words about experiences in prewar Turkey and India that would have interested Lawrence.
7. William Rothenstein (*Friends*, 287). Also, Lawrence had just been told that the author's name began with "M" (p. 202).
8. Lawrence said he rewrote 95 percent of the text in one month (Wilson, 627–28).
9. " . . . he possessed such a wide knowledge on so many subjects that the staff [of the American Mission School in Jebail, Syria, 1911–14] rightly named him the Encyclopaedia" (Fareedah el Akle in *Friends*, 77). "On the train from Cairo little Lawrence my supercerebral companion . . . [I] continue to wonder whether for all

288

his amazing knowledge, his sum total of pleasure is . . . any greater than mine"
(October 12 and 14, 1916 diary entries, Storrs, 186–87).

10. Unfortunately, I have lost the source and date (fall 1933?) of this letter.

11. October 21, 1932 letter to Mrs. Shaw (*British*) and January 2, 1932 to Manning
(Manning).

12. June 28, 1929 letter to F. N. Doubleday (Garnett).

13. October 5, 1933 letter to Edward Garnett (Garnett).

14. They are listed in *Friends*, 476–510.

15. Arnold Lawrence (*Friends*, 591).

16. The thesis was titled *The Influence of the Crusades on Military Architecture—
to the End of the XIIth Century*; a twelve-thousand-word limitation contributed to
the concision (Wilson, 64). Evidently there was no limitation on illustrations: it had
some 127 drawings, plans, and photographs!

17. April 26, 1929 letter to Marshall Field (*Bodleian*) and 1929 letter to Major
Archibald Beck (Weintraubs, 1–2).

18. " . . . I lent it to Lord Curzon about 1919; and I don't remember it since
(Except for a half-notion that he gave it me back & I burned it: but I don't remember
this well enough to swear to it" (Weintraubs, 1–2). Lawrence may have burned the
manuscript of his youthful Seven Pillars of Wisdom in August 1914. Sending an
account of the Arab revolt to *The Times* editor Geoffrey Dawson in November 1918,
he said, "Please burn it." He burned the translation of the French novel *Sturly* which
he had done for Cape in 1923–24. The dedication of *The Mint* manuscript he sent
Edward Garnett in 1928 read, "You dreamed I came one night with this book crying,
'Here is a masterpiece. Burn it.' Well as you please." Usually, after reading and
replying, he burned most of the many letters he received.

19. Ault, 128; Wilson, 97.

20. As *Crusader Castles* (London: Golden Cockerel, 1936; London: Michael
Haag, 1983; and, with introduction and notes by Denys Pringle, Oxford: Clarendon
Press, 1988).

21. June 28, 1927 letter to Graves, 49; this list omits Bagdad, cited in a 1923 letter;
see note 22.

22. Writing Robin Buxton September 22, 1923, Lawrence said, "The 'Seven Pillars
of Wisdom' is a quotation from *Proverbs*: it is used as title out of sentiment: for
I wrote a youthful indiscretion-book, so called, in 1913 and burned it (as immature)
in '14 when I enlisted. It recounted adventures in seven type-cities of the East (Cairo,
Bagdad, Damascus etc.) & arranged their characters into a descending cadence: a
moral symphony. It was a queer book, upon whose difficulties I look back with a
not ungrateful wryness: and in memory of it I so named the new book, which will
probably be the only one I ever write . . . " (Garnett).

23. A January 24, 1911 letter refers to "my monumental work on the Crusades"
(*Home*). He later told Herbert Baker, "I meant once to write a book on the back-
ground of Christ . . . . . Galilee and Syria, social, intellectual and artistic, of 40 B.C.
It would make an interesting book" (Garnett, 568). After lunching with Lawrence
in 1920, Evelyn Wrench (1935, 449) said, "He . . . is now writing a history of the
Crusades which he thinks will take him five years and then he expects to write a book
on Spinoza!" At that time, the "history of the Crusades" could only have been *Seven
Pillars* and "a book on Spinoza," a leg-pull. In 1923, Lawrence said, "I thought
of trying to write about . . . [Nebuchadnessar]: a psychological study of the Frederic
Manning manner" (Garnett, 410).

24. C. L. Woolley and T. E. Lawrence, *The Wilderness of Zin* (London: Palestine
Exploration Fund, 1914, reissued by Jonathan Cape, 1935).

25. In an October 1914 note to D. G. Hogarth, Lawrence protested "the insertion

of his name on the title page. His objections were over-ruled, since he had in reality contributed substantial sections of the text" (Wilson 1988, 46).

26. A short piece in the *Oxford High School Magazine*, 1906, written with a friend, was signed "Two Calcotripticians" (brass-rubbers); one in *Jesus College Magazine*, 1913, was initialled "C.J.G."

27. April 26, 1929 letter to Marshall Field, the American anthropologist (*Bodleian*).

28. A version of the Mesopotamian report, censored to remove the sharpest thrusts, appears in Wilson, 949–59. It still cuts; for example: Sir Percy Cox, the High Commissioner, "will not take orders or suggestions about his policy from anyone but London, and he knows London so well . . . this is only a diplomatic way of taking no orders at all." Twenty-Seven Articles for handling Arabs "expressed in command-ment form for greater clarity and to save words," is justly famous, though some imperceptive critics deem it Machiavellian (*Arab Bulletin*, August 20, 1917, reprinted in Mack, 463–67, and Wilson, 960–65). The analysis of Syria (*Arab Bulletin*, March 12, 1917) was used in *Seven Pillars* (Chapters 58 and 59), the language amended for a new audience and time. Thus, "German Zionist Jews, speaking a bastard Hebrew and German Yiddish" became "German Jews, speaking German or German-Yiddish"; "the only imposed government that will find . . . large body of adherents is a Sunni one" became "the only independent factor with . . . fighting adherents was a Sunni prince, like Feisal." *Secret Despatches* (1936 and 1991) contains many of Lawrence's wartime reports and *Evolution of a Revolt* (1968), his postwar pieces proselytizing for Feisal's cause.

29. Lawrence named the books he sought to rival as Rabelais, *Don Quixote, Leaves of Grass, War and Peace, The Brothers Karamazov, Thus Spake Zarathustra*, and *Moby Dick*; "my ambition was to make an English fourth" to the last three (Garnett, 360)—actually an Engish first, as all the models were foreign.

30. Arnold Lawrence (*Friends*, 589).

31. In letters, December 1920 to August 1927, to (in order) Robert Graves, G. B. Shaw, Edward Garnett, Harley Granville-Barker, Eric Kennington, Granville-Barker, E. M. Dowson, Sydney Cockerell, Edward Garnett, Robin Buxton, and Charlotte Shaw.

32. Review of *Seven Pillars, Sunday Times*, July 28, 1935.

33. Upon reading some pages of *Seven Pillars*, Sidney Webb remarked. "This fellow describes every blade of grass and slab of rock and grain of sand he walked over" (G. B. Shaw, in Cockerell 1956, 124).

34. " . . . there is such a thing as a book being too well written, too much a part of literature. . . . It should somehow, one feels, have been a little more casual, for the nervous strain of its ideal of faultlessness is oppressive. . . . On the whole I prefer the earliest surviving version, the so-called Oxford text. . . . the greater looseness of the writing makes it easier to read" (Graves 1927, 407–8). E. M. Forster and Vyvyan Richards agreed.

Lawrence should have taken Bernard Shaw's advice: "You have something to say; and you say it as accurately and vividly as you can; and when you have done that you do not go on fooling with your statement with the notion that if you do it over again five or six times you will do it five or six times better" (January 4, 1923 letter in *Letters*, 168).

35. Letter to Richards which Malcolm Brown (224) dates "early 1923" and Jeremy Wilson (1126), September or October 1922.

36. Cf. Jeffrey Meyers (2) about Lawrence's "paradoxical combination of affectation and honesty, exhibitionism and reserve, arrogance and humility, megalomania and self-abasement."

37. G. B. Shaw (1985, 853) to Prime Minister Stanley Baldwin, November 12, 1923.

38. Lawrence's technical writing is discussed by Rodelle Weintraub in Tabachnick 1984, 137–56.

39. Letters of March 16 and 20, 1928 to Charlotte Shaw (*British*) and March 22 and April 23, 1928 to Edward Garnett (Garnett).

40. Letters of July 23, 1929 to Colonel A. P. Wavell (*Bodleian*) and August 7, 1930 to Frederic Manning (246).

41. February 2, 1922 letter to his mother (*Home*).

42. February 25, 1928 letter to Charlotte Shaw (*British*).

43. July 14, 1931 letter (*Harvard*).

44. Lawrence's note on the crash is in Garnett, 713 and Wilson, 877.

45. A January 24, 1933 letter to Graves (170) contains the praise; letters of September 6, 1932 to Henry Williamson (Brown) and March 6, 1932 to Clare Smyth (136), the dismissal. Cf. his remark to Bertram Thomas: "what writing ambitions and faculties I did possess have flickered out. Yet they told me yesterday, from London, that my last report on the 8/28 dinghy engine we are testing was altogether the goods. So I am consoled. The bow still has a string" (Brown, 459).

46. August 31, 1924 letter to Charlotte Shaw (*British*) and December 12, 1924 to Granville-Barker (Salmon).

47. April 23 and August 6, 1928 letters to Garnett and Forster, respectively (Garnett).

48. May 3 and May 27, 1930 letters to F. L. Lucas (Garnett) and Edward Garnett (*Harvard*), respectively.

49. September 6, 1932 letter to G. F. J. Cumberlege (Garnett) and September 25, 1933 to A. S. Frere-Reeves (Wilson, 912).

50. December 9, 1933 letter (Brown).

51. December 21, 1927 letter (*Kings*).

52. July 19, 1928 letter to G. Bernard Shaw (Garnett).

53. August 26, 1922 letter to Edward Garnett (Garnett).

54. September 22, 1927 letter to Lawrence (Wrench, 135).

55. April 1, 1935 letter to John Buchan (Garnett). Because he believes parts of *Seven Pillars* are untrue, only partly true, or falsified for political reasons, David Fromkin calls it a novel. For reasons he does not give, he also calls *The Mint* a novel. He could not be more foolishly wrong. On the grounds he presents, every work of history, travel, biography, or public affairs would be a work of fiction (see "The importance of T. E. Lawrence," *The New Criterion* 10, no. 1 [September 1991]: 86–98).

56. G. B. Shaw remarked, "I only like to do things that I find easy, like writing plays. William Morris was like that. He found he couldn't paint so he gave it up. He said, 'Never do a thing that you find difficult, because another person who finds it easy will beat you at the game'" (Winsten, 42).

57. That is, he was not the child of a prominent or literary family whose circle might include writers and artists, but the illegitimate child of parents who socialized little because they came from radically different (landowning and working) classes, and were not married because the father already had a wife he had abandoned, who would not divorce him.

58. A copy of this will is in the Bodleian; a later will, dated August 28, 1926, leaving his property to his younger brother Arnold, asks him to consult Hogarth "in all points affecting my published or unpublished writings" (*Imperial*). Hogarth died in November 1927.

59. "I haven't, of intention, said enough: because I feared that people might say that in praising him [Churchill, for his 1921 Mid-East settlement] I was praising myself," Lawrence explained to Edward Marsh—if that is an explanation. It is more like a confession that, due to a strange combination of excessive sensitivity and self-centeredness, he identified the political decisions of a prime minister and his cabinet with those of a responsible minister who accepted his advice (November 21, 1925 letter, Brown).

Recognizing that *Seven Pillars* "often tells less than the whole truth" and gives "a one-sided account," Wilson (630) attributes this to Lawrence's "concealing politically damaging matters" such as non-Arab contributions to the desert war and "the bitterness of his experience at the Peace Conference." To an extent, these explanations conflict since, after the Peace Conference, there was less reason to present a one-sided story. The personal function of the story was to cast Lawrence's subsequent conduct—entering the ranks, remaining there, refusing honors and money from the use of his name and his knowledge of the Mid-East—in noble terms, to present it as an act of principle, not of self-degradation. That function would be embarrassed by a fuller documentation of what Lawrence averred in the footnote and elsewhere at greater length: that in 1921, *before* he entered the ranks, Britain remedied whatever political duplicity she showed the Arabs during the war.

60. See his June 26, 1930 letter to Frederick Manning (245).

61. April 1, 1929 letter (*Princeton*).

62. "B.B. [Bernard Berenson] said he had asked Lawrence (T.E.) to lunch in Paris [in 1919] and he had accepted and written it down in his engagement book. He never turned up and when B.B. reproached him later, he said that he saw him write it down. Lawrence said, 'Well, look at my engagement book!' He had accepted fifteen invitations for that day" (1928 journal entry by Cyril Connally, 137–38, following a conversation with Berenson in Florence).

63. Wilson, 580; Hassall, 456.

64. Graves said he met Lawrence "in February or March 1920 . . . [at] a guest-night at All Souls" (*Friends*, 325); Jeremy Wilson (627) places the meeting in November 1919.

65. October 1, 1927 and February 4, 1935 letters to Robert Graves (138, 183).

66. May 30, 1931 letter to Charlotte Shaw (*British*).

67. July 22, 1922 letter (*Letters*, 123). "Kipling . . . cast me into outer silence after reading it," Lawrence told Doubleday (October 22, 1926 letter, *Princeton*).

68. This invaluable copy edited by Garnett and corrected by Lawrence, thus showing what each wanted to omit and print of the Oxford text, can be examined at Harvard's Houghton Library.

69. True, when Edward Garnett had typescript copies made to protect the manuscript against loss, Lawrence said, "This I regret. I'd prefer it to be only in the single copy. Safer so, against dissemination" (Garnett, 602). However, he could have told Garnett to lock the copies up and show them to no one.

70. August 21, 1911 letter from D. G. Hogarth (175) to Doughty.

71. The foregoing account crediting Lawrence with initiating the 1921 publication of *Arabia Deserta* follows that of Michael Howard (26–27), chairman of Cape and Wren Howard's son. Edward Garnett tells a different story. "He [Cape] looked for the best reader he could find, chose me, and followed me blind. He had about four hundred pounds in cash. I had always been a great admirer of Doughty. . . . I said, 'Cape, you must publish this book in full. You will lose money on it, but it will make your name.' . . . he did publish it. He spent all his capital on that first book. And it made his name" (Jefferson, 196). But Garnett did not start to work for Cape until

early 1921. On January 10, 1921, Cape informed him that *Arabia Deserta* would be the firm's first book (Howard, 30).

72. January 13, 1921 letter (*Bodleian*).

73. January 7, 1923 letter to Cape (Garnett).

74. November 14, 1923 letter to Cape (Garnett).

75. "I'm afraid I can't write an introduction to them: partly because I don't like introductions: more because I'm not going to put forth anything more under the name of Lawrence" (March 30, 1923 letter to Cape, *Bodleian* and *Texas*).

76. Idem.

77. June 12, July 8, and September 13, 1923 letters to Cape (*Bodleian* and *Texas*). *The Forest Giant*, "Translated . . . by J.H. Ross," was published March 1924.

78. January 30, 1924 letter to Cape (*Texas*; Wilson, 734).

79. "I have been rather hoping that while you burned your MS that you might have another and earlier draft and that on reconsideration you would find it not as bad as you thought" (Cape to Lawrence, February 26, 1924, *Reading*).

80. Note on top of the first page of Lawrence's February 21, 1924 letter to Cape—Howard's son Michael identified the writing (Howard, 88)—and February 26 reply by Cape (*Reading*).

81. Lawrence to Cape, June 27, 1924 (*Texas*).

82. February 24, 1927 letter to D.G. Hogarth (*Bodleian*).

83. Lawrence to Cape, February 1, 1927 (*Texas*).

84. May 20, 1927 (*Reading*), Cape asked Lawrence if there was any book he wanted to translate; Lawrence evidently suggested none. February 9, 1928 (by which time he had been asked to translate the *Odyssey* for Bruce Rogers, the prominent American typographer), he said, "No translations, please. . . . I wanted to; and I know now that I couldn't pass them . . . . no second class work, such as my writing, justifies itself at all" (*Bodleian*). Cape's renewed offer of a retainer can be inferred from Lawrence's March 21, 1928 letter: "If I accepted your very generous offer of a permanent living to do nothing at all, I'd feel uncomfortably prompted to do something on paper for you: and I hope never to write anything again" (*Reading*). April 21, 1927, Cape wrote, "I have still not entirely abandoned the hope that one day you will decide to edit a review or magazine. . . . We would very much like to publish a Monthly. . . . which would have quality . . . but would not lapse into dullness" (*Reading*). Lawrence dashed that idea: "Nor will I edit a review. My critical opinion does not seem to jump well with the majority's. Why not ask E. M. Forster to do it? He is at a loose end. It is time there was an English literary magazine broader than the ranks of a single coterie" (May 15, 1927, *Texas*). When Cape suggested Rousseau, Lawrence declined (October 23, 1928, *Texas*).

85. " . . . if Heinemann [which Doubleday then owned] ever contemplate a leisurely translation of a French book, by an anonymous translator, I'd be grateful for the chance of doing it," he wrote Doubleday June 16, 1927. Doubleday must have said "yes," because on August 25, Lawrence drew back. "Don't send me any translation job, yet a while, please. . . . I shall write as soon as I'm free . . . and suggest it again" (*Princeton*).

86. May 17, 1928 to Garnett (Garnett). Lawrence was repeating what he had just written Bernard Shaw. "Writing books seems inevitable, somehow; but publishing them is an indulgence" (May 7, 1928, Garnett). That is a fair summary of his attitude. He had an urge to write but not to publish except in small editions for friends; open publication meant publicity and he had been punished enough by publicity he could not control to augment it voluntarily.

87. Letters of January 2, 1928 to Ralph Isham (Rogers), January 23, 1930 to

E. M. Forster (*Kings*), and April 22, 1932 to William Rothenstein (p. 190). Published in 1932, the *Odyssey* was available in England only in Rogers's expensive limited edition; the cheap Oxford University Press edition sold well in the United States.

88. December 27, 1932 letter to Cape (*Texas*).

89. "Books in payment. I have earned them, I think. Please ignore the editor, wholly and completely and for ever" (March 12, 1933 to Cape, *Texas*).

90. Cape referred to Burton or "anything else" September 28, 1933 (*Bodleian*). On March 7, 1934, he described *Danakil* as an "extraordinary travel book" written in Italian and then turned into English. "The job of revision is going to be a difficult one" (*Bodleian*). Two days later he evidently sent the manuscript, but there is no indication Lawrence worked on it. May 3, 1934, Lawrence wrote Cape, "I will not write anything of my own while I am in the R.A.F. Or afterwards? That is too soon to say. . . . Thanks all the same for your suggestion" (*Texas*).

91. On May 5, 1932, Cape wrote, "There is a strong probability I think that it [Heidenstam's *The Charlesmen*] will fall . . . unless something is done to give it a send off. . . . Have you any suggestions?" On October 19, he asked if Lawrence would write "an encomium" for the jacket "in exchange for free copies (*Reading*). Lawrence sent the blurb October 21, adding, "Sorry: but I oughtn't to puff any more books. It is vanity. Let us forget books. They are only meant to read." August 1, 1933, he says, "You will not need my puff to sell Brazilian Adventure [by Peter Fleming]. It is not a rare flower, like Gösta or the Heidenstam. Just English. . . . All the same, it's an excellent book" (*Texas*).

92. The title, *'Colonel T. E. Lawrence' in Arabia and After*, perpetuated the apostrophes that supposedly advised perplexed readers that the former Colonel Lawrence was no longer either a Colonel or a Lawrence.

93. The £70 figure was given April 16, 1934 to Morley; the round of publishers, March 20, 1934 to K. W. Marshall (*Texas*).

94. April 16, 1934 letter (*Texas*).

95. October 1925 letter from Robert Graves to Siegfried Sassoon (O'Prey, 159).

96. Graves, 10, 4; Graves's *On English Poetry* (1922) was dedicated to Lawrence and W. H. R. Rivers, and *My Head! My Head!* (1925), to Lawrence.

97. Graves, 12. Wilson (1118) says Graves greatly undervalued the chapters; Lawrence's literary agent had expected them to bring £1000 in the United States.

98. February 20, 1922, Lawrence wrote Rees of the *Sunday Times*, "There's a young poet I know, called Robert Graves. . . . he's hard up. In similar case Robert Nichols was cured by being able to write regularly for the Observer. I know the Sunday Times uses Gorse: but the world is rather tired of too much Gorse, and so you may be. In that case would you consider Graves? He might be worth a trial either for casual or for regular stuff. . . . I only suggest it as an experiment, for poets aren't, like bricks, good or certain building material" (*Texas*).

99. September 16, 1926 letter (Graves, 38).

100. Cf. Graves's October 27, 1920 letter to Edmund Blunden: " . . . Lawrence's edition of Doughty's *Arabia Deserta* is shortly out at £9 9/- a copy of which will be yours (for keeps) (only four review copies issued) if you arrange with [Middleton] Murry to review it yourself. Otherwise the *Athenaeum* [which Murry edited] will not get a copy: this is unofficial but from Lawrence's own lips. It wants to be reviewed as *literature* not as *Near Eastern Politics*, etc.; that's why Lawrence has hit on you for the job" (O'Prey). Lawrence or, as was often the case, Graves got the facts wrong. In return for an undertaking to review *Arabia Deserta*, Cape offered a complimentary set to two dozen selected journals and newspapers (Howard, 28).

101. " . . . I suggested to Ll.G. [Prime Minister Lloyd George] that the pension be awarded . . . and he agreed to it. . . . Of the present ministry, three or four are

Fellows of All Souls, & most of the others friends of mine. The Duke of Devonshire, & Lord Salisbury, & Amery, & Wood & three or four others would be glad to serve you in any way you wished. Please don't delay to let me know if, or when, anything comes to your mind" (November 6, 1922 letter to Doughty, in Garnett).

The idea of buying Doughty manuscripts evidently occurred to Lawrence when Doughty's name did not appear on the Civil List as expected. The purchase plan was adopted—and Doughty appeared on the next list (Gregory, 214–15). A year later, he received a large inheritance and resigned the government pension.

102. "Deeply attached to his strange follower though he was, he could not approve *The Seven Pillars of Wisdom*, which was submitted to him in 1924 in its least expurgated form, and between the lines of his letter of acknowledgement, one may read distressful surprise. He thought . . . that, in Lawrence's own interests, a good many passages should be omitted" (Hogarth, 204). "I've always wondered what the old man did think of my stuff. . . ," Lawrence wrote Cockerell. "I've always fancied that its matter shocked him as much as its manner!" (May 27, 1927 letter, Cockerell).

103. June 4, 1925 letter to R. P. Dougherty (*Yale*).

104. March 20, 1929 letter to Corporal W. Crampton (*Texas*), and August 1, 1933 to Edward Garnett: "Dunn, his name is. I have asked him to type out some of his poems, and they will come to you for judgement" (Garnett).

105. " . . . I have not stirred up the Observer at all. That is best done just before the time. I saw Yeats-Brown of the Spectator, who will get in touch with Heinemann's. . . . Evans [of Heinemann's] is a friend of Hugh Walpole: so get him to press H.W. to make one of his routine letters to the U.S.A. concern G-B [Gaudier-Brzeka, the subject of Ede's *Savage Messiah*]. . . . Remains the Times. . . . Eddie Marsh still feels to me the likeliest approach. I don't want all the propaganda of the book to be tainted with a smell of me!" (January 1931 letter, in Ede).

106. "You must . . . put up a scheme. . . . Do look round while this [£5] is being spent and find some sure way of doing something" (March 30, 1932 letter to Pike, *Texas*).

107. January 31, 1935 letter to Henry Williamson (*Bodleian*).

108. C. Day Lewis, *The Buried Day* (New York: Harper & Brothers, 1960), 216, reprinted with permission of The Peters Fraser and Dunlop Group Ltd. The story, "England's Great Man!", of dubious accuracy, in the *Evening Standard*, August 15, 1934, read:

Recently Mr Winston Churchill and Colonel T. E. (Aircraftman Shaw) Lawrence met at a country house of a British Minister.

The two men had a discussion . . . on the dearth of great men in the post-war period.

Mr Churchill scouted the idea that there were any great men in England at the present moment.

Aircraftman (Colonel T. E. Lawrence) Shaw was more optimistic. He claimed that he had discovered one great man in these islands.

His name is Cecil Day-Lewis. . . .

Mr Lewis's claim to greatness is based on his poetry. He has four volumes of verse to his credit.

Here is a sample . . . (S. Day-Lewis, 79–80)

Chapter 1. Introductions

1. January 2, 1923 letter to G.B. Shaw (Brown).

2. Cf. *Seven Pillars*, 29: " . . . he may imitate them so well that they spuriously imitate him back again." Lawrence told G.B. Shaw, "I pieced together pages from my *Seven Pillars* [for the introduction], with some few lines written expressly" (Brown, 217).

3. In his introduction to *Arabia Felix*, Lawrence says the famous Arabian travellers "just wrote a wander-book and the great peninsula made their prose significant."

4. "Your suggestion that Doughty's style had Swedish roots is very surprising," Cockerell wrote. "Is it not . . . more likely to derive from the old English writers which were his sole pabulum, deliberately chosen, when he was writing Arabia Deserta?" (April 9, 1928, *Bodleian*).

5. This is G. B. Shaw's succinct paraphrase, not quotation, in a July 14, 1944 letter to Sydney Cockerell (1956, 123). Graves's original comment was: "Doughty's book is great because it is written by a simple stupid man, a fanatic: all the while he despises the Arabs. Your book is great because you are too clever and know it and despise cleverness and because you have no fanaticism and your hatreds are capricious; and because you are unhappy and know it: and because you funked telling the whole story—which keeps the story human." Lawrence clipped this paragraph from a letter Graves had sent him and enclosed it in an August 18, 1927 letter to Charlotte Shaw (*British*).

6. Cape, June 24, 1924 letter to Lawrence (*Reading*), and February 22, 1926 letter, Lawrence to Cape (*Texas*).

7. "I will agree to finish it & to write, (if particularly required) a few lines about D.G.H. at the beginning, or end of it if

1) It is work which can be done by me out here [Karachi], away from libraries or reference books,

2) If it can be done without materials: I cannot have the originals of letters etc. sent out.

3) If it can be done anonymously. I will not sign anything, whether a revise, or an explanatory note" (handwritten draft, December 1927?, *Harvard*). Similar terms are stated in Lawrence's December 22, 1927 letter to Cape (*Bodleian*).

8. William D. Hogarth, January 1, 1928 letter (*Bodleian*).

9. Laura V. Hogarth, March 14, 1928 letter (*Bodleian*).

10. Replying to Lawrence's August 27, 1927 letter, Hogarth said, "I agree only too thoroughly about D's incapacity for, & consequent indifference to, Design" (September 18, 1927, *British*, RP 2185).

11. Her March 14 letter ends, "Some day will you do David's life for us? There is *no* one else. I ask this very seriously."

12. February 25, 1928 letter to Mrs. Shaw (*British*).

13. H.M. Tomlinson's son, then working at Harpers in New York, "is *dotty* about Mansoul. . . . His firm is reluctant unless he can secure an introduction by one of the Great. . . . Would I write to you? I would." This March 15, 1930 letter from Tomlinson to Lawrence was followed by one on May 13. "No [T. E.] Shaw, then no Mansoul for poor America; which could do with one" (*Bodleian*).

14. May 27, 1930 letter to Edward Garnett (*Harvard*).

15. December 3, 1923 (*Texas*).

16. January 17, 1924 letter (*British*).

17. Alex Dixon, a tank corps colleague; he notes that, at this time, Lawrence's "prime favourite [among books "which could make him laugh"] was . . . *Twilight of the Gods*" (*Friends*, 373, 376).

18. May 3, 1924 letter to Jonathan Cape (*Texas*).

19. May 24, 1924 letter to Edward Garnett (*Bodleian*).

20. The Foreign Office was displeased that Thomas made the trip without official permission. "I knew the mind of authority and so avoided the pitfall of seeking permission. . . . ," he explained. "The British official attitude . . . [is] inimical to exploration. . . . So my plans were conceived in darkness, . . . paid for by myself and executed under my own auspices" (Thomas, xxv). Of course, what displeased officialdom pleased Lawrence.

21. August 14, 1931 letter to Bertram Thomas (*Bodleian*).
22. August 22, 1931 letter (*Bodleian*).
23. October 28, 1931 letter (*British*).
24. December 7, 1931 letter (*Texas*).
25. December 16, 1931 letter to Cape (*Texas*).
26. December 9, 1931 letter (*British*).
27. Knightley, 237; the description is of Lawrence at forty-one, in February 1929.

Chapter 2. Reviews

1. *The Egyptian Problem* by Valentine Chirol, which Lawrence reviewed in *The Observer*, September 19, 1920, cannot be considered literary. Nor can D. G. Hogarth's *Hittite Seals*, which, on October 29, 1920, J. Middleton Murry, editor of *The Athenaeum*, asked him to review. On November 3, Lawrence said "yes"; November 16, Murry suggested 650 words, "As you say you definitely prefer to be brief" (*Bodleian*). The review would have been easy, as Lawrence had acquired many of the seals for Hogarth's Ashmolean collection; however, I have found no sign that it was submitted or published. In January 1921, *The Athenaeum* merged to become *The Nation and Athenaeum*, perhaps rendering the journal less hospitable to a technical scholarly monograph.

2. *Men in Print, Essays in Literary Criticism* by T. E. Lawrence, Introduction by A. W. Lawrence (London: The Golden Cockerel Press, 1940); includes A Note on James Elroy Flecker; the reviews of D. H. Lawrence, H. G. Wells, and Walter Savage Landor; and the long letter on *Tarka the Otter*. A recent French edition reprints all the foregoing but the *Tarka* letter and adds the translator's note on the *Odyssey* and the *Arabia Deserta* introduction (*Men in Print*, with an essay on Lawrence by Jil Silberstein [Paris: La Table Ronde, 1988]).

3. May 5, 1927 letter to Wrench, 131.
4. July 8, 1927 letter to Yeats-Brown (Brown).
5. June 23, 1927 letter (Brown).
6. October 13, 1927 letter to Yeats-Brown and November 2 reply (Wrench, 136).
7. August 18, 1927 letter to Yeats-Brown (Wrench).
8. September 6, 1927 letter to Yeats-Brown (Wrench); December 24, 1927 letter to Robert Graves (144).
9. October 13, 1927 letter to Yeats-Brown (Wrench).
10. "I got the Everyman Karamazoff to review. . . . But I review very slowly, and it wasn't finished, when Hogarth's death put a colon in my current" (November 15, 1927 letter to Edward Garnett *Bodleian*). On November 9, Lawrence received a wire about Hogarth's death.
11. Lawrence, September 15, 1927 letter to Charlotte Shaw (*British*).
12. July 8 and 14 letters to Yeats-Brown (Wrench).
13. August 18 and September 9 letters to Yeats-Brown (Wrench).
14. "Some Spectators came to me lately from India—have you put me back by

some accident on the free List? I wrote long ago saying that I had stopped writing, and that it must cease. Will you please check the List and make sure that I am crossed off'' (February 8, 1930 letter to Celia Simpson, Assistant Literary Editor of *The Spectator*, **British**).

15. March 19, 1929 letter to Marsh (Garnett) and March 3, 1933, to James Hanley (**Harvard**).

Chapter 3. Bric-à-Brac

1. Lawrence's diplomatic communications were most undiplomatic. He called the difficult old King "complacently absurd" in an August 7, 1921 telegram to Foreign Secretary Lord Curzon (Wilson, 657).

2. "I modelled & carved with some hope and vigour, for nearly four years: and did slowly gain the power to express something of my meaning in clay or stone" (May 12, 1927 letter to Charlotte Shaw, **British**). In 1935, he thought of taking up sculpting again. On his drawings and sketches, see Sarah Maline, "The Arabian Sketches of T. E. Lawrence," in *Lawrence, Jarry, Zukofsky* (Austin: Harry Ransom Humanities Research Center, University of Texas, 1987), 16–39.

3. A curious example is related by the sculptor Charles Wheeler. "On whatever subject he [Lawrence] spoke, and they were many and various, he did so with seeming authority. . . . he climbed with me up the ladders at the Bank of England, where I had been working for months, to see, behind the tarpaulins, the large stone statues I had carved on the Threadneedle Street façade. They had been severely criticised by one of the directors and the opinion of Lawrence of Arabia was thought to be sufficiently authoritative . . . to quell opposition or uphold it. . . . Fortunately for me his verdict was favourable" (Charles Wheeler, *High Relief* [Feltham: Hamlyn, 1968], 106).

4. September 25, 1923 letter to Cape (Wilson, 725).

5. "By the end of January [1924] he had hardly started to revise *Seven Pillars*. Realising that he had over-committed himself, he abruptly dropped the time-consuming translation work" (Wilson, 734).

6. Undated letter (**Texas**), evidently before January 30, 1924 when Lawrence told Cape he had burned the translation.

7. *Men*, 10. Arnold Lawrence placed the writing in 1926 and Mrs. Flecker, "in [19]23 or 24 when 'Hassan' was being played in London" (January 29, 1938 letter to A. W. Lawrence, **Bodleian**). In an April 29, 1925 letter to Robert Graves, Lawrence says, "If ever you see Rickword, tell him please that for days I struggled to put on paper my recollections of Flecker in Syria: a theme which I thought fitting for the Calendar . . . . . but my rotten little engine conked out" (**Harvard** and Graves, 29–30, where the date is given as April 24). Edgell Rickword edited *The Calendar of Modern Letters*, a literary monthly published 1925–27.

8. "It was the union of F and his wife which wrought the miracle" (p. 104).

9. January 29, 1938 letter from Hellé Flecker to A. W. Lawrence (**Bodleian**).

10. March 8, 1927 letter to Lawrence (**Bodleian**).

11. Henry Williamson, *Devon Holiday* (London: Jonathan Cape, 1935), 101.

12. May 30, 1931 letter (**British**).

13. July 17, 1928 letter to Charlotte Shaw (**British**).

14. "Alas, I am not a scholar. If I read Greek, it is for pleasure. I fear my version will inevitably try harder to convey my pleasure than to be an exact mould of the Greek. Yet accuracy is a good thing, in its way. Will you try to find a hide-bound

scholar, and ask him to snout through the sample chapter for literal errors? I'd like to avoid howlers'' (October 10, 1928 letter to Emery Walker and Wilfred Merton, in Rogers).

15. Henry Hazlitt (Mack, 520).

16. Bernard Knox, Introduction, *The Odyssey of Homer*, trans. T. E. Lawrence (New York: Oxford University Press, 1991), ix–xxii.

17. May 18, 1934 letter to C. J. Greenwood (*Harvard*).

Introduction to Part II

1. Cited in Cyril Connolly, *The Evening Colonnade* (New York: Harcourt Brace Jovanovich, 1975), 127.

2. Jeremy Wilson announced but then postponed publication of Lawrence's letters to Charlotte Shaw, the largest known collection of his letters to one correspondent.

Chapter 4. On Writers

1. Remark in a conversation with Ralph Isham (*Friends*, 307).

2. Herbert Baker (*Friends*, 250).

3. Cf. David Garnett: "*The Mint* can be closely compared with *The House of the Dead*. Both men had an enormous capacity for suffering, both had the power of lifting the lid on horror and of describing incidents that are symbolic and stay in the mind for ever" (*Friends*, 432).

4. Alfred Adler, *The Practice and Theory of Individual Psychology* (Totowa, N.J.: Littlefield, Adams, 1973), 286.

5. Doughty, 1902 and 1913 letters to D. G. Hogarth (114–15).

6. Wilfrid Blunt, *Cockerell* (London: Hamish Hamilton, 1964), 102 and elsewhere; this account plays up Cockerell's role and he was not modest.

7. *Friends*, 281. Forster's February 1924 letter to Lawrence is reproduced in *Letters*, 58–62.

8. Forster, December 12, 1926 letter to Florence Barger (Lago, 75).

9. Forster, August 9, 1927 letter (Lago, 80).

10. Forster, November 17, 1927 letter (Lago, 81).

11. February 16, 1928 letter (*Kings*; Lago, 85).

12. December 21, 1927 letter (*Kings*).

13. The obituary appears in Graves, 181–83 and Wilson, 921–23.

14. "Two or three letters in 1930 are about my poems: but blankly appreciative rather than critical in the old way" (Graves, 165).

15. From the jacket of *Boy* (New York: Knopf, 1932).

16. March 3, 1933 letter to Hanley (*Bodleian*); also April 7, 1933 letter, "I've had several tries . . . to get people interested in your doing books [i.e., reviews] for them. . . . Not much chance, I fear" (*Harvard*).

17. On the Knopf jacket of *Boy*, which also printed an extract from the July 2, 1931 letter of "Colonel T. E. Lawrence" and sentences of praise from Richard Aldington.

18. According to Anthony Rota, Modern Trends in Book-Collecting, *The Private Library*, 2d ser. 5, no. 3 (Autumn 1972): 156.

19. Hanley "Lawrence of Arabia," *Men Only* 14, no. 53 (April 1940): 21-23.

20. Geoffrey Grigson in Drabble, 87 and Howe 1985, 157.

21. "She incredibly old, wasted, sallow. . . . the mummied thing, the bird-like head cocked on one side . . . by disease, the red-rimmed eyes, the enamelled face. . . . Her bony fingers, clashing in the tunnel of their rings, fiddled with albums" (*Mint*, 184–85). Shaw wrote, " . . . need you savagely exult in her infirmities. . . . Be human, you young ruffian; and either scrap that description or recast it nobly and generously" (*Letters*, 177).

22. Gillian Avery and Sheila Sullivan in Drabble, 52 and 37.

23. See Lawrence's letters on the death of Frederic Manning (p. 207) and to the ailing F. N. Doubleday (Brown, 444). However, Lawrence refused, or was unable, to express his feelings upon his brother Frank's death in 1915.

24. Winston Churchill, for whom Lawrence was then working, was another subscriber (Maddox, 189).

25. August 1, 1927 letter to Edward Garnett (Brown).

26. December 17, 1933 letter to G. Wren Howard (Garnett).

27. "The word 'great' was often on his lips . . . [as] a synonym for manly self-mystification" (Graves, 9).

28. Lady Constance Chatterley tells her father Sir Malcolm that her lover Mellors "'was [her husband] Clifford's gamekeeper: but he was an officer in the army in India. Only he is like Colonel C. E. Florence, who preferred to become a private soldier again.'

"Sir Malcolm, however, had no sympathy with the unsatisfactory mysticism of the famous C. E. Florence. He saw too much advertisement behind all the humility. It looked just the sort of conceit the knight most loathed, the conceit of self-abasement" (D. H. Lawrence, *Lady Chatterley's Lover* [New York: The Modern Library, Random House, 1959?], 319).

29. "Mr. Williamson wrote it originally as a protest against the obituaries of D. H. Lawrence, but did not publish it. He was moving from one home to another when he sent in his T. E. Lawrence letters to the editor, and by accident included with them his own piece on Lady Chatterley. When the papers were returned he did no more than slit open the envelope without looking through the contents, and did not notice his mistake until the Letters were in print. He gave the story to a newspaper with specimens of the two hand-writings. . . . I have had the original of this Lady Chatterley note in my possession and have studied it with specimens of Lawrence's hand-writing. The hand-writing is certainly Williamson's" (Aldington, 339). Williamson, a friend of Aldington as well as Lawrence, was plainly the source for this story.

30. Jeffrey Meyers, *The Enemy, A Biography of Wyndham Lewis* (Boston: Routledge & Kegan Paul, 1980), 151.

31. January 24, 1933 letter to Robert Graves (170); the two others were Ernest Altounyan and E. M. Forster.

32. Henry Newbolt, who read the manuscript for John Murray, the firm that published it (Marwil, 107).

33. They were evidently introduced by William Rothenstein, who had done a portrait of Manning in 1899 (Marwil, 54). Two 1922 letters from Manning to Lawrence appear in *Letters*.

34. Manning applied for a commission and, for a short time, was a 2nd. Lieutenant. But he was a drunkard, was almost court-martialled, and was finally permitted to resign. His commanding officer wrote, "Manning is a gentleman but apparently has no strength of will and is quite unsuitable as an officer" (Marwil, 181).

35. January 28 and April 15, 1914 letters of Will Lawrence (*Home*).

36. November 26, 1923 and November 13, 1930 letters (*Letters*, 154, 156).

37. "G.B.S. incorporated all the suggested changes and excisions, rewriting where necessary to make his point more clear or to fill in around the alteration" (Weintraub, 217–18).

38. Williamson, February 23, 1929 letter to Lawrence and February 28 reply (*Bodleian*).

39. He must mean Bennett's novels, because he repeatedly praises Bennett's criticism.

40. Gertrude Bell had died July 10, 1926!

41. Hogarth's translation of *The House of the Dead* was published by Dent in 1911.

42. *Charles M. Doughty: A Critical Study* (London: Jonathan Cape, 1927).

43. Hogarth replied to this part of Lawrence's letter as follows: "I agree only too thoroughly about D's incapacity for, & consequent indifference to, Design. I have already said that only the lack of need for a plan has saved A.D.! Anything more chaotic, fuller of irrelevance, & less adequate as a working out of its main theme than 'Mansoul' could hardly be conceived. Yet, at past 80, he proclaimed it his best work! The *Titans* & the *Clouds* are little better. The *Cliffs*, absurd though much of it is, was his last coherent effort. *Adam Cast Forth* is his best just because it is but a fragment. . . . The *whole* thing wld have failed worse than *Dawn in Britain*! So we may give thanks!" (September 18, 1927, *British*, RP 2185).

44. The biography of Doughty that Hogarth was writing.

45. The foregoing extract is omitted by Graves (147–48) in reproducing this letter.

46. Garnett (756) reads "mists."

47. Garnett (824) comments: "A curious example of forgetfulness. The revaluation of Donne's poetry, which Leslie Stephen thought could interest nobody, was the work of Rupert Brooke and Geoffrey Keynes, men of Lawrence's generation and period, and of Sir Herbert Grierson of the older one."

48. In March, Forster had visited Lawrence, then stationed at the Tank Corps Training Centre, Bovington, Dorset. He stayed at an inn but visited Clouds Hill the next day.

49. That is, his homosexual rape at Deraa.

50. For the paper on Forster Lawrence wrote and rewrote but probably destroyed.

51. A draft article on Forster that Virginia Woolf sent him, published in *Saturday Review of Literature*, December 17, 1927.

52. A long passage of detailed textual comment is here omitted.

53. In his review of three D. H. Lawrence novels he wrote that Forster "rolled thunderstorms in teacups" (p. 76).

54. Brown (368) observes, "The Greek god Pan being associated with sudden fear . . . , Lawrence is presumably referring to Forster's use of sudden dramatic twists of fortune."

55. Contrast this charitable judgment with his own rejection of precisely that course: "If I'd aimed low [in *Seven Pillars*] I could have hit my target as squarely as Max Beerbohm or Belloc hits it" (p. 138).

56. After his grandfather Richard Garnett and father Edward.

57. The character's name is Benedict.

58. Ede had submitted *Savage Messiah*, his account of the French sculptor Henri Gaudier-Brzeska, to the Nonesuch Press. Garnett rejected it, "because I thought it gave a false impression of a great artist whom I had known slightly, but whom neither Ede nor Shaw [Lawrence] had ever met" (Garnett 1980, 194).

59. Graves (13) notes, "Sir John Squire had suggested that I should try the drama instead" (of poetry).

60. Graves had sent him "The Clipped Stater," a poem about an imaginary Alexander-cum-Lawrence dedicated "To Thomas Edward Shaw." The omnipotent, ill Alexander declares, "I must fulfill my self by self-destruction." Thought dead of fever, he enlists in a distant Asian frontier guard, suffers whipping, famine, thirst, goes long without pay. At last he is given a coin "clipped of its hair and neck," which he recognizes as a Silver Alexander with his own head stamped upon it (Graves, *Poems [1914-26]*, [Garden City, N.Y.: Doubleday, Doran, 1929], 167-70).

61. Graves had sent Lawrence an album of the *Jupiter*, Mozart's last symphony (no. 41 in C, K. 551).

62. In July 1928, Jonathan Cape issued Radclyffe Hall's *The Well of Loneliness* "in sombre black binding" at the relatively high price of fifteen shillings; Havelock Ellis wrote a prefatory note. Cape sent a copy to the Home Secretary, Sir William Joynson-Hicks, who threatened proceedings if the book were not withdrawn; Cape and Hall agreed to sell no more copies and to destroy the remaining stock. In September, The Pegasus Press published the book in Paris from plates supplied by Cape. Imported copies were seized and a trial held in November at Bow Street Court; the magistrate ordered the book's destruction (Howard, 103-10).

63. Portions of this letter were used on the jacket of *Boy*, in a Boriswood prospectus for *Boy*, and as a preface to Hanley's *La Maison Sans Issues* (see p. 116).

64. Evidently a request to use portions of Lawrence's July 2 letter to Hanley to promote *Boy* (see preceding note).

65. *The Observer* was owned by Lady Astor's husband Viscount Astor.

66. The prosecution of Boriswood for publishing the "obscene" *Boy*.

67. Forster, who had been active in the (futile) defense of *The Well of Loneliness*, discussed the case of *Boy* in a June 21, 1935 address to the Congrès International des Ecrivains in Paris. "We have had, of course, ridiculous cases in the past. . . . But none of them have been so fantastic as *Boy*, which asserts the right of Authority to prosecute after any lapse of time and at the initiative of any policeman in any provincial town" (E. M. Forster, *Abinger Harvest* [New York: Harcourt Brace Jovanovich, 1964], 68).

68. Lawrence was stationed near Max Gate, Hardy's home. Graves responded to this request for an introduction by writing a letter with great praise of Lawrence. "He is as unquestionably the greatest of our generation as Mr Hardy is of his. . . . Don't be surprised in whatever guise he appears, as a boy selling papers or as a decrepit cabman or a gypsy girl: he is like that—" (25 March 1923 letter, *Texas*).

69. Replying to Lawrence on March 15, Mrs. Hardy wrote, "You say the news struck you as a triumph. When I saw him after he had been laid out I was spell bound. On his face was a radiant look of *triumph*" (Brown, 365).

70. Cockerell and Mrs. Hardy were Hardy's literary executors.

71. Charlotte Shaw sent Lawrence an account of the service, which she and Bernard Shaw attended.

72. Hardy left an (auto)biography for Mrs. Hardy to publish under her name.

73. A satire on a writer who becomes the grand old man of letters by outliving his rivals.

74. An "emasculated version" (Howe 1985, 15) of a lost early novel; Mrs. Hardy angered Sydney Cockerell by issuing it without consulting him.

75. Cf. David Garnett (1980, 195): "I asked him [Lawrence] whether he had read Samuel Butler's *The Authoress of the Odyssey* [1879], but he had not. I have always found his evidence very convincing, and we discussed the Author's curious ignorance of masculine affairs, handling boats, etc."

76. Charlotte Shaw was reading Lawrence's translation—he sent her a book or more at a time—for clarity and errors; in this manner, she read and proofed almost everything he wrote, large or small, from the Oxford Text on.

77. The Greek scholar whom Rogers had asked to read Lawrence's translation for accuracy (see p. 95).

78. This extract is quoted by Fontana in her January 9, 1921 letter to Lawrence (*Bodleian*).

79. Graves had offered to send *Transition* because Joyce's *Work in Progress (Finnegans Wake)* was appearing in it. From the preceding letter to Charlotte Shaw, it is clear that Lawrence had already seen one or more copies. Despite his dismissive comments to her and Graves, Lawrence caught up with Joyce in *Transition* upon returning to England (see his April 1, 1929 letter to Hurley).

80. Cf. Brenda Maddox (360), ". . . Joyce's myriad references to rare and specialized works give a misleading impression of the depth and range of his reading. In his later life, with his dimmed sight, he certainly was not a great reader."

81. Lawrence himself in his review of Lawrence's novels: "Pages and pages are wasted in the effort to make the solar plexus talk English prose" (p. 76).

82. Home Secretary Sir William Joynson-Hicks, who "made many ill-judged efforts to suppress works of art, including books and pictures by D. H. Lawrence" (Garnett, 643).

83. "Sir Edward Marsh informs me that, having heard a rumour that Lawrence had read D. H. Lawrence's *Lady Chatterley's Lover* three times in borrowed copies, he sent him his own copy as a present as 'his need was greater'" (Garnett, 652).

84. This letter, printed in Garnett (687), appears to have been written by Henry Williamson, *not* Lawrence (see p. 131 and the accompanying note).

85. Lewis's "Mr. Zagreus and the Split-Man," in *The Criterion*, February 1924.

86. Lynne Farrington of the Department of Rare Books, Olin Library, Cornell, kindly deciphered these five lines, which were not clear in a photocopy.

87. For a drawing Lawrence had commissioned for *Seven Pillars*; Lewis neither did the drawing nor returned the money.

88. The correct title is *The Lion and the Fox*; Lawrence may have conflated it with David Garnett's *Lady into Fox*.

89. D. B. Wyndham Lewis, 1894–1969, writer and biographer, was not related to Percy Wyndham Lewis, 1882–1957, the novelist, critic, and artist.

90. In September, Graves and Lawrence had met in London after a gap of years. They spoke of Wyndham Lewis, whom Laura Riding had seen the previous day. Lewis "had asked her, if she saw Lawrence, to say that the matter [of the commissioned portrait] had slipped his memory; he would write to Lawrence immediately if she gave him his address, which she did" (Graves, 166). In a September 6, 1932 note to Lewis (*Cornell*), Lawrence said he would sit for a drawing, which Lewis evidently never did, or never gave him. A. J. Plotke says "there does exist a pencil-sketch of Lawrence purportedly drawn by Wyndham Lewis sometime in the late 1920s" ("Eric Kennington and *Seven Pillars of Wisdom*: A Reassessment," *Biography* 7, 2 [Spring 1984]: 178).

91. Probably, Jonathan Marwil (78–80) suggests, "The Organ Monkey," *The Outlook*, July 16, 1904; but how did Lawrence know the author of this unsigned piece?

92. Peter Davies's version of this conversation went as follows:

"My telephone bell rang, and an unknown voice addressed me out of infinity.

UNKNOWN VOICE: . . . I want to congratulate you as strongly as possible on 'Her Privates We.' It's magnificent, a book in a thousand. You've published a masterpiece. But tell me this: How did you get . . . . . to write it?

SELF: Thank you very much, and I'm delighted to hear you like it, but—

U.V.: Like it! It's not a question of like! The book's a classic! And it *is* by . . . . . , isn't it?

SELF: The author of 'Her Privates We' prefers to be known only as Private 19022. I've said so on the jacket of the book. So how can I answer your question? Besides, I don't even know who I'm speaking to.

U.V.: Oh, Shaw's my name, you probably won't know who I am, but I once wrote a book myself, called 'Revolt in the Desert.'

SELF: (*An ejaculation, indicative of impressed astonishment.*).

VOICE: But about Private 19022. You see, I've read '[Scenes and Portraits]' at least fifty times; that's a masterpiece, too, and the man who wrote it is the only man who could possibly have written 'Her Privates We.' I'm right, of course?

SELF: (*After a pregnant pause.*) You know, I'm not supposed. . . . When he went abroad, I promised him. . . . He can't have foreseen this, though . . . Oh well, here goes: You, Sir, and your method of attack combined, are too much for me, and must surely justify my surrender in the eyes of Private 19022. Yes, of course you're right. Only do please keep the secret, or I'm lost.

VOICE: I won't tell a soul [he promptly told Charlotte Shaw], though it's bound to come out before long. Meanwhile, will you let him know how enormously I admire and love his book? If people don't run to it in thousands, it'll be because they don't care to see themselves in a glass, magnificently. . . . I can't say half of what I feel about it on the telephone. Look here, I'll write to you now, and you can pass on my letter, or the substance or it, to him. (Peter Davies, *Colonel Lawrence and Others on "Her Privates We" by Private 19022* [London: Peter Davies 1930], 2–3).

93. This letter, reproduced in Davies (where the bracketed passage is paraphrased), was promised by Lawrence at the end of their telephone conversation (see preceding note).

94. The hero of *Her Privates We*; also the Lincolnshire town where Manning lived.

95. Presumably, when Lawrence met him in the early 1920s.

96. On February 11, 1930, Manning wrote Lawrence, "Was it some uncanny *flair* that led you to me; or did Will Rothenstein tell you that he has some letters from me with my regimental number on them, 19022?" (*Letters*, 128).

97. Though the Prefatory Note, little more than one hundred words, betrayed Manning to no one else, Lawrence must have seen his hand—in the substance as well as style—in passages such as: ". . . in recording the conversations of the men I seemed at times to hear the voices of ghosts. Their judgments were necessarily partial and prejudiced; but prejudices and partialities provide most of the driving power of life. . . . I have drawn no portraits. . . .

"War is waged by men; not by beasts, or by gods. It is a peculiarly human activity. To call it a crime against mankind is to miss at least half its significance; it is also the punishment of a crime. That raises a moral question, the kind of problem with which the present age is disinclined to deal" (*Her Privates We* [London: Peter Davies, 1930]).

Marwil (257) says, ". . . only someone who had reread the earlier book often (and recently) would have seen that the preface to the war book was 'pure *Scenes and Portraits*' . . . . if the two books are read successively, their expertly crafted dialogues, their ironies, their abiding compassion for man's effort to penetrate or simply to make peace with the mysteries of existence—all these suggest their common authorship."

98. The unexpurgated version of *Her Privates We*, published by Peter Davies at three guineas.

99. By issuing the booklet with an account of his conversation with Lawrence on the identity of the anonymous author of *Her Privates We*.

100. Manning wrote an Introductory Essay to *Epicurus, His Morals* (London: Peter Davies, 1926).

101. "Apologia Dei," dedicated "To T. E. Shaw," a new final chapter added to the edition of *Scenes and Portraits* issued by Peter Davies in November 1930.

102. A novel on which Manning had been working, on and off, since 1909; a one-hundred-page fragment survives (Marwil, 122–23). Writing Lawrence April 10, 1935, Peter Davies said he had told Manning's mother and sister nothing could be done with it and with an incomplete scene from a play unless Lawrence, and no one else, wrote an accompanying memoir on Manning (*Bodleian*). No answer is on record, but Lawrence is unlikely to have consented.

103. Lawrence underlined and starred the two passages referring to Manning's two main books.

104. "Lawrence declined . . . to make a public statement about the man he admired, silence which annoyed Rothenstein and hurt Manning's mother. Had they seen this letter to Davies they might have been less upset—and possibly fathomed the reasons for his silence" (Marwil, 301).

105. Chambers said, "I had read *White Jacket* and I'm positive that Lawrence [in *The Mint*] was actuated by Melville's writing" (*Lawrence of Clouds Hill*, BBC broadcast, December 3, 1958, transcript, 8, *Texas*).

106. At the initiative of Lawrence's brother William, then Vice-President of St. John's College Essay Society, Pound spoke to the society on Guido Cavalcanti in February 1913. "Will Lawrence visited Pound in London on 2 June [1913], and was introduced to [Rabindranath] Tagore" (Noel Stock, *The Life of Ezra Pound* [San Francisco: North Point Press, 1982], 132).

107. The subsequent sentences were deleted by Garnett (556), who may have considered them in poor taste.

108. Read had sent Lawrence a copy of Remarque's war novel; why he did so is not clear. In 1927, he had published a long review of *Seven Pillars* arguing that Lawrence had tried but failed to write an epic. Lawrence wrote Edward Garnett (who had sent him the review) a long rebuttal (December 1, 1927 letter in Garnett); Read had obviously stung him.

109. However, compare this view with the bitter sentences in the Introductory Chapter of *Seven Pillars* (deleted from the 1926 edition):

We lived many lives in those whirling campaigns, never sparing ourselves: yet when we achieved and the new world dawned, the old men came out again and took our victory to re-make in the likeness of the former world they knew. Youth could win, but had not learned to keep: and was pitiably weak against age. We stammered that we had worked for a new heaven and a new earth, and they thanked us kindly and made their peace.

110. An error: the protagonist of the novel is Paul Bäumer.

111. In conversation with Lawrence, Williamson (32–33) remarked, "When you said in your letter that Remarque's 'All Quiet' was the 'screaming of a feeble man', I immediately thought 'That's Williamson, too' [in *Patriot's Progress*]. I liked the book very much until half-way, when it seemed to me that the author had never been in a battle. The battle scenes seem to be descriptions from seeing war-film; also they have the tension of imagined dread, of non-experience."

Lawrence replied, "It's post-war nostalgia shoved into the war period. . . . He was too young to know how to write objectively."

112. Schwartz had sent Lawrence a signed, limited edition of Richardson's *Two Studies* (London: Ulysses Press, 1931).

113. *The Fortunes of Richard Mahony* (1917–29).

114. *Ultima Thula* (1929) is the third of the *Richard Mahony* trilogy.

115. A misprint for Minster (Lawrence's letter was typed).

116. According to David Garnett, this letter was sent to Laura Riding in response to a request for something on Rimbaud she could quote in the Seizin Press critical series (handwritten note on a typed copy of the letter in the *Bodleian*). The letter appeared in *Epilogue*, 1935, 1, and *The Private Library*, 2d ser. 6, 3 (Autumn 1973): 141. In the latter, Laura (Riding) Jackson enumerates many parallels between Rimbaud and Lawrence.

117. Marsh had asked Lawrence to present Sassoon the Hawthornden Prize he had been awarded for *Memoirs of a Fox-Hunting Man*.

118. At Sassoon's Hawthornden Prize ceremony in London, which Williamson was to attend.

119. Sassoon's home, or mansion, which Lawrence had visited.

120. At this time, Lawrence was quartered at the Ozone Hotel, near his last RAF station at Bridlington on the Yorkshire coast.

121. The day of his marriage the previous December.

122. The second volume of the seven-volume limited edition of Shakespeare published by the Nonesuch Press, 1929–33; David Garnett, then associated with the press, gave Lawrence a set in red leather.

123. In August 1922, Lawrence asked Shaw to read the two-columed Oxford Text of *Seven Pillars*; Charlotte Shaw read it at once but Shaw delayed until December.

124. Lawrence drove two-hundred miles from Bovington to London to see two parts of *Back to Methuselah*; the full play took five successive evenings (Weintraub, 84).

125. Lawrence's account of having to shoot the mortally wounded Farraj as the Turks approach ends with the statement that Farraj "wearily closed his eyes," before the shot is fired. However, to call his version of Deraa "plain narrative" is astonishingly deceptive. He rewrote it endlessly; scholars still reinterpret every word and debate what really happened.

126. Bernard Shaw visited Russia in the summer of 1931 with Lord and Lady Astor but without his wife Charlotte.

127. Cedric Hardwicke played Aubrey in *Too True to Be Good*. "Although it was always an open secret that Private Meek . . . was a portrait of Private Shaw, it has not been realised that Aubrey Bagot, ex–R.A.F. combat officer, represents another side of the same complex man—the 'Colonel Lawrence of Arabia' side" (Weintraub, 216).

128. Fully two years ago!

129. Dame Edith (1887–1964) and her brothers Sir Francis Osbert (1892–1969) and Sir Sacheverell (1897–1988).

130. In his January 20, 1928 letter to Edward Garnett (p. 105).

131. *The Pathway* (1928) is the last of four-novel sequence titled *The Flax of Dreams*; the other three are *The Beautiful Years* (1921), *Dandelion Days* (1922), and *The Dream of Fair Women* (1924).

132. John Brophy, to whom Lawrence also wrote the same day. Brophy gives his recollections of Lawrence in *Friends*, 437–43.

133. Brophy had evidently asked Lawrence about *The Gold Falcon*, for on February 7 Lawrence wrote, "Your 'Gold Falcon' I have not seen or heard of. I know Faber (Geoffrey) and have helped him with opinions, occasionally: but he did not offer me that. Let me see it, will you?" (*Texas*). Brophy, who so disliked *The Gold Falcon* and its depiction of Lawrence, had himself depicted Lawrence in his novel *Flesh and Blood* (1931).

Chapter 5. Literary Themes

1. The reviews are reprinted in Peter Faulkner, ed., *William Morris, The Critical Heritage* (London: Routledge & Kegan Paul, 1973), 409–17.

2. "The prose tales . . . were written very swiftly, poured out, as it were, from a brain overloaded and saturated with its pent-up stores of imagination. . . . Their author in later years thought, or seemed to think, lightly of them" (J. M. Mackail, *The Life of William Morris* [London: Oxford University Press, 1950; first published 1899], 1: 99, 102).

3. March 26, 1922 letter cited in Ronald D. Knight, *Colonel T. E. Lawrence Visits Mr and Mrs Thomas Hardy* (Weymouth, Dorset: R. D. Knight, 1985), 7.

4. May 3, 1935 letter from Lawrence to Charlotte Shaw (*British*).

5. Cf. E. M. Forster (59), "*Women have got out of hand*: is the burden of his [D. H. Lawrence's] Assorted Articles and I think they have."

6. Lawrence's *Odyssey* translation was among some two-hundred titles chosen by a committee to initiate the Walter Williams Library at the University of Missouri. The library was established by the Alumni Association of the School of Journalism to honor Williams, President of the University and, for twenty-six years, Dean of the School, the first university journalism school, which he had founded. ". . . the books were chosen from lists of the best books published [in 1932 and 1933] . . . including the American Library Association's Book List, and a list of '100 Best Books' selected by William Lyons Phelps, professor of English Literature at Yale" ("Walter Williams Library to be Presented" [press release], University of Missouri, Columbia, May 9, 1934 [Joint Collection University of Missouri Western Historical Manuscript Collection—Columbia and State Historical Society of Missouri Manuscripts]).

7. Cf. Goethe: "The monuments of antiquity . . . he almost always sees as ruins, as incomplete, and in this lies their attraction. His remark about his *Iphigenie*, 'incompletes stimulates', is valid in this context too. To reconstruct a picture from fragments, the image of a whole people from an empty amphitheatre, to read into the mutilated relief figures of a sarcophagus the forms of Greek gods and heroes: this is his way of seeing" (Richard Friedenthal, *Goethe: His Life and Times* [Cleveland: World Publishers, 1965], 240).

8. "But how I wish I believed in Garnett's critical instinct," she wrote Lawrence on 9 April 1928. "I don't, you know, one little bit. Each discovery I make about his views and his general philosophy of life incline me to trust him less and less. I think him conventional & *not* courageous" (**British**).

9. Graves said Bennett was "not a fraud but a financier. . . . Bennett will praise a book to oblige a friend . . . ; he will also praise books published by firms in which he has a financial interest" (letter to Lawrence, n.d. [1927?], *Bodleian*). Lewis called Bennett's criticism "a travesty of continental criticism. . . . he betrayed every standard [of the great Russian novelists] . . . in order to boost what was often the completest literary refuse" (W. K. Rose, ed., *The Letters of Wyndham Lewis* [London: Methuen, 1963], 208). Reviewing a book of Bennett's criticism, Murry saw "no evidence that Mr. Bennett ever had a subtle thought or saw things with other eyes than the auctioneer's" (*Athenaeum*, January 28, 1921, 96).

10. "To S. A.," original version (Knightley, 158); "Diversions" (Graves, 29); "Confession of Faith" (Garnett 1951, 291).

11. C. Day Lewis notes but does not resolve another Lawrencian contradiction. "He cannot surely have considered Wordsworth, Coleridge, Shelley and Keats as 'small

men'; but equally it is impossible to imagine him rating the 'Intimations' ode, 'Kubla Khan', 'Prometheus Unbound' or the 'Ode to a Nightingale' as *small* poems of big men'" (*Minorities*, 13).

12. E. H. R. Altounyan, *Ornament of Honour* (dedicated to T. E. Lawrence) (Cambridge: At the University Press, 1937). " . . . now that T.E. is gone I shall never be understood by a living soul," his daughter reports him saying (Taqui Altounyan, *Chimes from a Wooden Bell* [London: I.B. Tauris, 1990], 122).

13. Probably Les Trophées (1893) by José Maria de Heredia (1842–1905).

14. "Dr. Adams was an advocate of simplified spelling" (Garnett, 154).

15. The young son of Mrs. Rieder, a French teacher at the American mission school in Jebail, who had returned to England in the spring of 1912 after her husband died.

16. His brother Will.

17. *The Song of Renny* (1911) by Maurice Hewlett.

18. The underlined passage is taken from a letter of Richards on the *Seven Pillars*.

19. The first three titles are by Stephen Reynolds; *Jenny* is a slip for *Maggie* by Stephen Crane.

20. *On the Forgotten Road* (1909), mentioned—also without the title—in his September 12, 1912 letter home (p. 255).

21. These two books are by Elizabeth M. Roberts.

22. The brackets are on the photocopy of the original.

23. The poet and short-story writer (1868–1928) Hardy called "the best living woman poet."

24. Probably *A Final Burning of Boats* (1928).

25. The author of a book on Whitman that Doubleday gave Lawrence.

26. *Salammbô* (1862) by Gustave Flaubert, *Moralités légendaires* (1887) by Jules Laforgue, *Eothen* (1844) by Alexander Kinglake, and *Idle Days in Patagonia* (1893) by W. H. Hudson.

27. G. M. Trevelyan wrote three books on Garibaldi (1907, 1909, 1911) and *Scenes from Italy's War* (1919).

28. Aubrey Herbert, whom Lawrence liked enormously, was a Member of Parliament, son of Lord Carnarvon, polyglot wanderer in the Balkans and Near East, friend of nationalists, and sometime member of the Arab Bureau; he was also virtually blind. In February 1923, he sent Lawrence extracts from a travel book he was writing (*Ben Kendim*, 1924), compiled from diaries (Fitzherbert, 243).

29. Presumably, translating *Le Gigantesque* (*The Forest Giant* by Adrien le Corbeau).

30. A quote from Herbert Read's review of *Seven Pillars* in *The Bibliophile's Almanack for 1928*.

31. Marsh had just put on a show of paintings, presumably his own.

32. Ira Jones, an RAF Squadron Leader writing a biography, sought Lawrence's advice on writing. He picked up a menu card and wrote this passage (*Friends*, 348).

33. By Miss Black, then 81; she gave him a copy when he visited her August 17; "he took it very graciously and said, 'I shall tell you what I think of it quite sincerely'" (*Friends*, 535).

34. Ede's *Savage Messiah* (1931) is the story of the desperately poor young French sculptor Henri Gaudier-Brzeska and his platonic love, the Polish woman Sophie S. Brzeska, twenty years older, whose name he took.

35. The article on Forster that Lawrence drafted but never published.

36. Forster's lectures at Cambridge, published as *Aspects of the Novel* (1927).

37. Arnold Bennett wrote *Anna of the Five Towns* (1902), *Tales of the Five Towns* (1905), *The Grim Smile of the Five Towns* (1907), and *The Matador of the Five Towns* (1912).

38. With Lawrence's help, Dunn's *Poems—Group one* was published by Cape in 1934; he inscribed a copy "For T. E. Shaw. . . . For the only encouragement I ever received."

39. Published as *Minorities* (London: Jonathan Cape, 1971).

40. The choice was of who should next read a copy of the *Seven Pillars* 1922 text.

41. Osbert Burdett, *Critical Essays* (1925).

42. See chap. 4, n. 59 above.

43. Passages of Hewlett's translation of the *Iliad*.

44. *Artemision: Idylls and Songs* (1909).

45. "In Memoriam A. H.," a poem for Auberon Herbert, Capt. Lord Lucas, Royal Flying Corps, Aubrey Herbert's cousin, who was killed November 3, 1916.

46. Professor R. De la Bere edited (occasionally with help from Lawrence) the *Journal of the Royal Air Force College*, Cranwell.

47. Curtis edited *The Round Table*, a journal on Commonwealth affairs.

48. Contrast his remark to his biographer, the military historian Liddell Hart: "It's not how you say it, but what you say" (p. 272).

49. G. B. Shaw's *Too True to Be Good*.

50. Probably John Betjeman's *Ghastly Good Taste; or, A Depressing Story of the Rise and Fall of English Architecture* (1933).

51. A. R. Orage, who had edited *The New Age*, 1907–22, and *New English Weekly*, 1931–34, had just died.

Dramatis Personae of Authors and Correspondents

Acres, J. B.—member, Oxford University Air Squadron; RAF private, Cranwell.

Adams, Dr. W. B.—doctor, Beirut.

Altounyan, Ernest R., 1889–1962—surgeon, poet; *Ornament of Honour* (1937), poems about Lawrence dedicated to him.

Astor, Viscountess Nancy, 1879–1964—American, born Nancy Langhorne, married Viscount Waldorf Astor; M.P. for Plymouth 1919–45.

Baring, Maurice, 1874–1945—novelist, poet, playwright, translator; diplomatic service 1898–1904; journalist in Turkey, Russia, Balkans 1904–12; secretary to General Trenchard, Royal Flying Corps 1915–18; *The Puppet Show of Memory* (1922), *Daphne Adeane* (1926), *Selected Poems* (1930).

Barrie, Sir James M., 1860–1937—Scottish playwright, novelist; O.M. 1922; *The Admirable Crichton* (1902), *Peter Pan* (1911).

Bell, Gertrude M. L., 1860–1926—mountaineer, traveller, archeologist, government servant, writer; in Arab Bureau, Cairo 1916; Oriental Secretary, High Commissioner, Iraq; *The Desert and the Sown* (1907), *Letters* (1927).

Bell, Sir Thomas Hugh, 1865–1952—father of Gertrude; ironmaster; manager, Clydeside, during installation of turbine machinery in *Aquitania*, *Queen Mary*, warship *Hood*.

Belloc, Hilaire, 1870–1953—journalist, novelist, poet, critic, historian, biographer; Liberal M.P. 1906–12; *Cautionary Tales* (1907), *The Servile State* (1912), *Cromwell* (1927).

Black, Miss L. M. P., 1850–1936—wrote Lawrence in 1928, after reading *Seven Pillars*; he visited her several times in Devon.

Brophy, John, 1899–1965—novelist, reviewer; advertising copywriter; fiction critic, *Daily Telegraph*, BBC; *The Soldiers War* (1929), *Flesh and Blood* (1931), *The World Went Mad* (1934).

Brown, Curtis, b. 1866—operated literary agency representing Lawrence.

Buxton, Robert V., 1883–1953—in Imperial Camel Corps, Arabia; later, Lawrence's bank manager.

Cape, H. Jonathan, 1879–1960—errand boy, Hatchard's, at 16; travelling salesman, manager, Gerald Duckworth 1904–19; manager, Medici Society 1920; founded firm of Jonathan Cape 1921.

Chambers, A. E., 1896–1987—orderly RAF, Farnborough 1922; postal sorter.

Cockerell, Sir Sydney C., 1867–1962—secretary to William Morris and Kelmscott Press 1892–98; partner Doves Press 1900–1904; literary executor, Morris and Thomas Hardy; director Fitzwilliam Museum, Cambridge 1908–37.

Conrad, Joseph, 1857–1924—novelist, writer; Polish seaman, ship's master 1874–94; British citizen 1886; *Lord Jim* (1900), *The Secret Agent* (1907), *Under Western Eyes* (1911).

Coward, Noël, 1899–1973—actor, playwright, composer, entertainer; *The Vortex* (1924), *Private Lives* (1933), *Design for Living* (1933), *Brief Encounter* (1944).

Cummings, Edward E., 1894–1962—American poet, writer; *The Enormous Room* (1922), *Eimi* (1933), *Collected Poems* (1938).

Curtis, Lionel G., 1872–1955—barrister, writer, public servant; in South Africa 1899–1909, headed "Milner's kindergarten"; Fellow, All Souls, Oxford 1921; founder, editor *The Round Table*, quarterly on Commonwealth politics; Colonial Office 1921–24; founder Institute of International Affairs.

Custot, Pierre, 1880–1919.

Davies, Peter L., 1897–1960—virtually the adopted son of James Barrie; with his brothers, the model for Peter Pan; established Peter Davies, publisher 1926.

Day Lewis, Cecil, 1904–72—poet, detective story writer, translator; Professor of Poetry, Oxford 1951–56; Poet Laureate 1967–72; *The Magnetic Mountain* (1933), (as "Nicholas Blake") *Thou Shell of Death* (1936) with character based on Lawrence.

Dixon, Alex L., b. 1900—corporal, Tank Corps, Bovington 1923.

Dostoevsky, Fyodor, 1821–81—Russian novelist; *The House of the Dead* (1862), *Crime and Punishment* (1866), *The Brothers Karamazov* (1880).

Doubleday, Frank N., 1862–1934—American publisher; with Charles Scribner's Sons 1877–95; president Doubleday, Page 1900–1927; board chairman Doubleday, Doran 1928–34.

Doughty, Charles M., 1843–1926—traveller, poet, writer; *Travels in Arabia Deserta* (1888), *The Dawn in Britain* (1907), *Adam Cast Forth* (1908).

Dunn, George W. M., b. 1908—RAF Aircraftman, Plymouth; poet; *Poems—Group One* (1934).

Ede, Harold S., b. 1895—assistant Tate Gallery; *Savage Messiah* (1931).

Eliot, Thomas S., 1888–1965—American poet, playwright; to Britain 1915, British citizen 1927; editor *The Criterion*, quarterly, 1922–39; director Faber & Faber 1925; Nobel Prize, O.M., 1948; *The Waste Land* (1922), *The Sacred Wood* (1920).

Fairless, Michael, 1869–1901, pseudonym of Margaret Fairless Barber; *The Roadmender* (1902, reprinted 1921).

Flecker, H. James Elroy, 1885–1915—poet, playwright; British Vice-Consul, Beirut 1911–13; *The Golden Journey to Samarkand* (1913), *Collected Poems* (1916), *Hassan* (1922).

Fontana, Ralph A.,—British Consul, Aleppo 1911.

Fontana, Mrs. Winifred, b. 1880—wife of British Consul; to Britain, 1914.

Forster, Edward Morgan, 1879–1970—novelist, writer; Honorary Fellow, Kings College, Cambridge, 1945–70; O.M. 1969; *Howards End* (1910), *A Passage to India* (1924), *Aspects of the Novel* (1927), *Maurice* (1971).

Frere-Reeves, Alexander S., 1892–1984—William Heinemann, publisher's, director, managing director, chairman 1923–1960s.

Garnett, David, 1892–1981—novelist, writer; adviser, Nonesuch Press 1923–32; literary editor *New Statesman* 1932–34; *Lady into Fox* (1922), *The Grasshoppers*

Come (1931), *A Rabbit in the Air* (1932); edited *The Letters of T. E. Lawrence* (1938), *The Essential T. E. Lawrence* (1951).

Garnett, Edward, 1868–1937—critic, editor; father of David and son of Richard; abridged Doughty's *Arabia Deserta* issued as *Wanderings in Arabia* (1908); reader for Duckworth 190?–20, for Jonathan Cape 1921–37; *Friday Nights* (1922).

Garnett, Richard, 1835–1906—poet, bibliographer, biographer, translator, writer; worked for British Museum Library 1851–99; *Shelley* (1860), *The Twilight of the Gods* (1888), *The Age of Dryden* (1898).

Gerhardi, William, 1895–1977—novelist born of English parents in Saint Petersburg; *Futility* (1922), *The Polyglots* (1925).

Granville-Barker, Harley, 1877–1946—actor, playwright, author; manager, Court Theater 1904–7; influential director of Shakespeare, Shaw; *The Voysey Inheritance* (1905), *Prefaces to Shakespeare* (1927–45).

Graves, Robert, 1895–1985—poet, novelist, translator, writer; in Mallorca 1929–39, 1946–85; established Seizin Press with Laura Riding; Professor of Poetry, Oxford 1961–66; *On English Poetry* (1922), *Lawrence and the Arabs* (1927), *Goodbye to All That* (1929), *I, Claudius* (1934).

Greenwood, C. J.,—partner, Boriswood.

Guedalla, Philip, 1889–1944—historian, biographer, essayist; barrister 1913–23; *Palmerston* (1926), *The Duke* [Wellington] (1931), *The Hundred Days* (1934).

Hakluyt, Richard, 1552–1616—British Ambassador, Paris 1583–88; collected and published accounts of English explorations; *Principall Navigations, Voiages, and Discoveries of the English Nation* (1589).

Hall, M. Radclyffe, 1866–1943—poet, novelist; *The Well of Loneliness* (1928).

Hanley, James, 1901–85—Irish-born novelist, playwright; seaman 1914–24; butcher, clerk, railwayman, postman, journalist, 1924–30; *Drift* (1930), *Boy* (1931), *The Furys* (1935).

Hardy, Thomas, 1840–1928—novelist, poet; O.M. 1910; *The Return of the Native* (1878), *Tess of the D'Urbervilles* (1891), *The Dynasts* (1908), *Collected Poems* (1930).

Hardy, Mrs. Thomas, 1879–1937—Florence Dugdale, Hardy's second wife, married 1914.

Hart-Davis, Rupert C., b. 1907—actor, writer, publisher; with Heinemann 1929–33; director Cape 1933–40; founder, director Hart-Davis publisher 1946–68; knighted 1967; *Hugh Walpole* (1952), *The Arms of Time* (1979), *The Power of Chance* (1991).

Herbert, Aubrey, 1880–1923—linguist, diplomat, traveller in Mid-East, Balkans; Conservative M.P.; member Arab Bureau, Cairo 1915; protagonist of Albanian, Turkish nationalists; *Mons, Anzac and Kut* (1930).

Hogarth, David G., 1862–1927—Mid-East scholar, archeologist, traveller; Keeper, Ashmolean Museum, Oxford, 1908–27; Director, Arab Bureau 1916; Fellow, Magdalen College, Oxford; *A Wandering Scholar in the Levant* (1896), *The Life of C. M. Doughty* (1928).

Homer, ninth century B.C.?—Greek poet of the *Iliad, Odyssey*.

Hornby, Charles H. St. John, 1867–1946—printer; partner, W. H. Smith & Son, booksellers, printers, 1894; founder, Ashendene Press 1895–1935.

Howard, G. Wren, 1893–1968—founding partner Cape 1921.

Hudd, Walter,—actor; played Private Meek, a character based on Lawrence, in G. B. Shaw's *Too True to Be Good* (1932).

Hudson, W. H., 1841-1922—American, born in Argentina; naturalist, novelist; to England 1869, naturalized 1900; *The Purple Land* (1885), *Green Mansions* (1904).

Hurley, W. M. M., b. 1897—adjutant, RAF, Karachi, 1928; Felixstowe, 1932.

Isham, Ralph H., 1890-1955—American collector, businessman; Lieut.-Colonel, British army in France; bought Boswell papers 1927, gave them to Yale.

Jesty, Simon, pseudonym of W. W. Vickery.

Jones, Ira T., b. 1896—RAF squadron leader, Plymouth, 1929.

Joyce, James, 1882-1941—Dublin-born novelist; left Ireland 1902 for Trieste, Zurich, Paris; *Dubliners* (1914), *Portrait of the Artist as a Young Man* (1916), *Ulysses* (1922), *Finnegans Wake* (1939).

Kennington, Eric H., 1888-1960—painter, sculptor; official British war artist, World War I and II; did portraits for, and art editor of, *Seven Pillars* subscriber's edition.

Keynes, Geoffrey L., 1887-1982—surgeon, writer, publisher of fine limited editions.

Kipling, Rudyard, 1865-1936—poet, novelist; in India 1865-71, 1882-89; in U.S. 1892-96; Nobel Prize 1907; *Barrack-Room Ballads* (1892), *Kim* (1901), *Just So Stories* (1902).

Landor, Walter Savage, 1775-1864—poet, critic, writer; in Italy 1815-35, 1858-64; *Poems* (1795), *Imaginary Conversations* (1824-29).

Lawrence, Arnold W., 1900-1991—youngest brother and literary executor of T. E.; Reader, Professor of Classical Archaeology, Cambridge University, 1930-51; Director, National Museum, Ghana, 1951-57; *Classical Sculpture* (1929); editor, *T. E. Lawrence by His Friends* (1937), *Letters to T. E. Lawrence* (1962).

Lawrence, David H., 1885-1930—poet, novelist, essayist; travelled much in Europe, Australia, U.S., Mexico; *Sons and Lovers* (1913), *Women in Love* (1920), *The Plumed Serpent* (1926), *Lady Chatterley's Lover* (1928).

Lewis, Wyndham, 1882-1957—Canadian-born writer, artist, "vorticist"; to England 1888; in Canada and U.S. 1939-45; edited *Blast* with Ezra Pound, 1914-15; *Tarr* (1918), *The Art of Being Ruled* (1925), *The Lion and the Fox* (1927), *The Apes of God* (1930).

Liddell Hart, Capt. Sir Basil H., 1895-1970—military historian and journalist; military editor, *Encyclopaedia Britannica*; military correspondent *Daily Telegraph* 1925-35, *The Times* 1935-39; *'T. E. Lawrence' of Arabia and After* (1934).

Lucas, Frank L., 1894-1967—critic, poet, translator, writer; Fellow, King's College, Cambridge; *Time and Memory* (1929), *Cécile* (1930), *Eight Victorian Poets* (1930).

Machen, Arthur L., 1863-1947—Welsh journalist, translator, writer of supernatural tales; *The Great Good Pan* (1894), *The Three Impostors* (1895), *The Hill of Dreams* (1907).

Manning, Frederic, 1882-1935—Australian-born writer, poet; to England 1903; *Scenes and Portraits* (1909), *Her Privates We* (1930).

Marsh, Sir Edward, 1872-1953—writer, editor, translator, civil servant, art patron; private secretary to Winston Churchill 1906-29; edited *Georgian Poetry* (1912-22); literary executor of Rupert Brooke; translator of La Fontaine, Horace; proofreader par excellence for Churchill, Somerset Maugham.

Marshall, K .W.,—bookseller; member, Boriswood publishers.

Melville, Herman, 1819-91—American novelist, poet; sailor 1839-44; *Omoo* (1847), *White-Jacket* (1850), *Moby-Dick* (1851), *Clarel* (1876).

Merton, Wilfred—colleague of Emery Walker.

Morley, Frank V., 1899-1980—manager, London office, The Century Co.; vice-president, editor Harcourt, Brace; cofounder, director, chairman Faber & Faber; *River Thames* (1926), *Everybody's Boswell* (1930).

Namier, Lewis B., 1888–1960—historian, born Poland, to England 1907, British citizen 1913; political secretary Jewish Agency for Palestine 1929–31, 1940–45; professor University of Manchester, 1931–53; *The Structure of Politics at the Accession of George III* (1929), *England in the Age of the American Revolution* (1930).

Newcombe, Col. Stewart F., 1878–1956—director, Sinai Survey 1913–14; served in Arabia.

Palmer, E. S.—private, Tank Corps, Bovington, 1923.

Peake, Frederick G., 1886–1970—army officer, India 1906, Egypt and Sudan 1914, commanded Egyptian Camel Corps in Arabia 1918, founder and commander of Arab Legion in Trans-Jordan 1920–39.

Pike, Manning—printer of *Seven Pillars* subscriber's edition (1922).

Pound, Ezra, 1885–1972—American poet, critic, translator, editor, modernist leader; in England 1908–20, Paris 1920–24, Italy 1924–45, 1958–72, Saint Elizabeth's Hospital, Washington, D.C. 1946–58; *Personae* (1909), *Instigations* (1920), *Collected Poems* (1926).

Pugh, A.—sergeant, RAF, Cranwell, 1925–26.

Read, Sir Herbert E., 1893–1968—critic of art and literature, writer, poet, editor, anarchist; assistant keeper, Victoria and Albert Museum, London, 1922–31; editor, *Burlington Magazine*, 1933–39; itinerant professor; *Collected Poems* (1926), *The Meaning of Art* (1931).

Rees—at the *Sunday Times* 1922.

Remarque, Erich Maria, 1898–1970—German novelist, journalist; to U.S. 1939; *All Quiet on the Western Front* (1929), *The Road Back* (1931).

Richards, Vyvyan, 1886–1968—teacher, social worker; helped Robert Graves establish Seizin Press, 1928; *Portrait of T. E. Lawrence* (1936).

Richardson, Henry Handel, 1870–1946—penname of Ethel Florence Lindesay Richardson, Australian-born novelist, to England 1904; trilogy *The Fortunes of Richard Mahony* (1917–29).

Riding, Laura, 1901–1991—U.S. poet, critic, author; in England, Egypt, Spain 1926–39; managing partner Seizin Press; editor *Epilogue* critical series; *The Close Chaplet* (1926), *A Survey of Modernist Poetry* with Robert Graves (1927), *Poems* (1930).

Rieder, Mrs. André—French language teacher, American Mission School, Jebail, Syria; returned to England 1912.

Rimbaud, Arthur, 1854–91—French poet whose poetry exploded and stopped before he was twenty; he then wandered in Europe, Cyprus, Aden, Ethiopia.

Rogers, Bruce, 1870–1957—American book designer, typographer; with Riverside Press, Cambridge, Mass., 1895–1912; had own business 1912–17; associate, W. E. Rudge, printer, Mountain Vernon, N.Y., 1920–28; adviser, Harvard University Press, 1920–34; *PI* (1953).

Rothenstein, Sir William, 1872–1945—painter; official British war artist, World War I and II; Principal, Royal College of Art, 1920–35; *Men and Memories* (1931–32).

Sassoon, Siegfried L., 1896–1967—poet, novelist, writer; *The Old Huntsman* (1917), *Memoirs of a Fox-Hunting Man* (1928), *Vigils* (1935).

Schwartz, Jacob—literary agent?

Shakespeare, William, 1564–1616.

Shaw, Charlotte (Charlotte Payne-Townshend), 1857–1943—married George Bernard Shaw 1898.

Shaw, George Bernard, 1856–1950—Dublin-born playwright, novelist, music critic, writer, socialist, lecturer, vegetarian, wit; Nobel Prize 1925; *Man and Superman* (1905), *Pygmalion* (1913), *Saint Joan* (1923).

Sinclair, Upton, 1878–1968—American muckraking novelist, writer, socialist, unsuccessful political candidate; *The Jungle* (1906), *The Brass Check* (1919), *Oil* (1927).

Sitwell, Dame Edith, 1887–1964—critic, poet, biographer; *Façade* (1922), *Elegy for Dead Fashion* (1926), *Collected Poems* (1930).

Stark, Dame Freya, b. 1893—Mid-East traveller, writer; *The Valley of the Assassins* (1934), *The Southern Gates of Arabia* (1936).

Stuart, Vincent—at Tintern Press, 1934.

Thomas, Bertram, 1892–1950—explorer; in Mesopotamia with Army and as political officer 1916–22; political officer, Trans-Jordan 1922–24; thereafter financial adviser and prime minister, Sultanate of Muscat; *Arabia Felix* (1932), *The Arabs* (1937).

Tolstoy, Count Leo, 1828–1910—novelist, playwright, writer, wrestler with God; *War and Peace* (1869), *Anna Karenina* (1877), *What I Believe* (1883).

Tomlinson, Henry M., 1873–1958—novelist, journalist, essayist; *The Sea and the Jungle* (1912), *All Our Yesterdays* (1930).

Walker, Sir Emery, 1851–1933—process engraver, typographical expert; print seller 1883; process and general engraving 1886; established Kelmscott Press with William Morris 1891–98; cofounder Doves Press 1900–1909.

Warner, Richard,—cashier, Martins Bank.

Wavell, Col. (later, Field Marshall Lord) Archibald P., 1893–1950—on General Allenby's staff in Palestine, Syria, Egypt 1917–20; Commander, Middle East 1939; Commander, India 1941; Viceroy, India 1943–47; *The Palestine Campaigns* (1928), *Allenby* (1940), *Other Men's Flowers* (1944).

Wells, Herbert G., 1866–1946—science fiction and novel writer, popularizer, journalist, socialist; *The Time Machine* (1895), *The War of the Worlds* (1898), *The Outline of History* (1920).

Wilder, Thornton N., 1897–1975—American novelist, playwright, teacher; *The Bridge of San Luis Rey* (1927), *Our Town* (1938).

Williams, Walter, 1864–1935—American journalist, academic administrator; editor, *Columbia* [Missouri] *Herald*, 1890–1908; Dean, School of Journalism, University of Missouri 1908–35; President 1931–35.

Williamson, Henry, 1895–1977—nature and fiction writer; *Tarka the Otter* (1927), *The Flax of Dreams* (1921–28), *A Patriot's Progress* (1930), *Genius of Friendship, 'T. E. Lawrence'* (1941).

Wilson, John G., 1876–1963—proprietor, Bumpus bookstore, London.

Yeats, William Butler, 1865–1939—Irish poet, playwright, writer, editor; Nobel Prize 1923; *The Land of Heart's Desire* (1894), *A Vision* (1925), *The Oxford Book of Modern Verse* (1936).

Yeats-Brown, Francis, 1886–1944—assistant editor, *The Spectator*; *Bengal Lancer* (1930), *Dogs of War!* (1934).

Sources

Part I: Published Criticism

INTRODUCTIONS

Travels in Arabia Deserta by Charles M. Doughty. Introduction by T. E. Lawrence. Second edition. London: Philip Warner, The Medici Society, and Jonathan Cape, 1921 (first edition, Cambridge University Press, 1888).

The Twilight of the Gods and Other Tales by Richard Garnett. Introduction by T. E. Lawrence (T. E. L., May 24, 1924), illustrated by Henry Keen. London: John Lane, The Bodley Head, 1924.

Arabia Felix: Across the "Empty Quarter" of Arabia by Bertram Thomas. Foreword by Colonel T. E. Lawrence (T. E. S.). Appendix by Sir Arthur Keith. New York: Charles Scribner's Sons, 1932.

REVIEWS

"Novels of D. H. Lawrence." Review of *Women in Love, The Lost Girl*, and *The Plumed Serpent* (Secker, 3s. 6d. each), by C. D. *The Spectator*, August 6, 1927; text from *Men*, 25–29.

"Mixed Biscuits." Review of *Green Mansions* by W. H. Hudson, *The Polyglots* by William Gerhardi, *The Sea and the Jungle* by H. M. Tomlinson, *The Roadmender* by Michael Fairless, *The Terror* by Arthur Machen, and *Lost Diaries* by Maurice Baring (Duckworth's New Readers Library, 3s. 6d. each), by C. D. *The Spectator*, August 20, 1927.

"A Critic of Critics Criticized." Review of *Men of Letters* by Philip Guedalla (Hodder and Stoughton, 2s. 6d.), by C. D. *The Spectator*, August 27, 1927.

"Hakluyt—First Naval Propagandist." Review of *The Principal Navigations, Voyages, Traffiques and Discoveries of the English Nation, &c.* by Richard Hakluyt, Introduction by John Masefield, illustrated. In 8 vols. (April–October 1927), (J. M. Dent and Sons, £3 the set) [only vol. 1 reviewed], by C. D. *The Spectator*, September 10, 1927.

"The Short Stories of H. G. Wells." Review of *The Collected Short Stories of H. G. Wells* (Benn, 7s. 6d.), by C. D. *The Spectator*, February 25, 1928; this text is from *Men*, 33–38.

"The Works of Walter Savage Landor." Review of *The Works of Walter Savage Landor* (Chapman and Hall, Vols. 1–3); written February or March 1928 for, but not published by, *The Spectator*; this text is from *Men*, 57–59.

BRIC-À-BRAC

"Eric Kennington's Arab Portraits." *Catalogue of an Exhibition of Arab Portraits* prefatory note by T. E. Lawrence (Aden, August 25, 1921). London: Brown & Phillips, The Leicester Galleries, October 1921. This text is from Oliver Brown, *Exhibition: The Memoirs of Oliver Brown*, London: Evelyn, Adams & Mackay, 1968, 176–79.

Sturly by Pierre Custot, translated by Richard Aldington. London: Jonathan Cape, 1924; unsigned jacket blurb. This text is from a xerox copy kindly provided by Philip O'Brien; the original, in Lawrence's hardwriting (initialled E. L.) is in *Texas*.

"A Note on James Elroy Flecker." Written in late 1924 or early 1925; published as *An Essay on Flecker* by T. E. Lawrence. Corvinus Press, 1937 and Garden City, New York: Doubleday, Doran & Co., 1937. This text is from *Men*, 19–22.

Tarka the Otter by Henry Williamson. January 20, 1928 letter to Edward Garnett commenting on proofs of *Tarka* Garnett had sent Lawrence. This text is from *Men*, 41–54.

"*The Odyssey*: Translator's Note." *The Odyssey Of Homer*. London: Sir Emery Walker, Wilfred Merton and Bruce Rogers, 1932 (no signature) and New York: Oxford University Press, 1932 (T. E. Shaw).

La Maison Sans Issues by James Hanley. Introduction de Henry Miller, roman traduit de l'anglais par Jean-Claude Lefaure. London, Brussels: Nicholson & Watson, n.d. (1946?), prefatory extracts (translated into French) from Lawrence's July 2, 1931 letter to Hanley. The full letter is in Garnett, 727–29.

River Niger by Simon Jesty. Letter to C. J. Greenwood, May 20, 1934, signed T. E. S.; omissions, restored from the original in the *Bodleian*, are placed in brackets.

Part II. Literary Correspondence

This listing of Lawrence's letters is organized by correspondent (not author or theme). Where two sources are given, the first is the one whose punctuation and spelling has been followed. Lawrence's correspondents and the authors he discusses are identified in the Dramatis Personae above; a full reference for abbreviated forms is given in the bibliography; library letter collections are bold faced. Dates follow the British sequence of day: month: year. Pages are cited only when necessary, as the date suffices for publications with letters in chronological order. The following initials are used for frequently cited sources:

B	Brown	G	Garnett	P	*Princeton*
Bo	*Bodleian*	Gr	Graves	R	*Reading*
Br	*British Library*	H	*Harvard*	Ro	Rogers
C	Cockerell	Ho	*Home*	T	*Texas*
E	Ede	M	Manning	W	Williamson

Acres 15.1.26 G
Adams 19.4.13 G
Altounyan 9.1.33 G, B; 7.4.34 G, B; 9.12.34 G
Andrews 6.3.35 Weintraubs 94
Astor 8.1.30 *R*; 1931 or 32? *R*
Baring (both Smyth 338) 30.10.28 *T*, 18.12.28
Barker 4.5.34 *Bo*
Bell 4.11.27 B
Black 25.11.30 *T*, 2.9.31 *T*
Brophy (all *T*) 19.11.29, 8.2.30, 7.2.33 W 52, 13.2.33, 23.2.33

Brown 12.11.24 *H*
Buxton 25.6.25 *Bo*, 4.1.26 *Bo*
Cape 30.3.23? *Bo*, 28.3.28 *Bo*, 23.10.28 *T*
Chambers 10.3.23 G, 3.8.24 *Bo*, 5.12.24 *Bo*
Cockerell 22.10.23 G, 27.10.23 G, 25.12.23 C, 13.1.24 G, C; 19.3.24 G, C; 29.12.25
    G, C; 2.2.28 G, C; 22.3.28 C, 28.11.34 C
Coward 6.9.30 B, G; 5.10.30 G, 10.6.31 G
Curtis 27.3.23 G, B; 22.12.27 G
Davies early 2.30 Davies, 28.2.35 B, G
Day Lewis (both G) 16.11.34, 20.12.34
Dixon 9.11.34 *Bo*
Doubleday 20.3.20 G, 14.5.20 G, 21.7.20 *Bo*, 13.4.28 *P*, 16.10.28 *P*, 28.6.29 *P*, 2.9.30
    Bo, G; 18.9.30 G, B; 27.1.31 *Bo*, 2.12.32 G
Doughty (both G) 5.1.20, 7.11.20
Dunn 11.3.31 G, 21.10.31 *T*, 9.11.32 G, 15.12.32 G, *T*; 26.9.33 *T*, 19.7.34 *Bo*, 26.1.35
    Bo
Ede (all E) 16.4.28 G, 12.11.28, 25.12.28, 20.3.29 G, 28.3.29, 1.4.29, 10.4.29, 9.5.29,
    29.7.29 G, 2.1.30, 8.2.30, 2.1.32, 18.10.32, 25.9.33
Family (all Ho) 28.8.08, 8.10 B, 12.10 B, G; 31.3.11, 31.1.12, 20.2.12, 11.5.12, 12.9.12,
    6.3.13, 10.12.13, 4.1.28
Fontana 12.20? *Bo*, 2.5.28 *Bo*, 17.5.34 *Bo*, 28.11.34 B
Forster 20.2.24 G, 6.4.24 *Kings*, B; 30.4.24 Lago 56, 9.5.24 *Kings*, B; 24.7.24 G,
    17.6.25 B, 26.4.26 G, 11.1.27 *Kings*, 14.7.27 G, 8.9.27 G, 27.10.27 B, 21.12.27
    B, 16.4.28 G, 30.10.28 *Kings*, 12.12.28 G, 23.1.30 *Kings*, 8.2.30 *Kings*, 17.2.30
    Kings, 24.5.34 G
Frere-Reeves 19.2.30 *RAF Museum*, 7.1.35 *T*, B
Garnett, D. 30.11.27 *Bo*, *Fifty* 28–29; 16.2.28 B, *Bo*; 14.6.28 G, 4.5.29 G, 10.2.30
    Bo, 19.11.30 G, 10.6.31 G
Garnett, E. 23.8.22 G, 26.8.22 G, 23.10.22 G, 6.11.22 G, 12.11.22 G, 20.11.22 G,
    1.12.22 G, 7.12.22 G, 4.10.23 G, 3.12.23 *T*, 16.9. 24 G, 7.7.27 G, 22.9.27 G, 1.12.27
    G, 2.2.28 *Men* 42, 22.3.28 G, 14.4.28 G, 2.5.28 G, 17.7.28 *H*, 28.2.29 *Bo*, 14.3.29
    G, 10.4.29 *H*, 5.12.30 G, 12.10.32 *Bo*, 1.8.33 G, 10.8.33 G, 15.9.33 G, 5.10.33 G
Granville-Barker 23.10.32 Salmon 402, B
Graves 21.7.20 Gr, 9.1.21 *H*, Gr; 22.4.21 Gr, 21.5.21 Gr, 18.1.23 *H*, B; 20.3.23 B,
    Gr; 8.9.23 Gr; 9.5.24 *H*, Gr; 1924? Gr, G; 5.12.24 Gr, 5? 25 Gr, 25.6.25 Gr. B;
    29.8.25 Gr, 21.10.25 Gr, 11? 26 Gr, 28.6.27 *H*, Gr, 1927 Gr 64, 24.12.27 *H*, Gr;
    26.1.28 Gr; 29.3.28 *Bo*, Gr; 19.5.28 Gr, 5.8.28 Gr, 6.11.28 Gr, B; 26.11.28 *Bo*,
    Gr; 5.5.29 Gr, G; 13.9.29 B, 8.11.30 Gr, 12.11.33 *H*, Gr; 17.12.33 *H*, Gr; 4.5.34
    Gr, 13.1.35 Gr
Greenwood 17.7.31 G, 16.10.31 *Bo*, 12.10.32 G, 26.10.32 G, 16.4.34 G, 5.4.35 G
Hanley 2.7.31 G, 14.7.31 *H*, 21.8.31 G, 28.12.31 G, 7.12.32 *Bo*
Hardy 25.3.23 B, 2.12.23 G, 12.11.24 G, 15.1.28 G, B; 16.2.28 G, 16.4.28 G, 3.12.32
    B, 22.4.35 G
Herbert 3.23? Fitzherbert 243
Hogarth 21.1.24 *Bo*, 21.1.27 *Bo*, 27.8.27 G
Hornby 26.1.22 *Bo*
Howard 1932 *Bo*
Hudd 3.9.32 G
Hurley 1.4.29 G, B
Isham 2.1.28 B
Jones 1930? *Friends* 348
Judge 11.1.30 *Bo*

Kennington 10.4.22 G, 25.3.27 *T*, *Fifty* 18; 19.5.27 *T*, G; 16.6.27 *T*, G; 31.1.35 *T*
Keynes 28.1.34 *Bo*, 10.2.34 G, *Bo*; 6.8.34 G, *Bo*
Lewis 11.5.24 *Cornell*
Liddell Hart (both Liddell Hart) 5.3.30, 23.5.33
Lucas 9.12.27 *Bo*, 3.5.30 G
Manning 25.2.30 G, B; 21.3.30 M, 15.5.30 G, 24.6.30 M, 1.9.31 M, 2.1.32 M, 25.7.34
    M, 16.11.34 M, B
Marsh 12.4.25 G, 19.3.29 G, 18.4.29 G, 3.6.29 *Bo*, 7.7.31 *NYPL*
Marshall 29.1.31 *T*, 9.3.31 *T*, 9.4.31 *T*, 9.12.32 *T*, 20.10.32 *T*, 27.1.35 *T*, 1.2.35 G,
    7.3.35 *T*, G
Merton 29.11.32
Morley 21.10.32 *H*, 16.4.34 *T*
Namier 6.9.32 *Bo*
Palmer 15.3.27 Wilson 153
Peake 20.10.27 *Imperial*
Pound 4.20 Pound, B; 20.8.20 Pound, B; 7.12.34 B
Pugh 9.6.28 B
Read 26.3.29 B
Rees 20.2.22 *T*
Richards 27.2.20 *T*, G; 8.20 G, early 1923 B, 15.3.27 *Bo*
Riding 1932? Riding
Rieder 26.9.11 G, 12.9.12 G, 8.3.14 *Bo*, 24.4.14 G
Rogers 16.4.28 G, 30.6.28 Ro, 41.1.29? Ro, 30.7.29 Ro, 29.1.30 Ro, 10.2.30 Ro,
    12.2.30 Ro, 31.1.31 G, 20.8.31 Ro, G; 24.11.34 *Bo*, Rogers 1936
Rothenstein (all *H*) 12.5.27 G, 8.12.27 G, 14.4.28 G, 18.10.30 G, 22.4.32 B, 6.9.32,
    20.10.32 G, 5.5.35 G
Sassoon (both G) 6.9.34, 17.12.34
Schwartz 26.4.32 *H*
Shaw, C. (all *Br*) 6.3.24, 16.3.24 Dunbar 240, B; 19.3.24 Knightley 253, 26.3.24 B,
    30.8.24, 31.8.24, 29.11.24 Dunbar 243, 3.5.25, 31.5.25, 30.7.25, 5.11.25, 4.1.26,
    3.6.26, 22.8.26 B, 11.1.27 B, 23.3.27 Allen 44, 21.4.27, 4.5.27, 19.5.27, 26.5.27,
    16.6.27, 30.6.27, 14.7.27, 21.7.27, 8.8.27, 15.9.27, 29.9.27, 13.10.27, 8.12.27,
    2.2.28, 9.2.28, 25.2.28, 12.4.28, 26.4.28, 8.5.28, 17.5.28 Dunbar 268, 25.6.28,
    23.7.28, 4.8.28, 15.8.28, 18.8.28, 11.9.28, 18.9.28, 25.9.28, 16.10.28, 6.11.28,
    11.11.28, 7.11.28, 11.12.28, 18.12.28, 31.12.28, 10.7.29 B, 4.10.29 Wilson 1988
    26, 4.12.29, 2.1.30, 19.1.30, 6.2.30, 19.2.30, 25.2.30 B, 21.3.30, 4.4.30, 6.8.30,
    15.8.30 B, 24.10.30, 5.12.30, 29.4.31, 26.6.31 Weintraub 209, 9.1.32 Weintraub
    213, 27.1.32 Weintraub 218, 16.9.32 B, 23.8.33 B
Shaw G. B. (both G) 7.12.22, 20.12.23
Stuart 5.6.34 *Men* 14
Thomas 14.8.31 *Bo*, 22.8.31 *Bo*
Walker 25.12.28 *H*
Warner 18.10.32 G
Wavell 11.5.23 B
Whittaker 6.3.35 *Bo*
Williams 24.11.34 *Missouri*
Williamson 3? 28 W 19, 1928 W 22, 10.7.29 *Bo*, W; 1930 W 39, 25.3.30 G, 3.5.30
    B, W 41; 1.9.31 *Bo*, 1931? W, 13.2.33 W, G; 14.5.34 B, 11.12.34 W, G
Wilson 4.10.27 G
Yeats 12.10.32 G
Yeats-Brown 6.9.27 Wrench

Bibliography

Key words used for citations in the text and notes are included below; the specific edition cited is given; library letter collections are bold faced.

Aldington, Richard. *Lawrence of Arabia, A Biographical Enquiry*. London: Collins, 1955.

Allen, Malcolm D. *The Medievalism of Lawrence of Arabia*. University Park: Pennsylvania State University Press, 1991.

Ault, Warren O., "Oxford in 1907 (With a Glimpse of T. E. Lawrence)." *The American Oxonian* 46, no. 2 (Spring 1979): 121–28.

Bodleian: The Bodleian Library, Oxford, reserved collection.

British: The British Library, London.

Brown, Malcolm, ed. *The Letters of T. E. Lawrence*. London: J. M. Dent & Sons, 1988.

Buchan, John. "T. E. Lawrence." *Canadian Defense Quarterly* 16, no. 4 (July 1939): 371–8.

Buchan 1984: John Buchan. *Pilgrim's Way*. New York: Carroll & Graf, 1984.

Cockerell: Viola Meynell, ed. *Friends of a Lifetime: Letters to Sidney Carlyle Cockerell*. London: Rupert Hart-Davis, 1940 (357–73, letters from Lawrence).

Cockerell 1956: Viola Meynell, ed. *The Best of Friends, Further Letters to Sydney Carlyle Cockerell*. London: Rupert Hart-Davis, 1956.

Coleman, Verna. *The Last Exquisite, A Portrait of Frederic Manning*. Melbourne: Melbourne University Press, 1990.

Connally: David Pryce-Jones, ed. *Cyril Connally, Journal and Memoir*. London: Collins, 1983.

Cornell: Olin Library, Cornell University, Ithaca, New York.

Davies, Peter. *Colonel Lawrence and Others on "Her Privates We" by Private 19022* (pamphlet). London: Peter Davies, 1930.

Day Lewis, Cecil. *The Buried Day*. New York: Harper & Brothers, 1960.

Day Lewis, Sean. *C. Day-Lewis, An English Literary Life*. London: Weidenfeld and Nicolson, 1980.

Drabble, Margaret, ed. *The Genius of Thomas Hardy*. New York: Alfred A. Knopf, 1976.

Dunbar, Janet. *Mrs. G.B.S.: A Portrait*. New York: Harper & Row, 1963.

Ede: *Shaw-Ede: T. E. Lawrence's Letters to H. S. Ede 1927–1935*. Foreword and running commentary by H. S. Ede. London: The Golden Cockerel Press, 1942.

Ellis, Malcolm H. *Express to Hindustan*. London: John Lane, The Bodley Head, 1929.

Evolution: Stanley and Rodelle Weintraub, eds. *Evolution of a Revolt, Early Postwar*

Writings of T. E. Lawrence. University Park: Pennsylvania State University Press, 1968.

Fagles, Robert. "Epilogue: Homer and the Writers." In ed. George Steiner and Robert Fagles, 160–72. *Homer, A Collection of Critical Essays*, Englewood Cliffs, N.J.: Prentice-Hall, 1962.

Fifty: T. E. Lawrence/Fifty Letters: 1920–35. An Exhibition: October First to December Fifteenth 1962, Held at the Humanities Research Center, The University of Texas [Austin].

Fitzherbert, Margaret. *The Man Who Was Greenmantle, A Biography of Aubrey Herbert*. Oxford: Oxford University Press, 1985.

Forster: Philip Gardner, ed. *E. M. Forster, Commonplace Book*. Stanford, Calif.: Stanford University Press, 1985.

Friends: A. W. Lawrence, ed. *T. E. Lawrence by His Friends*. London: Jonathan Cape, 1937.

Furbank, P. N. *E. M. Forster, A Life*. Vol. II. New York: Harcourt Brace Jovanovich, 1978.

Garnett, David, ed. *The Letters of T. E. Lawrence*. New York: Doubleday, Doran, 1939.

Garnett 1951: David Garnett, ed. *The Essential T. E. Lawrence*. London: Jonathan Cape, 1951; Oxford: Oxford University Press, 1992.

Garnett 1980: David Garnett. *Great Friends*. New York: Atheneum, 1980.

Graves, Robert, ed. *T. E. Lawrence to His Biographer Robert Graves*. In *T. E. Lawrence to His Biographers Robert Graves and Liddell Hart*. Garden City, N.Y.: Doubleday & Co., 1963.

Graves 1927: Robert Graves. *Lawrence and the Arabs*. London: Jonathan Cape, 1927.

Gregory: Lennox Robinson, ed. *Lady Gregory's Journals 1916–1930*. London: Putnam & Co., 1946.

Harvard: The Houghton Library, Harvard University, Cambridge.

Hassall, Christopher. *Edward Marsh, Patron of the Arts, A Biography*. London: Longmans, 1959.

Hogarth, D. G. *Life of Charles M. Doughty*. Garden City, N.Y.: Doubleday, Doran, 1929.

Holroyd, Michael. *Bernard Shaw, Volume III, 1918–1950*. New York: Random House, 1991.

Home: M. R. Lawrence, ed. *The Home Letters of T. E. Lawrence and His Brothers*. Oxford: Basil Blackwell, 1954.

Howard, Michael S. *Jonathan Cape, Publisher*. London: Jonathan Cape, 1971.

Howe, Irving. "T. E. Lawrence: The Problem of Heroism." *The Hudson Review* 15, no. 3 (Autumn 1962): 333–64.

Howe 1985: Irving Howe. *Thomas Hardy*. New York: Collier Books, Macmillan, 1985.

Imperial: Imperial War Museum, London.

Jefferson, George. *Edward Garnett, A Life in Literature*. London: Jonathan Cape, 1982.

Kings: Kings College Library, Cambridge.

Knightley, Phillip, and Colin Simpson. *The Secret Lives of Lawrence of Arabia*. London: Thomas Nelson, 1969.

Knowles, Patrick. *"An Handful with Quietness."* Weymouth, Dorset: E.V.G. Hunt, 1992.

Lago, Mary, and P. V. Furbank, eds. *Selected Letters of E. M. Forster, Vol. Two, 1921–1970.* Cambridge: The Belknap Press of Harvard University, 1985.

Leeds: J. M. Wilson, ed. *T. E. Lawrence: Letters to E. T. Leeds.* With a commentary by E. T. Leeds. Andoversford, Gloucestershire: The Whittington Press, 1988.

Letters: A. W. Lawrence, ed. *Letters to T. E. Lawrence.* London: Jonathan Cape, 1962.

Liddell Hart, ed. *T. E. Lawrence to His Biographer Liddell Hart.* In *T. E. Lawrence to His Biographers Robert Graves and Liddell Hart.* Garden City, N.Y.: Doubleday & Co., 1963.

Mack, John E. *A Prince of Our Disorder, The Life of T. E. Lawrence.* Boston: Little, Brown & Co., 1976.

Maddox, Brenda. *Nora, A Biography of Nora Joyce.* New York: Fawcett Columbine, 1988.

Manning: L. T. Hergenham. "Some Unpublished Letters from T. E. Lawrence to Frederic Manning." *Southerly* 23 (1963): 242–52.

Marwil, Jonathan. *Frederic Manning, An Unfinished Life.* Durham, N.C.: Duke University Press, 1988.

Men: Men in Print, Essays in Criticism by T. E. Lawrence. Introduction by A. W. Lawrence. London: The Golden Cockerel Press, 1940.

Meyers, Jeffrey, ed. *T. E. Lawrence: Soldier, Writer, Legend.* New York: St. Martin's Press, 1989.

Minorities: T. E. Lawrence. *Minorities.* Edited by J. M. Wilson. Preface by C. Day Lewis. London: Jonathan Cape, 1971.

Mint: T. E. Lawrence. *The Mint* (unexpurgated text). London: Jonathan Cape, 1973.

Missouri: Special Collections, University Libraries, University of Missouri, Columbia.

NYPL: Berg Collection, New York Public Library.

O'Brien, Philip M. *T. E. Lawrence: A Bibliography.* Winchester: St. Paul's Bibliographies, 1988.

O'Prey, Paul, ed. *Robert Graves, In Broken Images, Selected Correspondence.* Mt. Kisco, N.Y.: Moyer Bell, 1988.

Patch, Blanche. *Thirty Years with G.B.S.* London: Gollancz, 1951.

Pound: Two Unpublished Letters [of T. E. Lawrence to Ezra Pound]. *Nine* 2 no. 3 (August 1950): 180–82.

Princeton: Princeton University Libraries, Princeton, N.J.

RAF Museum: Royal Air Force Museum, Herndon, London.

Reading: The Library, University of Reading.

Revolt: T. E. Lawrence: *Revolt in the Desert.* London: Jonathan Cape, 1927.

Riding: Laura (Riding) Jackson. "The Cult of Connection." *The Private Library*, 2d ser., no. 3 (Autumn 1973): 139.

Rogers: *Letters from T. E. Shaw to Bruce Rogers.* New York: W. E. Rudge, 1933.

Rogers 1936: *More Letters from T. E. Shaw to Bruce Rogers*, 1936.

Salmon, Eric, ed. *Granville Barker and His Correspondents.* Detroit: Wayne State University Press, 1980.

Secret: T. E. Lawrence. *Secret Despatches from Arabia*. London: The Golden Cockerel Press, 1939; London: Bellew Publishing, 1991 [Malcolm Brown, ed.].

Seven: T. E. Lawrence. *Seven Pillars of Wisdom, a triumph*. London: Jonathan Cape, 1952.

Shaw, G. Bernard. *Collected Letters*, 1911–1925. Edited by Dan H. Laurence. New York: Viking, 1985.

Shaw 1977: Bernard Shaw. *Flyleaves*. Edited by Dan H. Laurence and Daniel J. Leary. Austin, Tex.: W. Thomas Taylor, 1977.

Smyth, Clare S. *The Golden Reign*, London: Cassell, 1940.

Smyth, Ethel. *Maurice Baring*. London: Heinemann, 1938.

Storrs: *The Memoirs of Sir Ronald Storrs*. New York: G. P. Putnam's Sons, 1937.

Tabachnick, Stephen E., ed. *The T. E. Lawrence Puzzle*. Athens: University of Georgia Press, 1984.

Tabachnick 1981: Stephen E. Tabachnick. *Charles Doughty*. Boston: Twayne, 1981.

Texas: Harry Ransom Humanities Research Center, University of Texas, Austin.

Thomas, Bertram. *Arabia Felix, Across the "Empty Quarter" of Arabia*. New York: Charles Scribner's Sons, 1932.

Villars, Jean Beraud. *T. E. Lawrence or the Search for the Absolute*. New York: Duell, Sloan & Pearce, 1959.

Weintraub, R.: Rodelle and Stanley Weintraub. "Chapman's Homer." *Classical World* 67, no. 1 (September-October 1973): 16–24.

Weintraub, Stanley. *Private Shaw and Public Shaw*. New York: George Braziller, 1963.

Weintraub 1965: Stanley Weintraub. "Bernard Shaw's Other Saint Joan." *South Atlantic Quarterly* 65 (1965): 194–205.

Weintraubs: Stanley and Rodelle Weintraub. *Lawrence of Arabia, The Literary Impulse*. Baton Rouge: Louisiana State University Press, 1975.

Williamson, Henry. *Genius of Friendship, 'T. E. Lawrence'*. London: Faber and Faber, 1941.

Wilson, Jeremy. *Lawrence of Arabia, The Authorised Biography of T. E. Lawrence*. London: Heinemann, 1989.

Wilson 1988: Jeremy Wilson. *T. E. Lawrence*. London: National Portrait Gallery Publications, 1988.

Winsten, Stephen. *Days with Bernard Shaw*. New York: Vanguard Press, 1949.

Wrench, John Evelyn. *Francis Yeats-Brown, 1886–1944*. London: Eyre & Spottiswoode, 1948.

Wrench 1935: John Evelyn Wrench. *Struggle: 1914–1920*. London: Ivor Nicholson & Watson, 1935.

Yale: The Beinecke Rare Book and Manuscript Library, Yale University, New Haven, Conn.

Yeats-Brown, Francis. "Lawrence as I knew him." *The Spectator*, May 24, 1935, 872–73.

Index

Index of Letter Recipients